YOU BE THE JUDGE

20 True Crimes and Cases to Solve

YOU BE THE JUDGE

20 True Crimes and Cases to Solve

JUDGE NORBERT EHRENFREUND

SPHINX PUBLISHING
AN IMPRINT OF SOURCEBOOKS, INC.©
NAPERVILLE, ILLINOIS
www.SphinxLegal.com

First Edition: 2008

Published by: **Sphinx® Publishing, An Imprint of Sourcebooks, Inc.®**
Naperville Office
P.O. Box 4410
Naperville, Illinois 60567-4410
(630) 961-3900
Fax: 630-961-2168
www.sourcebooks.com
www.SphinxLegal.com

Library of Congress Cataloging-in-Publication Data

Ehrenfreund, Norbert.
You be the judge : 20 true crimes and cases for you to solve / by Norbert Ehrenfreund. -- 1st ed.
p. cm.
ISBN 978-1-57248-667-6 (pbk. : alk. paper) 1. Criminal justice, Administration of--United States--Digests. 2. Criminal law--United States--Digests. 3. Criminal procedure--United States--Digests. I. Title.
KF9223.A53E37 2008
364.1--dc22

2008019309

Printed and bound in the United States of America.
CHG—10 9 8 7 6 5 4 3 2

For Larry Treat (1903–1998), who inspired this book.

ACKNOWLEDGMENTS

Many people helped write this book, and I am deeply indebted to each of them.

First of all, I wish to acknowledge my debt for his inspiration to my late dear friend and former coauthor, Larry Treat. A nationally recognized mystery writer, Larry drafted several passages of the original manuscript.

I also wish to thank my wife, Jill, who not only typed the manuscript more than once but also made many important editorial suggestions.

Attorneys who offered their expertise were Richard Muir, Michael Marrinan, Jerry Wallingford, Nelson Brav, George Beall, Lou Boyle, Robert Grimes, Richard Sachs, Glen McAllister, Juliana Humphrey, Elizabeth Semel, Jeffrey Reilly, Tom Adler, Kerry Steigerwalt, and Harvey Levine. I am also grateful for the assistance of the late Judge Ben Hamrick and Judge William Mudd.

Contents

Introduction

Have you ever dreamed of being a judge? Have you ever been on a jury? Have you ever had the chance to decide the fate of another person by rendering a verdict of guilty or not guilty, liable or not liable? This is your chance. In the real-life cases that follow, you will be the judge, making the ultimate decision between right and wrong.

These cases are presented from the viewpoint of a juror observing the trial. The title *You Be the Judge* was chosen because in American jury trials, the juror is the real judge of the evidence, the one who decides with eleven other jurors whether the defendant is guilty or not guilty; in a death penalty case, whether the defendant should live or die; and, in a civil case, whether the defendant is liable, and if so, for what amount.

In 1992, Judge Ehrenfreund coauthored a book titled *You're the Jury*. Now he draws upon over forty-five years of experience as a trial lawyer and judge to bring readers a new work, expanding upon *You're the Jury* and adding many new cases to challenge the reader's sense of justice.

This book is based on real-life jury trials that have been shortened and slightly altered to protect the privacy of persons involved and also to protect readers from the tedium that often pervades the trial experience. Certain facts—including names, places, and dates—have been changed.

Various aspects of jury trials are missing—the long closing arguments have been shortened (in some cases omitted altogether), and there are no tedious delays for conferences between the judge and attorneys at sidebar or in chambers, no waiting in the hallway for court to begin, and no heated deliberations with other jurors who cannot understand your point of view. You will see only what the jury sees. The principal issues, however, remain the same as in the actual cases.

Many of these trials raise difficult questions because they go beyond the written law to the heart of one's own moral code. Could you, for instance, find a father guilty of kidnapping his 24-year-old daughter from a cult he believed was poisoning her mind? Does a wife who has been repeatedly battered by her husband have the right to kill him out of fear he will beat her again? Is it murder or suicide when a man helps a close friend die in order to avoid experiencing the ravages of AIDS? Is it rape or consensual sex when a woman consents to having intercourse and then in the throes of passion insists that her partner immediately stop, but he does not comply? There are civil trials here, too—a daughter's plea to the jury to let her 92-year-old mother die in peace, a woman's lawsuit for one million dollars in damages against her former lover for his intentional infliction of emotional distress, and a boy's suit against the government for violating his constitutional rights. Could you grant their wishes, based on the evidence?

Put yourself in the place of one of the twelve jurors as you listen to the details of each case. When the trial is over, you may turn to the general jury instructions in the back of the book; they present the law that applies to each case. Certain instructions of law are contained within the cases themselves. What would your verdict be? After you have made up your mind, read through the questions and answers that follow each trial, and finally, read on to see what the real jury decided.

The case is now in your hands.

Can You Believe This Witness?

STATE V. GENE GOODLIN

In this case, the State is seeking the death penalty for Gene Goodlin, who is charged with the cold-blooded murder of Bonnie Keeley.

Ben Keeley was the president of one of the largest banks in the city. While at work at his desk on the morning of December 5, 2007, Keeley received a call on his cell phone from his wife. "Ben," she said, "there is someone here who wants to speak with you."

A man's voice came on the line. He told Keeley he had a .22 pistol pointed at Mrs. Keeley's head. He instructed Keeley to place ten thousand dollars in a bag, fifty- and one-hundred-dollar bills only, take the bag to the phone booth at the food court two blocks from the bank, and await further instructions. The caller warned Keeley to be there with the money in forty-five minutes or his wife would be killed. He further instructed Keeley to bring his cell phone with him. As soon as Keeley hung up, he called the FBI. He had his cashier gather the money and was about to leave with the cash when the FBI called back to tell him that his wife had been found shot to death at the family residence. Acting under instructions from the FBI, a distraught Keeley took the money to the appointed spot at the food court and waited. Police and FBI agents were standing by in plain clothes, but after an hour no one showed up to collect the money and Keeley was allowed to leave.

For months, police agencies investigated the murder without any leads. The case finally started to break when a bankers' association offered a reward of one hundred thousand dollars for any information leading to the arrest and conviction of the killer. A few days later, a young man named Brock Olander came to the police station with a briefcase containing a .22 pistol, ammunition, and a silencer. He informed police that his roommate, Ellery Baldwin, gave him the briefcase for safekeeping. A police ballistics expert proceeded to test the weapon and examine the spent cartridges found at the murder scene, and concluded that the .22 in the briefcase was the murder weapon. Baldwin was questioned and confessed to being involved in the crime. Baldwin told detectives that he and his friend, Gene Goodlin, had hatched the scheme to rob the bank by holding Mrs. Keeley hostage but the plan went sour. Based on his confession, Baldwin was arrested and charged with first-degree murder as an aider and abettor. Goodlin was subsequently arrested and charged as the shooter. Before the two men were brought to trial, the district attorney offered a plea bargain to Baldwin whereby he would be allowed to plead guilty to the lesser charge of murder in the second degree, turn State's witness, and testify against Goodlin. At the trial, Goodlin's defense attorney claims that Baldwin is trying to frame Goodlin to save his own skin.

The deputy district attorney is Alice Gentry, a petite woman who always seems to be smiling despite the serious nature of the charge. "I will tell you right at the start," she says in a soft voice at the beginning of jury selection, "that I am going to ask you to choose the death penalty for this man. Can you do that?"

You look at Gene Goodlin—he's an average height and weight, has dark blonde hair, and is in his thirties. You want to study him but you try not to stare. He sits huddled between his defense team of two attorneys—on the one side, a young woman, Natalie Blake, apparently just out of law school and still in her twenties, and on the other side, Ed Hardin, short and burly, a familiar veteran of the courts. He sits back, saying little, holding a small black notebook in which he scribbles from time to time. Blake keeps pushing notes across the table to Hardin, who scans them briefly but tosses them aside as if they mean little to him. He is obviously an in-charge kind of guy. Blake is his assistant and never says a word in court.

You've thought about the death penalty before. Occasionally your family has discussed it at home. But you never thought you personally would have to decide if someone should live or die. When the issue was put to voters in the last election, you voted to support capital punishment. But this feels different. The immediate decision will actually be in your hands. You will have to decide, if the case goes that far, if the man sitting a few feet away should be put to death in the gas chamber or by lethal injection or should spend the rest of his life in prison. You look at him again and ask yourself, "Can I do that?"

After hearing opening statements, you realize that this case will rest primarily on the testimony of the prosecution witness Ellery Baldwin.

The district attorney calls Ben Keeley as her first witness. Keeley takes the stand looking every inch the bank president he is, a handsome man in his seventies with white hair, a paunch, and wearing a three-piece suit with a gold chain across his vest. He is obviously not enjoying the prospect of speaking in public about his wife's murder. Keeley testifies he has been the president of the national bank in town for twenty-seven years. He resided with his wife, Bonnie, for forty years in their family home. Their two grown children live elsewhere.

D.A.: Were you working at the bank on the morning of December 5, 2007?

Keeley: I was.

D.A.: And at that time did you receive a call on your cell phone of an unusual nature?

Keeley: I did. From my wife.

D.A.: I know this is hard for you, sir. But would you please repeat for us her words as best you remember?

Keeley: I recall every word. She said, "Ben, there is someone here who wants to talk to you."

D.A.: That's all?

Keeley: That was it.

D.A.: How was her tone of voice?

Keeley: Just normal. Nothing different about it.

D.A.: What happened next?

Keeley: A man's voice came on. He said, "Mr. Keeley, I am holding your wife at gunpoint. If she tries anything funny, this gun is going off."

Mr. Keeley pauses, wiping his eyes.

D.A.: Can you go on, sir?

Keeley: I'm all right. Then he said, "Here's what I want you to do. Put ten thousand dollars in a bag—only fifties and hundred-dollar bills. Take the bag to the phone booth at the food court two blocks down the street, and wait there for further instructions. Bring your cell phone and leave it on. Be there in forty-five minutes or it'll be all over for her. You understand?"

D.A.: And what did you say?

Keeley: What could I say? I said I understood—and he hung up.

D.A.: What next?

Keeley: I don't mind telling you I was scared. The bank has been robbed before, but not like this. I called the FBI. They told me to follow the caller's instructions and go to the food court with the cash. The FBI agent said he would have agents nearby in plain clothes.

D.A.: And did you follow the instruction?

Keeley: Well, I got our cashier to put the money together and I was starting to leave the bank with it when I got a call from the FBI agent.

D.A.: What did he say?

Keeley: It was terrible. He told me Bonnie had been found shot to death in our living room, two bullets in her head. Oh, God. I mean, we'd been married for forty years—

D.A.: Are you all right? Do you want a break?

Keeley: Let's continue. Get this over with.

D.A.: Did the agent say anything else?

Keeley: Yes. He told me to go to the food court with the cash and wait just as if I didn't know what happened.

D.A.: Did you do that?

Keeley: Yes. I went there and waited for an hour. Nobody showed up, so the FBI people came up and told me I could go.

D.A.: What did you do?

Keeley: I took the bag back to the bank and drove home. They were just taking her away when I got there.

D.A.: Do you have any idea who murdered your wife?

Keeley: No. I can't imagine—

D.A.: Mr. Keeley, do you think you could identify the voice of the man who spoke to you on the phone if you heard it again?

Keeley: I don't know. I could try.

D.A.: (*To Judge*) Your Honor, I will ask that the witness be permitted to hear the defendant's voice for the purpose of identification.

"Objection!" Ed Hardin, the defense counsel, is on his feet. "The defendant has a right to remain silent—a constitutional right to not testify."

D.A.: (*To Judge*) This is not testimony, Your Honor. The defendant will not be a sworn witness. He will not incriminate himself. It's the same as having him show the color of his eyes, or a mark on his arm, for the sole purpose of identification. He is not being asked to testify against himself—

Hardin: He is being made to speak when he has a right to remain silent—

Judge: Just a moment, Counsel. I will instruct the jury accordingly, but I will allow the witness to hear the defendant's voice for the purpose of identification only. (*The judge turns to the jury.*) Ladies and gentlemen of the jury, I will ask the defendant to rise and say a few words that were said by the caller. I admonish you that this is not testimony. He is not being sworn as a witness. It is being done for one purpose only, to see if the witness is able to recognize the defendant's voice. You are not to consider the words spoken for any other purpose.

Hardin: Mr. Goodlin will comply with the court's order, Your Honor, although I find it to be objectionable and very unusual.

Judge: The objection is overruled. I will ask the defendant to rise and say the first words spoken to Mr. Keeley by the caller. I have written them down: "Mr. Keeley, I am holding your wife at gunpoint." Will the defendant say those words, please?

Goodlin: "Mr. Keeley, I am holding your wife at gunpoint.

Judge: Thank you, Mr. Goodlin. You may be seated. Proceed, Counsel.

D.A.: You have heard the defendant's voice, Mr. Keeley. Can you identify it? Is it the same voice you heard over the phone?

Keeley: (*Pause*) I cannot say, ma'am. It is similar but I cannot say positively.

D.A.: Is it possibly the same voice?

Hardin: Objection! Anything is possible.

Judge: Objection overruled. The witness may answer.

Keeley: I just can't say, Your Honor. I suppose it's possible but it's also possible it is someone else's voice. I can't say any more than that.

D.A.: Thank you. Nothing further of this witness.

Hardin: No questions.

The next witness for the prosecution is Sophie Hellmann, a woman in her sixties and a long-time friend and next-door neighbor of Bonnie Keeley. Mrs. Hellmann testifies that she was watching television at her home on the morning of December 5, 2007.

D.A.: Did something unusual occur?

Hellmann: Yes. It was about ten-thirty. I thought I heard a loud voice, maybe a scream or loud laugh—I couldn't tell which—coming from Bonnie's house. I said to my husband—he's an invalid—I said, "Did you hear that?"

D.A.: What did he say?

Hellmann: He said he didn't hear anything.

D.A.: Did you hear any shots?

Hellmann: No.

D.A.: What's the next thing you heard?

Hellmann: A few moments later I heard the noise of a car engine revving up and then driving off at a high speed, real loud. It's a quiet residential neighborhood and we don't usually hear cars that sound like that.

D.A.: What did you do?

Hellmann: I sat there for a couple seconds. I know I should have reacted sooner, but I just sat there for a minute. I said to myself, "I'm going to look." Then I went to the front door and looked outside.

D.A.: Did you see the car?

Hellmann: No, it was gone. But from our front step I could see Bonnie's front door. It was wide open.

D.A.: Did that make you suspicious?

Hellmann: Well, yes, it did. That was unusual. I walked to her door and called to her.

D.A.: Did she answer?

Hellmann: No. No answer. I called again. No answer. So I peeked inside and kept calling with no response. I took a few more steps inside and I could see the back of their sofa and the top of Bonnie's head. "Bonnie," I called. "Bonnie!" Still no answer. I rushed over and there she was—oh, my God—

D.A.: What did you see?

Hellmann: She was lying on the sofa, dead as anything, blood dripping down from her forehead, her eyes wide open. I never saw a dead person before. I shook her but she was dead.

D.A.: What did you do?

Hellmann: I know I screamed. I picked up the phone to call the police, and just as I was doing that, I heard the police loudspeaker, calling for anyone inside to come out with their hands up. I went to the door and met the sergeant by the side of the door. He had his gun drawn. All of a sudden there were men in plain clothes rushing in.

D.A.: Did you tell them what you had observed?

Hellmann: I was screaming and crying. I loved Bonnie. She was my best friend. The sergeant calmed me down and I told him what I knew, which wasn't much. Then they took over.

D.A.: Two more questions. Did you ever see anything, anyone, to indicate who killed Mrs. Keeley?

Hellmann: No, not a thing.

D.A.: Have any idea at all who would want to murder her?

Hellmann: No. Everyone loved her.

D.A.: Thank you. That's all.

Hardin: No questions.

Police Sergeant Derrick Toms is called to the stand. He is with the city police force, but often works with the FBI on cases involving both agencies. He testifies that when Mr. Keeley made his call to the FBI, all law enforcement agencies were alerted. Together, police and the FBI organized a team to move in on the Keeley residence secretly to make every effort to save Mrs. Keeley's life.

D.A.: What happened when you arrived?

Toms: We drove by in plain clothes and saw the front door was wide open. We surrounded the house, not knowing if the man who had called Mr. Keeley was still inside holding Mrs. Keeley hostage. Then we made a loudspeaker announcement directed to the caller and told him to come out with his hands up. I was inside the front door with my weapon drawn. Then Mrs. Hellmann came out of the house. She'd been crying. She told us what had happened, that Mrs. Keeley was dead and the killer had fled. We were too late.

D.A.: Then what did you do?

Toms: I went inside and checked on the victim. She was dead all right. Two bullet entry wounds in her forehead.

D.A.: Did you and the other officers conduct a search?

Toms: I had a squad search the entire house. We checked for fingerprints that might be helpful. Especially on the phone, which we had reason to believe the caller had touched.

D.A.: Find anything of value?

Toms: Only two spent cartridges on the rug next to Mrs. Keeley's body. Nothing else.

The witness identifies the two cartridges and numerous photographs of the crime scene; all are admitted into evidence without objection.

D.A.: I take it you pursued your investigation?

Toms: We did. All over the state. The whole country. Months went by. Nothing. Not a clue. We interviewed all the neighbors near the Keeley residence to find out if anyone had seen or heard anything of value. Nothing. We were frustrated. At an impasse.

D.A.: Then did something happen that helped your investigation?

Toms: Yes. The bankers' association offered a one hundred thousand dollar reward for any information leading to the killer or killers. Two days later a guy came into the station with a briefcase.

D.A.: Did you meet him at the police station?

Toms: I did. I was home playing with the kids on my day off when they called me to come down and talk to him. When I got to the station, he handed me this briefcase and said it might be important. Olander was his name. Brock Olander.

The witness thereupon identifies a black briefcase, which is received in evidence as a government exhibit.

D.A.: Did you interview Mr. Olander?

Toms: Yes, he said—

D.A.: No, don't tell us what he said. That would be hearsay.

At this point, Hardin suddenly stands and addresses the judge. "Your Honor, the defense is aware that this conversation would be considered hearsay and thus inadmissible. But I wish to advise the court that we have no objection to the conversation coming into evidence."

Judge: Thank you, Counsel. There being no objection, the district attorney may proceed.

D.A.: Now you can tell us, Sergeant. Did he tell you how he got the briefcase?

Toms: Yes, he said he got it from his housemate, Ellery Baldwin. He said Baldwin knew he had a safe and wanted him—that is, Olander—to keep it for safekeeping.

D.A.: Did you find anything of value in the briefcase?

Toms: Yes. A .22 Ruger pistol with ammunition and a gun silencer. We had a ballistics expert examine the gun and compare it with the two empty cartridges found at the scene.

D.A.: Did you have the items in the briefcase examined for fingerprints?

Toms: We did. The gun, the ammunition, the silencer—they were all tested for prints.

D.A.: Did Mr. Olander ask about the reward?

Toms: He did and we thanked him but told him that would have to wait for further investigation.

D.A.: Your Honor, defense counsel and I have entered into the following stipulation with regard to certain evidence in the case—that if Dr. Jacob Ellstein were called as a witness, he would testify that he is a nationally recognized expert in the field of ballistics. Ballistics is the study of the functioning of firearms that includes the firing, flight, and effects of ammunition. Dr. Ellstein has examined the weapon in evidence as well as the ammunition found in the briefcase. He has also examined the empty cartridges found near the body at the crime scene. He has conducted a series of tests, including the firing of the weapon using the ammunition in the briefcase, and has compared the cartridges in his testing with those found at the scene. He has also examined a spent missile that was drawn from the body of Mrs. Keeley during the autopsy and made comparisons with the spent missiles in his testing. As a result of all his tests, and based on his training and experience, Dr. Ellstein concludes with virtual certainty that the weapon contained in the briefcase is the weapon that shot and killed Mrs. Keeley. That, Your Honor, is the extent of our stipulation.

Judge: Mr. Hardin?

Hardin: That is correct, Your Honor. We accept the stipulation.

Judge: (*To jury*) Ladies and gentlemen of the jury, you have heard the stipulation. A stipulation is an agreement between counsel as to certain facts in the case. You may receive the facts stated in the stipulation as having been conclusively proved. Proceed, Counsel.

D.A.: I have no further questions of the witness who is still on the stand.

Hardin: No questions.

Judge: The witness may step down.

Marva London is the next witness, a thirtyish, smartly dressed woman with a grim expression. She testifies that she is an employee of Continental Airlines and works at the airport as a ticket agent.

D.A.: A few days ago, did you see something in the local newspaper that caught your attention?

London: I saw a man's picture in the paper. When I saw it, I thought to myself, "That face looks familiar."

D.A.: Do you recall where you may have seen him?

London: I think it was at the ticket counter. I couldn't tell if it was him in the picture, but it looked similar.

D.A.: What is it you recall?

London: It was a slow time at the airport. I remember this man came up to me sort of excited and wanted to know the price of a ticket to Buenos Aires. I gave him the price. He said he would have to get the money. Then he left.

D.A.: Did he say anything else?

London: No. That was it.

D.A.: Do you remember when this occurred?

London: It was soon after I came back to working at the counter. So it would have to have been early December.

D.A.: This crime occurred December 5, 2007. Was it around that time?

London: Oh yes, that's right. I remember reading about this murder in the papers. It was right after that.

D.A.: Can you describe him?

London: Well, as best I recall he was average height and build, nothing distinctive, a young guy in his twenties or thirties, and he was wearing a black sweater.

You look at Mr. Goodlin. He seems to fit the characteristics described by the witness.

D.A.: Do you recall the color of his hair or the color of his eyes?

London: No. I only saw him for a few minutes—if that long.

D.A.: Do you think you could identify him if you saw him again?

London: I could try.

D.A.: Ms. London, I would like you to look around this room—take your time, look carefully—and tell us if you see that man in this courtroom.

The witness looks around. She puts on her glasses and focuses on the defendant seated at the defense table with his attorney. She leans forward as if to get closer. She turns to the judge. "Your Honor, may I step down and move closer?"

Judge: You may.

The witness steps down from the witness stand and walks to the defense table, examining the defendant up close. "Your Honor, could I please see the defendant in a standing position?"

Judge: I shall ask Mr. Goodlin to rise.

As Goodlin stands, the witness circles him, her eyes trained on his face. Finally, she returns to the witness stand. The audience is hushed, waiting for her response. The judge nods to the defendant, who resumes his seat.

London: I am sorry, Your Honor. He looks similar to the man I saw but I cannot say it is him. I cannot make a positive identification.

D.A.: Thank you, Ms. London. I have no further questions.

Hardin: No questions.

The D.A. calls Dahlia Yonatelli as her next witness. Ms. Yonatelli is a fairly attractive brunette in her early twenties and works as a receptionist for a computer company. She states that she knows the defendant and identifies him for the record.

D.A.: How do you know the defendant?

Yonatelli: We went out a couple of times.

D.A.: Was it before this crime occurred on December 5, 2007?

Yonatelli: Oh, yes. Weeks before then. It was around September and October.

D.A.: Did you like him?

Yonatelli: Of course. Would I go out with him otherwise? He was a nice guy. We went bowling together.

D.A.: Did he tell you of his plans?

Yonatelli: He said he had to leave town for awhile, if that's what you mean.

D.A.: Did he tell you why?

Yonatelli: I asked him that. He said it was his private business.

D.A.: Did you ask him when he was leaving?

Yonatelli: I did, and he said he needed to get the money together first.

D.A.: Tell us what happened the last time you saw him.

Yonatelli: We'd gone bowling, then to dinner. When he drove up to my place, we started making out and stuff in the car. It got pretty heavy, you know what I mean. At one point my head was leaning against his chest and all of a sudden I felt something in his inside jacket pocket. Real hard like a piece of metal. I asked, "What's this?" and started to slip my hand inside his jacket to see what it was and—oh God, he got very upset.

D.A.: What did he say?

Yonatelli: He pushed my hand away and said, "Don't touch it, it's loaded." I said, "What's loaded? You mean it's a gun?" And he said, "Yeah, sure it's a gun and be careful, it's loaded."

D.A.: What did you say to that?

Yonatelli: I was scared. I said, "Why are you carrying a gun when you're out with me?" And he said, "I got enemies, that's all. Nothing to do with you. I need it for protection." I asked him what kind of gun it was and he said, "It's a .22, don't worry about it."

D.A.: Did you ever see the gun?

Yonatelli: No. I didn't want to see it.

D.A.: What did you do next?

Yonatelli: Like I said, I was scared. I said good night and went inside.

D.A.: Did you see Mr. Goodlin again?

Yonatelli: Not until now. I mean, I liked the guy, but I didn't want to get mixed up in guns. He called me, but I just said I was seeing someone else.

D.A.: Thank you. That's all. The defense attorney may have some questions.

Hardin: No questions.

Brock Olander takes the stand for the prosecution.

D.A.: You lived in the same house with Ellery Baldwin?

Olander: Yeah. We shared the rent for a two-bedroom apartment. We'd been friends, but we didn't always get along.

D.A.: What do you mean?

Olander: He worked in a bakery and had strange hours. He'd get through with work at about midnight and come over with his friend Gene.

D.A.: You mean the defendant, Gene Goodlin?

Olander: That's right.

The witness identifies the defendant.

D.A.: Did they bother you?

Olander: They sure did. They'd stay up late and have loud music on. And also Ellery let Gene get into my liquor.

D.A.: Did you like Gene Goodlin?

Olander: He was okay, but I didn't like him getting into my liquor cabinet and getting drunk. He didn't smoke pot or use speed but he drank a lot.

D.A.: Did he ever ask you for money?

Olander: Oh, yeah, that—well, yes, he asked me for a loan—said he needed to get out of town and live abroad for awhile.

D.A.: Was this before the murder of Bonnie Keeley?

Olander: Yes, ma'am. It was definitely before that.

D.A.: Did you give him the money?

Olander: Heck no. I didn't have the kind of cash he wanted.

D.A.: Did he tell you why he wanted to go abroad?

Olander: I did ask him and he just said he had his reasons. I didn't pursue it.

D.A.: I want to ask you about the briefcase we have here in evidence.

She shows the briefcase to the witness.

D.A.: At some time after the crime in this case, did Ellery Baldwin give you this briefcase?

Olander: He did, but he didn't tell me what was in it. He just said he wanted me to keep it for safekeeping. I had a safe and he said he didn't have any good place to keep it. I asked him what was in it, but he just said it was his own private stuff and he didn't want anybody fooling with it. I just put it away in the safe and forgot about it.

D.A.: Did something happen that prompted you to look in the briefcase?

Olander: I thought about the briefcase when I saw the article about the reward. The story in the paper said police believed the victim may have been shot with a .22 pistol. A wild idea went through my mind that maybe the briefcase was somehow related to the case. I decided to open the safe and look inside the briefcase. There was a .22 in there, all right, and ammo, and a silencer. What was Ellery doing putting this stuff in my hands?

D.A.: Did that make you angry at Ellery?

Olander: It sure did. No wonder he didn't tell me what was inside. I could be in real trouble with the police if this gun was involved in the murder and it was found in my possession.

D.A.: So what did you do?

Olander: Well, I will admit I thought about the hundred thousand bucks. Sure, I'm no angel. I admit to thinking about the money. I mean, who wouldn't? That's a lot of cash. And I was mad at Ellery for putting me in danger. But, anyway, I took the briefcase down to the station.

D.A.: You talked to Sergeant Toms and gave him a report?

Olander: Yes. I gave the briefcase to him and told him how I got it.

D.A.: Did you ever talk to the defendant, Mr. Goodlin, about the briefcase?

Olander: No. I didn't know he was involved.

D.A.: Thank you. No further questions.

Judge: (*To defense counsel*) Cross-examination?

Hardin: No questions, Your Honor.

You notice that the judge is beginning to be disturbed by Ed Hardin's failure to cross-examine the prosecution witnesses. He stares at Hardin for a moment.

Judge: (*To defense counsel*) Are you sure you have no questions, Mr. Hardin?

Hardin: No questions, Your Honor.

D.A.: Your Honor, I am sure Your Honor and the jury will be pleased to know that I have just one more witness. The State calls Ellery Baldwin.

You look at the main door, waiting for Baldwin to appear. But unlike all the other witnesses, Baldwin enters through a back door, dressed in the orange jumpsuit of a jail inmate. He is escorted by a bailiff, his hands behind his back in handcuffs. There is a hush in the courtroom as the bailiff leads him to the witness stand and removes the handcuffs. You know from the D.A.'s opening statement and the evidence presented so far that Ellery Baldwin is the prosecution's principal witness. The case will stand or fall on his testimony. Baldwin is a lean, wiry man who seems a bit cocky, with a slight grin on his face as he states his name and awaits direct examination.

D.A.: Where do you reside?

Baldwin: You mean where do I live now? Right downstairs in the county jail.

D.A.: You are in custody, right?

Baldwin: Right.

D.A.: And that's because you have entered a plea of guilty to the charge of murder, the murder of Bonnie Keeley, is that right?

Baldwin: Yes, ma'am.

D.A.: And now you are awaiting sentence on that charge?

Baldwin: Yes.

D.A.: And you entered that plea voluntarily, of your own free will, correct?

Baldwin: Yes, ma'am.

D.A.: No one forced you to plead guilty, did they?

Baldwin: No, no one.

D.A.: And did you enter that plea because in truth and in fact you are guilty?

Baldwin: That's right. I mean, as an aider and abettor. But I didn't shoot her.

D.A.: I understand that. Now, did I or anyone else make you any promise as to what your sentence will be?

Baldwin: No, ma'am.

D.A.: Do you know Gene Goodlin, the defendant in this case?

Baldwin: Yes, ma'am. That's him right over there.

He points at Goodlin.

D.A.: Your Honor, may the record show the witness has identified the defendant?

Judge: The record may so show.

D.A.: How do you know Mr. Goodlin?

Baldwin: We met at a fitness center. He had a job showing customers how to use the equipment. I was going there to get in shape.

D.A.: Tell us how you came to be involved in the killing of Mrs. Keeley.

Baldwin: Well, ma'am, Mr. Goodlin needed a good amount of cash right away. He wanted to go to South America and live there awhile.

D.A.: Did he tell you why he wanted to do that?

Baldwin: He just said it was a private matter and I left it at that.

D.A.: So how did he plan to get the cash?

Baldwin: We hatched up this scheme to rob the bank.

D.A.: Whose idea was that?

Baldwin: We worked it out together. We agreed to split the proceeds.

D.A.: Tell us what happened.

Baldwin: We checked first to make sure Mr. Keeley was at the bank and Mrs. Keeley was home alone. Then we went to the front door and rang the doorbell. Goodlin carried a flower box with a gun inside it. Mrs. Keeley opened the door; he drew the gun on her and forced his way in. I stayed outside as the lookout.

D.A.: What happened next?

Baldwin: I waited a few minutes. I heard Mrs. Keeley scream. I couldn't hear the shots. Gene came running out of the house and we got in the car and drove off. We figured nobody saw us so we agreed to go back to our daily lives and act as if nothing happened.

D.A.: Did you ever ask Mr. Goodlin what happened in the house?

Baldwin: He just said the plan went bad. She didn't cooperate, and he had to shoot her.

D.A.: Is what you told us the same account you gave to the police?

Baldwin: Yes, ma'am.

D.A.: Have you told us the truth?

Baldwin: I have, it's the truth.

D.A.: Thank you. That's all I have.

This time Hardin is eager for cross-examination. "Didn't you leave something out when you told the jury about your plea of guilty?"

Baldwin: What do you mean?

Hardin: I'll tell you what I mean. You and Mr. Goodlin were both charged with murder in the first degree, right?

Baldwin: That's right.

Hardin: But you made a deal for a lesser charge.

Baldwin: I wouldn't call it a deal.

Hardin: What would you call it?

Baldwin: They call it a plea bargain.

Hardin: A bargain, eh? All right, Mr. Baldwin, let's call it that. You got a bargain for your plea, right?

Baldwin: Well—

Hardin: Your charge was reduced from first-degree murder to second-degree murder, isn't that right?

Baldwin: Yes, well, it wasn't reduced. I just pled guilty to second-degree murder.

Hardin: And the D.A. accepted it?

Baldwin: Yes.

Hardin: Instead of first-degree murder?

Baldwin: All right, yes.

Hardin: But with certain conditions, right?

Baldwin: What conditions?

Hardin: On the condition you turn State's witness and testify the way they want you to, right?

Baldwin: The only condition was that I tell the truth.

Hardin: And the so-called truth was what you agreed with the D.A. you would say, isn't that so?

Baldwin: That's right.

Hardin: So this was the deal, the bargain—let's just see if I have it right. One, you promised to turn State's witness and testify for the prosecution with the story you gave them. Two, they promised to let you plead guilty to the lesser charge of second-degree murder in which case the more serious charge of first-degree murder would be, in effect, dismissed. Have I stated the deal correctly?

Baldwin: That's one way of putting it.

Hardin: Is there another way?

Baldwin: Well, I don't know, I guess not.

Hardin: Another thing, Mr. Baldwin. You testified that no promises were made to you with regard to your sentence, isn't that so?

Baldwin: That's right. They told me they couldn't make any promises. They just said I would be sentenced according to law.

Hardin: Didn't the D.A. say that if you testified according to the plea bargain she would tell the judge at your sentencing hearing that you cooperated with the government?

Baldwin: Oh, yeah, she said that, but there was no promise about a lower sentence.

Hardin: Mr. Baldwin, we are generally not supposed to discuss penalty before the jury, but you are aware, are you not, that second-degree murder carries a lesser sentence than first-degree murder?

Baldwin: Of course. I know that.

Hardin: Substantially less, right?

D.A.: Objection!

Judge: Overruled. Goes to his state of mind. The witness may answer.

Baldwin: Yes.

Hardin: How much less?

D.A.: Objection! Your Honor, now counsel is going too far. Penalty is not to be considered by the jury.

Hardin: Your Honor, the jury is entitled to know the full nature of this bargain. If this witness was being paid in cash for his testimony, Your Honor would certainly allow it. Here he is being given a bargain, a much lesser sentence. The jury has a right to know what it is.

D.A.: This is ridiculous. I repeat, Your Honor, the jury is never permitted to consider penalty. I object!

Judge: That's enough, Counsel. The court is ready to rule. The witness has admitted he made a plea bargain. The jury is entitled to know its full extent. Proceed, Mr. Hardin.

Hardin: Mr. Baldwin, I will ask the question this way—what is the penalty for first-degree murder in this state?

Baldwin: Twenty-five to life.

Hardin: And what is the penalty for second-degree murder?

Baldwin: I believe it's fifteen to life.

Hardin: A difference of at least ten years in prison?

Baldwin: That's right.

Hardin: Thank you. Now let's turn to another subject.

Hardin rises from his seat and pauses a moment.

Hardin: Did you shoot Mrs. Keeley?

Baldwin: No! That's ridiculous.

Hardin: Is it?

Hardin approaches the court clerk and asks for State's Exhibit 5. There is a long silence as the clerk unlocks her file cabinet and pulls out the briefcase in evidence. Hardin takes the exhibit to the witness stand.

Hardin: Your Honor, so that we all feel safe, before proceeding I wish to inform the court that the gun inside this briefcase has been unloaded by the bailiff.

Judge: Thank you. Proceed.

Hardin: (*Handing the exhibit to the witness*) This your briefcase?

Baldwin: Yes.

Hardin: You gave it to Brock Olander for safekeeping?

Baldwin: Yes. He had a safe.

Hardin: And when you gave it to him, you said—and I quote his testimony—"He just said it was his own private stuff and he didn't want anybody fooling with it." Did you say that?

Baldwin: I don't remember my exact words, but something like that.

Hardin: You told him it was yours.

Baldwin: I guess I did, but—

Hardin: So the gun inside was yours?

Baldwin: At that time it was.

Hardin: What do you mean?

Baldwin: Gene gave it to me after the murder. I realize now I was stupid to take it, but I did.

Hardin: Oh? You didn't tell us that on direct examination.

Baldwin: Nobody asked me.

Hardin: No further questions.

D.A.: Mr. Baldwin, I have one question. I want you to turn to the jury and look them in the eye.

The witness does so.

D.A.: Do you swear under oath that Gene Goodlin shot Mrs. Keeley?

Baldwin: I swear to God.

D.A.: Your Honor, the prosecution has no further witnesses. The State rests.

Hardin: The defense will rely on the evidence presented, Your Honor. The defense rests.

Before closing arguments, the judge instructs the jury on the law. Several instructions stand out.

> The defendant has a constitutional right not to be compelled to testify. You must not draw any inference from the fact that the defendant does not testify. Further, you must neither discuss this matter nor permit it to enter your deliberations in any way.

In other words, a juror cannot even talk about the defendant's failure to testify in the jury deliberation room and must not let it affect the verdict. As to circumstantial evidence, the judge's instructions include the following remarks:

> Circumstantial evidence is evidence that, if found to be true, proves a fact from which an inference of another fact may be drawn. You may not find the defendant guilty of any crime based on circumstantial evidence unless the proved circumstances:
>
> 1. are consistent with the theory that the defendant is guilty of the crime; and,
>
> 2. cannot be reconciled with any other rational conclusion.
>
> It is not necessary that facts be proved by direct evidence. They may be proved also by a combination of direct and circumstantial evidence. Both direct and circumstantial evidence are acceptable as a means of proof. Neither is entitled to any greater weight than the other. If the circumstantial evidence permits two reasonable interpretations, one

pointing to the defendant's guilt and the other to his innocence, then you must adopt the interpretation that points to his innocence and reject the interpretation that points to his guilt. But if one interpretation is reasonable and the other unreasonable, then you must accept the reasonable interpretation only.

You are well aware of the most important instruction of all—in order to find the defendant guilty, the jury must be convinced by proof beyond a reasonable doubt.

The defense counsel begins closing arguments.

Ladies and gentlemen of the jury. You have heard from a series of prosecution witnesses and, except for one, they have all been credible. Except for one, we have no dispute with their testimony. Except for one.

And as to that one witness—and you all know who I mean—there hangs a heavy cloud over his testimony and a real doubt as to his credibility. I challenge the government's attorney to lift that cloud. I make that challenge because I know that nothing she can say—no matter how eloquent her closing remarks may be—she cannot make that cloud go away. She cannot erase the reasonable doubt that Ellery Baldwin has raised in this case.

Is there anyone else who has told us that Gene Goodlin did anything wrong? Anyone? Ben Keeley, the bank president—and how our hearts go out to him in this tragedy—heard a man's voice tell him his wife was in danger. Here in court Mr. Keeley even heard Gene Goodlin mouth the same words he, Ben Keeley, heard over the phone. Could Mr. Keeley identify that voice? "I cannot say," Mr. Keeley said. "I cannot say it is the same voice."

After the murder, an airline ticket agent, Marva London, was approached by a man seeking to fly to Buenos Aires but lacking the money for a ticket. Sounds suspicious. She saw him up close at the counter, says the man looked similar to the defendant's picture. Here in court she stepped down from the stand and went up to Mr. Goodlin face-to-face. You saw how carefully she looked him over. She was a good witness. She wanted to be sure. What did she say? "I cannot say," she said. "I cannot make a positive identification."

Cannot say. Cannot say.

Ladies and gentlemen, we don't convict a man for murder in this country on "cannot say." That is not the American way. That's not proof beyond a reasonable doubt. There has to be proof—not just maybe, not just probably, not just likely. No. We have to have proof—proof beyond any reasonable doubt. That's the law, and you promised under oath when you were sworn in as jurors that you would follow the law.

Dahlia Yonatelli was Gene Goodlin's girlfriend. One night in the car she felt a gun inside his jacket. He told her it was a .22. That was all. We may not approve of him carrying a gun, but was that a crime? Did he do anything wrong? I suppose thousands of people carry .22s. Can we say that was the gun that murdered Bonnie Keeley? No, we cannot say. Cannot say. It's a refrain that runs through this entire case.

So it all comes down to Ellery Baldwin. He is the only witness who tries to pin this murder on Gene Goodlin. The only one. The State's entire case depends on him. Can you believe Ellery Baldwin?

Mr. Baldwin made a deal with the D.A. He doesn't want to call it a deal. So we'll use his word for it—a bargain. In exchange for turning State's witness and testifying against Gene Goodlin, they let him plead guilty to second-degree murder and had his charge of first-degree murder dismissed. The district attorney doesn't like for us to put the bargain in those terms, but you heard Baldwin tell us what it was and you know that's what it comes down to. Now, let me put this to you. If the government paid Baldwin a thousand dollars, or even a hundred

> dollars, or any amount of cash for that matter, for testifying against Gene Goodlin, you would be disgusted. You would throw that testimony out the window in a second. And yet isn't that essentially what happened in this case? Wasn't Ellery Baldwin in effect paid for his testimony? In fact, he got a lot more than money for his testimony—he got at least ten years cut off his time in prison. He got at least ten years of freedom. And freedom, ladies and gentlemen, is priceless. Can you believe Ellery Baldwin in this scenario? Can you place your absolute faith in his testimony when you know what he's getting paid for it?—
>
> **D.A.**: Objection! Nobody's getting paid for anything!
>
> **Judge**: Overruled.

The defense attorney continues.

> Ladies and gentlemen, you are all good Americans. You want your courts to deliver justice, to deliver verdicts that are not tainted, not poisoned by questionable deals. If you are going to convict a man of a brutal murder, you want to be sure the only witness—or alleged witness—is being completely honest with you. Can you believe Ellery Baldwin? He has a motive to put the blame on Goodlin. He has a motive to fabricate. Can you say you are convinced beyond all reasonable doubt that he is telling you the truth?
>
> That's not all. There is another cloud of reasonable doubt in this case. Ellery Baldwin had the murder weapon in his possession. He tried to get Brock Olander to hide the gun for him in Olander's safe. Baldwin told Olander the gun was his. Now he tells us that Mr. Goodlin gave him the gun. Does that make sense? Does it make sense that Baldwin would take the gun from Mr. Goodlin knowing that he, Baldwin, would be in deep trouble with the police if he were ever found with it?

> Ladies and gentleman, I am about to close. I will not have the opportunity to speak to you again after the district attorney's argument. I will not have a chance to rebut what she says. Please keep in mind that there is not a single witness who corroborates Mr. Baldwin's story. Other than Baldwin, there is not a single witness who testified to seeing Gene Goodlin do anything wrong, anything suspicious. Other than Baldwin, it's all innuendo. Nothing positive. It's all circumstantial evidence. No direct evidence. No positive identifications. It's all, "cannot say." Even Mr. Olander, who was around Mr. Goodlin a lot of the time, told us that he had no indication Mr. Goodlin was involved. Those were his words. The judge told you that in a circumstantial evidence case, if there are two reasonable interpretations of the evidence, one pointing to guilt and the other to innocence, then you must—I repeat—must choose the interpretation pointing to innocence. That's the law and you promised to follow the law.
>
> All I ask you to do is to use your common sense, your sense of justice. If you do that, you will return the only reasonable verdict in this case—not guilty.

Hardin resumes his seat. Goodlin pats him on the shoulder as if to thank him for his remarks.

The D.A. frowns as she rises to make her closing statement.

> Ladies and gentlemen, let's get one thing straight at the start. Ellery Baldwin is guilty of murder in the second degree and that's what he pled guilty to. There is no evidence he ever shot anyone, ever threatened anyone, ever had a gun during the crime. He was the lookout, an aider and abettor to the murder, and that was all. His conviction is what he deserved—no more, no less. He received no promise of leniency for his plea. His plea was appropriate under the law, and he will face serious consequences for his crime. Yes, we did tell him we would let the judge know that he cooperated with us, but that was all. There was never any promise of any lesser sentence other than what the law

prescribed for second-degree murder. His plea was entirely voluntary. His decision to testify for the State was made of his own free will. That was not easy for him, but Ellery Baldwin had the courage to come in here and tell us the truth.

The defense counsel tries to make light of the other prosecution witnesses, as if their testimony did nothing to incriminate Mr. Goodlin. I disagree. Consider the evidence. Mr. Keeley could not positively identify the voice on the phone, but said it sounded similar. Ms. London, the ticket agent, could not positively identify the man at the ticket counter who was inquiring about a one-way ticket to Buenos Aires, but she testified he looked similar to the defendant. The man told her he needed to get the cash together for the ticket before he could buy it. Two witnesses—one saying the voice was similar, the other saying the physical appearance was similar. Is that just a coincidence? Olander told us that Mr. Goodlin asked him for a substantial loan before the murder. So we know Mr. Goodlin needed cash and a good amount of it. Remember Dahlia Yonatelli? She was the defendant's girlfriend for a while—until she found out he carried a gun. And what kind of gun was it, ladies and gentlemen? He told her it was a .22, the same kind of gun that was used to shoot Mrs. Keeley in cold blood. Another coincidence?

What about motive? Who had the motive to rob the bank and get a lot of cash? The judge has instructed you that motive is not an essential element of the crime and need not be shown, but it is a circumstance that you may take into consideration. There is no question that the defendant had the motive to steal for big money. Who had the motive? Who had the gun? Who looked similar and had a voice similar to the perpetrator of this terrible crime?

The D.A. walks to a position behind the defendant's chair and points down at him.

He is sitting right here, ladies and gentlemen. He is the only one who had the motive. He is the only one who had the gun. He is the only one who had the similar voice, the similar physical appearance. Every piece of evidence points to him and no one else. Oh yes. There is much more evidence in this case than just the testimony of Ellery Baldwin.

Ladies and gentlemen, this was indeed a brutal crime, a horrible crime. Bonnie Keeley cannot be here to tell us who shot her, but one person had the gumption to come forward and tell us who did. Defense counsel argues that Ellery Baldwin is lying to save his own hide. Well, certainly Baldwin would like a lesser sentence if he can get it, but there is no evidence he is lying. No witness has contradicted anything Baldwin has said.

You might be wondering why the district attorney would make such a deal as was made in this case, and yes, it was a deal, we admit that. It doesn't sound very pretty, but it's reality, something we had to do to get at the truth and get the killer in this crime. I will be frank with you. It's quite simple really, and I am not ashamed to tell you how it works. There was a big fish, Goodlin the shooter, and a little fish, Baldwin the lookout. We wanted the big fish and we had to make this deal to get him. There were no other witnesses to the murder. Without Baldwin as a witness, the real villain in this case could go free, walk right out the door. It's not something we like to do, but would the citizens of this community want us to do anything else? Would you rather we went to trial against Gene Goodlin without Baldwin's testimony? Of course not. You want the truth. You want as many facts as you can get.

Do your duty, ladies and gentlemen. This man is guilty of a treacherous, cold-blooded murder. He shot Bonnie Keeley in the head at close range. Not once, but twice. Don't let him get away with murder, ladies and gentlemen. He is guilty. Come back here after you deliberate and tell him so. Thank you.

WHAT IS YOUR VERDICT?

QUESTIONS FOR YOU TO CONSIDER

As you determine your verdict for this crime, here are some questions about the crime and the trial for you to think about.

1. A defense attorney in a criminal case is supposed to vigorously defend his or her client. Was the defense attorney negligent in his duty by failing to cross-examine any of the prosecution witnesses except Ellery Baldwin?

2. Assume you found Goodlin guilty as charged. Assume further that after the trial, you receive a call from Goodlin's daughter. She tells you that Goodlin had been an Eagle Scout, that he hated violence, that he worked as a volunteer in a program for children at juvenile hall where he served as a part-time teacher, that he was a kind and caring father, and that on Thanksgiving and Christmas he helped serve dinner to the homeless. You call Ed Hardin, the defense attorney, and ask, "Why wasn't this evidence presented at trial?"

3. What was the most effective part of the D.A.'s closing argument?

4. How many states authorize the imposition of the death penalty and how is it imposed?

AUTHOR'S ANSWERS TO THE QUESTIONS

1. The fact that the defense attorney failed to cross-examine any prosecution witnesses except Ellery Baldwin was not a sign of his negligence in this case. He had no reason to dispute their testimony. His sole strategy was to cast a cloud over Baldwin's credibility and thereby raise a reasonable doubt as to the guilt of his client. Whether he succeeded is up to you.

2. Evidence of a defendant's good character always opens up evidence of his bad character. If such evidence of Goodlin's good character had been presented by the defense on Goodlin's behalf, the prosecution could then have presented evidence of Goodlin's bad character that could not have been presented in the prosecution's case in chief. Such bad character evidence would have included the fact that Goodlin had pled guilty in federal court to manufacturing gun silencers and was out on bail awaiting sentencing for that crime at the time of the murder. That is why he needed enough cash to fly to Buenos Aires and live in South America until the federal case blew over. Federal cases don't blow over, but that was his plan. Furthermore, Goodlin had a prior felony conviction for robbery, which would have come out if he took the stand. The defense attorney had little choice but to keep silent as to Goodlin's character and keep him off the stand.

3. The most effective part of the D.A.'s closing argument was probably her candid admission to the jury as to the "deal" with Ellery Baldwin—the "use-the-small-fish-to-catch-the-big-fish" strategy. Jurors like to have such tactics explained to them.

4. As this book went to press, thirty-six states authorized the imposition of the death penalty. The sole method of execution in California for many years was the gas chamber. Now California allows a condemned prisoner to choose between lethal injection and the traditional method of the gas chamber. However, in October 2007,

the Supreme Court stayed the execution of a Mississippi prisoner who was scheduled to die by lethal injection. The stay was to remain in effect until the Supreme Court reviewed the question of whether lethal injection amounts to cruel and unusual punishment in violation of the Eighth Amendment of the Constitution. In April 2008, the Supreme Court ruled that the imposition of the death penalty by lethal injection does not violate the Constitution.

THE VERDICT

What was your verdict?

The real-life jury found the defendant guilty of first-degree murder.

The real-life defendant was sentenced to death.

At the penalty phase, factors in aggravation and mitigation were presented to the same jury that heard the guilt phase. In 1998, thirteen years after the real-life crime, the defendant was executed by lethal injection.

One Bullet Pierces Two Hearts

STATE V. ROY CARTWRIGHT

Roy Cartwright, 52, was romantically involved with Marlene Ransom, twenty-five years his junior. Almost every day, Roy would visit Marlene at her cottage and they would smoke and sip whiskey together, watch TV, and sometimes make love. Roy asked Marlene to marry him but she was not yet divorced from her estranged husband, so they had to put off wedding plans. Marty Hogan, 33, was Roy's best friend, but trouble started when Roy introduced Martin to Marlene. Martin and Marlene were attracted to each other. Martin began visiting Marlene, also.

One day, Roy bought a 7-millimeter rifle for the purpose, so he claimed, of going deer hunting, although he had never hunted deer before in his life and deer season was still three months away. Five days later, Roy was visiting with Marlene when Martin dropped by to see her. While Martin and Marlene were talking, Roy said he wanted to show them his new rifle. He went out to the trunk of his car, retrieved the rifle, and came back inside. Martin and Marlene were standing near each other at the other side of the room. When Roy unwrapped the rifle, a shot went off. The bullet went through Marlene's heart, out her back, through Martin's heart, out his back, and through the wall behind him. Marlene and Martin were killed instantly by the same bullet. From the location of the entry and exit wounds, and the position of the bodies, it was obvious that Marlene was standing directly in front of Martin when the shot was fired. Roy went home, wrote a suicide note that said he was sorry, placed the end of the rifle barrel in his mouth, and pulled the trigger. The bullet ricocheted off his palate and tore through his cheek, and Roy survived to be prosecuted for double murder. Roy claimed he did not mean to kill his two best friends, and that he was holding the gun up when it fired accidentally. Was the shooting accidental or intentional? If it was intentional, whom did Roy intend to kill? Martin? Marlene? Or both?

District Attorney Alan Weckstein arouses your curiosity in his opening statement when he says that this is the most bizarre murder he has ever prosecuted.

"One bullet," he says, and he pauses as his deep-set eyes fix you with a penetrating stare. "One bullet—and it pierced the hearts of two innocent persons, Marlene Ransom and Martin Hogan, and left them dead. We will prove that this man, Roy Cartwright, fired that shot and did so with the premeditated and deliberate intent to kill them both."

Weckstein seems satisfied that he has impressed you. He yields the podium to young Donald Ryder, a small, bouncy man who is the attorney for the defense.

Ryder is obviously incensed at the D.A.'s statement and states sharply in his opening: "Roy Cartwright never intended any harm. This was an accident, pure and simple. He is a gentle, law-abiding man, and he has already suffered far beyond what most human beings are ever called upon to experience. Roy's grief will burden him for the remainder of his life."

You look at the defendant, who sits motionless, staring straight ahead—a stocky, balding, humorless-looking man in his fifties.

"And why was the accident so tragic?" Ryder continues. "Because that bullet caused the death of Roy's two best friends. The judge will tell you that it is not a crime if a shooting is the result of an accident—"

"Objection!" Weckstein jumps up from his seat. "He's instructing the jury. That's Your Honor's job."

"Sustained." The judge turns to the jury and looks over his spectacles. "Ladies and gentlemen of the jury, I wish to instruct you that what counsel says in their opening statements is not evidence and not to be considered for a moment as evidence. The only evidence will come from the witness stand or by stipulation of counsel. And I will instruct you on the law. No one else will do that. Proceed, Counsel."

The first witness for the prosecution is a grizzly looking man in his seventies, Frank Kersey. He testifies he is the caretaker of Family Cottages, a residential complex of about twenty studio cottages where Marlene Ransom had lived for the last seven years. On the morning of July 7, 2005, he was making his rounds when he heard a sharp bang. As he neared the rear of cottage number nine, he heard the sound of running water. He went toward the sound and noticed that the water pipe about four feet high behind cottage nine had sprung a leak and water was pouring out of a hole in the pipe. Then he noticed a hole in the back wall of cottage nine, about the same height as the pipe. He heard what he thought was a low moan inside the cottage.

"And did you investigate further?" D.A. Weckstein asks.

> **Kersey**: I figured something was up. I knew Marlene was inside, since her car was still there. So I went around to the front.
>
> **Weckstein**: Tell the jury what you saw.
>
> **Kersey**: The door was ajar. I called for Marlene, but there was no answer. I peeked in, and…oh, my God…

Weckstein: Just take it easy and tell us what you saw.

Kersey: It was the most horrible sight. There was Marlene and this guy lying together on the floor in a puddle of blood. I took one look and figured they were dead. I got out of there and called the cops.

Weckstein: You know the defendant, Roy Cartwright?

Kersey: Sure, I seen him around there a lot.

Weckstein: Did you see him there that morning?

Kersey: I seen his car leave earlier. But I didn't think—

Weckstein: That's all, thank you.

Ryder begins his cross-examination politely, almost deferentially. "Have you any reason to think Roy here would shoot Marlene?"

Kersey: Who? Him? Nah. He loved her. He was tender-like to her. He'd never do anything like that, not unless it was an accident.

Ryder: You were around cottage number nine many times when Roy was there visiting her?

Kersey: Sure, lots of times.

Ryder: Ever hear Roy and Marlene argue?

Kersey: Never.

Ryder: Ever hear Roy act hostile to anyone?

Kersey: No, never.

The next witness is police officer Guy Robb, the first officer on the scene. He testifies the first thing he did was to check the pulse and heartbeat of Marlene Ransom and Martin Hogan, and he found they were both dead.

Blood was still coming out of both their chests. Their bodies lay on the floor together, Hogan's head propped up against the back wall. Both lay on their backs, eyes open. Ransom's body lay partly on top of Hogan's, and both were still warm to the touch. He turned the bodies over and saw blood oozing from their backs.

He looked about the room for evidence. On the back wall above the bodies, forty-nine inches from the floor, he noticed a hole that indicated that a bullet had passed through the wall. He searched the room for any empty cartridges but found none. On the bed near the front door he found a large piece of wrapping paper from a gun store.

Officer Robb further testifies that after the bodies were removed, he searched outside the cottage for the expended bullet or bullets. He still was not sure how many shots had been fired. He saw the hole in the water pipe and then saw another hole in the wall of the cottage next door, about ten feet from number nine, also about the same height as the other holes. He went inside the cottage next door after receiving permission from the frightened occupants, and on the floor of the kitchen found what he was looking for—a spent rifle bullet.

The prosecution then calls Emily Masterson. She is a timid woman, about 30 years old, and as she raises her hand to take the oath, you can tell she is reluctant to testify. When she gets to the witness stand, she stops and asks, "Your Honor, do I have to testify?"

> **Judge**: We just want the truth.
>
> **Masterson**: I don't want to testify unless you order me to, Your Honor.
>
> **Judge**: Then I will have to order it.

Mrs. Masterson testifies that she is Cartwright's only child from his former marriage. He had been living with her and her daughter—his granddaughter—at the time of the shooting. She had wanted him to end the relationship with Marlene because she knew Marlene had been unfaithful to him. Yet her father was obsessed with Marlene, and insisted he was going to marry her. On the morning of the shooting, Mrs. Masterson was in the kitchen of her home, about two miles from Family Cottages, when she heard a loud bang and a cry of pain from her father's room. She rushed in to find him lying on his bed holding a rifle in his hands, the muzzle up against his face, one side of his face covered with blood. He could not talk, but she realized he had tried to kill himself. She called an ambulance, and he was taken to the hospital. After leaving him at the hospital with the doctor's assurance he was out of danger, she returned home and found a note on his bed.

Weckstein shows her a piece of paper. "Is this the note?"

Masterson: Yes.

Weckstein: You recognize the handwriting?

Masterson: Yes, it's Dad's.

Weckstein: Please read it to the jury.

Mrs. Masterson is close to tears as she reads the note: "Marlene is dead. Please take care of my body."

Mrs. Masterson also identifies the rifle Weckstein shows to her as the rifle she took from her father after he shot himself.

The defense attorney, Ryder, has only a few questions. "You know your father better than anyone. What is his reputation?"

Weckstein is on his feet. "Objection, Your Honor! The question is vague. Reputation for what?"

Judge: Sustained.

Ryder: I'll rephrase it, Your Honor. Mrs. Masterson, what is your father's reputation for being a law-abiding citizen?

Masterson: He was never in any trouble in his whole life. Quiet, respects the law. He has a good reputation for being decent in every way.

Ryder: What is his reputation for being nonviolent, peaceful?

Masterson: He never hurt anyone.

She is about to leave the stand when Weckstein remembers something else. He approaches her with a small envelope and places it on the witness stand before her. "Would you open that, please?"

She takes out a small metal object.

Weckstein: You recognize what that is?

She looks at it and nods her head. "Yes, it looks like what I found in my father's pocket after he shot himself."

Weckstein holds it up for all to see. "Looks like an empty cartridge of a bullet, doesn't it?"

Masterson: I believe so, yes.

Weckstein: "That is all, thank you."

The next witness is Jason Wilkes, a young clerk from Krane's Gun Shop. He testifies that he sold a Mauser 7-millimeter rifle to a man on July 2, 2005. He identifies the same rifle that Mrs. Masterson identified as the one he sold. He also identifies a purchase slip for the rifle of $156.22, taken from his records. He cannot be sure the defendant is the man who bought the rifle, but Roy Cartwright looks similar to the person. He remembers the purchaser was unfamiliar with rifles and had to be shown how to load one.

He identifies the wrapping paper that Officer Robb found on the bed as the paper he used to wrap the rifle.

The last witness for the prosecution is Dr. David Featherman, the autopsy surgeon. He examined the bodies for the cause of death and found that each died from a bullet wound to the chest and heart.

"Was it the same bullet?" Weckstein asks.

"Objection! Beyond his expertise."

"Sustained," the judge says. "That's for the jury to decide."

But the judge allows the doctor to describe the path and position of the bullet that entered and exited each body, based on his examination of the entry and exit wounds. The doctor testifies that the bullet that killed Marlene Ransom entered her body on a path at a right angle to her body, and the position of the bullet at entry was also perpendicular to her body. The point of entry measured forty-eight inches from her toes.

He explains that the bullet exited her back slightly higher than where it was at entry. Upon exiting, the missile changed course because of the obstacles encountered while passing through her body, moving a little upward as well as slightly sideways.

The doctor explains that when the bullet entered Martin Hogan's body, it was not traveling straight as it was in Ransom's case, but rather in the same tumbling motion it exhibited when it exited Ransom's back. This tumbling—rolling forward over and over—upon entry into Hogan's chest indicated the bullet had struck something else before reaching that point. Further, the height of her exit wound and his entry wound were almost precisely the same—about forty-nine inches.

> **Weckstein**: Can you tell us, Doctor, the position of the bodies at the time the shot was fired; that is, how close they were to each other?

Featherman: I can make a very good guess.

Ryder: Objection!

Judge: Sustained. No guessing here.

Weckstein: Well then, Doctor, can you at least tell us if the two victims were seated or standing, or even lying down, when the shot or shots were fired?

Ryder: Objection! He was not there.

Judge: Sustained.

Weckstein sits down, apparently exasperated by the judge's ruling.

"Your witness, Counsel," he says to Ryder, who remains silent for a few seconds before beginning cross-examination.

Ryder: On the basis of all your training and experience, Doctor, are you able to tell this jury if the shot or shots were fired intentionally or accidentally?

There is a long pause.

Featherman: I cannot say that, no.

Ryder: Any sign of struggle?

Featherman: None I could observe.

When the doctor leaves the stand, Weckstein announces he has no further witnesses, and the prosecution rests.

Ryder opens the defense case with a number of witnesses who testify to Roy Cartwright's good reputation for two character traits—for being a nonviolent, law-abiding citizen, and for being a thoroughly honest gentleman. One such witness is Dale Stearns, manager of The Right

Spot, a restaurant where Martin Hogan worked as a short-order cook. Stearns also testifies that Hogan and Cartwright were the best of friends, that Cartwright ate most of his meals at his restaurant, and that he never heard a hostile word between them. Another witness is the Reverend Dudley Haseltine, pastor of the church Cartwright regularly attended. The minister testifies Cartwright is highly respected by other parishioners. The defendant's granddaughter, Melissa Masterson, age 14, testifies along the same lines. No one ever heard Cartwright say a hostile word about Marlene or Marty.

Ryder stands as if to make an announcement. "The defense calls Roy Cartwright."

The defendant walks to the stand slowly, solemnly, shoulders sagging. When the clerk asks him if he swears to tell the truth, he almost shouts, "I do!" You can see the scar across the side of his cheek where the bullet went through.

Cartwright testifies he retired from the Navy after twenty-four years of service as an aviation chief machinist mate, divorced his wife of many years, then became acquainted with and eventually fell in love with Marlene Ransom, twenty-five years his junior. They started having an intimate relationship while she was still married and living with her husband. One day she asked Cartwright to move into the cottage next to the one she shared with her husband, which he did gladly. After that, whenever her husband beat her up—which was often—she would come over to Cartwright's place with her eyes black and blue and stay with him for a few days, then return to her husband. When her husband left her, Cartwright asked her to marry him. She said she could not because she was not divorced yet. His grown daughter, Emily, persuaded him to move into her place a few miles away, but he and Marlene continued to see each other often.

Cartwright says he was in love with Marlene and believed she was in love with him, and it did not make him jealous that she sometimes saw other, younger men. He believed they would marry when she obtained her divorce.

He explains that his best friend was Martin Hogan. A few weeks before the shooting, he brought Marty over to Marlene's cottage and introduced them to each other. He could tell Marlene liked Marty, but that did not bother Cartwright; he knew she loved him.

He admits that five days before the shooting, he bought a Mauser 7-millimeter rifle at Krane's Gun Shop because he decided to go deer hunting. He put the rifle in the trunk of his car and kept it there. On the morning of July 7, about 9:00 a.m., he drove over to Marlene's house with some shirts she had promised to iron for him. He also brought in a bottle of Seagram's whiskey, and they both took a nip from time to time while they talked and she ironed the shirts. Then the phone rang and Marlene answered it.

Ryder paces back and forth as he continues direct examination.

Ryder: Do you remember what Marlene said on the phone?

Cartwright: I didn't pay much attention until the very end when I heard her say, "Come on over, Roy's here."

Ryder: Did you know to whom she was speaking?

Cartwright: After she hung up she told me it was Marty who called.

Ryder: Then did he arrive later?

Cartwright: Yes, about fifteen, twenty minutes later.

Ryder: Did you and Marty greet each other?

Cartwright: Sure. Why not?

Ryder: Then what happened?

Cartwright: Marlene offered him a drink, but he said he didn't want a drink until he got off work.

Ryder: So, what did you three talk about?

Cartwright: Well, she talked about this nice apartment that Marty and two other bachelors shared together—she had been over there at a party one night recently. She said it was a really nice place and that when she got some of her bills caught up and a little money ahead, she would get a nice place like that.

Ryder: Did the subject of the rifle come into the conversation?

Cartwright: Not at first.

Ryder: Later did it?

Cartwright: Well, Marlene was saying how bad her place was to live at, and she asked Marty to come over to the window so they could look out and she could show him what a mess it was in the back.

Ryder: And did they go over to the window?

Cartwright: Yes.

Ryder: Were they standing close together?

Cartwright: Yes.

Ryder: Touching?

Cartwright: Almost, yes.

Ryder: And where were you?

Cartwright: I was by the front door, so I said, "I'll show you the gun I bought."

Ryder: What did she say?

Cartwright: She said, "Oh, okay."

Ryder: Did you have the gun there?

Cartwright: No, it was in the trunk of my car.

Ryder: And where were they when you went out to get the gun?

Cartwright: They were still looking out the window by the kitchen.

Cartwright then testifies how he went out to the car, got the rifle, and brought it into the house. It still had the wrapping paper on it, so he stopped at the foot of the bed near the door and was just taking the wrapping paper off when it suddenly discharged.

Ryder: Did you say anything before the gun fired?

Cartwright: I think I said, "Well, here's the gun."

Ryder: That's all?

Cartwright: Yes.

Ryder: Did you mean for the gun to go off?

Cartwright: No, I didn't.

Ryder: What happened?

Cartwright: Well, it hit Marlene and Marty.

He says he stood there for a moment stunned. He looked at them both lying on the floor. The next thing he remembers is going out to the car with the gun, and then going back in to look at them again. He did not know what to do. Then he went back to his car, drove to his daughter's place, and wrote a suicide note to her. He sat on his bed, put the end of the rifle barrel in his mouth, with the butt end between his knees, and pulled the trigger with the intent to kill himself. But somehow the bullet went through his cheek, and he did not die; he was taken to the hospital, where the doctors treated him, sewed up his cheek, and after a few days released him to the police. Tears fill his eyes when he says he loved Marlene. And Marty was his best friend. He never intended to hurt either one.

Up to this point, the prosecutor, Weckstein, has hardly raised his voice.

"You may cross-examine, Mr. Weckstein," the judge says, but Weckstein is bent over in his seat searching through the black briefcase on the floor beside him. You wait while he continues to poke through his case. Finally he finds what he is looking for—a small, metal object, which he slips under his notebook. Now he speaks.

Weckstein: You ever fire a rifle before that morning?

Cartwright: Well, I—

Weckstein: Did you?

Cartwright: Well, yes, when I joined the Navy. I was on the rifle range at Camp Lewis, Washington. I was just 19 then.

Weckstein: You were 19? So that was, let's see—you're 55 now-that was thirty-six years ago, right?

Cartwright: Yes, I guess so.

Weckstein: And you've not fired a rifle since then?

Cartwright: No.

Weckstein: Not until you shot and killed Marlene and Marty—

Ryder: Objection, Your Honor. He never said he shot them.

Judge: Sustained.

Weckstein: Did you hear that? Your attorney says you didn't say you shot them. Did I misunderstand? Didn't you shoot them?

Cartwright: Well, not, not really. I—

Weckstein: Didn't you shoot and kill them both with your rifle?

Ryder: Objection, Your Honor. The prosecutor won't let Mr. Cartwright finish his answer.

Judge: Sustained. Mr. Cartwright, you may finish your answer.

Cartwright: Well, no, I didn't really shoot them, not like you make it sound. It was an accident. The gun just went off.

Weckstein: Oh, I see, you had nothing to do with it?

Cartwright: Well, yes, I had the gun in my hand. But I didn't mean for it to fire.

Weckstein: It just went off?

Cartwright: Yes.

Weckstein: Did you know it was loaded?

Cartwright: Well, no. I forgot.

Weckstein: Who pulled the trigger?

Cartwright: Who pulled the trigger? Well, I don't know. It went off.

Weckstein: You don't know who pulled the trigger?

Cartwright: Well, I don't know how—

Weckstein: Did Marlene pull the trigger?

Cartwright: No, sir.

Weckstein: Did Marty pull the trigger?

Cartwright: No, sir.

Weckstein: Anyone else in the room?

Cartwright: No, sir.

Weckstein: I will ask you again, Mr. Cartwright. It's a very simple question. Please listen to my question. Who pulled the trigger?

Cartwright: I presume my hand must have done it.

Weckstein: Was your hand on the trigger?

Cartwright: I don't know.

Weckstein: When's deer-hunting season?

Cartwright: What?

Weckstein: I said, when is deer-hunting season?

Cartwright: Well—

Weckstein: You say you bought the rifle to hunt deer, right?

Cartwright: Yes, sir.

Weckstein: So, I ask you again: when is deer-hunting season?

Cartwright: Well, I don't know, sir.

Weckstein: You don't know?

Cartwright: But I was going to find out—

Weckstein: You mean you bought this rifle to hunt deer and you have no idea when the season is?

Cartwright: Well—

Weckstein: Did you know deer-hunting season was still three months away when you bought the rifle?

Cartwright: Well, no, but, like I say, I was going to find out.

Weckstein: All right, Mr. Cartwright, I am going to ask you to step down from the witness stand and come over here in front of the jury box and show this jury just how you were holding the rifle when it went off.

"I object, Your Honor," Ryder says. "He has called for a demonstration that cannot be conducted under the same circumstances that existed at the time. It is nothing more than a show-off question—"

"I resent the accusation that I am showing off, Your Honor." Weckstein replies. "I made a very reasonable request. He testified he was holding the gun a certain way when it went off. The jury has a right to see precisely how he was holding it. He is the only one who knows. There are no other witnesses alive."

Judge: Objection overruled.

Cartwright reluctantly steps down from the witness stand and stands in front of you. You notice the beads of sweat on his forehead. Weckstein picks up the rifle. As he walks toward the defendant with it, he informs the court that the rifle has been checked for safety by the bailiff. It is not loaded, the safety lock is on, and there is no possibility he could harm anyone. He hands the rifle to the defendant and asks him to take the position he was in when it went off.

Weckstein: How far was Marlene from you when the gun went off?

Cartwright: Oh, about ten feet.

Then Weckstein asks a young woman in the courtroom to come forward. "Your Honor, this is one of our secretaries. She happens to be the same height as Marlene Ransom. I will ask her to stand at the same distance from the defendant that Marlene was when the gun went off." He places her about ten feet from Cartwright. "This is how far she was?"

Cartwright: About that, a few inches farther. (*The woman steps back.*) That's it.

Ryder: Your Honor, I object!

Judge: Overruled.

Cartwright is holding the rifle down around his knees with the barrel pointed upward. The woman is facing him about ten feet away.

"Hold that position!" Weckstein shouts, and he pulls out the object he had concealed before. Now you can see it is a steel tape measure. He puts one end of the tape on the rifle and draws it out at the same angle in which it is pointed until it reaches a place on the woman's chest. He turns to the defense attorney.

Weckstein: Do you stipulate this could be the same spot the bullet entered Marlene's body, Counsel?

Ryder: No, I'll take no part in this circus.

Judge: The record may show the tape has been placed approximately at the same point where the evidence shows the bullet entered Ms. Ransom's body.

Weckstein: Thank you, Your Honor.

Weckstein turns back to the defendant to continue his cross-examination.

Weckstein: So the line shown by this tape would have been the line of fire, right, Mr. Cartwright?

Cartwright: I guess so.

You can see that the line of fire is not at a right angle.

"Just one moment, please," Weckstein says. He reminds you of a director of a play in rehearsal, instructing the characters what to do onstage.

Now he directs the defendant to hold the rifle at shoulder height, the way he would if he were actually aiming it. Ryder's objection is again overruled. Cartwright does as he is directed, and again Weckstein extends his steel tape from the end of the rifle barrel to the female stand-in to show how the bullet entered horizontally.

Weckstein: Isn't it a fact, Mr. Cartwright, that the way you are holding the rifle now, at shoulder height, is the way you held it when it fired?

Cartwright: No, no way. Absolutely not!

Weckstein: And that is your testimony, even though the angle of entry from this position, at a right angle to the body, is exactly the angle of entry the doctor found in this case?

Cartwright: The doctor wasn't there. I was there. I know. As God as my witness, I swear I am not lying. It was an accident. No way did I hold the rifle like this!

Finally, Cartwright resumes his seat on the stand. As Weckstein puts the rifle away, he asks, "By the way, Mr. Cartwright, this rifle throws out an empty cartridge off to the side every time it is fired, right?"

Cartwright: That's what I understand, yes.

Weckstein: Do you know what happened to the empty cartridge when you fired the fatal shot?

Cartwright: Oh, God, no. I was too shocked to notice that. I loved her so.

Weckstein: I show you this empty cartridge that your daughter says she found in your pocket. Do you have any idea how it got there?

Cartwright: Well—

Weckstein: Well, what?

Cartwright: Well, I guess I must have picked it up.

Weckstein: While your two best friends lay dying in front of you, you had the presence of mind to pick it up?

Cartwright does not answer. He leaves the stand and the defense rests.

There are five possible verdicts for both of the victims:

1. guilty of first-degree murder
2. guilty of second-degree murder
3. guilty of voluntary manslaughter
4. guilty of involuntary manslaughter
5. not guilty

WHAT IS YOUR VERDICT?

QUESTIONS FOR YOU TO CONSIDER

As you determine your verdict for this crime, here are some questions about the crime and the trial for you to think about.

1. What was the position of the two victims, Marlene Ransom and Martin Hogan, at the time they were shot?

2. What was the most damaging piece of evidence against Cartwright, showing a premeditated and deliberate intent to kill?

3. Whom did Cartwright intend to kill—Marlene Ransom, Martin Hogan, or both?

4. Cartwright killed two people with one shot. If he intended to kill both, he should of course be found guilty of killing both. But suppose that you—as some jurors did—find that he intended to kill only Martin Hogan and killed Marlene Ransom, the woman he loved, by mistake or accident. This could be the case if Cartwright aimed at Hogan and Marlene stepped in front of him at the last second before Cartwright could hold his fire. What would your verdict be then? Would you still find Cartwright guilty of two crimes or only one? Should he be punished for murdering a person he did not intend to kill and to whom he bore no malice?

5. What is the significance of Cartwright's picking up the empty cartridge from the floor?

AUTHOR'S ANSWERS TO THE QUESTIONS

1. An attentive jury could figure out the relative position of the two victims when they were shot. On the basis of the doctor's testimony regarding the entry and exit wounds, the bullet holes in the wall and water pipe were also relevant to this issue. The entry wound to Marlene Ransom's chest showed the bullet entered straight on, at a right angle to her body and without any tumbling motion. This meant the bullet had not yet passed through any other object—it must have struck her first. The angle of entry supported the inference that Cartwright held the rifle at shoulder length when the shot went off. The entry wound in Hogan's chest, on the other hand, showed the bullet had started to tumble at that point as a result of its passage through Ransom's body. How close was she to him? Since the position of the bullet upon exiting her back and entering his chest was the same, and since the height of her exit wound and his entry wound were also the same, it would be reasonable to conclude she was immediately in front of him, her back touching his chest. Were they standing, sitting, or lying down when shot? The bullet hole in the wall behind them and its subsequent path through the water pipe outside showed they must have been standing, because of the line of fire. A likely scenario is that Marlene stepped in front of Martin to prevent Cartwright from shooting him, hoping that Cartwright would never pull the trigger to shoot her.

2. Cartwright bought the rifle five days before the shooting and kept it in the trunk of his car. He had no reasonable explanation for buying it. He said he bought it to go deer hunting, but deer season was months away, and he had never hunted deer in his life. The purchase of the rifle was the strongest evidence of a deliberate and premeditated intent to kill one or both of the victims.

3. The question of whom Roy Cartwright intended to kill was never resolved by the jury. Some jurors believed he intended to kill

only Martin out of jealousy but that Marlene stepped in front of Martin at the last moment before Cartwright could stop himself from pulling the trigger. One juror thought Martin stepped behind her to protect himself. Another thought Martin was in the act of embracing her. No one believed it was an accident.

4. When a person murders one person and another is accidentally killed by the same act, the law is in conflict as to how many murders he or she committed. One court's view is that in such a case, the intent to kill is transferred by law to the unintended victim, and the defendant should be held equally responsible for both deaths he or she caused. This is known as the *doctrine of transferred intent*. But other courts say he or she should be convicted only for the victim he or she intended to kill; otherwise there would be no difference in penalty between the killer who intends to kill only one and the killer who intends to kill both.

5. After firing the fatal shot, Cartwright picked up the empty cartridge from the floor and left with it in his pocket. This act of concealing the evidence was very telling on the issue of deliberation. It certainly was not the normal reaction of a poor soul who had just accidentally shot his two best friends.

THE VERDICT

What was your verdict?

The real-life jury found the defendant guilty of murder in the second degree in the case of both victims.

This verdict was apparently a compromise between those jurors who wanted a verdict of murder in the first degree and those who favored a lesser degree of manslaughter. Jurors are not supposed to compromise, but they often do.

The defendant was sentenced to five years to life in prison on both counts, to be served concurrently (at the same time).

Stop or I'll Shoot

STATE V. ARMANDO COSIMI

Armando Cosimi is the manager of City Drugs, a store so large that it occupies an entire city block. During the year prior to the incident in question, Cosimi had become increasingly disturbed by the excessive amount of shoplifting in his store. In fact, his superiors warned him that unless he found ways to curb the thefts, his position as manager could be in danger. On the morning of December 17, 2007, Cosimi was at work at his desk on the second floor when he received a call on his cell phone from a female clerk downstairs. "Aisle nine," the clerk said. "Looks like trouble." Cosimi went outside his office to the balcony, where he observed a teenager removing scissors, each in a plastic container, from a shelf on aisle nine and slipping them inside his shirt. Cosimi went back to his desk, retrieved a .22 pistol from the drawer, and went downstairs with the gun in his belt. He saw the young man leave the store without paying and followed him outside. Cosimi caught up to and confronted him, saying, "I am the store manager. You'd better come back with those items." The suspect laughed at Cosimi and said, "I wouldn't take that crap you sell even if you were givin' it away." When Cosimi said he would have to place him under arrest, the thief swung at Cosimi with his fist and ran off. Cosimi pursued him and shouted for him to stop, but the shouts were ignored. "I've got a gun," Cosimi yelled, drawing the weapon from his belt. "Stop or I'll shoot!" Again, the warnings were ignored. Cosimi fired at the ground just behind the fugitive thief. The bullet ricocheted off the sidewalk and struck the boy in the head, killing him instantly. Cosimi was in tears as the police arrived and arrested him. He is now on trial for the charge of involuntary manslaughter.

Mirya Donner takes the stand first. She testifies she was on duty as a clerk at City Drugs on the day of the incident. The D.A. questions her.

D.A.: What were your duties, specifically?

Donner: I had two main duties: one, help the customers, and two, watch for shoplifters.

D.A.: During the morning of December 17, did you see anything unusual?

Donner: Well, it wasn't so unusual anymore, but yes, I could see a young guy through the mirror, taking some things off the shelf.

D.A.: What else did you see him doing?

Donner: The items were scissors in plastic containers and he was placing them inside his shirt.

D.A.: What did you do?

Donner: I immediately called Mr. Cosimi on my cell phone and told him we had trouble on aisle nine.

D.A.: Can you describe the boy you saw?

Donner: He was a kid, maybe 13 or 14, long red hair, looked like he needed a bath.

D.A.: What's the next thing you saw?

Donner: I saw the kid button up his shirt with the merchandise inside. Mr. Cosimi came down and we both watched him walk out.

D.A.: Did he ever pay for anything?

Donner: No. He just walked past the cashier stand.

D.A.: What did Mr. Cosimi do?

Donner: He followed the boy outside and confronted him in the parking lot. I was still inside and couldn't hear what he said.

D.A.: What happened next?

Donner: The boy swung at Mr. Cosimi, hit him in the shoulder, and then took off running. Mr. Cosimi followed him. I went to call the police.

The defense counsel goes to the podium to begin his cross-examination. Like the district attorney, he is a well-dressed young man of average height and weight without distinctive features. At the start of trial, the judge introduced both men by name, but since then, the judge has always addressed them only as "Mr. District Attorney" and "Mr. Defense Attorney," and as a result, you have forgotten both their names. The judge is short, stooped, and elderly. You think of him also not by name, but as "Your Honor."

Defense Counsel: How was the boy dressed?

Donner: He was wearing a blue shirt that hung over his pants. A red handkerchief around his neck.

Defense Counsel: Gang colors?

D.A.: Objection!

Judge: Sustained.

Defense Counsel: So the last thing you saw was Mr. Cosimi running after the thief, is that correct?

Donner: That's correct. A few moments later I heard a shot, but I didn't see anything else.

Defense Counsel: Did you ever see Mr. Cosimi threaten the thief with a gun?

Donner: No, I never saw a gun.

Defense Counsel: Thank you, that's all.

D.A.: I have one more question for the record. Ms. Donner, do you see in the courtroom the person known to you as Mr. Cosimi, the man you have been talking about?

Donner: Yes, I do. He is right there with his attorney (*pointing*).

D.A.: Your Honor, may the record show that the witness has identified the defendant?

Judge: The record may so show.

The next witness is Colin Pinkert. He also works as a clerk at City Drugs and was outside the store on the day of the incident when he noticed Mr. Cosimi speaking in an angry voice to a teenager in the parking lot.

D.A.: What were you doing at the time?

Pinkert: I was busy arranging our stock of Christmas trees. The next thing I knew, the guy laughed and struck Mr. Cosimi in the shoulder and took off running. Mr. Cosimi started running after him.

D.A.: What did you do?

Pinkert: I realized it must be a shoplifter so I started running after the guy, too.

D.A.: Did you hear Mr. Cosimi say anything?

Pinkert: He kept shouting, "Stop! I'm warning you!" words like that, but the guy just laughed and ran on. He was a pretty fast runner and Mr. Cosimi was losing ground.

D.A.: What did Mr. Cosimi do?

Pinkert: I was still a little behind Mr. Cosimi when I saw him pull the gun out of his belt and he yelled, "I have a gun. Stop or I'll shoot."

D.A.: Did the fellow stop then?

Pinkert: No, he just kept going. He was, well, sort of giggling. Almost like he was enjoying the whole thing.

D.A.: Did you say anything to Mr. Cosimi?

Pinkert: I shouted, "Fire in the air. Fire in the air." But Mr. Cosimi pointed the gun in the guy's direction. I can't say if it was pointed directly at the guy, but it was pointed in his general direction. So I yelled the same thing again: "Fire in the air!"

D.A.: Did he fire in the air?

Pinkert: No, I'm afraid not.

D.A.: What happened?

Pinkert: Mr. Cosimi pulled the trigger—

D.A.: How far was he from the fellow when he did that?

Pinkert: About thirty yards.

D.A.: Go on.

Pinkert: The guy went down right away, and I realized he'd been hit. We both ran up to him. Blood was coming out of the back of his head. I knelt down and looked at him. I said to Mr. Cosimi, "The guy's dead."

D.A.: What did he say?

Pinkert: He said, "Are you sure?" I said, "Yes, I'm positive."

D.A.: What did he say then?

Pinkert: I swear he turned white as a sheet. "Oh my God," he said. "What have I done? Forgive me, oh Lord." He started to cry. I mean, openly cry like a baby. "I didn't mean to kill him," he said. "I meant to shoot at the ground." His body was shaking. I tell you I never saw a man cry like that.

D.A.: What happened next?

Pinkert: He still had the gun in his hand. The way he was crying and shaking I was afraid what he might do with it—I mean to himself. I told him to put the gun down and he put it down on the curb. A couple minutes went by and a crowd gathered around. Then the police came on the scene sooner than I'd expected. They must have been called before the shooting.

D.A.: One more question. I will ask you to step down and stand before the jury.

The witness does so.

D.A.: Now please show us as best you recall exactly how Mr. Cosimi's arm was extended with the gun when the shot was fired.

Pinkert: Yes, sir.

The witness extends his right arm parallel to the floor.

Pinkert: It was like this. Straight out.

D.A.: Your Honor, may the record show the witness has extended his arm straight out, parallel to the ground?

Judge: Yes. Approximately parallel.

The defense counsel begins cross-examination. "Mr. Pinkert, isn't it true that after the shooting, you had the belief that the fatal bullet had traveled directly from Mr. Cosimi's gun to the victim's head?"

Pinkert: Yes. We all thought so. So did he.

Defense Counsel: And in fact isn't that what you told the police?

Pinkert: Yes.

Defense Counsel: And did you later find out you were wrong?

Pinkert: I did. I was wrong about that. We all were.

Defense Counsel: How was that?

Pinkert: When the police completed their investigation, they told us that the bullet did in fact strike the ground first—the sidewalk—and then bounced off or ricocheted off and struck the back of the guy's head.

Defense Counsel: So it was not a direct shot?

Pinkert: No, it was not.

Defense Counsel: And so Mr. Cosimi did what he said he meant to do—fire into the ground?

Pinkert: He would have had to, yes.

Defense Counsel: Does that change your testimony that he was holding the gun parallel to the ground?

Pinkert: Well, I didn't mean to mislead the jury. I only said what I recall. I realize he must have had the gun lowered a bit.

Defense Counsel: Was Mr. Cosimi still running hard when he fired the shot?

Pinkert: Yes, sir.

Defense Counsel: So he did not stop to take aim?

Pinkert: No, sir.

Defense Counsel: Thank you. Just a few more questions if I may. When you and Mr. Cosimi were chasing the victim, did you see any people in the street in front of you?

Pinkert: At first, yes, but then we turned into a residential section and there was no one out on the street where it happened.

Defense Counsel: So when Mr. Cosimi fired, there was no danger to anyone in the street?

Pinkert: That's true.

Defense Counsel: So it's your testimony that he was careful not to strike anyone?

D.A.: Objection! That's for the jury to decide.

Judge: Sustained!

Defense Counsel: Nothing further.

Police Officer Stratton Cain takes the stand in uniform. He has been a patrolman for the city for six years and was on duty the morning of December 17, 2007.

D.A.: On that morning, did you have occasion to go to the vicinity of 5100 Charmain Drive in this city?

Cain: I did. I was alone in my police car when I got the call and drove to the scene immediately.

D.A.: Upon arrival, did you observe a man sitting at the curb?

Cain: Yes. I knew we had a homicide on our hands. One of his employees pointed him out to me as the shooter and I went over to talk to him. That's him right there (*pointing at Mr. Cosimi*).

D.A.: Your Honor, may the record show the witness has identified the defendant?

Judge: It may. Proceed.

D.A.: What did he say, if anything?

Cain: He was very emotional, tears in his eyes. Before I could say anything, he said, "I didn't mean to kill him. I meant to shoot at the ground. I swear to God I didn't mean to kill him." I took him into custody and placed him in the backseat of my police vehicle.

D.A.: Nothing further of this witness.

The cross-examination begins.

Defense Counsel: Was he cooperative?

Cain: Very much so.

When the witness steps down, the D.A. rises to address the court.

D.A.: Your Honor, there are a number of facts in this case as to which there is no dispute. Defense counsel and I have agreed to enter into a stipulation as to those facts—that is to say, we agree they can be admitted into evidence without objection and the jury may consider such facts as proven.

Judge: You may state the stipulation.

D.A.: First of all, counsel stipulate that the cause of the victim's death was a gunshot to the back of the head. Secondly, we stipulate that if Abraham Kovitz were called to the stand, he would testify that he is a criminalist employed by the city police department, that he is recognized nationally as an expert in both criminalistics and ballistics, that he has examined a spent bullet that was drawn from the head of the victim at the autopsy, that he has examined and tested the shooter's .22 caliber pistol, and that he has also examined the scene of this incident and all photographs taken at the scene. Upon such examination, he has determined that the said bullet came from the defendant's pistol; that the damaged condition of the bullet was such that in his opinion the bullet struck another surface before striking the victim; further, that his personal examination of a mark on the pavement at the scene and of photographs of the same indicate that the mark on the pavement was probably made by the same bullet or one similar to it; and, that the said mark measured about ten feet from the spot where the victim fell to the ground. Oh yes, and one more thing—that Mr. Kovitz also examined the angle at which the bullet entered the victim's head and that said angle showed that the bullet entered from a lower position, moving upward at about a forty-five degree angle and therefore not perpendicular; that based on all his examinations and on his training and experience, it is Mr. Kovitz's expert opinion that the bullet did in fact first strike the pavement about ten feet behind the victim and then ricocheted to the back of the victim's head. That is the stipulation, Your Honor.

Defense Counsel: We so stipulate, Your Honor.

Judge: Very well. Thank you, Counsel, for saving the court's time with this stipulation. (*Turning to the jury*) Ladies and gentlemen, you have heard the stipulation. A stipulation is an agreement between counsel as to the facts. You may consider the facts contained in the stipulation as having been conclusively proved. Let's proceed.

D.A.: The State rests, Your Honor.

The defense opens its case by calling three witnesses who state that they are familiar with Mr. Cosimi's reputation for law-abidingness, nonviolence, and honesty, and that his reputation as to these character traits is excellent in every respect. The D.A. has no cross-examination of the character witnesses and there is no evidence to impeach their testimony. In response to the judge's question as to how many other witnesses defense counsel intends to call as to the defendant's good character, defense counsel answers that he has five additional witnesses waiting in the hallway who will testify along similar lines. The district attorney objects to the additional testimony as being cumulative and the judge sustains the objection.

As his final witness, defense counsel calls the defendant, Armando Cosimi, to the stand. Cosimi is a small man with a black moustache and a sad face. When he raises his hand to be sworn, you can see his hand shaking. You suspect his emotions are very near the surface. From his facial expression, you worry that he might begin to cry at any moment. He holds a little black book in his other hand and when the judge asks him what it is, he states that it is a Bible that he wishes to keep with him when he testifies. There being no objection, direct examination by defense counsel proceeds. Cosimi speaks in a voice so soft that the judge has to ask him to speak up.

"I am sorry, Your Honor," he says. "I never did this before."

From the outset of his testimony, Cosimi corroborates the testimony of the other percipient witnesses. When he received the call from his clerk, he went outside to the balcony and saw what was happening in aisle nine. He returned to his desk, retrieved his .22 pistol, and went downstairs with the gun in his belt. He watched the young man walk outside without paying, his shirt stuffed with merchandise. Cosimi says he followed the teenager outside to confront him in the parking lot.

Defense Counsel: What did you say to him?

Cosimi: I said, "Sir, pardon me, I am Armando Cosimi, the store manager. Would you please give me the scissors that you have under your shirt?"

Defense Counsel: What did he say?

Cosimi: He said—uh, Your Honor, I don't wish to say in this company, it is a bad word—should I say it, Your Honor?

Judge: Tell us the exact words. We are all adults here. We want the truth.

Cosimi: He said, "Listen, you fucker. I don't have them." I asked him again and he said, "I wouldn't take the crap you sell in there." Then I said, "Then I will have to place you under arrest."

Defense Counsel: What did he do?

Cosimi: He said, "Go to hell, fucker" and he swung at me with his fist, striking me in the left shoulder. Then he started to run.

Defense Counsel: Did you run after him?

Cosimi: Yes. I was fed up with these kids getting away with our merchandise. I wasn't going to stand for it. Like my clerk said, I kept shouting at him to stop. I warned him. I saw him getting away and finally I pulled out the gun. "Stop or I'll shoot," I said, but he didn't stop. He just laughed at me and kept running. I decided to fire a warning shot into the ground and that's what I did.

Defense Counsel: Did you have any thought of hitting him?

Cosimi: God, no! I didn't want to hurt him. I didn't want to hurt anybody. I just wanted our property back. I just wanted to scare him so he would stop. I never thought the bullet could possibly bounce that way. (*Turning to the jury*) Please believe me. I didn't want to hurt anybody!

Defense Counsel: How did you feel when you saw what happened?

Cosimi: How did I feel? How did I feel? I killed a boy. I took a guy's life. It was an accident, but I fired the shot. How did I feel? My God, I have a boy myself the same age.

Mr. Cosimi nods to a group of people in the front row behind the defense counsel's table. You turn to look at them. They have been present every day of the trial in the same seats, and you have already figured out who they are—his wife, always dressed in black, and their four children. One is a boy of about 14. The boy is wiping his eyes. You cannot help feeling sorry for Cosimi, but then you check yourself. Sympathy must play no part in the verdict. If he did the crime, he must pay the price.

Cosimi: I feel for his parents. I want to say to them that I am sorry. I went to the jail and cried on the bed.

Defense Counsel: Your witness.

The district attorney begins cross-examination.

D.A.: Did I understand you to say this was an accident?

Cosimi: It was an accident, yes. I never meant to hit him.

D.A.: When you took your loaded gun downstairs to confront the boy, that wasn't an accident, was it?

Cosimi: No.

D.A.: You did that deliberately, right?

Cosimi: Right.

D.A.: And when you were chasing the boy down the street, you deliberately pointed the gun in his direction, right?

Cosimi: Yes, you can say that.

D.A.: And when you pulled the trigger, you did that deliberately?

Cosimi: Yes. But I didn't intend to hit him.

D.A.: Just answer the question, please. You intended to pull the trigger, isn't that so? Yes or no.

Cosimi: Well—

D.A.: Pulling the trigger wasn't an accident, was it?

Cosimi: No.

D.A.: So all these acts that I have just mentioned—taking the loaded gun, aiming the gun in his direction a few feet away from him, pulling the trigger—all these acts were intentional and not accidental, right?

Cosimi: All right, yes.

D.A.: And in fact, didn't you tell your staff at a meeting last fall that you were fed up with all the shoplifters, that they were getting away with too much stuff, and stronger measures had to be taken to stop them—didn't you tell them that?

Cosimi: Who told you that?

D.A.: I'll ask the questions here, Mr. Cosimi. It's for you to answer them. Did you say that to your staff? Yes or no.

Cosimi: I don't recall the exact words.

D.A.: If I told you that one of your staff would testify that you said it—

Cosimi: All right, all right, I said it, so what? My God, I certainly wasn't thinking of anything like this.

D.A.: And in fact weren't you under pressure to do more to stop the shoplifters?

Cosimi: What do you mean?

D.A.: Didn't your executive officer at the Chicago headquarters, your CEO, warn you that you better find a way to stop all the stealing going on in your store, or you might be looking for another job?

Defense Counsel: Objection! Calls for hearsay.

D.A.: It is an exception, Your Honor. Goes to his state of mind.

Judge: Overruled. You may answer.

Cosimi: How'd you find that out?

D.A.: Just answer the question. Yes or no, Mr. Cosimi. Did your CEO say that?

Cosimi: Well, yes, but that didn't mean—

D.A.: Let me ask you this, Mr. Cosimi. When you were aiming your gun just a few feet behind the boy, were you confident of your accuracy?

Cosimi: Well, I passed the firing test.

D.A.: When was that?

Cosimi: That would have been in 2006. About eighteen months ago.

D.A.: Eighteen months. Ever fire the gun since then?

Cosimi: No, sir. I didn't have to.

D.A.: Ever fire your gun while running with it?

Cosimi: No.

D.A.: When you passed the test were you running with the gun?

Cosimi: No, that was at the firing range.

D.A.: Thank you, that's all.

Cosimi: (*As he is stepping down*) I just wanted to say one more time that—

D.A.: Objection. There is no question pending.

Judge: Sustained. The witness may step down.

Both sides rest their cases. The judge allows various items that have been received in evidence to be passed among the jury. They include the unloaded pistol; five pairs of scissors taken from inside the victim's shirt (you notice that each package has a price tag of $3.79 attached); the damaged bullet that was removed from the victim's head at the autopsy; a spent cartridge from the defendant's pistol found at the scene; and, various photographs of the scene, including some that show the mark on the pavement caused by the bullet upon striking the pavement and also a close-up view of the entry wound in the victim's head.

The judge turns to the jury.

Ladies and gentlemen, both sides have rested and all admissible evidence has been received. That means you shall hear no further evidence. Before we hear closing arguments from counsel, I wish to instruct you further on the pertinent law.

The crime of involuntary manslaughter is the killing of a human being without the intent to kill when the fatal act involves a high risk of death or great bodily harm and is done without due caution. The term *due caution* refers to a reckless act committed without proper regard for human life.

When a person commits an act by accident under circumstances that show no criminal intent or purpose, he does not thereby commit a crime and must be found not guilty.

I remind you also of the reasonable doubt instruction given previously. The defendant is presumed to be innocent and the State has the burden of overcoming that presumption by proof beyond a reasonable doubt. If you have a reasonable doubt, you must find the defendant not guilty.

Remember that you must not be influenced by mere sentiment, conjecture, sympathy, passion, prejudice, public opinion, or public feeling.

Counsel may proceed with closing arguments.

The defense counsel proceeds to give his closing argument.

Ladies and gentlemen, this is an unusual case for the jury because, unlike almost every other case, there is no dispute as to the facts, no argument between prosecution and defense as to what happened. The only question is how to apply the law to the facts. Thanks to a thorough police investigation, there is no longer any dispute as to how Mr. Cosimi was holding the gun when he fired. We know now that he could not have held it—as one witness testified—straight out, parallel to the ground. We know that was not possible because the bullet struck the ground first, which means that Mr. Cosimi had to have been pointing the gun downward, groundward. Had the police known that when they first arrived on the scene, they may not have arrested Mr. Cosimi at all. They would have realized that the shot was an accident. But the police thought, as did everyone else at the time, that the bullet traveled directly from Mr. Cosimi's gun to the victim's head. I say thank goodness for an excellent investigation by the police because it showed us the truth and that Mr. Cosimi had no intent to harm anyone, that the victim's death was due to a freak accident that no one could have foreseen. Who could have predicted that the bullet would bounce off the ground and take a bizarre path to the back of the boy's head? That was incredible and it would be grossly unfair to hold an innocent man responsible for it.

The district attorney revealed his plan of attack in this case during the cross-examination of Mr. Cosimi. He tried to get around the law that an act done by accident is not a crime. But try as he might, he could not and cannot get around it. The law is there in black and white. The judge just told you what it is. I quote what the judge said: "When a person commits an act by accident under circumstances that show no criminal intent or purpose, he does not thereby commit a crime and must be found not guilty." That's it. It's all there in those words. You took an oath to follow the law and that's all I ask you to do. Was the killing unintentional? No one disputes it. Mr. Cosimi is a good citizen. His reputation as a peaceful man, an honest man, is impeccable. You may be sure that if it were otherwise, if there was the slightest stain on Mr. Cosimi's record, the district attorney would have brought it out. Mr. Cosimi had no intention of harming the boy. He only wanted his property back. His spontaneous reaction, bursting into tears, crying like a child, when he realized what happened, is the best evidence that he had no criminal intent.

Was the killing done in the performance of a lawful act? There is no evidence otherwise. Mr. Cosimi was only trying to catch a fleeing

> thief. He was only trying to warn the thief to stop. Was the killing an accident? Absolutely. As freakish and unlikely as anyone could imagine. And that's exactly why they're called freak accidents.
>
> The district attorney was very clever in his examination of Mr. Cosimi. He brought out that carrying the gun, aiming the gun at the ground behind the boy, and pulling the trigger were all intentional acts, and so they were. But notice that he left out the most important fact of all, the most critical fact of all, in his line of questioning. He never asked Mr. Cosimi if the bullet's path to the boy's head was intentional or accidental. He didn't ask it because he knew the answer he would receive and he did not want that answer.
>
> Ladies and gentlemen, they are trying to hang a bad conviction on a good man. Don't let them do it. I urge you to do the right thing. Find Mr. Cosimi not guilty. Thank you.

Next, the district attorney offers his closing argument.

> Ladies and gentlemen of the jury, there is only one question in this case, and that is whether the defendant fired his gun without due caution, that is, without proper regard for human life.
>
> We know he fired intentionally. The pulling of the trigger was no accident. We know that from his own admission on the stand. He meant to pull the trigger. He meant to fire in the direction of the boy thirty yards ahead of him. The defendant is not a stupid man. When he pulled that trigger, he knew he was not a trained sharpshooter. He knew his shot could go astray. He knew a shot at the pavement could very well bounce off and strike something else ahead. He took a chance and fired without proper regard for the life of this poor boy. The boy was a thief. No question. We may not like the way he treated the defendant outside the store. We may not like the way he struck the defendant and ran off laughing at him. All that we concede. But does that mean he deserved to die for his crime? Did he deserve the death penalty for his petty theft?

> Keep your eye on the ball. Please do not let your dislike of this boy and his behavior prevent you from doing the right thing in this case, from doing justice. Please do not send out the message to this community that it is perfectly all right for a store manager to shoot a deadly weapon in the direction of a boy who has just taken about twenty dollars' worth of merchandise. The defendant tells us he looked about to make sure there was no one else up ahead who could be endangered by his shot; he wants us to know he was careful not to hit anyone else. But he was not careful enough. There was someone in the line of fire and he knew it and that was not due caution; that was a reckless act. I know you may feel sorry for the defendant. He is a sympathetic man. He is not your typical criminal, if there is such a thing. He is the kind of man who draws out our sympathetic nature. Here (*pointing*) in the front row are his wife and children sitting here every day. No doubt one of the reasons they are here is to play on your sympathy for—

"Objection!"

"Sustained!"

> I am sorry. I assure you I did not mean to criticize the defendant for having his family here. He has every right to do that. They all do it. I might do it myself if I were in his position. But this is not the time or place for sympathy. You must judge this case on the facts and the law and nothing else. His Honor has told you that you must put such feelings aside and not allow them to affect your verdict.
>
> The simple fact is that the defendant is guilty. He fired his gun recklessly and without proper regard for human life and therefore he is guilty of this crime—involuntary manslaughter. It is up to you to tell him so. Thank you. The case is in your hands.

WHAT IS YOUR VERDICT?

QUESTIONS FOR YOU TO CONSIDER

As you determine your verdict for this crime, here are some questions about the crime and the trial for you to think about.

1. Why does the prosecution always have the last word in criminal trials? Isn't that unfair to the defendant, who already has all the resources of the State against him?

2. You may have noticed that in closing arguments, the district attorney always referred to the accused as the defendant, never by name. The defense counsel, on the other hand, always referred to the accused by his name—Mr. Cosimi—and never called him the defendant. Why is this so?

AUTHOR'S ANSWERS TO THE QUESTIONS

1. The rationale for why the prosecution is given the last word is that the prosecution has the burden of proving the defendant guilty beyond a reasonable doubt, which is a rather heavy burden. The defendant has no such burden and does not have to prove anything. But, of course, as in any argument, someone always has to have the last word. This order of argument is steeped in criminal trial tradition and is a major advantage for the prosecutor because it deprives the defense attorney, no matter how much he or she is yearning, of any chance to answer.

2. The manner in which each counsel refers to the accused individual is often part of a planned tactic. The district attorney wants to dehumanize the person on trial as much as possible, to have jurors view the person as a figure without human qualities. The defense, on the other hand, seeks the opposite: to portray the defendant as a person with a name, a human being just like the jurors.

THE VERDICT

What was your verdict?

The real-life jury found the defendant not guilty.

Rape or Consensual Sex?

STATE V. MAURICE VERNON

Rape is an ugly word and an ugly crime because the violation is so outrageous to both the mind and body of the victim. Jurors frown when they learn for the first time that they have been assigned to a rape case, and they usually make an effort to be excused. Many jurors feel embarrassed by explicit talk of sex in the courtroom. But the matter you are about to witness is one of first impression and almost sure to be different from any rape trial you have ever heard about.

Kate Samson and Maurice Vernon knew each other from high school where they were students together. After graduation, they started dating regularly to the point of embraces and long kisses, but never to the point of sexual intercourse. Suddenly he stopped calling her and the relationship seemed to be over. They met again months later at a party given by a mutual friend in a spacious residence with a swimming pool. They danced and drank together. The attraction was still evident.

When most of the guests were gone, Kate and Maurice put on their bathing suits and swam in the pool together. Next to the pool was a small guest cottage. The couple entered the cottage, undressed, and began fondling each other on the bed. He entered her without objection although it was her first sexual experience. During the heated act of intercourse, Kate suddenly cried out for Maurice to stop and begged him to withdraw, but he ignored her cries and continued to the point of climax. The incident occurred on a Friday evening. Kate waited until the following Tuesday before she went to the police and registered a complaint of forcible rape.

Both the D.A. and the defense attorney are young women in their late twenties. The defendant is a blonde man who looks barely 20. After a brief opening statement, the D.A. calls Kate Samson to the stand. She is a shapely brunette whose hair covers one eye. She gives her age as 18 years.

D.A.: Ms. Samson, how long have you known the defendant?

Samson: About two years.

D.A.: Now would you please describe for us how you met.

Samson: Well, we knew each other casually back in high school. He was a senior. I was a junior. Just casual. Nothing serious. We didn't date or anything. Then after I graduated, I went to City College and he was there. We got better acquainted.

D.A.: What do you mean by that?

Samson: Well, we'd have snacks or lunch together on campus. Then we decided to go to a movie. That was our first real date.

D.A.: Did anything of a sexual nature occur between the two of you?

Samson: We held hands, if that's what you mean. He kissed me good night. That was it.

D.A.: Did you go out again?

Samson: Yes, we went to the beach one afternoon. We had a little picnic.

D.A.: Anything physical?

Samson: Well, yes, in the car. We were making out a lot. But it went no further than that. He was always the perfect gentleman.

D.A.: Did you continue to date after that?

Samson: Well, as a matter of fact, he didn't call for quite a while that summer. I heard he was going out with someone else.

D.A.: When did you see him next?

Samson: We both went to this party—the same party. My girlfriend, Jean Littmeyer, from high school—she was having a little high school reunion party. And we both came.

D.A.: Please tell the jury what happened there.

Samson: Jean has a big house. Two stories. Lots of rooms and a big pool. There were about thirty kids there. Maury and I danced together and late in the evening when most of the guests had left, we decided to go for a swim in the pool. We were alone in the pool. We fooled around in the water. He started pulling me under and kissing me underwater.

D.A.: Did you object?

Samson: Nah, it was all in fun. I still liked him.

D.A.: What happened next?

Samson: Some guys brought some beers out to the pool. Maury and I each drank one although we weren't supposed to be drinking.

D.A.: Go on.

Samson: We, uh, kept playing around in the pool for awhile. By that time it was getting dark. When we got out, we were the only ones around the pool. There was this little guest cottage off to the side. The door was ajar. Maury looked inside and waved for me to come on over. I wasn't sure what he meant. He took my hand and led me inside.

D.A.: Did you resist at all?

Samson: Well, I guess not. He sort of pulled me in but I didn't really resist. I said, "What are we doing?" He kissed me and said, "You are a beautiful creature." Then he locked the door. I said, "Maybe we shouldn't do this." And he says, "Oh, but maybe we should."

D.A.: Were you afraid?

Samson: Not really. He was always the gentleman.

D.A.: And so, then what? Tell us exactly what happened.

Samson: We still had our swimsuits on. Still standing by the door. Suddenly he grabbed my shoulders, took me in his arms, and—there was a long kiss. Very passionate.

D.A.: You didn't resist?

Samson: Uh, no. I guess I was into it as much as he was. I'll be frank with you. I liked the guy.

D.A.: Please continue. I know this may be difficult for you, but we are in court now. And we have to know the truth.

Samson: I had on a two-piece suit. He slowly unhooked my top at the back and removed it. The embrace continued. He began, um, touching me, touching my breasts. Then we sat on the bed. We looked at each other. Suddenly there was a knock on the door and Jean called out, "Kate?" She asked, "Are you all right?"

D.A.: Did you answer?

Samson: I said, "It's all right, Jean. I'm fine." And she went off.

D.A.: You left off where you were sitting on the bed. What next?

Samson: Maury looked at me and took off his trunks. He nodded down to my suit bottom. I took it off and we lay down on the bed together, embracing, touching. It was kind of a wild scene. I'd never been in that situation before.

D.A.: Now, Kate, I have to ask you a very personal question. Perhaps the answer is obvious to you, but I have to ask it for the record. (*Samson nods affirmatively*). Did he place his penis inside your vagina?

Samson: Yes.

D.A.: And you consented?

Samson: I—I didn't object.

D.A.: Did it hurt?

Samson: At first, yes. But I expected that. It was the first time for me.

D.A.: Did you let him know it hurt?

Samson: I think I winced out loud, or something like that. He knew it hurt me.

D.A.: How do you know that?

Samson: Because he said, "I'm sorry if I hurt you. I don't want to hurt you." I said, "It's all right."

D.A.: Then what happened?

Samson: Well, we continued to have intercourse. I want to be honest about this. I know it's a serious matter. But I guess I was into it as much as he was, if you know what I mean.

D.A.: We appreciate your sincerity in answering some very tough questions. Now, then, did he say something that upset you?

Samson: He sure did. He kept telling me how wonderful I was and then he said—this is right in the middle of the act—he whispered, "You're wonderful, Peggy, I'm crazy about you."

D.A.: You heard him say, "Peggy"?

Samson: Distinctly. Then he said it again. "You're so beautiful, Peggy," he said.

D.A.: Who is Peggy?

Samson: I couldn't believe it when he said it. Then I remembered. Peggy was the girl he dated that summer.

D.A.: Did that make you mad?

Samson: Sure it did. He's making love to me, and imagining he was making love to her. I felt terrible and I got very angry.

D.A.: What did you do?

Samson: I yelled, "Stop, please stop," in a loud voice.

D.A.: Did he stop?

Samson: No, he did not. He just kept on.

D.A.: And did you keep asking him?

Samson: I begged him to stop.

D.A.: Did he hear you?

Samson: Oh, yes. He said, "Please don't say that. Please don't ask me to stop now. You're wonderful. I can't stop." I yelled, "Stop, Maury. No, I don't want this." I tried to push him away but he was too strong. He just went on.

D.A.: To a climax?

Samson: Uh, for him, yes. Not for me.

D.A.: What happened then?

Samson: He rolled over and we both lay back. He tried to kiss me, but I turned my face away. I was disgusted, and felt I had been used. I was mad at him because he didn't stop when I asked him to. He had to have his way. He didn't care about my feelings at all. What was I? Just a substitute—a stand-in for Peggy? He didn't care about me. Didn't care at all. (*Tears come to her eyes.*)

D.A.: May we take a recess, Your Honor?

Judge: Yes. We'll take a recess. Ladies and gentlemen, please don't talk about the case with anyone. Don't let anyone talk to you about it. Fifteen minutes.

When court resumes, Ms. Samson is back on the stand, still dabbing her eyes with a tissue, but more composed.

Judge: (*To the witness*) Are you all right, Miss? May we continue?

Samson: I'm okay. I'm sorry if I caused a recess.

Judge: Let's proceed.

D.A.: Now, when he tried to kiss you and you turned away, what did he say?

Samson: He said, "What's the matter? What's wrong?" And I said, "You know what's the matter. I begged you to stop."

D.A.: What did he say to that?

Samson: He said, "What did you expect me to do? You got me all excited. I thought you wanted it. What are you so mad about?" I answered, "You wouldn't understand."

D.A.: What did you do then?

Samson: I got up and got dressed—all I had there was my bathing suit—and I started out the door.

D.A.: Did you say anything else to him before you left?

Samson: Yes, I said, "I hope you and Peggy are very happy."

D.A.: Thank you, Ms. Samson. The defense attorney may have some questions.

Defense Attorney: Did you go to the police that night?

Samson: No.

Defense Attorney: Did you go to the police the next day, Saturday?

Samson: No, I was thinking about it. I didn't know what to do.

Defense Attorney: What about the following day, Sunday? Did you report this to the police then?

Samson: No. I wasn't sure if it was a crime, what he did. I thought about it all day.

Defense Attorney: The next day, Monday—did you report it that day?

Samson: No. It was a holiday.

Defense Attorney: Did you expect him to call you over the weekend?

Samson: Well, yes. I thought he would call and apologize. He knew what he did was wrong.

Defense Attorney: But he didn't call?

Samson: No.

Defense Attorney: And that made you all the angrier?

Samson: Well, sure, you could say that. He didn't even care.

Defense Attorney: So, finally, on Tuesday, after waiting over the weekend for his apology, you went to the police and filed charges?

Samson: What I did, I called a friend of mine who went to law school for a year and asked her—I didn't say it was about me—I asked her about the rape law. She said if there is sex without consent then that is rape. So I figured that's what he did because I told him to stop and he didn't. There must be a law against it. And I filed charges.

Defense Attorney: Did he call you after that?

Samson: Finally, yes. But the police had told me not to talk to him so I just hung up.

Defense Attorney: Thank you. Nothing further.

The next prosecution witness is Alpha Moberly. He testifies he was the detective assigned to the case. After receiving Ms. Samson's complaint, he phoned Maurice Vernon and asked him to come down to the station for some questions. He came right down.

D.A.: Did you advise him as to his constitutional rights?

Moberly: Yes. First I identified myself. I told him he didn't have to talk to me. That he had a right to remain silent. That he had the right to see an attorney before speaking to me. And that anything he said could be held against him in a court of law. All the Miranda elements.

D.A.: Did he agree to talk to you?

Moberly: Yes. He said he understood his rights and was willing to talk. He said he had nothing to hide.

D.A.: And then what did he tell you?

Moberly: It turned out to be very short. He was very cooperative and simply verified just about everything Ms. Samson had told us. He admitted they started out having consensual intercourse just like she said. Yes, at one point during the act she told him to stop. He didn't deny that. But he said he was all heated up and full of passion—as he described it—and just couldn't stop. There really wasn't any dispute in the two stories.

D.A.: What happened next?

Moberly: I told him I had to arrest him for the felony of rape and took him into custody.

The defense counsel begins cross-examination. "Did he know why she asked him to stop?"

Moberly: I asked him that. He said he didn't know why since she seemed to be enjoying it.

Defense Attorney: What did he say when you told him he was being arrested?

Moberly: He said, "What did I do wrong? I didn't know I was doing anything wrong. She consented of her own free will."

Defense Attorney: What did you say to that?

Moberly: I just told him that he had confessed to the crime. I had no choice but to take him in.

Defense Attorney: Was he cooperative?

Moberly: Oh, yes. Very much so. Confused, but very cooperative.

When the detective leaves the stand, the D.A. announces, "Your Honor, the State has no further evidence and the State rests."

Then the defense attorney stands and also makes a surprising announcement: "Your Honor, the defense will rely on the evidence presented and the defense rests."

The testimony is over—with no word from the defendant and only two prosecution witnesses.

The defense counsel begins the closing arguments.

Ladies and gentlemen, this case is very unusual because there is no argument as to the facts. Both sides agree about what happened. Unlike most juries, you don't have to go back to the jury room and argue about who was telling the truth and what the true state of the evidence is. No, the only argument in this case is whether the law of rape applies to this strange set of circumstances.

The State generally prosecutes people who have some idea that they are violating the law when they commit the crime in question. The robber, the burglar, the thief, the murderer—they all know very well they are doing wrong even if they may not know the law precisely. Oh, yes, the D.A. will say ignorance of the law is no excuse. But we do not have an ignorant man here. He knows very well what rape is, and in this case he had no reason to believe he was violating the law against rape. He had no idea he was doing wrong. Ms. Samson consented, in fact led him to believe she wanted intercourse as much as he did. She was—to use her own words—into it as much as he was. This is a serious crime with serious consequences. No, we cannot speak of punishment here and I shall not do that. But they want to brand Maurice Vernon a rapist—a perpetrator of forcible rape—for the rest of his life.

The D.A.'s theory of the case is that Maurice is guilty because he continued when Ms. Samson asked him to stop. But let's be realistic, for heaven's sake. This is the real world. She led him to believe she wanted to have intercourse with him; he had every reason to believe she had no objection. And then to expect him to suddenly stop after she led him to the highest point of excitement and passion? That is simply not realistic. It defies common sense, it's not fair, it is not the real world. Surely the law of rape was not meant for this situation. Surely the legislators of our state, in their infinite wisdom, did not anticipate this scenario when they passed the law of rape. We all know what they had in mind when they made forcible rape a crime, one of the oldest crimes in history. They had in mind a man forcing himself upon a woman, overcoming her resistance by his brute strength, and penetrating her body over her frightened objections. That is what we all understand to be forcible rape—an outrage to the deepest sensibilities of the female victim, and that is a far cry from what happened in this case.

Ladies and gentlemen, you represent the conscience of this community. You have on your shoulders a heavy burden—to do the right thing. The people out there are hoping and relying on you to do the right thing. For the sake of justice, assume that profound burden; do the right thing, make the right decision.

> Not guilty is the only verdict that makes sense. Thank you.

Next, the D.A. speaks.

> Ladies and gentlemen, when you were sworn in as jurors in this case, you promised to follow the law whether you agreed with it or not. What you have just heard is a desperate plea for you to ignore the law. That's exactly what the defense attorney asked you to do, although, of course, she didn't put it in those words. The law of rape is simple. A man has sex with a woman against her will, without her consent—that's rape. That's exactly what happened in this case once Mr. Vernon continued to have sex with Kate after she told him—begged him—to stop. At that point he was acting in violation of the law. He knew it was wrong, but simply favored his own sexual impulses over her wishes and therein lies the outrage to her feelings. He didn't care what she said. He was determined to gratify his lust.
>
> The reason for her wanting him to stop is not relevant. The law says a woman has a right to say no, whatever the reason, and *no* means *no*. That's it. Oh, I know you may not like Kate for submitting to sex at the outset. You may not like her for various reasons. But that, too, is irrelevant. The only question is: did he have sex with her without her consent? And there is only one answer to that. This argument is short because there are no facts in dispute. Did she consent to him continuing? No. Did she resist? She certainly did. She tried to withdraw, even tried to push him off, to no avail. As the detective said, Mr. Vernon confessed to the crime when he admitted he heard her say "stop" and kept on ignoring her. This is all we need to know. All I ask is that you follow the law. If you do, you will return the only proper verdict: guilty of forcible rape.

The judge, also a young woman, reads a long list of instructions of law. Three of her instructions are as follows:

1. Rape is an act of sexual intercourse with a female victim accomplished by means of force and against her will.

2. The defendant is presumed to be innocent and the State has the burden of overcoming that presumption by proof of guilt beyond a reasonable doubt.

3. The defendant has a constitutional right not to be compelled to testify. Jurors must not hold the defendant's failure to testify against him. Jurors are not allowed to discuss his failure to testify in their deliberations nor allow it to enter into their consideration of the case.

WHAT IS YOUR VERDICT?

QUESTIONS FOR YOU TO CONSIDER

As you determine your verdict for this crime, here are some questions about the crime and the trial for you to think about.

1. As a juror, you are supposed to follow the law whether or not you agree with it. Suppose you find that under strict adherence to the law of rape, the defendant is guilty since he had intercourse with Kate against her will. But the unusual facts of the case bother you. You feel that since she consented to penetration, it would not be fair to convict him of such a serious crime. Do you have the power to ignore the law and acquit the defendant?

2. Why did defense counsel decide not to call the defendant to the stand in this case? Didn't the jury want to hear his side?

AUTHOR'S ANSWERS TO THE QUESTIONS

1. Yes, it seldom happens, but the jury has the power to disregard the law and acquit the defendant. This is called *jury nullification*. Judges do not tell jurors they have such a power because they do not wish to encourage it. In 1972, the U.S. Supreme Court ruled in the case of *U.S. v. Dougherty* that "the jury has an unreviewable and unreversible power… to acquit in disregard of the instructions on the law given by the trial judge."

2. Defense counsel faced a hard choice as to whether to let her client testify. There may be many reasons why she decided as she did. First of all, the jury had already heard his side of the case by way of the detective's testimony. Mr. Vernon may have had nothing to add. Why risk his getting hurt on the stand by subjecting him to cross-examination? Also, she may have determined that he would simply not be a good witness. The choice of whether to call the defendant as his or her own witness is often the toughest decision a defense attorney has to make in a criminal trial.

THE VERDICT

What was your verdict?

The real-life jury found the defendant guilty.

Revenge of the Battered Woman

STATE V. MARIA CARVALHO

This case was tried in Lisbon, Portugal, in response to a request by the Portuguese government for a demonstration of a U.S. jury trial. In 1990, the Portuguese government invited Judge Ehrenfreund and a team of American lawyers to come to Lisbon to dramatize a mock criminal trial with English-speaking Lisbon citizens serving as jurors. At the time, the major difference between U.S. jury trials and those in most of Europe was in the role of the judge and that of the jury. In England, for example, the judge sums up the evidence for the jury as he or she sees it. The judge is supposed to be objective, but in reviewing the case, he or she has the power to give the jurors a lead or suggestion as to how to decide.

This is not so in the United States. Our judges rarely comment on the evidence; it is considered bad form to do so. In some foreign countries, judges and jurors sit together, confer together, and decide together in a joint effort unheard of in the United States. Our judges and juries have separate roles. The judge decides the law; the jury decides the facts. The American judge must always be on guard not to show the slightest leaning toward one way or another. At the time of this trial, Portugal was recovering from the injustices of a long dictatorship and was seeking to install a new democratic legal system. Trial by jury—American style—was under consideration. When Judge Ehrenfreund asked the Portuguese officials what kind of trial they wished to see, they described a scenario that has challenged justice systems, not only in the United States and Portugal, but also throughout the world—the case of a wife continually battered by her husband to the point where she resorts to violence to either defend herself or seek revenge.

The opening statements reveal the following facts:

Maria Carvalho lived with her husband, Miguel, and their 2-year-old daughter in a small apartment in Lisbon's Alfama district. They had a happy relationship until Miguel started drinking to excess, which resulted in bitter arguments. As the arguments became more heated, Miguel began beating Maria until she would collapse on the bed crying. After each beating, Miguel would become remorseful, beg Maria to forgive him, and they would reconcile. Soon the cycle would begin again. One night Miguel came home intoxicated, and when Maria scolded him, he struck her many times. As Maria lay on the bed sobbing, Miguel threatened to beat her again if she didn't stop crying like a child. Then he lay back on the sofa and fell asleep in a drunken stupor. As Maria lay in bed listening to Miguel snore, she was frightened that he might awake any moment and beat her again. She thought of his gun in the drawer nearby. One interpretation of the evidence is that Maria eventually picked up the gun, went over to the sofa, and shot and killed Miguel. Another interpretation of the evidence is that the angle of the bullet entry and exit wounds in Miguel's body shows that Miguel could have risen from the sofa to attack Maria when he was shot.

Was it murder or did Maria shoot Miguel in self-defense?

Imagine that you are one of the English-speaking citizens of Lisbon who has been selected for this case. You are nervous because many people in your country of Portugal, as well as in other countries, are watching what the jury does in this case. The room is a large, stark chamber with thick, sturdy columns. Once part of a prison, with barred windows as a grim reminder of its past, now it is a courtroom jammed with several hundred lawyers, judges, and scholars from many lands who have come to see their first American jury trial.

The accused is Maria Carvalho, a pale, harmless-looking woman slumped beside her attorney. The charge is murder.

"You may feel some sympathy for Maria," the prosecutor, Maurice Sands, says in his opening statement. "But sympathy has no part in this case. Do not let it sway you. She is a murderess and must pay the price for her deed."

Maria Carvalho's attorney, Philip Bourne, stands behind her with one hand on her shoulder as he makes his opening statement.

"Maria shot her husband because there was no other way out for her. She shot him out of fear he would beat her again, as he had done so many times in the past."

You look at Maria Carvalho. The tears are already beginning to form in her eyes.

The first witness for the prosecution is Ilde Diaz, next-door neighbor to Miguel and Maria Carvalho and their 2-year-old daughter. She testifies that on the morning of January 3, 1990, at about 5:00 a.m., she heard three shots coming from the direction of the Carvalho apartment. She was lying awake in bed at the time, and after hearing the shots, she dressed and looked out in the hallway. She noticed the Carvalhos' front door open. She rang the bell, knocked several times, announced her presence, and finally, when no one responded, went inside. There she saw the body of Miguel

Carvalho lying faceup on the sofa. He wore only a bathrobe, and she could see a considerable amount of blood in the area of his chest and shoulders. He appeared to be dead, so she immediately called the police. No one else was present.

The prosecutor, Sands, asks her about the shots.

Sands: You are sure you heard three shots?

Diaz: Yes, quite sure.

Sands: Tell us how they were spaced as to the time between each shot.

Diaz: The first two came in rapid succession, one right after another, boom-boom. The third came a bit later.

Sands: How much later?

Diaz: That's hard to say.

"I will ask you to try to remember in this way," Sands says. He looks up at the big clock on the wall. "I am looking at the clock. Imagine you are in your bed at the time of the shots. When I say 'Now!' think of that as the second shot. Then think to yourself the time that passed, and say, 'Now' when you heard the third shot."

The audience is hushed. Along with everyone else, you and the other jurors watch the red second hand as it goes around. When it reaches twelve, the prosecutor shouts, "Now!" The witness has her eyes closed. One second, two, three, four, five, six—"Now!" she says.

"Thank you, Mrs. Diaz. Your Honor, may the record show six seconds passed between the two 'Nows'?"

Judge: The record may show so.

Under cross-examination, the witness testifies she often heard arguments between the couple, especially during the month before the shooting. She could hear the loud voice of Mr. Carvalho and at times the screaming of the defendant. She could never make out the words. On the evening before the shooting, she heard another such argument. This time she also heard the sounds of breaking glass and furniture falling over.

Sands returns to the podium for redirect examination.

Sands: What time was it when you heard this argument?

Diaz: About 10:00 p.m.

Sands: Did you hear anything sounding like an argument after that?

Diaz: No.

Sands: Before the shots were fired at about 5:00 a.m., did you hear any argument, anything at all?

Diaz: No, nothing.

Sands: You said you often heard arguments between the couple. Ever see the defendant, Mrs. Carvalho, after one of these arguments?

Diaz: Oh yes, many times.

Sands: Ever see any marks on her body?

Diaz: No.

Sands: Black eyes, bruises, anything like that?

Diaz: No, I never did.

Sands is finished with the witness, but Bourne still has a question.

Bourne: How did she look after these arguments?

Diaz: Very depressed.

Bourne: Frightened?

Sands: Objection! Calls for a conclusion.

Judge: Overruled. You may answer.

Diaz: You might say she looked scared, yes.

Bourne: Thank you.

Officer Stefano Tavares was the first police officer on the scene. He testifies he found the victim lying on his back on the sofa, clothed only in a robe. The deceased had visible wounds to his right hand, left shoulder, and chest. The sofa where the victim was lying was soaked with blood. The room had a bed and a sofa. After the body was removed, Tavares searched the apartment with other members of the homicide squad. He found no weapons. There was one spent bullet embedded in the wall above the sofa where the body was discovered, and about five feet above the floor. Except for the blood on the sofa, he found no other traces of blood. Several bottles of alcohol, including wine, vodka, and brandy, stood open on the table. In the dining room, the officer noted an overturned chair and what appeared to be pieces of smashed glass. He also found a small amount of cocaine and items used for sniffing it.

The prosecution next calls its forensic pathologist, Dr. Duarte Vasconcelos. He performed the autopsy and says the gunshot wound to the chest was the principal cause of death. The doctor testifies he found a through-and-through bullet wound to the right hand, entering the palm just under the index finger and exiting the back of the hand. The palm of the right hand showed tattooing and powder burns, indicating the bullet was fired at close range. A second bullet struck the left shoulder and was still lodged in the back behind the shoulder. The third shot was also a through-and-through wound, entering just above the breastbone at about a forty-five degree angle to the chest. He explains he was able to determine the path of entry and exit from careful examination of the wounds. The doctor draws a diagram with the body in a horizontal position to show how the bullet entered the chest and exited the back.

He found no tattooing or powder burns in the wounds to the shoulder or the chest, indicating those shots were fired at a greater distance than the shot to the hand, at least four feet from the body. There was a small amount of cocaine found in the victim's blood and urine. The victim's blood alcohol level was .18%, well above the amount at which an individual is considered too intoxicated to drive a car.

Bourne takes the doctor on cross-examination.

Bourne: Any way to tell in which order the three shots were fired, Doctor?

Vasconcelos: No way I can say that.

Bourne: You testified the shot to the hand occurred at close range. How close?

Vasconcelos: One can't say exactly. But within a foot or so.

Bourne: Would that be consistent with the victim trying to strike Maria with that hand when the shot was fired?

Sands: Objection! Beyond his expertise.

Judge: Sustained.

Bourne: Doctor, I notice you drew your diagram with the body lying down. Is it your testimony the body was in that position when the shot was fired?

Vasconcelos: I cannot testify to that, no. I can only say this is the angle at which the fatal bullet entered the body. I'm afraid I assumed he was in that position because the body was found on the sofa, lying down, with blood on the blanket.

Bourne: So that position is just an assumption.

Vasconcelos: Yes, from what I was told by the police.

Bourne: Thank you, Doctor. By the way, how tall was Mr. Carvalho?

Vasconcelos: Let me check my notes. Ah, yes, he measured five feet eleven inches.

Bourne: And weight?

Vasconcelos: One hundred seventy-six pounds.

Bourne: Your Honor, I will ask my client to stand so the jurors may observe her approximate height and weight.

Maria Carvalho stands up, and you look at her size. She is only about five feet three inches tall, about 120 pounds in weight.

The prosecution calls another neighbor to the stand. Luis Caetano testifies he lived in the apartment directly opposite the Carvalhos. He knew them both, especially Maria, since they had grown up in the same neighborhood of Lisbon. He recalls having a conversation with Maria on the day before Christmas in 1989. She told him she feared she would have to kill her husband because he was violent toward her. She also told him her husband had beaten her on several occasions during the last three years, to the point where she was considering leaving home with her child.

Sands pauses before resuming direct examination. "You would see her often?"

Caetano: Yes.

Sands: Ever see the effects of a beating—marks, bruises, anything like that?

Caetano: No, I never did.

Sands: Did you ask her about that?

Caetano: Yes.

Sands: And what was her response?

Caetano: She said her husband was always careful to hit her only on the torso, or ribs, so it would not show.

As is his habit, Bourne wastes no time on cross-examination. "You knew Maria well?"

Caetano: Yes.

Bourne: You consider her honest, truthful?

Caetano: Yes. Of course.

Bourne: Thank you.

The final witness for the prosecution is a woman who is brought in under guard. Her name is Teresa Salazar, and she testifies she is currently being detained at the Lisbon detention facility for women, awaiting trial on a charge of selling narcotics. She says that on the morning of January 5, 1990, she was having breakfast with another inmate, Maria Carvalho, at the jail. During the course of the conversation, Maria told her she was glad she killed her husband, that he treated her badly, and that she knew for some time she would have to kill him to get away from him. The witness further testifies that the defendant also told her that if she got out, she would not hesitate to harm any member of her husband's family if they tried to take her child away from her. The witness said she made some notes of the conversation immediately afterward, because she knew they would be important to the police, but the piece of paper was confiscated before the trial during a routine search of jail lockers.

Bourne takes the witness on cross-examination. "Did the police tell you it might be better for you in your own case if you testified for the prosecution here?"

Salazar: No.

Bourne: No promises of benefit of any kind?

Salazar: No.

Bourne: What did they tell you?

Salazar: They asked me if I would cooperate, and I said I would.

Bourne: Why?

Salazar: Well, so the truth would come out.

Bourne: And you hoped that by telling what you call "the truth" you might get a break from the police?

Salazar: No, they made no promises. They even said they couldn't make any promises.

Bourne: Didn't they say they would tell your judge you cooperated?

Salazar: Well, yes, but no promises of leniency.

Bourne: But you hope you will get a break, that the judge will go easier on you if he knows you helped the police?

Salazar: Well—

Bourne: Well what?

Salazar: Well, of course, if I can get a better deal for myself, fine, I don't want to go to prison.

Bourne: Just a few more questions. Have you been convicted of a felony?

Salazar: What's that got to do with it? I'm not on trial. Do I have to answer, Your Honor?

Judge: You do.

Salazar: Yes, I have been convicted of a felony.

Bourne: How many?

Salazar: Oh, for God's sake. All right. Two.

Bourne: What were they for?

Salazar: One was selling cocaine. One was credit card fraud.

Bourne: Thank you. That's all.

The prosecution rests and Bourne begins the defense case by calling the defendant's mother, Eliana Viriato. She testifies that on the morning of January 3, 1990, at about 5:15 a.m., she received a phone call from her daughter, who was crying. She asked her parents to come pick her up right away. Mrs. Viriato testifies she and her husband drove to the apartment, where Maria was waiting outside with her child. She hysterically told her parents she just shot her husband, and they drove her to the police station, where she turned herself in.

Sands cross-examines in a kindly manner. "Did she have the gun with her?"

Viriato: No, we didn't see any. And we didn't ask her about it.

Sands: Did she seem to be in possession of all her faculties?

Viriato: Well, she kept crying all the time.

Sands: But did she seem to know what she was doing, what she was saying?

Viriato: Yes.

Now a psychiatrist, Dr. Fritz Mannheim, takes the stand for the defense. He has impressive credentials. He testifies that at the request of Mr. Bourne, he interviewed Maria five times in the Lisbon jail after her arrest. He directed a psychologist to give her the standard psychological tests. He says he found no major organic deficiency, but she was suffering from major depression resulting from the way her husband treated her, and at the time of the shooting she was suicidal and saw no hope for herself or her child. Dr. Mannheim says he tried to get her to tell him what happened, but the events were unclear in her mind. This failure to recall, the doctor says, is consistent with a woman suffering from such a mental illness; she wants to leave such an experience behind and not relive it in any way, either with her psychiatrist or in the courtroom. The doctor testifies Maria was suffering from *battered woman's syndrome,* resulting from a cycle of emotional and physical abuse by her husband, from which she could see no options for escape.

Sands begins questioning, with a note of cynicism in his voice. "Doctor, do you consider the defendant your client?"

Mannheim: Oh, no, I was simply asked to evaluate her for the court.

Sands: Who is paying you for your services?

Mannheim: Mr. Bourne is taking care of that.

Sands: How much are you being paid?

Mannheim: Well....Do I have to answer that, Your Honor?

He turns to the judge.

Judge: You do, sir.

Mannheim: One hundred fifty an hour for services out of court and—

Sands: And more if you testify?

Mannheim: Yes. Two hundred fifty an hour as a witness in court.

Sands: And if your opinion is adverse to the defense, you do not testify?

Mannheim: I testify if I am called as a witness.

Sands: And it's to your advantage to testify?

Mannheim: I consider your line of questioning insulting, sir.

Sands: By the way, Doctor, is there any scientifically verifiable test to determine mental illness?

Mannheim: Well, no.

Sands: It's a matter of subjective determination, isn't that true?

Mannheim: One may say that.

Sands: And there is no scientifically verifiable test to determine what Maria Carvalho was thinking on the morning of January 3, 1990?

Mannheim: That is true.

Sands: And isn't it also true that reasonable psychiatrists, qualified experts such as yourself, might disagree as to such a diagnosis?

Mannheim: That is also true, yes.

Bourne gets up immediately for redirect examination. "Doctor, based on all your training and experience, do you have an opinion as to why Maria shot her husband?"

Mannheim: I do.

Bourne: Tell the jury, please.

Mannheim: In my opinion, she believed she had to shoot him in order to protect herself and her child from further abuse and possibly being killed.

The next witness for the defense is a criminologist from the Lisbon Police Department who testifies he took blood and urine samples from the defendant immediately following her arrest on January 3, 1990, and found no evidence of alcohol or cocaine in her body.

A detention officer who works in the women's detention facility testifies that she inspected the items seized in the search of Teresa Salazar's locker and found no notes of a conversation with the defendant.

Defense Attorney Bourne casually announces that Maria Carvalho will be his next witness. You feel relieved. You wanted to hear her testify. Now you will. She seems a pathetic little figure as she walks slowly to the stand and is on the verge of tears even before the first question is asked. She testifies she and Miguel were very much in love when they married five years ago. They both had good jobs and looked forward to a happy life. With the birth of their child, another dream was fulfilled.

But then came changes in Miguel's behavior. He started drinking and using cocaine. He became abusive to her, not so much physically as emotionally, always putting her down, humiliating her, screaming at her, threatening her with violence in front of their little girl. At times, although not often, he would actually beat her with his fists. He never struck her in the face. After each bout of violence, he would be remorseful and they would reconcile.

This went on for the last year and a half of their marriage and seemed to get worse around Christmas 1989. Maria became quite depressed and often lacked the energy to get up in the morning; she felt there was no way out and thought of killing herself. On the night of January 2, 1990, Maria and Miguel had another bitter argument. She wanted him to stop using cocaine, and he resented her telling him how to live his life. He punched her in the shoulder, and she finally went to bed crying while he stood over her and threatened to hit her if she didn't stop "acting like a child." The night passed. He slept on the sofa, the one on which he would be found dead.

Maria awoke while it was still dark. She was very depressed and thought of killing herself. She lay back thinking how she would do it. She remembered his gun was in the drawer next to the bed. After that, she cannot recall what happened. She knows she must have shot him from what others have told her, but she has no recollection of how it happened.

Sands drops his sympathetic demeanor as he begins cross-examining. "Did you have to shoot to defend yourself?"

Carvalho: I don't know. I can't remember.

Sands: Did he attack you that morning?

Carvalho: I can't say.

Sands: You say you were very depressed and suicidal. Did you ever seek counseling or any medical assistance for your condition?

Carvalho: No, I didn't think it could help.

Sands: It didn't occur to you that it might be an alternative to killing your husband?

Bourne: Objection!

Judge: Sustained.

Sands: Did you ever report any of these beatings to the police?

Carvalho: No. What good would that do?

Sands: Did you have a chance to get away?

Carvalho: Well, yes, but—

Sands: You could have gone to the police?

Carvalho: Yes.

Sands: You could have gone to neighbors? To your parents?

Carvalho: No, I really couldn't. They had no room.

Sands: Did you ever try any of these things?

Carvalho: I couldn't! I couldn't! I felt so trapped. (*She is sobbing now.*) I can't explain—

Sands: No, I guess you can't explain. Thank you, ma'am.

Bourne recalls Officer Tavares to the stand. He was the officer who made the search of the apartment. "Officer, you testified earlier you noted the blood on the sofa where the victim was lying?"

Tavares: Yes, sir.

Bourne: Notice anything else on the sofa?

Tavares: What do you mean, sir?

Bourne: Did you find a bullet there behind his back?

Tavares: I didn't see any bullet, sir.

Bourne: You looked for the bullet?

Tavares: I looked sir, yes, sir, but there was a lot of blood there. When I didn't see any I figured it must still be in his back.

Bourne: So your answer is you found no bullet on the sofa?

Tavares: That is correct, sir.

Bourne: See any bullet hole?

Tavares: You mean in the sofa, sir?

Bourne: That's exactly what I mean. If a bullet came out his back it would have left some kind of hole in the sofa, wouldn't it?

Sands: Objection!

Judge: Sustained!

Bourne: I will ask you again. Did you see any bullet hole in the sofa?

Tavares: Sir, as I said, the sofa was covered with blood—

Bourne: So, you didn't see any bullet hole?

Tavares: No, sir.

Bourne: Thank you, Officer. Your Honor, I wish to recall Dr. Vasconcelos as my final witness.

As the doctor resumes the stand, Bourne approaches the large diagram the doctor drew earlier.

Bourne: Doctor, you drew this diagram showing the angle of the bullet that entered the chest?

Vasconcelos: Yes, sir.

You can tell the doctor is wondering what the attorney is getting at.

Bourne: You said you drew the victim in this horizontal position because you assumed that was his position when shot?

Vasconcelos: Yes.

Bourne: The bullet did come out his back, did it not?

Vasconcelos: It had to, yes.

Bourne: And knowing the path of the bullet, would it be your opinion that if he were lying down on the sofa in this horizontal position, faceup, the bullet would have gone into the sofa upon exiting his back?

Sands: Objection!

Judge: Overruled. You may answer, Doctor.

Vasconcelos: I would say so, yes.

Bourne then turns the diagram on its side. "Suppose, Doctor, we look at your diagram this way—in this position, with the victim in a standing position, the shooter down below. Is this also consistent with your finding as to the angle of entry?"

Vasconcelos: It is.

Bourne: That's all. Thank you, Doctor, you've been very helpful.

There are four possible verdicts you can reach in this case:

1. guilty of first-degree murder
2. guilty of second-degree murder
3. guilty of voluntary manslaughter
4. not guilty

WHAT IS YOUR VERDICT?

QUESTIONS FOR YOU TO CONSIDER

As you determine your verdict for this crime, here are some questions about the crime and the trial for you to think about.

1. The pathologist's diagram showed the victim lying in a horizontal position when shot. How did the defense attorney put this diagram to the defendant's advantage?

2. In order to prove first-degree murder, the prosecution must show that the killing was willful, deliberate, and premeditated with malice aforethought. What two pieces of evidence in particular could be used by the prosecutor to attribute these qualities to Maria Carvalho prior to the shooting?

3. How did the defense attorney damage the credibility of a key prosecution witness, the jail inmate Teresa Salazar?

4. What evidence of noise or lack of noise prior to the shooting was helpful to the prosecution in rebutting the defense claim of self-defense?

5. What glaring error of investigation was made by the police officer who searched the apartment?

6. Suppose you found that Maria Carvalho was not in immediate danger when she killed her husband, but shot him out of a reasonable fear that he would harm her seriously in the near future. Does that justify her action in your mind? Could her attorney use the battered woman's syndrome evidence to help her?

7. Suppose you found that Maria Carvalho was not in immediate danger, but fired in an honest but unreasonable fear that she was. What would your verdict be? In this situation, would the battered woman's syndrome evidence have greater relevance?

AUTHOR'S ANSWERS TO THE QUESTIONS

1. The defense attorney in this case made several smart moves. One of the best had to do with his handling of the pathologist's diagram showing the victim lying in a horizontal position when shot, the bullet entering his body from above.

   Bourne simply turned the diagram on its side, which then showed the victim in a vertical or standing position, the bullet now appearing to enter from below. This position would lend credibility to the defense argument that Maria got the gun out to commit suicide after the fight the previous evening, as she testified, and when her husband advanced toward her in the bed to beat her again, she fired upward from the bed to defend herself. And there was the State's own diagram to show how it happened.

2. Two pieces of evidence in particular could be used to support the element of deliberation and premeditation: the testimony of the neighbor Caetano that Maria told him several days before the incident she was thinking of killing her husband if the violence continued, and the fact that she waited six seconds—ample time to weigh her decision—before firing the third shot.

3. By eliciting from the female prisoner, Salazar, her admission that she hoped to gain favor with the prosecution by her testimony, the defense counsel impeached her credibility. Her notes of the alleged conversation with the defendant were never found in the jail locker, which also damaged her status as a witness.

4. There were no sounds heard by the neighbors just before the shots to indicate any struggle or beating—no screaming or crying of a woman in fear. The lack of such evidence supports the prosecutor's argument that Maria fired not in self-defense, but in cold blood.

5. Three shots were fired. One bullet was found in the wall. Another was still lodged in the victim's shoulder. Where was the third bullet? Apparently the police never found it. The officer who searched the apartment made a glaring mistake in failing to search for the third bullet or a bullet hole in the sofa where the body was found. It was obvious from cross-examination that he neglected to make a careful probe because of so much blood in that spot. The fact that there was blood on the sofa behind the victim's back doesn't mean he was shot there. He could have been shot while standing, then fallen back on the sofa. Evidence of either the bullet or bullet hole would have been the strongest possible circumstantial evidence that the victim was shot while lying down on the sofa.

6. Under existing U.S. law, the right of self-defense is available to the killer only when the danger to one's life is immediate, not at some future time. Therefore if Maria fired because she feared her husband would harm her in the near future, the right of self-defense is not available to her. The law says that no matter how severely her husband may have injured her in the past, her use of deadly force is not justified unless it appeared necessary to protect her from immediate death or great bodily injury. Evidence of the battered woman's syndrome will not help her in this situation.

   There is considerable criticism of this law of self-defense, and some lawyers argue that it is too rigid, that deadly force should be justified even when the danger isn't so immediate, such as when the woman feels so trapped by an abusive relationship that she sees no other way out. There seems to be growing support for a change in the law, which would give a battered woman in certain abusive relationships the right of self-defense when she kills to avoid an inevitable fatal result, i.e., when she kills not in defense of an immediate threat, but to prevent abuse that she reasonably believes will occur in the future.

7. As part of the changes occurring throughout the United States in this area of the law, some states now allow evidence of battered woman's syndrome to help the defendant who is not actually in immediate danger but has an honest belief that she is because of past abuse. If the jury finds that the woman defendant had an honest but unreasonable belief that she was in immediate danger, the jury is instructed that the verdict should be voluntary manslaughter rather than murder. Such a finding does not, however, warrant acquittal.

THE VERDICT

The real-life jury found the defendant guilty of murder in the first degree.

The defense attorney's use of the State's diagram was a simple but brilliant stroke; however—as so often happens with brilliant strokes in jury trials—the jury did not accept it.

The jury sentenced the defendant to twenty-seven years to life in prison.

Assisted Suicide or Murder?

STATE V. STEPHEN SARKO

Dying of AIDS, Leo Melnik begged his roommate, Steve Sarko, to help him die before the pain and suffering became worse. This was at a time in the early 1990s when AIDS was a speedy death sentence and treatment just a dream. Both men were gay, loved each other, and had lived together compatibly for many years. Melnik proposed a plan to Sarko whereby Sarko would tie Melnik's wrists behind his back while Melnik lay on the bed facedown. Then Sarko would wind a sash around Melnik's neck, attach it to his wrists behind him, and then to his raised ankles. In this position Melnik could strangle himself by stretching out his feet. All Sarko would have to do is hold Melnik's body so he would not fall off the bed.

At first Sarko refused. How could he help kill someone he loved? But Melnik pleaded with him. It would be suicide, not murder. Melnik would do the actual killing. He reminded Sarko of how he had watched a close friend suffer with AIDS before dying. Surely Sarko would not want Melnik to go through such misery. "If you really love me," Melnik said, "you will do it."

Finally, Sarko consented. First the two men prayed together, after which Sarko tied Melnik up according to plan. He stood by and held the body until Melnik choked himself to death. Frightened of the consequences, Sarko fled the scene and left Melnik's corpse on the bed.

Was it murder or suicide?

Eventually, police arrested Sarko and the D.A. brought him to trial on the charge of aiding and abetting a deliberate and premeditated murder.

D.A. Jack Kornbluth makes his opening statement. "Sarko may not look like a murderer now," he says, "but I assure you he will look different to you when you hear what he did."

Sarko's attorney is Tim O'Connor, a white-haired Irishman who was a D.A. until he threatened to fight the judge in another case. Then he became a defense attorney.

"What Stephen Sarko did," O'Connor says, "was help his dying friend commit suicide. That is all. What we have here is not a murder of any kind, but an act of friendship and love."

The prosecution calls Linda Kerry as its first witness. She is the director of nursing at Valley Hospital. Leo Melnik was a practical nurse on her staff. He failed to show up for work on the evening of October 10, 1991, which was unusual for him. When he did not show up the following evening, she became concerned. Her phone calls to his number were unanswered, so she called the police and asked them to check his apartment.

On cross-examination by O'Connor, she states that her staff treats patients who have AIDS.

O'Connor: You are aware that AIDS is usually fatal?

Kerry: Yes.

O'Connor: Once you have it, you are likely to die?

Kerry: In many cases, right.

O'Connor: Did Leo Melnik have AIDS?

Kerry: I have no idea.

O'Connor: Was he ever tested for AIDS?

Kerry: You mean by our hospital?

O'Connor: Yes—before you hired him?

Kerry: No. We cannot demand that an individual be tested for AIDS. That might be considered discrimination. So we don't do it.

Irina Melnik takes the stand. She is the victim's mother. Mrs. Melnik lives in Moberly, Missouri. She testifies that her son left his hometown in Missouri while still in his teens, when he realized he was homosexual. He moved to the West Coast, where he had lived for the past seventeen years, to be in a friendlier atmosphere. She often discussed his homosexuality openly with him. She knows he attempted suicide three years ago, but he never told her he had AIDS. As far as she knew, he was in good health, even ran several miles a day to stay in shape. She also phoned the police when she could not reach him on the phone.

Tom Jessup testifies he was the first police officer on the scene. He received a radio call in his patrol car on the evening of October 11, 1991, to check on Leo Melnik in his apartment at 2005 Fifth Avenue. When he rang the bell and banged on the door without getting an answer, he inquired of neighbors. They said they had not seen Melnik or his roommate, Stephen Sarko, for several days.

Finally, Officer Jessup kicked in the door. Seeing no one in the living room, he opened the door to the bedroom. There, lying on the bed, facedown on the pillow, was a fully clothed man who fit the description of Leo Melnik. The officer checked for rigor mortis. He felt the skin, lifted an arm and let it drop, and determined Melnik had been dead several hours. Melnik's hands were behind his back, but they were not tied. The officer found no ropes or bindings of any kind. He saw no blood on the bed or anywhere else in the apartment. He searched the apartment for possible murder weapons but found none.

While he was still in the apartment, the phone rang, and he answered it. It was Melnik's mother calling from Missouri, asking to speak with her son. The officer had to tell her the truth. "That," he says, "was one of the hardest things I ever had to do."

Another police officer, Detective Christine Cusimano, is called to the stand. She was a member of the homicide team investigating the case. Officer Cusimano arrived on the scene soon after receiving Officer Jessup's call for assistance. She inspected the body, noticed abrasions on the wrists and ligature marks across the front of the throat. In her opinion, these marks were caused by the tightening of an object, such as a rope, around the neck. The apartment was neat, showing no sign of a struggle, no sign of any forced entry. She found a card on the desk that read, "AIDS and the Doctors of Death. Dr. Marvin Rosenberg."

Investigation led Cusimano's team to Sarko in his cousin's apartment across town. When they found him, he seemed very frightened. After being advised of his rights, Sarko admitted he had been Melnik's roommate, that he helped him commit suicide and then left the body on the bed because he was afraid of the consequences. He broke down in tears and refused to answer any more questions without the advice of an attorney. He was placed under arrest and charged with murder.

Dr. David Zuniga testifies as the medical examiner who performed the autopsy. The cause of death was asphyxia by ligature strangulation. He found ligature marks on the neck and wrists, and bruising of the tongue by the teeth of a clenched mouth. Dr. Zuniga also examined the victim's colon. He found purple spots in the intestines, and after examining them under a microscope, he concluded Melnik had a cancer called Kaposi's sarcoma. The doctor testifies this is an indication the decedent was infected with HIV.

D.A. Kornbluth hones in on the AIDS question. "You are certain Mr. Melnik tested positive for HIV, which is associated with AIDS?"

Zuniga: Yes.

Kornbluth: Does that mean he was going to die from it?

Zuniga: Not necessarily. Some people with this virus may never get sick.

Kornbluth: They could live indefinitely?

Zuniga: Yes.

Kornbluth: Through their natural course in life?

Zuniga: It's possible, yes.

Kornbluth: And when people die of AIDS, do they die because their immune system breaks down?

Zuniga: Yes.

Kornbluth: And do they suffer from various illnesses before death?

Zuniga: Yes—usually pneumonia, sometimes malignancies, until they finally succumb to some fatal infection.

Kornbluth: And did you see any evidence that Mr. Melnik suffered from pneumonia or any other serious illness before his death?

Zuniga: I did not.

Kornbluth: And he was of normal weight for his size?

Zuniga: His weight was normal. There was no indication of any abnormal weight loss.

O'Connor begins cross-examination with a hypothetical question.

O'Connor: Doctor, if a man's wrists were bound behind his back, and a cord was wrapped around his neck and tied to his wrists, would it be possible for that person to choke himself to death?

Zuniga: It's possible. But doubtful.

O'Connor: Why do you say doubtful, Doctor?

Zuniga: Because usually a person will lapse into unconsciousness first before dying from strangulation. And so it's unlikely that while unconscious he would be able to keep up the pressure or tension necessary to strangle himself to death.

O'Connor: But it could happen?

Zuniga: Possibly.

The prosecution rests.

Now Stephen Sarko takes the stand in his defense, a frightened look on his face.

O'Connor starts right off with the fact that Sarko is gay. "Let's start with your sexual orientation. What is that?"

Sarko: I am a homosexual.

O'Connor: How long have you been a homosexual?

Sarko: All my life.

O'Connor: When do you first recall having a homosexual encounter?

Sarko: I had encounters at age 5 or 6.

He testifies he was working in a bookstore around the time of Melnik's death. A year before meeting Leo Melnik, he had been involved with a man named Eddie Wilmont. They were not only lovers, but also best friends. Then Eddie contracted AIDS. As his illness became serious, he asked Sarko to live with him, to help him in his final days. So Sarko moved in with Eddie, tended to his needs, helped get him to the hospital. Sarko watched the horror of the ordeal, how Eddie suffered. After Eddie died, he moved back to his own place and began looking for another friend and lover. One day when he was about to cross the street near the park, a car went by slowly and the driver cruised him.

O'Connor: What do you mean, he "cruised" you?

Sarko: He looked me up and down, checked me out. He expressed certain, um, certain meanings with his eyes.

O'Connor: What did you do in response?

Sarko: I looked at him the same way.

O'Connor: This form of cruising—is that a common experience?

Sarko: Everybody does it.

O'Connor: How many times have you been cruised like that?

Sarko: Hundreds of times.

Sarko says the driver turned the car around and asked him where he was going, and he got in. They went to the apartment of the driver, Leo Melnik, and that started their relationship. They lived together for a year before Leo's death, a close monogamous bond. The two also discovered they were both dedicated distance runners. Together they would run five, ten miles a day through the streets and parks of the city before work in the morning. Often they ran side by side in ten-kilometer and marathon races sponsored by the city. They were both in excellent condition as far as anyone could tell. Both had steady jobs. They were the envy of their gay community. Then one night just after they had had sex, they were lying in bed and Leo told Sarko he had AIDS and knew he was going to die.

O'Connor: What did you say?

Sarko: I said, "Leo, you look fine. You run fine." But he said he knew what would happen. He felt bad inside. We stayed awake all night. We cried together and I held his hand. He talked about how he was going to die.

O'Connor: Did you have sex after that?

Sarko: Yes, but I used a condom so I wouldn't get AIDS, too.

O'Connor: What did he want you to do?

Sarko: He wanted me to contact a secret organization, The Black Mask, where a person who has AIDS—if he wants to die—he can call this organization and they will help him die. He said they operate a big business in New York and San Francisco helping people who really want to die. Leo wanted to pay them five thousand dollars to help him die, but I didn't know how to contact the people.

O'Connor: So then what did he say?

Sarko: Then he asked me if I would help him do it, if I would help him strangle himself.

O'Connor: What did you say to that?

Sarko: I said, oh God, no. I couldn't do that. He offered me his ATM card and gave me the password to get the money out; he wanted to give me his gold rings, even his car. But I said no, I didn't know how to drive anyway.

O'Connor: Did he finally persuade you to help him?

Sarko: He knew how to get to me. He looked at me and said, "Steve, you don't want me to go through what your friend Eddie went through, do you?"

Sarko agreed to help Leo die. They went through another night during which they both got down on their knees and prayed together. Leo told Sarko what to do, and Sarko followed his instructions. Leo lay on the bed facedown with his hands clasped behind his back. Sarko tied Leo's hands with a belt that Sarko took from his own trousers.

O'Connor: What did he ask you to do then?

Sarko: He asked me to leave him like that with his hands tied behind his back, so I did. I told him I loved him, that's why I was doing it. I went into the other room. I was real tired, because we hadn't slept for two nights. I went to sleep, and when I got up and went in, he was dead. But I didn't kill him.

Up to this point, you have hardly noticed the nondescript-looking D.A., Jack Kornbluth. Short in stature, with thick glasses and thin graying hair, he has asked all his questions from his seat at the counsel table, never raising his deep voice. You haven't even heard him make an objection. Now for the first time he gets up from his chair, moves to the podium, and glares at the defendant.

Kornbluth: Did you call the police?

Sarko: No.

Kornbluth: Did you take care of the body, the body of your best friend?

Sarko: No, I didn't.

Kornbluth: In fact, you went into the kitchen and had a drink, didn't you?

Sarko: Yes.

Kornbluth: And you left right away, didn't you—just left him there like that.

Sarko: I was scared.

Kornbluth: Scared of what? You hadn't done anything wrong, had you?

Sarko: I was scared of all the implications.

Kornbluth: You weren't too scared to take his ATM card and go down to the bank and withdraw two hundred dollars. You weren't so scared that you couldn't do that, were you?

Sarko: No.

Kornbluth: Did you do that?

Sarko: Yes, he wanted me to.

Kornbluth: You took the gold rings?

Sarko: Yes. He gave them to me.

Kornbluth: Tell us the truth. Isn't it a fact you killed him because you were mad at him?

Sarko: Mad at him? God, no. I loved him. No.

Kornbluth: Come on Mr. Sarko, level with us—weren't you mad at him because he didn't tell you he had AIDS until after you had sex with him? Didn't that make you mad?

Sarko: Oh no, no, no, you've got it all wrong. That wasn't it. Not that at all.

Sarko is beginning to break. The D.A. just stands there and looks at him for a long time.

Kornbluth: Come on, Steve. Why don't you tell us the truth—why don't you level with this jury? You'll feel better if you open up.

Sarko: I didn't kill him. I swear it.

Kornbluth: All right. Then tell us how he died.

Sarko: I told you.

Kornbluth: With his hands behind his back? Come on.

Sarko: He wanted me to tie his neck up. But I wouldn't do that.

Kornbluth: How did he want you to tie his neck up?

Sarko: He had this deal on his neck.

Kornbluth: What kind of deal?

Sarko: A sash.

Kornbluth: What sash?

Sarko: Like off a robe.

Kornbluth: He had that on his neck?

Sarko: He had it around his neck, and he wanted me to tie that to his wrists so he could choke himself, but I wouldn't do that.

Kornbluth: So you just tied his hands?

Sarko: Right. I just tied his hands and I left him alone with that deal around his neck. He said just to go and leave him, and I went into the living room. And I closed the door. I went to sleep, and when I went back in there he was dead.

Kornbluth: Just like that?

Sarko: Yes.

Kornbluth: Steve—

Sarko: I swear—

Kornbluth: Come on, Steve. A man just doesn't die from having his hands tied behind his back. You don't expect this jury to believe that?

Sarko: I didn't kill him.

Kornbluth: How did the marks get on his neck?

Sarko looks down. He is shaking his head.

Kornbluth: How did the marks get on his neck, Mr. Sarko?

Sarko: Well—

Sarko is visibly shaken.

Kornbluth: Steve, I know you want to open up. You're going to feel a lot better if you tell us the truth. For his sake, for your own soul, just tell us what happened in that bedroom.

Sarko: Well, I didn't want to—

Kornbluth: Go ahead, let it out. Don't make his death a lie. You want to tell us.

Sarko: When his hands were tied, I tied the sash on—

Kornbluth: See now. That's better. Now you're starting to tell us the truth—

Sarko: I tied his hands like this, with the sash onto them.

Kornbluth: Okay. It's around his neck. Then you tied the sash to his hands, right?

Sarko: Yes. That's what he asked me to do.

Kornbluth: What was he doing?

Sarko: Doing? He was trying to choke himself.

Kornbluth: And you let him do it?

Sarko: I was scared. I didn't want him to go through what Eddie went through.

Kornbluth: Now you're being truthful. Tied his feet, too?

Sarko: Yes.

Kornbluth: You feel better now?

Sarko: Yes.

Kornbluth: But you still haven't told us everything, have you?

Sarko: What do you mean?

Kornbluth: I mean, he needed some help to die, didn't he?

Sarko: I helped him.

Kornbluth: How did you help him?

Sarko: I tied him.

Kornbluth: I know you tied him. Did you hold him?

Sarko: What?

Kornbluth: Did you hold him after he was tied?

Sarko: I just held his body.

Kornbluth: You held it?

Sarko: Yeah. To keep from falling off the bed. He said, "Please hold me so I can do it."

Kornbluth: Did he choke?

Sarko: Yes, sir, he did; he choked.

Sarko is crying openly now, no longer trying to hold back the tears. His body is shaking, as if something deep inside is being forced out. You look at the other jurors. Some are crying, too. Even the judge looks on the verge of tears.

Kornbluth: Go ahead, let it out, Steve, let it out.

Sarko: I didn't do this—I didn't do this for his money, or rings. I swear.

You can't make out all the words through the sobbing.

Kornbluth: Go ahead.

Sarko: He was bucking. I had to put my hands on his back to hold him down.

Kornbluth: You were there the whole time?

Sarko: Yes. Standing beside him.

Kornbluth: You didn't choke him with your hands?

Sarko: No! No! He was doing that himself—

Kornbluth: Never pulled on the sash?

Sarko: Oh, no—

Kornbluth: Just enough weight on his back with your hand?

Sarko: Yeah.

Kornbluth: Until it started to choke him?

Sarko: Yes. Then he kicked one last time. The belt broke—and that—that was it.

Kornbluth: He was gone?

Sarko: Yes.

Sarko leans back, exhausted. The judge hands him a tissue from the bench. There is a long pause. Finally the crying stops.

"We're in recess," the judge says.

You can reach five possible verdicts in this case:

1. guilty of first-degree murder
2. guilty of second-degree murder

3. guilty of voluntary manslaughter

4. guilty of involuntary manslaughter

5. not guilty

WHAT IS YOUR VERDICT?

QUESTIONS FOR YOU TO CONSIDER

As you determine your verdict for this crime, here are some questions about the crime and the trial for you to think about.

1. Do jurors have the right to allow their sympathy or pity for a defendant to influence their verdict?

2. What is the biggest mistake the defendant made as a witness?

3. What well-known tactic of cross-examination did the D.A. use effectively on the defendant?

4. Did the defendant have a motive to murder Melnik?

5. If you were the defense attorney for Stephen Sarko, would you want men or women on your jury, or would it make any difference, assuming all other factors are equal?

6. After leaving the body in the apartment, Sarko did one thing that placed him in a particularly bad light with the jury. What was it?

7. In his cross-examination of Sarko, the prosecutor made a number of statements imploring Sarko to tell the truth. Should defense counsel have objected?

AUTHOR'S ANSWERS TO THE QUESTIONS

1. This is the type of case in which jurors may feel pity or sympathy for the defendant. But jurors must not allow themselves to be influenced by such emotions. Their duty is to determine the facts and to apply the law to those facts. They must not be swayed by mere sentiment, conjecture, sympathy, passion, prejudice, or public opinion. In reality, however, sympathy often does influence verdicts.

2. The defendant's biggest mistake as a witness was to lie to the jury in his direct examination. He lied when he testified on direct examination that he merely tied Melnik's hands behind his back. He thereby lost some of the sympathy jurors may have felt for him. Jurors are instructed that a witness who willfully lies in one material part of his testimony is to be distrusted in others. Not until he broke down under the D.A.'s cross-examination did the truth finally come out.

3. The D.A. used one of the oldest devices in history to persuade Sarko to tell the truth. It can be summed up in several ways: confession is good for the soul, you'll feel better if you tell the truth, the truth will set you free. The confessional of the Catholic Church and the psychiatrist's couch are examples of the same theory. It doesn't often work in the public setting of the courtroom, but it did this time.

4. Did Sarko have a motive to kill? Melnik did not tell Sarko he had AIDS until after they had sex together. It would be reasonable for Sarko to be very upset by this, and thereby have a motive to kill Melnik. Of course, Sarko denied such thoughts.

5. Defense attorneys differ on whether to seek male or female jurors in a trial against a male homosexual, or whether it makes any difference. Most attorneys, however, tend to favor female jurors, because women are considered more tolerant of gay men than are straight men.

6. After leaving the body in the apartment, which was a bad move by itself, Sarko went to the bank and drew out two hundred dollars on Melnik's ATM card. This act greatly damaged his cause with jurors. They saw it as a particularly cynical act of greed, lacking in remorse, and supporting the element of malice.

7. Yes, defense counsel should have objected to the prosecutor's statements imploring Sarko to tell the truth on the grounds that they were not questions at all. Cross-examination should be limited to questions without comments by the examiner. Such statements as "You'll feel better if you open up" and "Why don't you tell us the truth" proved to be effective, but it was improper cross-examination and most judges would have sustained an objection. In this case, the prosecutor got away with it.

THE VERDICT

What was your verdict?

The real-life jury found the defendant guilty of murder in the second degree.

The defense had high hopes for a verdict of voluntary manslaughter, which carries a lesser sentence, but this case was won by the district attorney's effective cross-examination. His unique posture as father/confessor trying to help the defendant gained the trust of the jury. Sarko hurt the defense when he lied under direct examination.

The defendant was sentenced to fifteen years to life in prison.

I Won't Let Rosa Die

ELISE WARNER, GUARDIAN FOR ROSA MOSCINI, V. GUNTHER MARX, MD

Rosa Moscini, 92, is being kept alive by means of a feeding tube. She is practically a vegetable as she lies in a coma in the nursing home, unable to speak or feed herself. Her eyes are open, but there is no sign she recognizes anyone. The doctors cannot say how long she will last—it may be months, even years. Elise Warner, 65, Rosa's daughter and guardian, wants the doctor to remove the tube so her mother can die a peaceful death. Mrs. Warner tells the doctor her mother would never have wanted to live this way. But Rosa's doctor, Dr. Gunther Marx, says his hands are tied. Rosa left no instructions of any kind as to this situation. Dr. Marx says if he removes the tube, Rosa will die, and he is not in the business of helping patients die; his job is to help them live. Hastening Rosa's death would be against his medical and ethical principles. He refuses to remove the tube.

Mrs. Warner sues the doctor for specific performance, which means she wants the court to order Dr. Marx to remove the tube. There is a disturbing angle to Mrs. Warner's request. When Rosa dies, Mrs. Warner will inherit a large sum of money. You must decide whether the feeding tube that is keeping Rosa alive should be removed.

"I wish to introduce the parties to this action," the judge, an attractive woman in her late thirties, says to the jury. "This is the plaintiff, Mrs. Elise Warner."

Mrs. Warner stands, biting her lips. She is a gray-haired woman, and she seems frightened, overwhelmed by the courtroom scene. When Mrs. Warner sits down, her attorney, Josephine Keegan, touches her arm as if to reassure her client.

The defendant, Dr. Gunther Marx, then rises when the judge introduces him. He is balding, with a beard, and looks very uncomfortable. You notice that he avoids looking at Mrs. Warner except for occasional stealthy glances.

"The question the court must decide," the judge says, "is whether a feeding tube that now keeps Rosa Moscini, age 92, alive, should be removed at her daughter's request so that Mrs. Moscini may be allowed to die. The daughter, Elise Warner, is the plaintiff in this action.

"Although such cases are generally tried by the judge alone, the parties have requested a jury to decide certain questions of fact. Your answers will guide the court in making its final decision."

The portly man on the stand is Peter Warner, the plaintiff's first witness. He testifies he is 43 years old and lives with his wife and four children in San Francisco. He is Elise Warner's son.

The plaintiff's attorney, Keegan, conducts the direct examination. "You are the only grandson of Rosa Moscini?"

Warner: Yes.

Keegan: And the only son of Elise Warner, Mrs. Moscini's daughter, the plaintiff in this action?

Warner: That's correct.

Keegan: You saw your grandmother often?

Warner: Oh, yes, ever since I can remember. When I was growing up, I used to spend summers at her house in Santa Monica.

Keegan: You had many talks with her?

Warner: Yes.

Keegan: Based on your knowledge of your grandmother, do you have an opinion as to whether she would want to be kept alive in a coma the way she is now?

Dr. Marx's attorney, Elizabeth Rico, a small, wiry woman, jumps to her feet. "Objection! Calls for speculation."

"Sustained," the judge says. "Counsel, you'll have to lay a better foundation before I will allow the witness to give such an opinion."

Keegan nods respectfully and resumes her questioning.

Keegan: All right, did you have a chance to observe your grandmother's attitude toward life?

Warner: Yes. She was full of life. Spent a lot of time giving herself to others. I can't believe she'd ever want to be lying in bed like a vegetable this way.

Keegan: She ever tell you that?

Warner: No, unfortunately the question never came up. But she was always active, going all the time.

Keegan: Wanted to be involved in everything?

Warner: That's right.

> **Keegan**: I will ask you again. In your opinion, would your grandmother want to be kept alive by a feeding tube in a nursing home?

"Same objection," the defense attorney says. "She never told him whether she would or not, Your Honor. How would he know? It's pure speculation."

"Objection sustained," the judge says.

This time Keegan resists the judge's ruling. "But Your Honor, it's the only way we can show what Mrs. Moscini would want in her condition—through those who knew her, her attitude toward life. She did not sign a living will instructing the family what to do if she lost her faculties; she did not sign a durable power of attorney for health care; she did not sign a directive to doctors; she did not specify what she would want in any other form except by implication in the way she lived. These circumstances go to show what she would want done."

The judge pauses. "All right," she says, "I'll reverse my ruling. The witness may answer."

"I'll try, Your Honor," Peter Warner says. "My grandmother was very strong-willed; she took hold of life, always up early and doing things. If somebody got sick, she was the one who took care of them. If in those days there was such a thing as a living will or whatever the term is, she would have signed it. She would never have wanted to live the way she is now. And that's not an opinion, ma'am, that's a fact."

Elise Warner takes the stand. She is the guardian and conservator for her mother, Rosa Moscini. For many years after her father's death, her mother lived alone with a housekeeper. When her mother reached her late eighties, she began to grow senile and needed more care. She was showing signs of Alzheimer's disease. When Mrs. Warner tried to place her in a nursing home, her mother escaped in a wheelchair and had to be pursued in the street. She was moved into Mrs. Warner's home, but the situation was difficult because Mrs. Warner's husband was ill with cancer. Mother and daughter had minor arguments, nothing serious. They loved each other, and Mrs. Warner wanted only the best for her mother.

Then one day, about a year later during the summer of 2005, Mrs. Moscini choked on some food, causing asphyxiation. The paramedics came to the house and had to resuscitate her. Mrs. Moscini was rushed to the hospital. She suffered severe brain damage, never recovered, never regained consciousness, and has not spoken to anyone since. She is totally unable to care for her bodily needs. She was moved to a nursing home where she is fed with a tube, called a *nasogastric tube,* which enters through her nose, passes through the back of her throat, down her esophagus, and into her stomach. The nurses feed her fluids and nourishment this way, since she is unable to eat or swallow anything on her own.

Mrs. Warner is crying quietly.

Keegan: Did you ask Dr. Marx to remove the tube?

Warner: Yes.

Keegan: What did he say?

Warner: He said she would die.

Keegan: What did you say?

Warner: I said, "For God's sake, that's what she would want. That's what her family wants. For her own good. This is abhorrent to her."

Keegan: His reply?

Warner: He said he could not do that because the nurses would report him.

Keegan: He refused?

Warner: Yes. He said he was terribly sorry, but his hands were tied. He said I would need a court order.

The crying is more obvious now. She asks the judge for a tissue to wipe her eyes. "Please," she says to the jury. "Please, somebody, let my mother die in peace. She'd never want to live like this."

Keegan: When your mother was competent, did she ever express to you her views about being kept alive this way?

Warner: She hated the thought of it.

Keegan: Did she ever say anything specific?

Warner: When she was much younger, in her sixties, I remember she was part of a group of volunteers that would visit the old age home. She'd go to help them, read to them, entertain them on their birthdays. There were people there the same age she was, but she thought they were old. She told me it was terrible to live that way; she said, "I'd rather be dead than live that way."

Keegan: How many times did you hear her say that?

Warner: Several times.

Now Dr. Marx's attorney, Elizabeth Rico, takes the witness on cross-examination. She is less than five feet tall, but her voice booms out in clear, stentorian tones.

Rico: You say you once heard Mrs. Moscini say she'd rather be dead than live in a nursing home?

Warner: Yes.

Rico: How long ago was that?

Warner: Oh, about thirty years ago.

Rico: In her whole lifetime did you ever hear her say anything else along those lines?

Warner: Oh, let's see. I remember once a good friend of hers had a stroke and she said she'd never want to be in that situation.

Rico: How long ago was that?

Warner: About—she was about fifty then.

Rico: About forty years ago?

Warner: Yes.

Rico: And you never had any conversation with her as to how she wished to be cared for if she was in a comatose state?

Warner: She didn't believe she could ever become comatose, so the subject never came up.

Rico: So your answer is no, you never had any such conversation?

Warner: Correct.

Rico looks at Mrs. Warner for several seconds before continuing. "I know this may not seem polite, but I must ask it—it's become relevant."

Warner: Go ahead, you have your job to do.

Rico: Your mother's estate—you would inherit the bulk of that upon her death, isn't that true?

Warner: I don't need that money, I'm very comfortable financially. I'm not interested in her money. You're not suggesting—

Rico: Please, Mrs. Warner, I'm not suggesting anything. I'm just asking a question.

Warner: This is an insult to our family—

Rico: Please just answer the question—would you be the sole inheritor of her estate?

Warner: Yes, but I've discussed that with her. I'll keep that money in trust for Peter's children, my grandchildren.

Rico: But you would get control of it on her death?

Warner: Yes.

Rico: And you could invade the principal of that trust if you wanted to?

Warner: I don't know. I really haven't thought about that.

Rico: How much is it worth?

Warner: Oh, for God's sake. *(She turns to the judge.)* Do I have to answer, Your Honor?

Judge: I am sorry, Mrs. Warner, but you have to answer, yes.

Warner: I'm not sure how much it is.

Rico: Would the amount of $600,000 sound about right?

Warner: I don't know, well, yes. Yes! My God!

Rico: Thank you, that's all.

Mrs. Warner remains on the witness stand, sobbing audibly for several minutes, before she steps down.

The plaintiff rests.

Rico opens the defense case by calling Dr. Marx to the stand. Up to this time, he has been seated beside his lawyer at counsel's table. It is obvious from the expressions on his face so far that this trial has been a very unpleasant experience for him. Dr. Marx testifies he is a licensed physician with a specialty in internal medicine and cardiology. He first began to see Rosa Moscini professionally ten years ago, and has been her primary physician ever since. She was competent when he first saw her for a hypothyroid condition, which still exists. Mrs. Moscini had three children. He noticed her mental status began to change with the death of her only son about seven years ago. Then a daughter, Elise Warner's sister, died, and now Elise is left as the only surviving child. As each child died, Mrs. Moscini's mental condition became worse. She suffered a cardiopulmonary arrest last year from choking on some food at home, and she never recovered.

Rico continues the direct examination of her client. "You understand you are not being sued for money?"

Marx: I understand that.

Rico: You are in court because you are the physician in charge, and Mrs. Warner wants you to remove the tube. You refuse to do that, is that correct?

Marx: That's correct. I cannot do that. I respect Mrs. Warner's wishes. It troubles me to see the anguish she is going through, but I cannot do what she asks.

Rico: Why not?

Marx: If I removed the tube, Mrs. Moscini would die. I didn't become a doctor to put my patients to death. I am not in the business of killing people. I am in the business of helping people live.

Rico: Even if it is the request of her daughter and family?

Marx: I cannot do it.

Rico: Even if Mrs. Warner is acting as her conservator, her guardian?

Marx: I cannot do it! It is against my principles.

Rico: What principles?

Marx: My ethical principles, first of all. She never told me she'd want me to let her die in this situation.

Rico: In all the years—

Marx: In all the years I treated her, she never expressed her views to me if it came to this.

Rico: So you don't know what she'd want you to do.

Marx: I have no idea. I'm not about to guess.

Rico: You've told us about your ethical principles. What about your medical principles?

Marx: Look, the woman has severe damage to the brain. She may never recover. But she is not what you'd call brain-dead. It is still possible she could improve somewhat. When I have been in the room to examine her, her eyes open and sometimes appear to be tracking. When I move from one side to the other, the eyes appear to move. Whether that's reflex or not, I can't be sure. When I put the stethoscope to her chest, there's response; she appears to respond to touch.

Rico: Is she in pain?

Marx: There is no certain medical evidence she is in pain, no.

Rico: Can she talk?

Marx: No.

Rico: Is she comatose?

Marx: Only partly comatose. Not completely.

Rico: Does she understand anything?

Marx: I don't know if she comprehends anything.

Rico: Is it your opinion, Doctor, that it is medically inappropriate to withdraw the feeding tube?

Marx: Yes, it is.

Rico: Assuming you were ordered to remove the tube, would you be personally concerned about repercussions from the State Board of Medical Quality Assurance, or the American Medical Association?

Marx: Yes, I would be.

Rico: Your witness.

Keegan cross-examines the doctor. "Dr. Marx, you have testified that you don't know what Mrs. Moscini's views are—"

Marx: That's correct.

Keegan: —as to having the tube removed.

Marx: Correct.

Keegan: Doctor, suppose Mrs. Moscini signed a sworn statement, while competent, requesting that if the situation came up, she'd want the tube removed and to be allowed to die in peace. Suppose—

Rico: Objection, Your Honor! There is no such statement and counsel knows it! This is pure speculation.

Keegan: Your Honor, this isn't a trick. Yes, I am quite aware no such document exists. But I pose this hypothetical question to enable the court to understand the doctor's state of mind.

Judge: Objection overruled. The doctor may answer.

Marx: If she requested it?

Keegan: Yes.

The doctor pauses, reflects. He shakes his head. "No, I still could not do it. I would not want to be involved."

Keegan: Why?

Marx: Because it's wrong, that's why. It's morally and ethically wrong! It's medically wrong!

Keegan: Doctor, as a licensed physician in this state, are you aware of any regulations that would subject you to disciplinary action for complying with a court order to remove the tube?

Marx: No, I am not.

Keegan: Then why—

Marx: But I remember a few years ago, two doctors in California were charged with murder for withdrawing the artificial feeding mechanism from a patient, resulting in his death.

Keegan: Do you know what happened to that case, Doctor?

Marx: Well, I'm not sure.

Keegan: Isn't it a fact those charges were dismissed?

Marx: That may be. But if I removed the tube, I think my professional standing would suffer.

Keegan: Even if the court ordered it? Even if the family wanted it? Even if—

Marx: I'm sorry. I have to live with myself.

The doctor leans back, exhausted. He looks at the jury. "Don't ask me to do it. I could not do it." He turns to the judge. "May I add something, Your Honor?"

Judge: Go ahead.

Marx: I don't know of any other doctor who would do it, either.

Keegan: Have you asked?

Marx: I have asked. I have talked to my colleagues. I put a notice on the bulletin board. I have not found anyone who would do it.

As the doctor leaves the witness stand, the juror in front of you stands up. "Your Honor," she says, "I have a request. Is it possible for the jury to visit the nursing home to see Mrs. Moscini for ourselves?"

The judge seems taken aback by the request. She summons the attorneys to the side bar for a conference outside of your hearing. Then she announces to the jury that counsel agree the request is reasonable under the circumstances; the jury will be taken by bus to the nursing home tomorrow, provided the medical staff at the nursing home can assure the judge that the visit will present no additional danger to the patient. Court is adjourned.

In the courtroom the next morning, the judge instructs the jurors on their conduct at the nursing home. No testimony will be taken. The visit is to observe Rosa Moscini only. There must be no discussion of her condition among jurors.

When the jury bus pulls up to the nursing home, you are confronted with a strange scene. As you disembark, a group of about twenty-five persons carrying picket signs begins to march in a circle near the entrance. "Don't pay attention," the judge shouts. You try to avert your eyes, but you cannot help seeing a large sign, "Let Rosa Moscini Live," and another, "Thou Shalt Not Kill."

As you enter, the pickets are chanting, "Let Rosa live! Let Rosa live!" The judge and her bailiff hurry all of you inside. As soon as the doors close behind you, the judge gathers the jurors around her in the reception room.

"What you have just seen and heard must be stricken from your minds," she says. "Disregard it. It is not evidence in this case. Treat it as though it never happened."

In the room occupied by Rosa Moscini, you and the other jurors gather around her bed in a semicircle. You see an emaciated woman lying in bed, with a small tube from each nostril attached to a feeding apparatus. Her eyes are open, but you cannot tell if she sees anything. At times her eyes appear to track a moving person. The jurors stand silently. The only sounds are some moans and grunts coming from Rosa Moscini's mouth. Once or twice she belches; she chews. One of the jurors, the woman who requested to visit, goes up to her and calls out her name, but there is no response—just a blank stare. Now you go up to her. You ask the nurse if it is all right to hold Mrs. Moscini's hand, and the nurse nods approval. You take her hand in yours. You squeeze it slightly. No response. You are near tears. The hand is warm, but it drops like a dead thing.

After a while the judge signals it is time to leave. "We'll go out the back way," she says, "to avoid the demonstrators. Court resumes at 1:00 p.m."

When court resumes after lunch, the plaintiff's attorney, Keegan, calls one final witness in rebuttal, Dr. Robert Sugarman. He testifies he is the consulting neurologist in the case.

> **Keegan**: You were contacted by Dr. Marx to examine Rosa Moscini?
>
> **Sugarman**: Yes.

Keegan: Dr. Marx is an expert in cardiology, pertaining to the heart?

Sugarman: That's right.

Keegan: So he contacted you because you are an expert in neurology, pertaining to the brain?

Sugarman: Exactly.

Dr. Sugarman testifies he has examined Mrs. Moscini on several occasions, the last time being this morning before the jury arrived at the nursing home. He says there has been no significant change in her condition over the past year.

Keegan: Is she still in a coma?

Sugarman: Some people call it a coma. I call it a vegetative state.

Keegan: Which means?

Sugarman: It means her bodily functions are all going on. The heart is going. The blood is pumping. But mentally she is not functioning.

Keegan: Can you explain, Doctor?

Sugarman: The brain is divided into two basic parts, the brain stem and the cerebral cortex. The brain stem is the core of the brain; it connects the brain to the spinal cord and to the rest of the nervous system.

Keegan: Is it functioning in Rosa Moscini, Doctor?

Sugarman: At the most primitive level, yes.

Keegan: What about the cerebral cortex?

Sugarman: The cerebral cortex is not functioning. This is the so-called gray matter, the lumpy-looking stuff everybody thinks of as the brain. The jury may have seen Mrs. Moscini react in some way, but if she did it was as reflex, not voluntary. All voluntary movement originates in the cortex. Thinking, understanding language—they are functions of the cortex.

Keegan: Did you see any signs of cortical functions?

Sugarman: No, she's lost those functions.

Keegan: Permanently?

"Yes." The doctor pauses. He looks at the jury. "Yes. Permanently."

After closing arguments, the judge hands the jury a verdict form that reads as follows:

"Should the feeding tube that is keeping Mrs. Moscini alive be removed? Answer yes or no."

WHAT IS YOUR VERDICT?

QUESTIONS FOR YOU TO CONSIDER

As you determine your verdict for this crime, here are some questions about the crime and the trial for you to think about.

1. In this tour of duty as a juror, this was your first civil case. What is the difference in the burden of proof required in a civil case compared to a criminal case?

2. In a right-to-die case such as the one you just heard, where the final decision means life or death, should the plaintiff's burden of proving that the patient should be allowed to die be greater than in the usual civil case?

3. During the trial, a juror stood up and asked for more evidence—specifically, to visit and observe the patient, Rosa Moscini. Should such requests be allowed by the court?

4. In the Moscini trial, both attorneys as well as the judge were women. Do you find that scenario unusual?

5. The doctor testified that removing the tube and allowing Mrs. Moscini to die would be medically and ethically wrong. Should this opinion of the doctor's be a determining factor in the final decision?

AUTHOR'S ANSWERS TO THE QUESTIONS

1. In the normal civil trial, the plaintiff has the burden of proving his or her case by a *preponderance of the evidence*. This means the evidence in favor of the plaintiff must have more convincing force, however slight, than the evidence opposed to it. The civil plaintiff has no burden of proof beyond a reasonable doubt. This burden is much lighter than the burden required in a criminal case, in which the State must prove its case beyond any reasonable doubt.

2. There is a strong current of opinion that because of the consequences involved, the burden of proof in right-to-die cases should be greater than in the usual civil trial. In 1990, the United States Supreme Court approved a burden of proof heavier than the usual preponderance of the evidence. In the case of *Cruzan v. Missouri Department of Health*, the Supreme Court held that a state could require plaintiffs to prove a comatose patient's wish to die by *clear and convincing* evidence. In the context of our case, clear and convincing means the plaintiff must persuade the trier of fact that the patient held a firm and settled commitment to withdrawing the feeding tube.

3. Judges differ on whether to allow jurors to ask questions or request more evidence. The practice is disfavored due to the danger of opening the door to a barrage of questions by jurors, thereby removing control of the case from the attorneys. Some judges, without encouraging it, will allow jurors to submit written questions, which the judge will consider in conference with counsel. After all, the goal of the court is a fair trial, and if the juror's question or request helps further that goal, it should at least be considered.

4. The scenario in which both attorneys and the judge are women is no longer unusual. One of the most remarkable changes in jury trials—in fact in the entire legal system—over the past century has been the inclusion of women as attorneys and judges. In fact, there was

a time when women were not even allowed to serve on the jury. In California, for example, prior to 1917, a jury was defined as "a body of men," and women were not qualified for jury service. A state law was passed in 1917 that expressly extended this right to women. The federal courts, however, did not allow female jurors until 1919.

5. Under existing law, the doctor's medical and ethical opinion should not be a determining factor in the court's final life-or-death decision. What is involved here is the constitutional *right of privacy*: the right of the individual to refuse medical treatment. This right takes precedence over the doctor's medical and ethical beliefs, and must not be abridged. The individual's wish is the determining factor. In this case, of course, the court was faced with the factual question of what the patient's wish was, since she was in a comatose state and could not express it to the court.

THE VERDICT

What was your verdict?

The real-life judge in this case returned a verdict to remove the patient's feeding tube.

The judge found in the plaintiff's favor that there was sufficient evidence Mrs. Moscini would have wanted the tube removed, that it was in her best interest to do so, and that Mrs. Warner was motivated by the best interests of her mother rather than financial gain. The judge ordered the doctor to grant Mrs. Warner's request, but the doctor still refused on the grounds it was against his personal ethics. The judge tried to find another doctor in the county who would remove the tube, but was told all took the same position. Mrs. Moscini was moved to another county, where she died before the tube was ever removed.

Does He Need Marijuana to Stay Alive?

STATE V. SAM KEPNER

The year is 1991, long before doctors were allowed to prescribe marijuana for medical purposes in any state.

The judge is a smart-looking African American woman with her hair pulled back into a bun. She is young, but she knows her job.

The deputy district attorney, Jean Stanley, rises to make her opening statement. She is an attractive woman in her forties with short blonde hair, and she wears a dark pantsuit. She does something that seems a bit startling. Instead of facing the jury, she turns her back on you, walks over to the defendant's table, and points down at him. Her pointed finger is only a few inches from the defendant's face. Now she looks at the jury. "Ladies and gentlemen, this man is guilty." She pauses for effect. "He is guilty beyond any reasonable doubt and we will prove it. He is guilty of cultivating and possessing illegal marijuana in his home, and when you have heard all the evidence, I know you will do your duty and tell him so. And you know what? He won't even deny it. He'll admit the charges right here in open court. That's right. He will admit he broke the law. Oh, yes, he'll give you some lame excuse about needing the stuff, the contraband, for his health. But don't you believe it. You will see how weak that story is. The second count charges possessing marijuana for sale. He is guilty of that charge also. Just use your common sense. That's all I ask. Don't leave your common sense out in the hallway. Thank you, and I am confident that as good Americans, you will do the right thing."

Slowly, the judge turns to the defense attorney. "Do you wish to make your opening statement now, Ms. Vornanen, or do you wish to reserve?"

The defense attorney stands. Maida Vornanen is a tall, determined-looking young woman in a long skirt. "I certainly want to do it now, Your Honor," she says. "Right now."

"Sounds so simple, doesn't it?" Vornanen says. "The district attorney has it all wrapped up in a pretty little box. All you have to do is go out and find him guilty. Lock the door and throw away the key. Nothing to it. Only she forgot one thing. She forgot to tell you about the defense. 'A lame excuse,' she calls it. Well, we'll see about that. She forgot to tell you that Sam Kepner had to have that marijuana to save his life. Without it, he would die of AIDS. The judge will tell you that under the law of necessity, that means he is not guilty—"

"Objection!" shouts the prosecutor, jumping up. "She's instructing the jury on the law. That's Your Honor's job."

"Sustained." The judge turns to face the jury. "Ladies and gentlemen of the jury. I wish to instruct you that what counsel says in their opening statements is not evidence, and not to be considered as evidence. And I will instruct you on the law. No one else will do that. Proceed, Counsel."

"Thank you, Your Honor," Vornanen says, even though the judge has just ruled against her. "I only wish to remind the jury that there is another side to this story, and I ask you to please, please keep an open mind until all the evidence is in. Thank you."

The D.A. calls her first witness. "Call Sergeant Martin to the stand." A husky man in uniform enters, is sworn, and takes the witness box.

Stanley: Your name?

Martin: Mathew Martin.

Stanley: Rank?

Martin: Sergeant, city police department.

Stanley: Your assignment?

Martin: Narcotics.

Stanley: Now, Sergeant, on the morning of August 14, 1991, what were you doing?

Martin: I was driving through the residential section of east San Diego.

Stanley: Did you observe anything unusual?

Martin: Yes. As I was passing this residence on Karfer Street, I noticed a solid wooden fence along the front of the house.

Stanley: Was that unusual?

Martin: Well, it was the height of this fence, about seven feet high. I thought that was unusual.

Stanley: Notice anything else? I mean, of an unusual nature?

Martin: Yes, ma'am, I did. I noticed some green leaves just over the top of the fence—on the inside of the fence.

Stanley: What was unusual about that?

Martin: They looked like marijuana leaves.

Vornanen: Objection! That's a conclusion.

Judge: Sustained. You may rephrase your question.

Stanley: You've been a police officer how long?

Martin: Twenty-three years.

Stanley: Seen a lot of marijuana leaves?

Martin: Hundreds of times.

Stanley: Testified as to the identity of marijuana?

Martin: Many times, yes.

Stanley: So, when you saw what you believed to be marijuana leaves, what action did you take?

Martin: I parked the car and walked over to the fence for a closer look.

Stanley: Was your first impression confirmed?

Vornanen: Objection! Leading.

Judge: Sustained.

Stanley: What did you think when you got closer?

Martin: My impression was confirmed.

Stanley: What did you do next?

The sergeant testifies that he went back to the station, obtained the papers necessary for a search warrant, found a judge at the courthouse who signed the warrant, and returned to the residence.

Stanley: Alone?

Martin: No, ma'am, I had a squad with me this time. We didn't know if we would run into trouble.

Stanley: Did you run into any trouble?

Martin: No, ma'am. We rang the doorbell. Mr. Kepner, the gentleman sitting right there (*he points*) let us in.

Stanley: Your Honor, may the record show the witness has identified the defendant?

Judge: It may. Proceed.

Stanley: What happened next?

Martin: I showed Mr. Kepner the warrant and asked if we could search the house. He was very cooperative and we proceeded to search.

Stanley: Find anything of interest?

Martin: Yes, ma'am. We found lots of marijuana plants, some small, some big. They were growing on the patio in back and on the one in front. A few inside, too.

Stanley: How many marijuana plants?

Martin: May I review my notes?

Vornanen: No objection.

The sergeant studies his notes. "We found seventeen plants."

Stanley: Are you sure they were all marijuana?

Martin: Well—

Vornanen is on her feet. "Your Honor, I think we can cut this short if I can just have a moment with my client."

Judge: Go right ahead.

You watch Vornanen as she whispers to the defendant. He is nodding. She writes something on a paper and pushes the paper over to him. He picks up a pen and writes on the same paper, quickly, as if signing it. She pats him on the back and stands again.

"Your Honor, the defendant will stipulate that all the plants were marijuana, that they all belonged to him and his partner, and that he knew they were marijuana."

There is a gasp from the audience.

The judge looks at the defendant.

Judge: Mr. Kepner. You heard the stipulation?

Kepner: Yes, Your Honor.

Judge: You realize it is an admission as to certain elements of the crimes charged?

Kepner: I do, Your Honor.

This is the first time you hear Sam Kepner speak. His voice is strong.

Kepner: I do, Your Honor, but I am still not guilty.

Judge: Thank you. The jury will decide that.

Now the judge turns to the jury. "Ladies and gentlemen, you have heard the stipulation. You may accept the facts stated in the stipulation as having been proved. They are no longer in contention. Proceed, Counsel."

There is whispering in the audience, but it stops when the judge clears her throat and looks sternly across the room.

Stanley: What else did you find?

Martin: We found equipment for growing such plants in the growing room. In the kitchen we found powdered dried marijuana in plastic containers; also cooking pans and utensils that looked like they had marijuana residue on them.

Stanley: Anything else?

Martin: Oh yes, I almost forgot, we found books on how to grow marijuana; also a cookbook on how to use it in cooking.

Stanley: You mentioned a "growing room." What was that?

Martin: Well, there was one room that seemed like it was set aside just for growing plants. It had special lights and fans and a watering apparatus. Stuff like that. Several small plants just getting started.

Stanley: Lights? What are they for?

Martin: They help the plants grow faster.

Stanley: Now, Sergeant, I want to ask you about another area. You have been working in narcotics for how many years?

Martin: Nineteen years.

Stanley: And have you testified as an expert as to whether marijuana was possessed for sale? That is, for the purpose of selling it?

Martin: Oh, yes. About seventy-five times.

Stanley: And do you have an opinion as to whether the marijuana you found in this case was being cultivated for sale?

Martin: I do.

Stanley: What is that opinion?

Martin: In my opinion, it was possessed for sale, yes.

Stanley: On what do you base your opinion?

Martin: On the amount. So many plants. I doubt anyone would have so much marijuana just for his own use.

Stanley: Thank you, Sergeant. Now can you tell this jury how much this marijuana sells for on the open market?

Vornanen: Objection!

Judge: Overruled. He may answer.

Martin: Well, I can tell you this. I've bought and sold marijuana as an undercover officer for many years. I believe I know the prices. The marijuana in this case is particularly strong because it was grown under controlled conditions. Highly controlled, I might add. Therefore it sells for a lot more than the stuff smuggled in from Mexico.

Stanley: How much more?

Martin: This stuff sells for about four to five thousand dollars a pound. That's ten times as much as what we see from Mexico.

Stanley says, "Your witness," and takes her seat.

Vornanen looks like a tiger that can't wait to pounce. "You say he had this marijuana for the purpose of selling it?"

Martin: Yes.

Vornanen: For four to five grand a pound?

Martin: That's what I said.

Vornanen: Sounds like big business, doesn't it?

Martin: Could be.

Vornanen: Big business means files and records and lists of customers, doesn't it, Sergeant?

Martin: I don't know what you're driving at.

Vornanen: Sergeant, you've made hundreds of arrests over the years for possession of marijuana for sale, haven't you?

Martin: Yes.

Vornanen: And you've searched those people's homes and apartments whenever you do, right?

Martin: Yes. That's standard.

Vornanen: Sergeant, you know what a Pay and O sheet is, don't you?

Martin: Yes.

Vornanen: Just tell the jury what a Pay and O sheet is, please.

Martin: Well, it's a record of sales, what customer bought what, with dates and so forth, and phone numbers.

Vornanen: It's a business record, right? A ledger?

Martin: You might call it that. It's not that formal.

Vornanen: And every time you arrest a drug peddler in his home, you find such a record, right?

Martin: Not every time.

Vornanen: Most of the time?

Martin: Well—

The sergeant pauses. He knows where the defense attorney is going.

Vornanen: Most of the time, Sergeant?

Martin: Well, yes, you could say that.

Vornanen: Tell this jury, Sergeant: did you search for such a record in this case?

Martin: Well, yes, yes we did.

Vornanen: A thorough search?

Martin: Yes.

Vornanen: And that's because if Sam Kepner was selling his marijuana at anywhere near four to five thousand a pound, you would expect to find such a record, right?

Martin: Well—

Vornanen: Isn't that right, Sergeant?

The sergeant looks at the D.A. briefly.

Vornanen: Isn't that right, Sergeant?

Martin: Well, yes. I guess I did.

Vornanen: Thank you. Now, Sergeant, would you please tell this jury: did you or didn't you find such a record, any Pay and O sheet, or anything else showing any kind of business transactions?

Martin: Well. No, I did not.

Vornanen: Did anyone else?

Martin: No. No one did.

Vornanen: No lists of customers?

Martin: No.

Vornanen: No lists of phone numbers?

Martin: No.

Vornanen: Thank you, Sergeant. Now let's move on.

You think to yourself, "This lady knows her job."

Vornanen: There are a few other things you usually find when you are searching the rooms of marijuana dealers, aren't there, Sergeant?

Martin: What do you mean?

Vornanen: Marijuana sellers deal in cash, don't they?

Martin: That's true.

Vornanen: And so you usually find large amounts of cash either on the person or somewhere in his residence, right?

Martin: Sometimes.

Vornanen: Come on, Sergeant, isn't it true that you usually find cold cash in pretty substantial amounts?

Martin: Well, I—

Vornanen: Most of the time?

Martin: All right.

Vornanen: Did you search Sam Kepner?

Martin: Yes.

Vornanen: Find any cash?

Martin: Actually, I found a five-dollar bill and three singles.

Vornanen: A grand total of eight bucks. You hoped to find more, didn't you?

Martin: Well, I don't know what I—

Vornanen: You searched the entire place?

Martin: I already answered that.

Vornanen: You hoped to find a bundle of cash, didn't you?

Martin: I don't know what I hoped for.

Vornanen: Did you find any other cash?

Martin: A few bills.

Vornanen: Nothing substantial?

Martin: No.

Vornanen: Oh, by the way, Sergeant, Sam Kepner wasn't alone in his house, was he?

Martin: No. His partner, Clyde Lambron, was there also.

Vornanen: Really? You didn't tell us about that on your direct examination, did you?

Martin: I wasn't asked.

Vornanen: Did you arrest both men?

Martin: Yes.

Vornanen: Who was Clyde Lambron?

Martin: He lived there, too.

Vornanen: They were partners. They were homosexual partners, right?

Stanley: Objection!

Judge: Sustained.

Vornanen: Did you find any cash on Lambron?

Martin: Some change. That's all.

Vornanen: What happened to him? Isn't he being prosecuted?

Martin: Clyde Lambron is dead. He died a few weeks ago.

Vornanen: What did he die of?

Stanley: Objection! Irrelevant!

Vornanen: Your Honor, I will prove the relevance in due time.

Judge: Very well. I will allow the question. Subject to a motion to strike.

Vornanen: I will ask you again, Sergeant Martin: what was the cause of death?

Martin: I understand Clyde Lambron died of AIDS.

Vornanen: Thank you. By the way, did you question Sam Kepner after the arrest?

Martin: Yes.

Vornanen: What did he say?

Stanley: Objection! Calls for exculpatory evidence.

Vornanen: I just want to know what he said.

Judge: Don't argue, Counsel! Will you both please approach the bench.

The lawyers walk up to the bench and speak to the judge at the side. You watch them but you cannot hear what they are saying because they are whispering. The court reporter is there, too, taking down every word. Judging by Vornanen's facial expressions, she seems to be losing the argument. Finally the attorneys return to their tables.

Judge: The objection is sustained. Proceed, Counsel.

Vornanen: Just a few more questions, Sergeant. Aren't commercial scales also usually found in a search of a marijuana seller's home?

Martin: Sometimes.

Vornanen: Find any?

Martin: No.

Vornanen: And baggies? Plastic baggies used for packaging? Aren't they commonly found also?

Martin: That's true, yes.

Vornanen: Find any marijuana in little packages ready for sale?

Martin: No.

Vornanen: I ask you this, Sergeant. Please answer yes or no. Did you find anything—I repeat, anything—to indicate sales of marijuana? Files? Records? Cash? Scales? Baggies? Anything like that?

Martin: No, but that doesn't mean—

Vornanen: Thank you, Sergeant. You've answered the question. That's all I have, Your Honor.

Judge: Thank you, Counsel. Then we'll take our recess for the day. Ladies and gentlemen of the jury, I remind you that you are not to speak to anyone about the case—not husband, wife, no one. And don't let yourself form or express any opinion about the case. And don't let anyone talk to you about it. Keep your mind open. See you in the morning at 9:00 a.m. Court is adjourned.

The next morning, the D.A. quickly winds up her case. Another officer testifies he took photographs of the scene and identifies them on the stand. The photographs are passed among the jury and they corroborate Sergeant Martin's testimony. The D.A. stands before the judge and announces, "Your Honor, because of the stipulation, the State has no need for further witnesses and the State rests."

The judge says to Vornanen, the defense attorney, "You may present your case."

Vornanen: We call Doctor Bergstrom.

A small, wiry man in a light-colored suit takes the stand.

Vornanen: State your full name, please.

Bergstrom: Gary Edson Bergstrom.

Vornanen: Your profession?

Bergstrom: I'm a physician.

Vornanen: What type of physician?

Bergstrom: Internal medicine.

Dr. Bergstrom then outlines his background and experience as a doctor. He has been practicing medicine for fifteen years with an office in the Mission Hills section of San Diego. He testifies that although he is not a specialist in treating AIDS, he has many HIV-positive patients who come to him. With such patients, he often works with a specialist. Those patients often develop AIDS.

Vornanen: What does "HIV positive" mean?

Bergstrom: It means you're infected with the HIV virus. The blood test tells us that.

Vornanen: And this virus that often turns into AIDS, does it have any cure?

Bergstrom: No, I'm afraid not.

Vornanen: Would it be fair to say that treatment for the HIV condition is still in the experimental stage?

Bergstrom: Yes. That would be a fair statement.

Vornanen: What does the virus affect in the body?

Bergstrom: The immune system.

Vornanen: Can you tell us, Doctor, how the HIV virus develops into AIDS?

Bergstrom: When a person has HIV, it means the immune system is very weak, very vulnerable. The person is extremely susceptible to a whole range of illnesses, any of which, even a common cold or the flu, could develop into AIDS. That's the great danger of an HIV-positive status.

Vornanen: What is the life expectancy of someone who is HIV positive?

Bergstrom: I'd say it's about a year and a half. Three years at the most.

Vornanen: Did you tell Sam Kepner that?

Bergstrom: He asked me and I told him.

Vornanen: So how do you determine if a person has advanced from HIV to AIDS?

Bergstrom: Mostly it's the blood count—the CO4 count, we call it—it's way down and then the person gets sick. A person with HIV can look healthy, not sick. Like Mr. Kepner there. He looks perfectly healthy. But he's HIV positive and could get AIDS any time. A person with AIDS is definitely sick. He looks sick. He has symptoms. The immune system is too weak to fight back.

Vornanen: You treated Mr. Kepner?

Bergstrom: Yes, and also his partner, Mr. Lambron.

Vornanen: Did Mr. Lambron develop AIDS?

Bergstrom: Yes. We tried to help him but to no avail. We treated him with AZT—that's one of the medications—but he only got worse.

Vornanen: Did Mr. Kepner show any signs of AIDS when he came to your office?

Bergstrom: I thought so. I have my notes here.

The doctor reviews his notes.

Bergstrom: First of all, he told me he was HIV positive. He complained of mucus in his throat, a bad cough, herpes on his mouth, and he was unable to sleep or eat.

Vornanen: What did you write?

Bergstrom: I wrote "probable AIDS."

The doctor goes on to tell how he tested Kepner for the blood count and then concluded that Kepner was HIV positive. He tried to treat Kepner with AZT and other medications but the defendant refused to take them. "Mr. Kepner said they were worthless. He saw how they killed his friend, Clyde, and he didn't want that to happen to him."

Vornanen: Did you ever prescribe marijuana?

Bergstrom: No. I can't do that even if I wanted to. It's against the law.

Vornanen: Thank you, Doctor. Your witness, Counsel.

Cross-examination begins.

Stanley: Does the defendant have AIDS now?

Bergstrom: No.

Stanley: Other than having HIV, is there anything wrong with him?

Bergstrom: No.

Stanley: All those things he complained of, a cough and so on, they can be treated, can't they?

Bergstrom: Yes.

Stanley: And when you wrote "probable AIDS"—that was based on what he told you?

Bergstrom: Yes.

Stanley: You don't think he has AIDS now?

Vornanen: Objection! Asked and answered.

Judge: Sustained.

Stanley: No further questions.

Then Vornanen calls the defendant as a witness. He identifies himself as Samuel Carl Kepner. He identifies photographs of his home where he has lived for eight years. He describes how he built high walls around the house to provide privacy for himself and Clyde Lambron.

Vornanen: Who is Clyde Lambron? What was your relationship with him?

Kepner: Clyde was my companion for life—till death do us part.

Tears come to Mr. Kepner's eyes. The bailiff hands him a tissue and he wipes his eyes.

Vornanen: Can we continue? Are you all right?

Kepner: Yes. I'm sorry.

Vornanen: Why did you move to this property?

Kepner: We both knew we were dying. We wanted to create a sanctuary, a safe and secure oasis where we could live—until—where we could be together until—the end.

Vornanen: Before you went to see Dr. Bergstrom, did you go to a public health clinic?

Kepner: Yes.

Vornanen: Why?

Kepner: Because I thought I had AIDS.

Vornanen: What made you think that?

Kepner: Well, I knew I had all the criteria for the high-risk group. I was a homosexual. I hung around a lot of people. Was involved with a number of people. Y'know, free love. At some point I began feeling sick. And one day I was watching television and there was a documentary about HIV and AIDS. And I thought—oh, oh, I've got that.

Vornanen: What happened at the clinic?

Kepner: I was tested and the nurse said, "You are HIV positive and likely to get AIDS very soon, so get your affairs in order and take care of your friend."

Vornanen: Was your friend Clyde Lambron?

Kepner: Oh no, that was before Clyde. My friend then was Peter. He had AIDS and he died, too.

Vornanen: Was he taking AZT?

Kepner: Yes, and it never helped him. The medications never helped him and they never helped Clyde. They both died in my arms.

Vornanen: So that's why you refused to take the medications?

Kepner: Yes, ma'am. I saw they were worthless.

Vornanen: You took care of Peter and Clyde?

Kepner: Yes. Totally. Fed them, dressed them. First Peter. I watched him die. Then Clyde. Same thing. It was terrible.

Vornanen: When you finally went to Dr. Bergstrom, what did he tell you?

Kepner: He said the most important thing was to stay healthy, to eat well, sleep well, keep my weight up. He said I had to do that to keep from getting AIDS.

Vornanen: So what did you do?

Kepner: I didn't want to go the way of Peter and Clyde. So I did the only thing that helped me.

Vornanen: And that was?

Kepner: Cannabis.

Vornanen: By cannabis you mean marijuana?

Kepner: Yes.

Vornanen: Was marijuana a cure?

Kepner: No, it's not a cure. But it treats the symptoms.

Vornanen: How do you use it?

Kepner: I eat it. It's like eating anything else. Like a fruit. I cook it, put it in soups and stews, make brownies with it. I eat it fresh, too. It keeps my weight up, gives me an appetite. Also helps prevent nausea.

Vornanen: Are you able to work?

Kepner: Yes. I'm a gardener.

Vornanen: Was there a difference between when you had cannabis available and when you didn't have it?

Kepner: Oh, God, yes. A tremendous difference. Three years ago the police took my cannabis away. I began to lose weight, got a sore throat. Became really sick. When I got a new supply I began to recover.

Vornanen: Any other differences?

Kepner: Yes. I don't think about death every three seconds.

Vornanen: So when you don't have cannabis, you find yourself obsessing about death?

Kepner: Constantly. Because, I mean, after all, I really am dying.

Vornanen: At one time years ago I believe you had a stomach ulcer. Tell us about that.

Kepner: Yes. It bled profusely. I lost a lot of blood and had to have a transfusion.

Vornanen: Did you get relief from the bleeding ulcer?

Kepner: Absolutely. With the cannabis.

Vornanen: And how did you get into growing marijuana?

Kepner: I didn't want to go out and find a criminal to get my supply. So I studied up on how to grow it.

Vornanen: And when you found out you were HIV positive, how did you use it?

Kepner: I didn't smoke it. I began to eat it. I have some every day. Breakfast, lunch, dinner.

The witness describes how he grows the marijuana plants, how he waters them, how he gives them light so they can grow faster, how he dries the seeds, how he designed the strain of marijuana he was cultivating, how he eats the top bud of the plant.

Vornanen: Do you eat the bud just plain?

Kepner: I pick it off the plant just like you'd reach up and grab an apple and chew it like tobacco. It's an amazing taste. It's great.

Vornanen: Do you believe that this cannabis—this marijuana—is keeping you alive and well?

Kepner: Oh, I know it is.

Vornanen: What other ways do you consume it?

Kepner: Well, as I mentioned, I add it to soups and stews and brownies. I also make peanut butter balls. I grind it up in the food processor and it turns out like a dough. And I sprinkle two tablespoons of ground cannabis on my dry cereal every morning.

Judge: Mr. Kepner, I notice sometimes you use the word cannabis and sometimes marijuana. Are they synonymous?

Kepner: Yes, Your Honor. Marijuana is a slang term. Cannabis is the formal word.

Vornanen: You mentioned several effects from using marijuana. Any others?

Kepner: Yes, it makes you hungry. Increases your appetite.

Vornanen: Are you a smoker?

Kepner: No. I do not smoke cigarettes or joints.

Vornanen: Are you afraid to be without marijuana?

Kepner: I would die without it.

Vornanen: Nothing further. You may cross-examine.

Stanley: You went to the doctor because you thought you were in a high-risk group?

Kepner: Yes. Because the nurse told me I had HIV and would probably die in a year or two. And what I saw on TV. And also because of seeing my friends die of AIDS.

Stanley: Why did you move to this house where you grew the marijuana?

Kepner: Because it was a private place where my lover and I could build our sanctuary and grow the food we needed to exist.

Stanley: You don't have AIDS now?

Kepner: I hope not.

Stanley: You're not dying now.

Kepner: Ma'am, call it what you want. I am HIV positive. I have been told I only have two years to live. I could get AIDS any moment and die. I know the marijuana is keeping me alive. That is why I don't have AIDS. I don't sell it. I need it for myself to stay alive so I don't die like Clyde and Peter.

Stanley: But you feel healthy now?

Kepner: Yes, thank God.

Stanley: No further questions.

After a recess, Vornanen calls Dr. Lowell Malone.

Dr. Malone, a tall, distinguished looking man with a gray moustache, testifies he is a psychiatrist and professor of psychiatry at a prestigious southern university. He was formerly assistant chief of psychiatry at the Veterans Administration Hospital in Washington, D.C. He impresses you with his background and demeanor on the stand. Dr. Malone is also certified by the American Society of Addiction Medicine and is recognized as an expert in pharmacology, which, as he explains, is the use of medications to take care of various illnesses. Dr. Malone testifies he has treated cancer patients with marijuana and has designed a study involving marijuana for about two hundred cancer patients. He found that marijuana, both in the smoked and pill form, was effective for some patients in controlling nausea and vomiting caused by anticancer chemotherapy.

Vornanen: Had these patients been treated with conventional medications?

Malone: Yes. All the patients in our study were treatment failures on conventional drugs.

Vornanen: After completing your work with cancer patients, did you then begin working with persons who had the HIV virus or AIDS?

Malone: Yes.

Vornanen: Are there any cures for HIV or AIDS?

Malone: No there are not. Nothing.

Dr. Malone describes in detail how weight loss in people with HIV or AIDS causes the weakening of the immune system and leads to profound weakness. He calls this the *wasting syndrome*.

Vornanen: Does marijuana help stop the wasting syndrome?

Malone: It can, yes. In some patients. Our studies show marijuana stimulates the appetite and allows people to eat more and thereby offsets the weight loss.

Vornanen: Is this an ongoing study?

Malone: Yes. I haven't yet analyzed all the data statistically.

Vornanen: From what you know so far, what is the best way to stave off AIDS and eventual death from AIDS?

Malone: The best way is to maintain a good weight, appetite, and quality of life.

Vornanen: Do you know why marijuana works to do this?

Malone: No, but I still feel it works for some. Different drugs may or may not work for different human beings.

Vornanen: One more question, Doctor. If a patient with HIV came to you and told you he was taking marijuana and that it was keeping him from contracting AIDS, would you advise him to stop?

Malone: No. I wouldn't. I know from my studies and the scientific literature that what he says is true.

Vornanen: Even though you both knew it was illegal, you wouldn't advise him to stop?

Malone: No. I'm an adviser about his medical care, not his legal problems.

Vornanen: No further questions.

Stanley cross-examines Dr. Malone.

Stanley: Doctor, is a person who is HIV positive, without any other disease or ailment—is he in a life-threatening situation?

Malone: Yes. They have a viral infection that overwhelmingly kills people eventually. Because there's no cure for HIV.

Stanley: Let's talk about weight loss, Doctor. Isn't it true that weight loss can be a symptom of many other problems, other than HIV?

Malone: Yes. Many.

Stanley: Including depression?

Malone: Yes.

Stanley: Including anxiety?

Malone: Yes.

Stanley: Stress?

Malone: Yes.

Stanley: What are some others?

Malone: Cancers can produce weight loss. And, of course, weight-reduction regimens can produce it, too. There are probably many others.

Stanley: And in fact aren't there a number of conventional methods for treating people with HIV who are losing weight?

Malone: There are a few. But they don't work for everyone. Marinol is a medicine approved for appetite stimulation in AIDS patients. It is helpful to some patients, but for others it is no help at all.

Stanley: Have you done any research involving the eating of marijuana?

Malone: I have not. But some HIV and AIDS patients would eat brownies that contained marijuana and claimed this was helpful.

Stanley: Thank you. I have no further questions.

Two neighbors of the defendant then testify for the defense. Both say Kepner was a good neighbor, they never noticed any problems, and they knew he and his partner were homosexuals. They never noticed any unusual pedestrian traffic going in or out of the house.

Both sides rest. The judge says she wishes to instruct the jury on the law before counsel make their closing arguments.

> Ladies and gentlemen of the jury, as to the first charge there is no dispute that the defendant cultivated and possessed marijuana in his home, and that he knew what it was and knew it was illegal. So don't waste your time on that question.
>
> The case for the defendant rests on the proposition that it was necessary for him to cultivate and possess the marijuana in order to keep from contracting AIDS and dying from AIDS. This is called the defense of medical necessity. In this regard, the law is as follows—a person is not guilty of a crime when he commits an act, otherwise criminal, through necessity. The defense must prove by a preponderance of the evidence each of the following five elements:
>
> 1. the act charged as a crime was done to prevent a significant and imminent evil, namely the threat of bodily harm to oneself;
> 2. there was no reasonable alternative;
> 3. the harm caused by the act was less than the harm that was avoided;
> 4. the defendant had a good-faith belief that his act was necessary to prevent the greater harm; and,
> 5. the defendant did not substantially contribute to the creation of the emergency.

As to the second count, which charges possession of marijuana for the purpose of selling it, in order to find the defendant guilty, you must find beyond a reasonable doubt that he had the specific intent to sell his marijuana.

The closing arguments begin. Stanley waives her right to make the first argument. "I will reserve my remarks," she says, "until I have heard from the defense."

Vornanen's arguments are quite lengthy.

> Ladies and gentlemen, Sam Kepner is an accused citizen with a death sentence already hanging over his head. He knows he is HIV positive, he knows there's no cure for it, he knows he is likely to contract AIDS and die, and he knows it could happen any moment if he fails to maintain his health. He also knows that marijuana is the best way for him to stay alive and so he takes it, eats it, every morning, noon, and night. The question for you to ask is: was his action reasonable under all the circumstances known to him? If so, you must find him not guilty.
>
> You don't have to rely solely on his testimony. Fortunately we have been able to summon good doctors, experts in their field, who corroborate Sam's testimony and agree that what he did was reasonable under the circumstances. The district attorney will argue that he refused to try all the alternatives such as AZT and therefore he has failed to fulfill the necessary elements required to prove his case. But what would you do? He saw how those alternative medicines failed to help his closest friends. The other medicines might be helpful to some people, but they didn't help Peter and Clyde. They died in his arms. He didn't want to go the way they did. Wasn't that reasonable? Are you going to say he should have waited until he was about to die before he used marijuana?
>
> And whom did he harm? Did he steal from anyone? Rob anyone? Threaten anyone? You heard from his neighbors. Did he bother

> anyone? Sam Kepner didn't hurt anybody. He just helped himself. He just did what he had to do to keep from dying.
>
> As to the second count of possessing marijuana for sale, there's not a single shred of evidence he intended to sell it. Just give Sam Kepner what he deserves— justice.

The district attorney goes to the podium for her closing argument.

> Ladies and gentlemen of the jury, when you were selected for this jury, I asked all of you one question. That question was: do you promise to follow the law? And you each answered that you would. All I ask you to do now is keep that promise.
>
> The judge has just told you what the law is in a case like this where the defendant's only defense is that his act of cultivating and possessing marijuana was necessary. The judge listed five elements, each of which the defendant must prove in order to make his case. I contend that he has failed in at least two of those elements. First, the judge said the defendant must prove that the harm or evil that the defendant was trying to avoid was imminent. Imminent! That means just about to happen; that means right away. Not two or three years off, but right away. Look at the defendant. He is not sick. He is perfectly healthy. He can go on like this for years and not get AIDS. So there is nothing imminent about it at all. His case fails on that point alone. What else? The judge also told you that the defendant must prove that there were no reasonable alternatives. He never tried the medication called AZT. He refused to take it. We don't know if it would work for him or not because he never tried. The doctor told us it works for some, not for others. So the defendant has failed to show there were no reasonable alternatives. That's two out of five of the elements he is required to prove.

> Keep your promise, ladies and gentlemen: follow the law. If you do, you will find the defendant guilty of count one because there is no doubt he cultivated and possessed the illegal substance, marijuana.
>
> As to count two, I have to concede that charge is weak. I leave it up to you. Thank you.

The judge reminds the jury that there are two counts and the jury may find the defendant guilty or not guilty of either count. Deliberations begin in a private room.

WHAT IS YOUR VERDICT?

QUESTIONS FOR YOU TO CONSIDER

As you determine your verdict for this crime, here are some questions about the crime and the trial for you to think about.

1. Why would the defense attorney stipulate in the jury's presence that the plants were marijuana, that Sam Kepner owned them and had full knowledge they were marijuana? Wasn't she giving away the main part of the case?

2. Did the prosecution make a mistake in charging possession of marijuana for sale?

3. Suppose you are a person who is prejudiced against homosexuals, but at the same time you cannot help feeling sorry for Sam Kepner, who is HIV positive and likely to die of AIDS within two or three years. Should such feelings enter into your jury deliberations?

AUTHOR'S ANSWERS TO THE QUESTIONS

1. The defense attorney knew all those admitted facts would come out anyway. By admitting them at the outset, she gave the impression that the defense was being completely open with the court and not trying to hide anything. Her sole defense was that of medical necessity and she was in no way giving that defense away.

2. The district attorney's office loses the jury's trust every time it tries to convict a defendant on little or no evidence. In this case, the prosecutor, Jean Stanley, made a wise decision to admit her case was weak on that count and to refrain from argument. A wiser decision would have been to omit the charge at the outset and focus on the first count.

3. It may be difficult, but a juror must not be influenced by pity for or prejudice against a defendant. A juror must be able to set such feelings aside and judge the case strictly on the evidence and the law. A juror's inability to do so should have been disclosed to the court during the jury selection process.

THE VERDICT

What was your verdict?

The real-life jury found the defendant not guilty.

Sam Kepner made a favorable impression on the jury as a sympathetic and sincere person who was only doing his desperate best to save his life. The medical witnesses for the defense were instrumental in winning an acquittal. Furthermore, the D.A. made the mistake of charging Kepner with a second count of possessing marijuana for sale when there was no evidence of intent to sell.

Death of a Bully

STATE V. JAMES ALFORD

Two reliable witnesses saw the defendant fire eight shots into the body of a helpless victim. There is no evidence of a struggle or self-defense—it appears to be simply a shooting spree at close range with the victim sitting unarmed in his car.

The D.A. is a tall man with a clipped moustache, dapper in his three-piece suit with a chain across his vest. He calls his first witness, a middle-aged woman.

D.A.: State your name please, and spell your last name.

Meskey: Sheila Meskey—M-E-S-K-E-Y.

D.A.: On the morning of August 19, 2006, where did you reside?

Meskey: Same place I live now. My house at 213 Hackley Road, here in this city.

D.A.: Who else lived at that residence?

Meskey: I'm a widow. I live alone. Well, not really. I live with my cat Jolie. She's practically a person.

There are chuckles from the jury. The judge smiles.

D.A.: Describe the physical nature of that street.

Meskey: It's a big hill with a canyon on one side. I live near the top of the hill. It's a two-lane street. A quiet, residential neighborhood.

D.A.: And on that morning of August 19, did something unusual occur?

Meskey: It did indeed. I was out in front, trimming the hedges, when I saw these cars side-by-side, coming up over the hill and starting down, coming toward me.

D.A.: Can you describe the two vehicles you saw?

Meskey: The one on the left was a black BMW—I could tell that because we had a BMW—and the other car was a white pickup. I don't know the model.

D.A.: Was that unusual?

Meskey: Well, yes, since it's only a two-lane road. Two cars coming side by side like that.

D.A.: What happened next?

Meskey: As they started down the hill, the BMW pulled over on the shoulder of the road and stopped. The pickup pulled over to his right and stopped beside the BMW.

D.A.: So the pickup was on the road and the BMW was off on the shoulder?

Mary Caggiano, the defense attorney, rises in her seat. “Objection! He’s leading the witness!”

Judge: Sustained!

D.A.: All right. You tell us how the two cars were positioned.

Meskey: The white pickup was in the street on the right side of the road. The BMW was off the road, on the shoulder, which wasn’t very wide to begin with.

D.A.: How close were the cars from each other?

Meskey: Real close. Maybe inches between them.

D.A.: What did you see next?

Meskey: I saw the driver of the BMW immediately roll down his window and start shouting at the other driver. He was very angry.

D.A.: What did the other driver do?

Meskey: He just sat there smiling—actually, laughing.

D.A.: You could see the faces of both men?

Meskey: Yes. Quite clearly. They were only about thirty feet away from me.

D.A.: What happened next?

Meskey: Well, the driver of the pickup started yelling, too. He leaned over and opened his window on the right side. He yelled something at the man in the BMW—

D.A.: Excuse me for interrupting, but before we go further, do you see the driver of the BMW in the courtroom now?

Meskey: Yes. He's my neighbor up the hill, Jim Alford, sitting right there with his lawyer.

D.A.: Your Honor, may the record show the witness has identified the defendant?

Judge: It may.

D.A.: Now, Mrs. Meskey, would you please tell this jury what you saw the defendant do?

Meskey: He picked up a gun, leaned out the window, and fired two quick shots at the other guy. I recognized him, too.

D.A.: You mean the victim?

Meskey: We all knew him as Wilbur. I never met him personally, thank God.

D.A.: Objection.

Judge: Sustained.

D.A.: Mrs. Meskey, I shall ask you to keep your personal comments to yourself. Just answer the question. Do you understand that, ma'am?

Meskey: I'm sorry. I couldn't help it. What's your question?

D.A.: How far away was the defendant from the other man when he fired the weapon?

Meskey: Oh, I'd say about from here to the jury box.

D.A.: About ten feet?

Meskey: Maybe a little less. Maybe seven or eight feet.

D.A.: What kind of weapon was it?

Meskey: I don't know anything about guns.

D.A.: Was it a handgun as compared to a rifle?

Meskey: Oh, yes. Not a rifle. Like a pistol or revolver.

D.A.: Were there more shots?

Meskey: Yes, two or three more.

D.A.: Did he hit the other driver?

Meskey: I saw the other guy slump over, his truck started to roll, and that's all I know. I screamed and ran into the house to call 911. That's the last I saw.

D.A.: Did you see or hear anything else while you were calling 911?

Meskey: While I was talking to the police, I heard this boom, like a crash, and then some more shots coming from down the hill.

D.A.: How many shots?

Meskey: I didn't count, but it sounded like four or five or so. I'm not sure how many.

D.A.: The shots you heard down the hill—were they one right after another or was there a break in between?

Meskey: There was about two or three shots quick in succession. Then there was a little break of a couple seconds. Then two or three more. I couldn't see anything.

D.A.: Did you ever see the driver of the white pickup—the one you call Wilbur—did you ever see him attack or threaten to attack the shooter?

Meskey: No, nothing like that. Wilbur just sat smiling in his car until he saw the gun.

D.A.: Did you ever see Wilbur with any gun in his hand?

Meskey: No. Far as I could tell he just had his hands on the steering wheel.

D.A.: Thank you, Mrs. Meskey. Your witness, Counsel.

Caggiano: Mrs. Meskey, I ask you to think back to that moment when you saw the two vehicles side-by-side coming down the hill. When you first saw them, how far apart were they?

Meskey: When I first saw them, they were about ten feet apart.

Caggiano: Let's be clear. They were parallel with—um—they were side-by-side, right?

Meskey: Yes.

Caggiano: And the driver of the black BMW, Mr. Alford, was in the right lane, the proper lane, correct?

Meskey: Yes.

Caggiano: And the driver of the white pickup was in the other lane, the only other lane, correct?

Meskey: That's true.

Caggiano: On that two-lane street, that wasn't the proper lane to be in, was it?

D.A.: Objection!

Judge: Overruled! You may answer, Mrs. Meskey.

Meskey: No. No it wasn't. Unless he was trying to pass.

Caggiano: You watched these cars as they came over the hill?

Meskey: Yes.

Caggiano: And saw the white pickup try to pass?

Meskey: I couldn't say, no.

Caggiano: Now think back, Mrs. Meskey. While they were still parallel, didn't the white pickup start to close this distance of ten feet and veer closer to the black BMW?

D.A.: Objection, Your Honor. What's all this have to do with whether the defendant committed murder? Motion to strike.

Caggiano: We will prove its relevance later, Your Honor.

Judge: All right. I'll reserve ruling on the motion to strike. You may proceed.

Caggiano: You have the question in mind, Mrs. Meskey?

Meskey: You want to know if the white pickup started to come closer to the BMW? Well—

Caggiano: Think about it, Mrs. Meskey. Picture it in your mind. Take your time.

Meskey: Well—

The witness grimaces. She looks at the D.A. There is a long pause.

Meskey: Well, yes. I do recall it. Yes, he did veer to the right, closer to the other car, to Mr. Alford's BMW.

Caggiano: Thank you. And how close did he come?

Meskey: How close?

Caggiano: Yes, how close? Less than ten feet?

Meskey: Yes.

Caggiano: Less than five feet?

Meskey: Mmm, yes.

Caggiano: In fact, didn't the white pickup come within inches of the BMW?

Meskey: Oh, dear, it's hard to remember exactly how far.

Caggiano: You remember talking to my investigator, Sam Morelli, about a week ago?

Meskey: Mr. Morelli? Oh, yes. I remember.

Caggiano: And do you remember telling Mr. Morelli that the white pickup came within inches of the other car?

Meskey: Well, it was awfully close, I remember that.

Caggiano: What you told Mr. Morelli was true, wasn't it?

Meskey: Yes.

Caggiano: And what you're telling us now is the truth, right?

Meskey: Of course.

Caggiano: The truck—so close that the BMW veered off to the side of the road to avoid being struck?

D.A.: Objection! Your Honor, even if the defendant's car was forced off the road, and I am not conceding that it did, but if it did, that's no defense to shooting a man down in cold blood!

Caggiano: I will tie it up, Your Honor.

Judge: Objection overruled. Proceed, Counsel.

Caggiano: Mrs. Meskey, you were the only witness. The jury wants to know the truth. Did the white pickup force the BMW off the road?

D.A.: Objection! She's not qualified to give that opinion!

Caggiano: We don't need an expert to tell us what happened, Your Honor. She was right there. A lay person can give her opinion whether one car forced another off the road.

Judge: Don't argue in front of the jury, Counsel. Objection overruled. Proceed.

Caggiano: In your own opinion, based on what you saw, Mrs. Meskey. Did it appear to you the BMW was forced off the road?

Meskey: (*Looking at the judge*) May I answer, Your Honor?

Judge: If you have an opinion, you may answer.

Meskey: I don't know what anyone else would say, but in my opinion—

Caggiano: Yes?

Meskey: You could say he was forced off the road. You could say that.

Caggiano: Thank you. Now, Mrs. Meskey, how long have you lived at that location?

Meskey: Let's see, we came in—oh, it's been twenty-three years now.

Caggiano: So you are familiar with the physical area?

Meskey: Oh yes, yes.

Caggiano: You gave us a brief description of that street. Could you describe the area immediately to the side of the shoulder where the BMW was stopped.

Meskey: Well, yes, there's a drop-off there.

Caggiano: How steep is that drop?

Meskey: About fifteen feet. There used to be a brook running along there when we came but now it's all dried up and just rocks.

Caggiano: How wide is the shoulder before the drop-off?

Meskey: Not very wide. Three feet or so.

Caggiano: So if a car was pushed off the shoulder it would tumble down into that bed of rocks?

D.A.: Objection! On two grounds. Speculation and leading.

Judge: Sustained. You may rephrase your question, Mrs. Caggiano.

Caggiano: Thank you, Your Honor. Is that a dangerous spot?

D.A.: Objection! Calls for expert opinion.

Judge: No, overruled. The witness may answer.

Meskey: It is dangerous. We've tried to get a railing there. And a car did go off there once. It wasn't nice.

Caggiano: And when the white pickup came to a stop, was it pointed in the direction of the black car?

D.A.: Objection! Your Honor, I regret having to object so much but she is leading the witness, practically putting words in her mouth.

Judge: Counsel, this is cross-examination of your witness. She is allowed to lead. The witness may answer.

Meskey: Was it pointed at—oh, dear. I'm not sure I—

Caggiano: You remember what you told my investigator?

Meskey: Oh, dear, did I say that? I, uh—

Caggiano: Let me show you the investigator's report.

Attorney Caggiano takes a document up to the stand, stating, "Your Honor, I have shown counsel this report so it's no surprise to him." She shows Mrs. Meskey the document and asks the witness to read it.

Caggiano: Does that refresh your memory, Mrs. Meskey?

Meskey: Oh, yes—yes, I recall it now. Okay, now, what was the question again?

Caggiano: Was the white pickup pointed at the black car when they came to a stop?

Meskey: Yes. Yes, it was.

Caggiano: I wonder if you would do something for us, Mrs. Meskey. Would you kindly come up here to this board, and on this large sheet of paper, would you draw for us the positions of the two vehicles and the fifteen-foot drop as you saw the scene when the shooting started?

Meskey: Oh, gosh, I'm not an artist, I—

Caggiano: Just do your best, Mrs. Meskey. Would you do that for us, please?

Mrs. Meskey leaves the stand, goes up to the board, and draws a picture of the scene.

Caggiano: Thank you, Mrs. Meskey. Your Honor, may this drawing be marked as Defense Exhibit A and received in evidence?

Judge: Received in evidence. The jury may have the drawing in the jury room during deliberations.

Caggiano: No further questions.

D.A.: I just have a few questions on redirect, Your Honor. Mrs. Meskey, as to whether the BMW was actually forced off the road, you are not an expert in such matters, are you?

Meskey: No, I'm certainly not.

D.A.: Have you ever seen a car forced off the road before?

Meskey: No, I can't say I have.

D.A.: And did you ever see the white pickup touch or come in contact with the BMW?

Meskey: No. I didn't see that.

D.A.: Thank you, Mrs. Meskey, you may step down. We will call Tom Cunningham.

A teenage boy enters the courtroom and takes the stand. He testifies his name is Thomas Cunningham. He is 16 years of age and a junior at Donly High School. He appears to be shaking but his voice is clear.

D.A.: Are you nervous?

Tom Cunningham: Sure, a little. I never did anything like this before.

D.A.: Just calm down. All we want is the truth. Where do you live, Tom?

Tom Cunningham: 290 Hackley Road.

D.A.: In this city and county?

Tom Cunningham: Yes.

D.A.: Who do you live with?

Tom Cunningham: My mom and dad. I have an older sister but she was away.

D.A.: Now, Tom, do you remember where you were on the morning of August 19, 2006?

Tom Cunningham: The morning of the shooting?

D.A.: Yes.

Tom Cunningham: I was at home alone. I was in the living room watching TV.

D.A.: Did something unusual occur?

Tom Cunningham: Yes, sir.

D.A.: Just relax, Tom. Tell the jury what you heard.

Tom Cunningham: Yes, sir. I heard a loud crash just outside in the front yard. I ran to the window and looked out.

D.A.: What did you see?

Tom Cunningham: I saw this car. Well, it wasn't a car. It was a white pickup truck, smashed into the tree in our front yard.

D.A.: Did you see the driver of that car?

Tom Cunningham: Yes, sir. I saw a guy in the driver's seat. He was slumped over on the steering wheel.

D.A.: Was he moving?

Tom Cunningham: Not that I could tell, no, sir.

D.A.: What happened next?

Tom Cunningham: I was only at the window for a second when this black car pulled up immediately behind the white pickup. The driver, Mr. Alford, got out and ran up to the pickup.

D.A.: Did Mr. Alford have—the driver of the black car—did he have anything in his hand?

Tom Cunningham: Yes, sir. He had a gun—a little gun—like a revolver.

D.A.: Tell us what you saw him do.

Tom Cunningham: Like I said, he ran up to the pickup—

D.A.: Which side did he run to?

Tom Cunningham: The passenger's side.

D.A.: Then what?

Tom Cunningham: He pointed the gun at the guy behind the steering wheel and started firing.

D.A.: How many shots did you see him fire?

Tom Cunningham: I remember two quick shots, one right after another.

D.A.: Was that window open?

Tom Cunningham: I couldn't tell for sure, but I didn't see any glass breaking or anything like that.

D.A.: What did you do next?

Tom Cunningham: As soon as I saw the shots I ran to the phone to call the police.

D.A.: You dialed 911?

Tom Cunningham: Yes, sir.

D.A.: While you were on the phone, did you hear anything else?

Tom Cunningham: Yes, sir. There was a pause. Then I heard more shots. Bang, bang—just like that, all one after another—three or four more shots.

D.A.: After you called 911, did you see anything else?

Tom Cunningham: I ran back to the window. Mr. Alford was just getting into his car. I saw him drive off. Up the hill.

D.A.: What did you do next?

Tom Cunningham: I was—well, yeah, I'll admit it—I was scared. I didn't know if I should go outside or not. I didn't know if there would be any more shooting. But then I saw the neighbors coming out and gathering around the pickup, so I went out, too.

D.A.: Did you see the man slumped at the steering wheel?

Tom Cunningham: Yes, sir. He had a lot of blood on his head and face. He looked like he was dead. Then the police came and I told one of the officers about what happened.

D.A.: Now Tom, I want you to look around this courtroom, look very carefully, and tell us if you see the man who fired those shots that morning.

The courtroom is silent. Tom looks about at everyone.

Tom Cunningham: Yes, sir. I see him. Mr. Alford. He is sitting right there at that table (*pointing*).

D.A.: What is he wearing?

Tom Cunningham: He's wearing a gray suit and a blue tie.

D.A.: Thank you, Tom. Your Honor, may the record show the witness has identified the defendant, James Alford?

Judge: The record may so show. Anything further of this witness, Counsel?

D.A.: Nothing further, Your Honor. Counsel may examine.

Caggiano, the defense attorney, pauses in her seat, studying the witness. Then she rises to begin her cross-examination. As she goes to the podium, you can't help feeling a bit sorry for her. How can she possibly defend this case? She is so short her head barely reaches over the podium.

Caggiano: You knew this man, the man who was shot?

Tom Cunningham: I didn't know him personally. But I knew about him. Most everybody in the neighborhood knew about him. They called him Wilbur the Bully—

D.A.: Objection! Motion to strike.

"Sustained! Motion granted." The judge looks at the jury. "Ladies and gentlemen of the jury, once again I must ask you to strike the last statement from your mind and treat it as if you never heard it." He turns to the boy on the stand. "And young man, I will admonish you to just answer the question. We have certain rules here just like you have in a ball game and we all must follow them. Do you understand me?"

The witness looks frightened. "I'm sorry, Your Honor. I was just—"

Judge: Proceed, Counsel.

Caggiano: Let's do it this way, Tom. Have you talked to people in the neighborhood about him? Yes or no.

Tom Cunningham: Yes.

Caggiano: What was his name?

Tom Cunningham: I just knew he was Wilbur. I never knew his last name. Everybody called him Wilbur.

Caggiano: And, having talked to people in the neighborhood about Wilbur, are you familiar with his reputation in that community for violence or threats of—

D.A.: Objection! Your Honor, counsel is proceeding as if this were a self-defense case.

Caggiano: Your Honor, the defense has a right to—

Judge: That's enough, Counsel. We'll not argue the law in front of the jury. I will see counsel privately. Counsel will approach the bench.

The two attorneys go up to the judge's bench on the side opposite the jury box. The court reporter takes her machine and joins them. They all whisper as if to keep you from hearing. But as they converse, the whispers become louder and more animated.

You notice the judge is trying to admonish counsel to keep their voices down, but from time to time you hear phrases from the angry D.A. like, "That's not self-defense. That's crazy," and "Where's the proof?" And from Caggiano: "I will have the proof, Your Honor, I promise." All the while, young Tom Cunningham sits dumbly and uncomfortably on the witness stand. Finally, the sidebar exchange ends and the parties return to their places.

Caggiano: I will ask you again, Tom—are you familiar with Wilbur's reputation in that neighborhood for violence or threats of violence?

Tom Cunningham: Well, if you mean forcing people off the road and—

Caggiano: No, Tom, just answer the question. Yes or no. I will repeat it. Are you familiar with his reputation for violence or threats of violence?

Tom Cunningham: Yes.

Caggiano: And what is it, that reputation?

Tom Cunningham: Terrible! His reputation was terrible. That's the truth. My mother said—

Caggiano: No, Tom, that's it. You've answered the question. Thank you. You've been very helpful.

Caggiano sits and the D.A. returns to the podium for redirect.

D.A.: Now, Tom, unfortunately the man you know as Wilbur—Wilbur Forrest is his true name—unfortunately he can't be here to defend himself, can he?

Tom Cunningham: No, sir.

D.A.: And that's because he was shot in cold blood by this man seated right here (*pointing*), right?

Tom Cunningham: Yes, sir.

D.A.: Now, Tom, I want you to think very carefully and tell this jury. Have you ever seen Wilbur Forrest strike anyone?

Tom Cunningham: No.

D.A.: Here you ever overheard him threaten anyone with violence?

Tom Cunningham: No, but my mom—

D.A.: I didn't ask you about your mom. I am asking you what you saw or heard. Ever seen him do anything violent?

Tom Cunningham: Uh, no, sir. Can't say I have.

D.A.: Did you see him do anything, anything at all, to provoke this shooting?

Tom Cunningham: No, sir.

D.A.: Thank you, son. That's all. You may step down.

The next witness for the prosecution is Dr. Anthony Krautzer of the county coroner's office. Dr. Krautzer testifies that he performed the autopsy on the body of Wilbur Forrest.

D.A.: Tell the jury, Doctor, what is an autopsy?

Krautzer: The autopsy I did in this case consisted of an external examination of the body and then an internal examination of the head, chest, and abdominal cavities. This was done to document any trauma and natural disease present.

D.A.: In general, Doctor, what were your findings?

Krautzer: In general I found a number of bullet wounds, both entry and exit wounds, where the bullet went through one part of the body and out another. Otherwise he appeared healthy.

D.A.: How many entry wounds altogether?

Krautzer: Eight in all. Two went through his head. The other six went through the chest and abdomen. Most of the bullet wounds entered the right side.

D.A.: And, for the record, Doctor, what was the cause of death?

Krautzer: Multiple gunshot wounds.

The doctor then identifies photographs of the deceased and shows with diagrams where the bullets entered and exited the body.

D.A.: Thank you, Doctor. Mrs. Caggiano may have some questions.

Caggiano: Doctor, from your report, I notice one bullet struck the right cheek and went through his head, is that correct?

Krautzer: That is correct.

Caggiano: And that bullet was fatal by itself, was it not?

Krautzer: Yes. That one shot was fatal, or lethal, by itself. That is true.

Caggiano: And that bullet would have killed the victim instantly, is that correct?

Krautzer: Yes.

Caggiano: Can you tell us which bullet or bullets were fired first?

Krautzer: No. I cannot say.

Caggiano: Can you tell us the distance the shooter was from the victim by the nature of these wounds?

Krautzer: No, there were no powder burns such as would occur at close range. I can only say he was not close up.

Caggiano: Doctor, if that fatal shot to the head was the first shot, then the victim would have been dead when all the other shots were fired, right?

D.A.: Objection! Speculation!

Judge: Overruled.

Krautzer: That is probably correct. If the shot to the head was the first one, then the victim would have been dead or close to it when the other shots were fired, yes, one could say that.

Caggiano: Thank you, Doctor. That's all.

The next witness is police sergeant Anthony Mangerini, who testifies he is a detective on the police force and was in charge of the investigation at the crime scene.

D.A.: What did you do first?

Mangerini: First I went to the victim. That's always our first priority. When I arrived, a crowd of neighbors was standing around the white pickup. The victim was still slumped over the steering wheel, his head covered with blood. I felt his pulse and determined he was dead. Other squad cars arrived. We moved the crowd back and roped off the area.

Thereupon the D.A. shows the detective a number of photographs for identification. Once identified and explained by the witness, the photographs are passed among the jury. You study each exhibit as it is passed to you. The photographs show the victim inside the vehicle as the detective found the scene on arrival. They also show the bullet holes in the vehicle and the position of the vehicle embedded against the tree. The detective testifies that once the body was removed, he and his officers took statements from witnesses, especially from Tom Cunningham, who was the only actual eyewitness.

D.A.: What did you do next?

Mangerini: Well, of course, our primary concern at that point was to find and arrest the shooter. Mrs. Meskey had reported the shooting near the top of the hill that occurred immediately before the second series of shots down below. So I drove up there with my partner to examine the scene and interview Mrs. Meskey.

D.A.: Did something of an unusual nature occur when you arrived?

Mangerini: Yes. No sooner had I exited my police unit when a gentleman came out of a house nearby and approached me. He came up to me and said, "I'm the man you're looking for, Officer."

D.A.: Did he do or say anything else?

Mangerini: Yes. He reached into the pocket of his jacket, pulled out a gun—it was a .45—and handed it to me.

D.A.: What did he say?

Mangerini: He said, "You may want this."

D.A.: Detective Mangerini, do you see that man in the courtroom?

Mangerini: Yes. He is the defendant, sitting right there (*pointing*).

D.A.: Your Honor, may the record show the witness has identified the defendant?

Judge: Yes.

D.A.: (*To the detective*) Did you ask him any questions before he spoke?

Mangerini: No, nothing. He just started speaking voluntarily.

D.A.: What did you do next?

Mangerini: I arrested the defendant, handcuffed him, and took him into custody. One of my partners took him to the station.

D.A.: Did you do anything after that?

Mangerini: Oh, yes. We still had a lot to do. We examined the scene near the top of the hill and found four shell casings—cartridges—on the ground. We interviewed Mrs. Meskey.

D.A.: Did you examine the gun?

Mangerini: Yes. It was a .45 caliber revolver. It still had two bullets unfired.

D.A.: How many bullets does it hold?

Mangerini: Seven altogether.

D.A.: So if ten shots are fired, the shooter would have to stop and reload in order to fire any more, is that correct, Officer?

Mangerini: That's right.

D.A.: Could you determine how many shots were fired altogether in this case?

Mangerini: We found four cartridges up on the hill and six down below around the area of the white pickup. Ten altogether.

D.A.: You are speaking of cartridges that are automatically ejected from the side of the weapon every time a bullet is fired, is that right, sir?

Mangerini: Yes, that's right.

D.A.: So, in this case, if the shooter fired a total of ten shots, that would mean he had to stop after seven bullets were expended, take the time to reload the weapon, and fire again, is that right?

Mangerini: That's true.

D.A.: Thank you, Detective Mangerini. Your witness, Counsel.

Caggiano: Did Jim Alford ever try to resist arrest?

Mangerini: Oh no, just the opposite.

Caggiano: He was cooperative?

Mangerini: Completely, yes.

Caggiano: Did he show any remorse for his conduct?

Mangerini: He had tears in his eyes when he came up to me. When he sat in the police car on the way to the station, he broke down crying.

Caggiano: Did he say anything?

Mangerini: He just kept saying, "I am sorry, I am so sorry. Oh, God, what have I done?"

At that point Caggiano turns to the judge. "Your Honor, I wish to go into a different subject with Sergeant Mangerini. And I wish to make him my own witness for the purpose of this examination."

D.A.: Objection, Your Honor. The State hasn't rested yet. This is highly irregular.

Caggiano: It will save court time, Your Honor.

Judge: I will allow it in the interest of saving time. Sergeant Mangerini, up until now you've been a witness for the prosecution. You are now being called as a witness for the defense. Mrs. Caggiano, you may proceed.

Caggiano: Thank you, Your Honor. Sergeant Mangerini, did you know the victim in this case, Wilbur Forrest?

Mangerini: I met him. I talked to him.

Caggiano: How did it happen that you met him and talked to him?

Mangerini: Well, a group of neighbors came into my office with a complaint, and they said—

D.A.: Objection! Hearsay!

Judge: Sustained!

Caggiano: Let me phrase it this way, Sergeant. As a result of talking to a group of neighbors, did you then speak to Wilbur Forrest?

Mangerini: Yes, I warned him about—

D.A.: Objection, Your Honor. This is also hearsay!

Judge: Sustained!

Caggiano: But, Your Honor, this will show—

Judge: Don't argue with the court, Counsel. The court has ruled. Proceed.

D.A.: Motion to strike!

Judge: Motion is granted. The witness's last statement about warning Mr. Forrest is stricken. The jury is admonished to disregard it.

Caggiano: Without telling us what they said, how many neighbors did you talk to?

Mangerini: There were about ten in the group that came to see me.

Caggiano: And was my client, Jim Alford, in that group that came to your office with a complaint?

Mangerini: He was. In fact he appeared to be the spokesman. He did most of the talking.

Caggiano: And so it was as a result of this meeting at the police station that you went to see Wilbur Forrest?

Mangerini: That's right.

Caggiano: And have you also spoken with other members of that neighborhood about him?

Mangerini: Yes.

Caggiano: And as a result of all those conversations, did you form an opinion as to Mr. Forrest's reputation in that community for violence and threats of violence?

Mangerini: Yes.

Caggiano: What was that opinion—good or bad?

Mangerini: Bad.

Caggiano: Thank you, Sergeant. That's all I have of this witness, Your Honor.

The D.A. stands as if to ask a question, then pauses. "No, I have no questions, Your Honor. The witness may step down."

Judge: Does the State have any further evidence?

D.A.: Nothing further. The State rests.

After a fifteen-minute recess, Caggiano begins the case for the defense. She calls Ellen Cunningham.

Caggiano: Was it your son Tom who testified earlier in this case?

Ellen Cunningham: Yes. I was very proud of him.

Caggiano: And you live on the same street as the defendant, Jim Alford?

Ellen Cunningham: Yes. We are neighbors. Jim lives up the hill from us.

Caggiano: Did you also know Wilbur Forrest?

Ellen Cunningham: I knew him only as Wilbur. We had a name for him but I understand I am not allowed to say it here in court.

Caggiano: Have you talked to neighbors about him?

Ellen Cunningham: I certainly have. We were all afraid of him.

Caggiano: Just answer the question, please. As a result of discussing him with your neighbors, did you form an opinion as to his reputation for violence or threats of violence?

Ellen Cunningham: Yes.

Caggiano: Please tell the jury what that reputation was.

Ellen Cunningham: It was awful. I'd like to say it again. We were all afraid of the man.

Caggiano: And have you formed your own opinion as to Wilbur Forrest's character trait for violence or threats of violence?

Ellen Cunningham: I certainly have. He threatened me enough times.

Caggiano: What do you mean?

Ellen Cunningham: A few times he forced me off the road when I was driving.

D.A.: Objection!

Judge: Overruled. The witness may explain her answer.

Ellen Cunningham: Thank you, Your Honor. One evening, about two months before the shooting, my husband and I were going out to dinner with the Alfords, Jim and Dahlia. My husband was driving. I was sitting up front with him. The Alfords were in back. We've been friends with them for years. It was dark out. Suddenly a pair of headlights appeared in our rearview mirror. The car behind us was closing rapidly. It got so close I thought it was going to hit us. I told my husband to pull over to let him pass. So my husband pulled off on the shoulder and stopped. The car behind pulled over in front of us and stopped so we couldn't drive forward. My husband asked the driver if there was a problem and the driver said, "You know what the problem is and don't—" Must I say the exact word, Your Honor? I never said it before but if I must—

Judge: We want the truth. You should state the exact language he used.

Ellen Cunningham: Well, I'm embarrassed to say it, but he said, "Don't fuck with me. I know where you live," and then he drove off.

Caggiano: Who was the driver?

Ellen Cunningham: It was Wilbur. Wilbur Forrest. He looked very agitated.

Caggiano: Was there a second time a similar incident occurred?

Ellen Cunningham: The next time I was driving in the neighborhood alone. Two-way road. He was coming toward me in the opposite direction. As he came near me, he veered into my lane and was coming straight at me. I had to suddenly swerve off the road to avoid a crash. He slowed down and laughed and went on. It was frightening.

Caggiano: Was there a third incident?

Ellen Cunningham: Yes. I was driving with my son Tom. Then the same thing—

D.A.: Objection, Your Honor. This is cumulative.

Judge: Overruled. Please continue, Mrs. Cunningham.

Ellen Cunningham: This time he came toward me again on a two-lane road. Again he suddenly veered into my lane and was heading straight at our car. Again I had to turn off the road to avoid a crash, but I almost hit a tree. This time he threw something at our car as he went by. I was so scared. Especially for Tom.

Caggiano: Did you take any action as a result?

Ellen Cunningham: Yes. I said, "This is it. I've had enough." I went to court and got a restraining order against him.

Caggiano: Thank you, Mrs. Cunningham.

The D.A. has no questions, but as Mrs. Cunningham starts to leave, she turns to the judge. "Your Honor, may I say something else?"

Judge: Does it pertain to this case?

Ellen Cunningham: It certainly does, Your Honor.

Judge: Briefly, you may speak.

Ellen Cunningham: Your Honor, I don't like to see anyone dead. I am sorry it had to end this way. But Jim Alford is a hero in our neighborhood for what he did. We were all scared of this man. At last we can live in peace.

The D.A. jumps to his feet and pounds the table. "Objection, Your Honor! Motion to strike!"

The judge assents. "Motion granted. Ladies and gentlemen of the jury, the last statement is out of order, absolutely inadmissible. You are to disregard it completely. Strike it from your minds. You may step down, Mrs. Cunningham."

The next witness is Margaret McLoud. She testifies she is a teacher at an elementary school. She lives in the same neighborhood as the defendant. Mrs. McLoud describes several incidents involving Wilbur Forrest. The first occurred at about 6:00 p.m. on a day the previous November. She was driving her car with her husband. Forrest began tailgating her. She slowed down and pulled off to the side of the road to let him pass, but instead he pulled alongside her car and started pushing her farther off to the side. She testifies she was frightened because there was a steep hillside to the right. She managed to drive off but Forrest began tailgating her again. This time he pulled in front of her and stopped, blocking her way. He eventually drove off. A second time, she was driving alone when he came at her with his white pickup. At the last minute, he moved out of the way. A third time she was riding with her 17-year-old daughter and he did the same thing.

> **Caggiano**: Did you have any idea why he seemed to be targeting you?
>
> **McLoud**: He knew I was going to be a witness against him at his trial.
>
> **Caggiano**: Did you take any actions as a result of these incidents?
>
> **McLoud**: We had several community meetings with the neighbors and the police. We needed help. There were about thirty of us at the first meeting. The man had us all terrified. We didn't know what he would do next. The police were concerned and listened to our complaints but they couldn't do anything.

Thereupon a parade of witnesses for the defense take the stand to testify about Wilbur Forrest's threatening conduct. Caggiano calls thirteen neighbors who one by one describe incidents similar to those reported by the first two witnesses. They tell of their frustration in seeking protection from law enforcement. After the sixth witness, the D.A. objects on grounds the testimony is cumulative and adds nothing new to the case. The objection is overruled.

After thirteen witnesses, the D.A. again objects. Caggiano responds that she has more witnesses waiting in the hall, twenty-nine in all. "Your Honor, the evidence is necessary to show Mr. Alford's state of mind at the time of the shooting. We will show he had knowledge of each incident." But this time the judge sustains the objection and Caggiano calls the witness that you and everyone else has been waiting for. Amid a courtroom packed with spectators, the defendant takes the stand.

Caggiano: State your name, please.

Alford: James Willis Alford.

Caggiano: Your occupation?

Alford: I am a retired Army officer.

Caggiano: Your rank at the time of retirement?

Alford: Major.

Caggiano: How long did you serve in the United States Army?

Alford: Twenty-seven years.

Caggiano: How old are you, sir?

Alford: I'm 57 years old.

Caggiano: And were you decorated for your combat service in the Vietnam War?

D.A.: Objection! This is all very interesting, Your Honor, but what does it have to do with whether this man committed murder? It's irrelevant.

Caggiano: It goes to his character, Your Honor.

Judge: I will allow it to a degree but don't go too far with it, Mrs. Caggiano.

Caggiano: Thank you, Your Honor. Do you recall the question, Mr. Alford?

Alford: I do. I received the Bronze Star medal.

You study the man on the stand. He sits tall and straight with a military bearing and a blond crew cut. He seems like a nice man who got caught up in a tragic set of circumstances through no fault of his own. As he testifies, you begin to feel sorry for him. But then you remember you promised to put aside any feelings of sympathy. Over objection, he describes his family life. He lives with his wife, Margaret, to whom he's been married for thirty-two years. They have two grown sons and three grandchildren.

Caggiano: Did you shoot Wilbur Forrest?

Alford: Yes, I must have.

Caggiano: What do you mean?

Alford: It's hazy in my mind. But I know from the evidence that I did.

Caggiano: Tell the jury why you shot him.

Alford: I was terrified. When he said, "You and your whole family will be dead," I just lost it. I know it was wrong and I'm sorry. I didn't know what he would do next. I was afraid for my family.

There follows lengthy testimony by James Alford as to how he came to shoot and kill Wilbur Forrest—how it began when he heard stories from the neighbors, especially the women, about being forced off the road by Forrest; how he, Alford, formed a neighborhood group and went twice to the police for help but nothing was done; how after the second meeting with the police, Forrest began threatening him and forced him off the road four times, twice when Alford was with his wife and young granddaughter. Alford further speaks about how one of the women who had been assaulted by Forrest finally persuaded the district attorney to file charges for criminal assault; how he, Alford, and other neighbors testified at the trial but the jury could not agree and the trial ended in a hung jury; how after the trial, Forrest got out on bail and was waiting for a new trial; how as soon as Forrest got out, he began making new threats, threats of increasing violence, that those who testified against him had better watch out; how the entire neighborhood was frightened of the man.

Caggiano: What did he do to you just before the shooting?

Alford: First he forced me off the road on that hill with the deep drop on the side. He stopped next to me and turned his wheels toward my car. I opened my window—his was open on the passenger side—and I yelled at him.

Caggiano: What did you say?

Alford: I said, "You're crazy. I've had enough of you." Something like that.

Caggiano: What did he say?

Alford: That's when he said, "You and your whole family will be dead."

Caggiano: What did you think when he said that?

Alford: I knew at that point that he was going to harm me and my family.

Caggiano: When was he going to do that?

Alford: At any moment. Right then.

Caggiano: What did you do when he said that?

Alford: I don't remember firing the first shot. But I was very scared. That's when I must have shot him.

Caggiano: Thank you. The D.A. may cross-examine.

D.A.: Was it an accident?

Alford: Was it—well, what do you mean?

D.A.: You know very well what I mean. Did you shoot and kill Wilbur Forrest accidentally?

Alford: Well, no, obviously not.

D.A.: Obviously. So you meant to shoot him?

Alford: Yes.

D.A.: And you meant to kill him?

Alford: I don't remember thinking that. I don't remember what I was thinking.

D.A.: Mr. Alford, you expect us to sit here and believe that you don't remember?

Caggiano: Objection!

Judge: Sustained.

D.A.: You prepared for this shooting, didn't you?

Alford: I had a gun, if that's what you mean.

D.A.: And the gun was loaded?

Alford: Yes.

D.A.: With a bullet in the chamber?

Alford: Yes.

D.A.: And you had it in your car beside you in case you saw him, right?

Alford: I had it for protection.

D.A.: And you intended to use it on him, right?

Alford: If I had to, yes.

D.A.: So that's it. You only intended to shoot him if you had to?

Alford: That's right.

D.A.: Did you have to on this occasion?

Alford: Well, I thought so.

D.A.: Was he attacking you when you fired?

Alford: He had just forced me off the road!

D.A.: His car was stopped?

Alford: Yes.

D.A.: His car was not moving?

Alford: No, but it was pointed—

D.A.: Just answer the question. Was his car moving? Yes or no.

Alford: No.

D.A.: Did he have a gun?

Alford: I didn't see one.

D.A.: Was he shooting at you?

Alford: No.

D.A.: Did he have anything in his hand, any weapon?

Alford: No.

D.A.: Did he strike you or your car in any way, before you fired?

Alford: No.

D.A.: So I will ask you again, Mr. Alford. Just answer the question. Was he attacking you when you fired?

Alford: Well, if you put it that way—

D.A.: How would you put it? Was he attacking you, yes or no?

Alford: Well, no, but—

D.A.: Thank you. You've answered the question. Now, you say the only reason you had the gun was for protection?

Alford: Yes, to protect my family and myself. The man was a menace.

D.A.: How many shots did you fire?

Alford: I don't remember. Whatever the detective said.

D.A.: He found ten shell casings altogether. So you fired ten shots?

Alford: That must be right.

D.A.: And you want us to believe that you needed to fire all ten shots for protection?

Alford: Like I said, I don't recall what I was thinking at the time.

D.A.: Your gun was a .45 caliber Colt Commander semiautomatic, right?

Alford: Right.

The D.A. shows the gun to the defendant and the defendant identifies the weapon as his.

D.A.: It fires seven shots, right?

Alford: Right.

D.A.: The detective found four casings up on the hill, six more down below. That's more than seven, isn't it?

Alford: Yes, right.

D.A.: So you had to reload the weapon, didn't you, Mr. Alford?

Alford: It seems so, yes.

D.A.: When you went down below, you found Mr. Forrest's truck smashed up against a tree, didn't you?

Alford: I don't remember that.

D.A.: He was slumped over the wheel, bleeding from the head, wasn't he?

Alford: That's what the witness said. I simply don't recall.

D.A.: Did you need protection then?

Alford: No, I guess not.

D.A.: Did you need protection from a man dead or dying?

Alford: I've answered that.

D.A.: In fact, you took the time to reload your weapon, didn't you?

Alford: I must have. I don't recall it.

D.A.: Why did you reload your gun?

Alford: I don't know.

D.A.: I'll tell you why you reloaded, Mr. Alford. You took the time to reload it because you wanted to make absolutely sure he was dead, isn't that so?

Alford: I told you. I don't remember that.

D.A.: Is it because you don't remember?

The D.A. approaches the stand.

D.A.: Or is it that you just don't want to remember?

Caggiano: Objection, Your Honor. Counsel is badgering the witness.

Judge: Sustained. I will ask the district attorney to move back behind the counsel table.

D.A.: Tell us then, Mr. Alford, what were you thinking when you reloaded your gun?

Caggiano: Objection, Your Honor. The witness has already said he doesn't remember.

Judge: Sustained.

D.A.: All right, let's try it this way, Mr. Alford. How long does it take to reload a .45 Colt Commander?

Alford: It depends on whether you put the seven bullets in the magazine one by one or if you just put a loaded magazine into the grip.

D.A.: Which did you do?

Alford: My mind was in a fog. I simply don't remember.

D.A.: You have no memory of firing six bullets into the body of a dead man?

Alford: I'm sorry, sir. I do not.

D.A.: Then I have nothing further.

Both sides rest, which means the presentation of evidence is over. The judge gives lengthy instructions on the law, going on for about forty minutes. He explains that the defendant is presumed innocent and can be proven guilty only by proof beyond a reasonable doubt. To get off on self-defense, the defendant must show the attack on him was immediate, not a threat to harm him in the future. You must not consider pity for the defendant.

The D.A. waives opening argument and Mary Caggiano goes to the podium to speak to the jury members for the last time.

> Jim Alford had reason to be terrified. He had reason to believe that Wilbur Forrest was about to kill him and his family. "You and your whole family will be dead," Forrest shouted at him, after almost pushing Alford off the road into a deep canyon. Alford knew the man meant what he said. Alford knew Wilbur Forrest was like a bomb about to explode. What was he to do? There was every reason to believe that Forrest was about to carry out his threat immediately—his whole demeanor, the threat he shouted. And Forrest's car was pointed right at him, only inches away. He had reason to be terrified all right because of what Forrest had done before. Forrest had already forcibly maneuvered him off the road four times in the past. He had similarly shunted

> elderly women off the road, dozens of them, laughing at them while he did so. But now he was threatening to do much worse.
>
> Ladies and gentlemen, we were not there. We did not have to live through it, and who among us can fully imagine the raw fear that gripped the neighborhood, unless we were there ourselves? A fear created by the evil actions of this one man? Who can say what Jim Alford felt when that man told him he would kill him and his whole family? This jury speaks for the conscience of the community. Jim Alford did everything he could to avoid this confrontation. Twice he organized the neighbors and went to the police to plead for help. Little was done. Jim Alford knew Wilbur Forrest was out to get him because he was the leader in the community's struggle to stop the violence.
>
> What are you going to say to Jim Alford in your verdict? Are you going to say: sorry, but you should have waited until Wilbur Forrest pushed you off the cliff before you acted to defend yourself? Are you going to say to Jim Alford: you should have waited until Wilbur Forrest killed your wife and the rest of your family before you took action to protect them?
>
> No, ladies and gentlemen, you don't have to leave your common sense outside that courtroom door. Do the only thing that is based on reason and good judgment and common sense. Find Jim Alford not guilty.

The D.A. responds with his closing argument.

> Ladies and gentlemen of the jury, let's put one matter to rest right at the start. I am not here to offer a sweeping defense of Wilbur Forrest and his actions. He did some bad things. He was wrong to force those people off the road. Yes, he frightened many persons in the neighborhood. If he broke the law, he deserved to be charged and punished for what he did. Wilbur Forrest was a nuisance and, more than that, a bully. I concede all of that. But that does not make it all right to kill him in cold blood; that doesn't make it all right to fire eight bullets

into his body, some of those fired when he lay helpless and bleeding and dying in his truck. No, that is not the American system of justice. It is not the American way to say it was all right to murder Wilbur Forrest just because people disliked him. That is not the law. Wilbur Forrest was still a human being, a human being and a citizen, with *certain unalienable rights* as our Founding Fathers put it, first among which is the right to life.

I know you feel some degree of sympathy for James Alford. Under the circumstances, that is understandable. But you all promised at the beginning of this trial you would follow the law. And the judge told you that under the law, you must put any feelings of sympathy aside and judge the case on the evidence and the law of homicide. That is all I ask you to do here today.

The defendant is charged with murder in the first degree—a willful, deliberate, premeditated killing—and, ladies and gentlemen, he is guilty of that charge beyond any reasonable doubt. The evidence supports every element of the charge.

Willful: This was no accident. He admits that.

Deliberate and premeditated: This was no sudden impulsive act. He prepared for it. He carried a gun with the intent to shoot Wilbur Forrest if, as he says, he had to. So he thought about shooting and killing Wilbur Forrest beforehand. That's deliberate and premeditated right at the start. The gun was loaded and ready to fire at the slightest provocation. But even if you still have a question in your mind when he fired the first shots, what did he do next? He decided to get out of his car and fire again—four shots altogether at the first scene. But now comes the clinching evidence of deliberation and premeditation: He doesn't stop after he sees his victim slumped over the wheel and bleeding in the head. No. He decides to follow Forrest down the hill, and gets out and fires again at a helpless dying man. Does he stop when all the bullets in his gun have been fired and the gun is empty? No. He makes a conscious decision to reload and then fires again. That, ladies and gentlemen, is deliberation and premeditation beyond any doubt whatsoever.

Self-defense? This is not a self-defense case. The law says that the right of self-defense only applies when one is actually being attacked; the attack has to be immediate, right now, not a promise of attack in the future. Defense counsel wants you to twist the law and say that one can use self-defense when the other party threatens to attack in the future. But that is not the law. According to the defendant's own testimony, Wilbur Forrest said, "You and your whole family will be dead." *Will be*—that's in the future. There was no attack going on when Mr. Alford fired. The cars were stopped; they were not even touching—that act of forcing him off the road was over. Forrest had no gun or weapon of any kind; he was simply sitting in his vehicle and never struck the defendant or the defendant's car. That, ladies and gentlemen, is simply not self-defense under the law of this state.

I ask you to remember your oath, follow the law, and do what must be done—find the defendant guilty of murder in the first degree.

There are four possible verdicts in this case:

1. guilty of first-degree murder
2. guilty of second-degree murder
3. guilty of manslaughter
4. not guilty (on grounds of self-defense)

WHAT IS YOUR VERDICT?

QUESTIONS FOR YOU TO CONSIDER

As you determine your verdict for this crime, here are some questions about the crime and the trial for you to think about.

1. What was the biggest problem for the district attorney in this case?

2. Did James Alford fire in self-defense?

AUTHOR'S ANSWERS TO THE QUESTIONS

1. Sympathy for the defendant and intense dislike of the victim Wilbur Forrest were the district attorney's main obstacles to conviction. You could almost hear the jurors saying to themselves: he got what he deserved. The law is clear that jurors must set aside any feelings of sympathy, passion, public opinion, or public feeling in reaching their verdict. But in a case like this, that rule is not easy to follow and some jurors may choose to ignore it. This is called *jury nullification*. Jury deliberations are conducted in secret and never recorded, so no one knows how the jury arrives at its verdict. The district attorney was right to face the problem at the outset in his closing argument.

2. This was a close question for jurors. One could argue it was not self-defense because Alford was not actually being attacked at the time he fired. Forrest's car was stopped. He had no weapon. And he was not in the process of assaulting Alford at the time of the shooting. His threat to kill Alford and his family was in the future tense. "You and your whole family will be dead."

   The answer comes down to the meaning of the word "immediate." The law states that in order to claim self-defense, "the danger must be… immediate… or must so appear at the time to the slayer as a reasonable person, and the killing must be done under a well-founded belief that it is necessary to save one's self from death or great bodily harm."[1] Was Wilbur Forrest's threat immediate?

---

[1] *CALJIC 5.12, California Jury Instructions, Criminal, 6th ed., Committee on Standard Jury Instructions, Criminal, of the Superior Court of Los Angeles County, California (St. Paul, MN: West Publishing Co., 1996), p. 242.*

THE VERDICT

What was your verdict?

The real-life jury found the defendant guilty of murder in the second degree, which was then reduced by the court to manslaughter.

Sympathy for the defendant and dislike of the victim persuaded the jury to reduce the charge from first- to second-degree murder, but the circumstances of the shooting were too damning to warrant a not guilty verdict. At the sentencing hearing, the judge reduced the verdict to voluntary manslaughter. Although the case is based on an actual trial, the facts regarding the self-defense theory have been changed to some degree.

The defendant was sentenced to ten years in state prison.

While the Children Waited in the Car

STATE V. TYRONE WASHBURN

Tyrone Washburn was a popular junior high school teacher with an excellent reputation. He lived with his wife and two children, ages 7 and 9. There is no history of domestic dispute. From all appearances, they were a happy family.

At 1:45 a.m. on March 13, 2006, Washburn called police to his residence. He told them he had just found his wife's dead body, fully dressed, in the garage. When the police arrived, he led them to the crime scene. Elena Washburn had been strangled to death and tests confirmed she had been dead for several hours by the time police arrived. A bloody trail led from the living room through the kitchen to the garage. The police search showed that someone had tried to mop up the blood in the kitchen. Police found no sign of forcible entry through doors or windows and no sign of ransacking. Washburn told police he had no idea who would want to kill his wife. On the morning before the murder, the family had breakfast together, after which he went out to the car with the children. His habit was to drop them off at their school on his way to work. Elena was a social worker and drove her own car. Evidence showed that when Washburn got inside the car, he remembered a report he had forgotten and went back to the house to retrieve it. The children waited in the car for about ten minutes before he returned.

Washburn testified that when he came home that evening at about 5:30 p.m., Elena's car was in the driveway. Elena's routine at the end of the day was to get the children from the babysitter's house and bring them home. But when Washburn arrived home and went inside the house, neither she nor the children were there. He drove to the sitter's house and got the children. Elena was still missing when he returned. He said he did not notice any blood on the floor. At about 1:30 a.m. he finally looked in the garage, and there she was.

The police arrested Washburn for the murder of his wife.

Washburn's defense lawyer has the look of a County Cork Irishman, with a ruddy complexion and a fine mop of white hair. At the other end of the counsel table, closest to you, sits the prosecutor, Madeline Smith, an attractive woman in her thirties, nearly six feet tall, with a full mane of tawny hair. She seems to dominate the courtroom with her unusual height.

"We will prove," she says in her opening statement, "that on the morning of March 12, 2006, Tyrone Washburn cold-bloodedly strangled his wife in the living room of their home and then dragged her body into the garage and left it there, all this while their two children waited outside in the car to be driven to school."

There is a long pause. The judge is looking at Mr. O'Connor, waiting for him to give his opening statement. Finally, the older defense attorney shuffles to his feet.

"As Your Honor knows," he says, "the opening statement is not evidence. The evidence will come from the witness stand. We will waive opening statement and let the evidence speak for itself."

The first witness called by the prosecution is Officer Dale Chambers, investigator for the homicide bureau. He testifies he was called to the Washburn residence at 1:45 a.m. on March 13 and found the defendant waiting for him at the front door. Washburn told him he had just discovered his wife's dead body and led the officer to the garage. There Chambers observed the body of the decedent lying on her stomach on the concrete floor in a small pool of blood. She was fully dressed, with a gold chain, which was broken, still partly around her neck. She appeared to have bled profusely from the nose. Next to the body was a trash can tipped over on its side. Beside the can were several lamb chop bones, an empty milk carton, and an empty doughnut bag. A trail of blood in the garage led to the body. Chambers noticed a ligature mark about her neck.

Deputy District Attorney Smith continues her direct examination.

Smith: Did you draw any conclusions as to how that mark occurred?

Chambers: Yes, by some object that had been wrapped around her neck.

Smith: Such as the gold chain that she had on her chest?

Chambers: Yes, ma'am.

Officer Chambers testifies that the body was cold to the touch. From his sixteen years' experience on the force, he believed she had been dead for some time. She had bloody wounds on her hands. He tells that he then proceeded to inspect the house.

Smith: Did you find any sign of ransacking?

Chambers: No, ma'am.

Smith: Any sign of forcible entry through doors or windows?

Chambers: I examined all the locking mechanisms, all the doors and windows. In my opinion, there was no evidence of forced entry.

The house was dusted for fingerprints, but they did not turn up anything. They were all from the Washburn family and the maid. While Officer Chambers was critiquing the case with the other officers on the investigation team in the living room, one of them noticed a wet spot on the carpet. Detective Marsha Dykes reached down and touched it, brought her finger up, and saw that it was blood. It was hard to see because the color of the carpet was dark red.

Smith: Did you do anything as a result?

Chambers: Yes, ma'am. We called the evidence technician and asked him to test for blood.

Smith: How did he do that?

Chambers: Well, it was getting light, and you need complete darkness to do the test he uses, so we came back the next night. He sprayed the living room carpet with luminol. It's a luminous spray, and when it comes in contact with blood, it illuminates, same as what phosphorus does at night.

Smith: What happened?

Chambers: To my surprise, the living room floor illuminated with this bright phosphorescent color.

Officer Chambers testifies that they sprayed further throughout the house and discovered a bloody trail from the living room through the kitchen to the garage. One of the officers found a wet mop in the kitchen closet, so they sprayed the mop also, and it lit up with the same phosphorescence.

Smith: Notice anything special about the kitchen floor?

Chambers: Yes. From the tests it looked like someone had tried to mop up the blood.

Smith: Did it look like an inside job?

O'Connor: Objection!

Judge: Sustained.

O'Connor begins his cross-examination. But first he walks over to the clerk and picks up the necklace that has been marked as an exhibit.

O'Connor: This the necklace you found on the body?

Chambers: Yes, sir.

O'Connor: And you think she was strangled with this little necklace?

Chambers: That's my opinion.

O'Connor hands the necklace to the officer on the stand.

O'Connor: Here, take it in both hands. See how strong it is. Go ahead. Just give it a light tug.

The officer hesitates.

Smith: Objection, Your Honor!

But before the judge can rule on the objection, the officer pulls the necklace apart with one pull. He looks surprised.

O'Connor: Easy to break, wasn't it?

Chambers: I guess so.

O'Connor: Want to change your mind, Officer, about the necklace being strong enough to strangle a woman to death?

Chambers: Well—

O'Connor: Do you?

Chambers: I could be wrong on that, yes, sir.

O'Connor: Thank you, that's all.

A police criminologist, Pat O'Malley, testifies he inspected Tyrone Washburn's body the day after his wife's body was discovered, but could find no scratch marks or blood.

Next, the D.A. calls the county coroner, Dr. Kiro Yoshino. He performed the autopsy on Elena Washburn. Dr. Yoshino testifies that in his opinion, Elena died of strangulation by an object pressed around her neck. The markings on her body indicate she had been dragged to her death. He found no defensive wounds that would indicate she had been in a struggle. There was no evidence of a sexual attack.

Now the D.A.'s questions focus on the time of death.

Smith: Did you form a conclusion as to the time of death?

Yoshino: Yes. In my opinion she was killed around breakfast time the day before she was found.

Smith: Your reasons for that opinion?

Yoshino: There was practically no food in her stomach. That means she had not eaten that day.

Smith: Any other basis for your opinion?

Yoshino: Yes. The police investigator told me she was very cold to his touch when he found her. In his opinion she had been dead for many hours.

O'Connor: Objection. Hearsay.

Judge: Overruled. An expert may use hearsay to form an opinion.

Smith: One more thing. She was found lying on her stomach. Do you have an opinion as to when she was placed in that position?

Yoshino: Yes. She had been lying on her back for several hours before being turned over.

Smith: How can you say that?

Yoshino: Lividity.

Smith: What?

Yoshino: The process of lividity. When a person dies and lies in a certain position, the blood tends to congest at the lowest spot. This leaves a large bluish discoloration.

Smith: And did you find such a spot on the decedent?

Yoshino: I did, on her back, indicating she'd been on her back for several hours. Later, someone turned her over on her stomach, which was how she was found.

O'Connor begins his cross-examination by attacking the testimony as to time of death. "You say you relied on the officer's opinion as to time of death?"

Yoshino: Partly, yes.

O'Connor: Did that officer have any medical training?

Yoshino: I assume—

O'Connor: Do you know?

Yoshino: No, I'm afraid not.

O'Connor goes back to the clerk's desk and picks up the necklace again. "In your opinion, how was she strangled—that is, with what instrument?"

Yoshino: Some sort of garrote.

O'Connor: Some sort of what?

Yoshino: A garrote—a cord or wire used for strangling.

O'Connor: Was she strangled with this necklace?

Yoshino: Not in my opinion. It's not strong enough.

The prosecution calls Detective Marsha Dykes as the next witness. She testifies she interviewed Washburn at his home the morning after the body was found. He was not under arrest and was cooperative in every respect. Washburn told her he and Elena had been married twelve years and had two children, Maria, age 9, and Morgan, age 7. They had a good relationship. He had no idea who would want to kill her. On the morning of March 12, 2006, he, Elena, and their children had a light breakfast together. She had orange juice and toast. He and the children went out to his VW and got in the car. He took the children to school every morning on his way to work. Elena had her own car, a van, which she would drive to her job as a county social worker. When he got in the car with the children, he remembered a report he needed that was still in the house, so he went back to look for it while the children waited in the car.

Smith: Did he tell you how long he was in the house while the children waited outside?

Dykes: Yes, he said it was only a few minutes—not more than ten or so. He couldn't find it right away.

Smith: Did he tell you if he saw Elena in the house then?

Dykes: Yes. He said she was still in the kitchen doing the dishes. It was about 7:45. He kissed her good-bye and drove off with the children. He said he never saw her alive again.

Washburn carefully described to Detective Dykes where he'd been that day—classes all morning with a half hour break in the middle of the morning, then meetings in the afternoon. He came home at about 5:30 p.m. and saw Elena's van in the driveway but didn't see her when he went inside. The children were not home either, so he called the sitter, who usually picked them up from school and took care of them until Elena came by to take them home. The children were still at the sitter's house. Elena had not picked them up. So Washburn went to get the children and brought them home. When Elena did not appear for dinner, he searched the house for her but did not look in the garage. Her sack lunch was still on the kitchen table, her car keys on the living room couch. He fried lamb chops for dinner and also served the children doughnuts and milk.

Smith: Did he say what he did with the lamb chop bones and the other trash?

Dykes: I asked him that and he said he put the bones and the doughnut bag and the milk carton in the trash basket in the kitchen.

Smith: Did you ask him if he emptied the trash later that evening?

Dykes: I did.

Smith: His answer?

Dykes: He said he did. Right after dinner.

The detective further testifies that Washburn said he got very worried as it grew late. Finally after midnight he decided to look in the garage, and that is when he found his wife.

Smith: Did you ever talk to him again?

Dykes: Yes, two days later he phoned me. He said he wanted to correct one thing in his statement. He then told me he remembers now he did not empty the trash in the garage.

O'Connor begins cross-examination. "Did you check out his alibis?"

Dykes: I did, and they all checked out for the most part.

O'Connor: As far as you could tell he told you the truth?

Dykes: Yes.

O'Connor: Did you arrest him?

Dykes: No, not then.

O'Connor: When did you arrest him?

The detective checks her report. "We finally arrested him April 12, 2007."

O'Connor: More than a year later?

Dykes: Yes.

O'Connor: Why did you wait so long?

Dykes: We wanted to be sure. We wanted a thorough investigation. After all, he had a good reputation. We wanted to check out all possible suspects.

O'Connor: Find any?

Dykes: No.

O'Connor: So that was why you arrested him—because you couldn't find any other suspects?

Smith: Objection.

Judge: Overruled. You may answer.

The detective glares at O'Connor. "Counselor, we arrested him because we had the evidence."

The next witness is Washburn's neighbor, Jim Martin. He testifies that on the morning of March 12, he saw Washburn driving down the street. He remembers the time, about ten o'clock. He remembers Washburn was going toward his (Washburn's) house. Martin said he was chatting with another neighbor, Oscar Ramirez, at the time.

O'Connor's brow is knitted as he begins his cross-examination. "Mr. Martin, I am confused. Didn't you testify before the grand jury in this case that you were not sure of the date, and not sure what time this happened?"

Martin: That is true, sir. I didn't remember then.

O'Connor: What made you change your testimony?

Martin: The police had me hypnotized last night to jog my memory. Now I remember.

O'Connor: Hypnotized?

Martin: That's right, sir.

O'Connor turns to the judge. "Your Honor, I object to this testimony. There are scientific studies to show a witness may not tell the truth under hypnosis. Testimony is not trustworthy if it has been brought on by hypnosis. I move that the testimony of this witness be stricken and the jury admonished to disregard it."

The judge ponders this motion for a moment, then says, "Objection overruled. Please proceed."

O'Connor grimaces but goes on. "How can you be so sure it was March 12?"

> **Martin**: Because that was the day I prepared my tax returns. I brought them in to my accountant after lunch, and he told me he'd have them ready the next day. So I went back the next day, signed them in his office, and mailed them on that day. That's why I'm sure.

The D.A. calls her final witness, Ray Deems. He testifies he is a private investigator for the All-Safe Insurance Company, which held a $5,500 policy on the life of Elena Washburn, with Tyrone Washburn as the beneficiary. Deems says his company wanted to find out if Washburn had killed Elena, because if he did, he would not be entitled to the money. About two months after the murder, Deems interviewed Washburn at his home.

D.A. Madeline Smith pauses noticeably before her next question. "What did he say?"

> **Deems**: At first, nothing different from the police reports.
>
> **Smith**: Then what?
>
> **Deems**: Then he said something I didn't expect.
>
> **Smith**: What was that?

Smith looks at the jury as if to make sure everyone is listening.

"Mr. Washburn said, 'I didn't look in the garage because I knew she was in there the whole time.'"

The D.A. lets the answer sink in before she sits down. You hear a buzz of conversation from the audience. "You may inquire, Mr. O'Connor," she says politely.

O'Connor stares at Deems before beginning cross-examination. "Were those his exact words?"

Deems: Something like that.

O'Connor: You took notes?

Deems: Didn't have to. (*He points to his head.*) It's all up here.

O'Connor: Is it up there word for word?

Deems: Not word for word, no.

O'Connor: You can't tell us verbatim?

Deems: No

O'Connor: Could he have said, "I didn't look in the garage because I was afraid she might be in there?"

Deems: I don't think so.

O'Connor: Is it possible he said it that way?

Deems: Anything's possible. But that's not how I remember it.

O'Connor: And this interview was over a year ago?

Deems: Yes.

O'Connor: You knew this was a very important statement.

Deems: Yes.

O'Connor: And how long after he said this did you report it to the police?

Deems: Don't know. Didn't keep track.

O'Connor: Three months?

There is a long pause. Deems doesn't answer.

O'Connor: Three months, Mr. Deems?

Deems: Well, yeah, about that.

O'Connor: So it wasn't important enough to report for three months?

Deems: Well—

O'Connor just waits.

Deems: Well, he said something like that. That's all I can say.

O'Connor is finished with cross-examination. The prosecution rests.

O'Connor opens the defense case by calling Elena's sister, Rosa Aguirre. She knew Tyrone for fifteen years. The family was very close. Tyrone was a loving husband and father.

O'Connor: Tell the jury his reputation for being a peaceful, nonviolent person.

Aguirre: Very good. He never once harmed my sister. He'd never dream of striking her. That wasn't like him. They loved each other—

She starts to cry.

Aguirre: I just know Tyrone never did this—

Smith: Objection, Your Honor. That's for the jury to decide.

Judge: Sustained. Just answer the question, madam, thank you.

Other witnesses also testify to Washburn's reputation as a peaceful, law-abiding person. The principal of Washburn's school testifies that he has known the Washburns for years, and they had a loving relationship.

A minister of the Unitarian church, the Reverend Guy Walton, testifies he attended a meeting with Washburn on the afternoon of March 12, during which Washburn did not appear nervous or upset about anything. He was his usual self.

Three witnesses testify they saw Elena alive during the day of March 12. A neighbor, Perla Francisco, says she saw Elena standing in the front doorway as Washburn and the children drove off in the morning. Another neighbor, Sara Mardikian, says she was looking out her window around noon, waiting for her daughter to come home from school, when she noticed Elena's van pull into the driveway. She also noticed the van leave about a half hour later.

The D.A. cross-examines. "Was she driving?"

Francisco: I guess so. She always does.

"Objection, Your Honor," the D.A. says. "She's guessing."

"Objection sustained," the judge replies. "Please do not guess, madam."

"Move to strike the last answer as to who was driving," the D.A. says, "and I ask the court to admonish the jury to disregard it."

"Motion granted," the judge says. He turns to you. "Ladies and gentlemen of the jury, the last answer as to whether Elena Washburn was driving the car is stricken from the record. You will disregard it and treat it as though you never heard it. Proceed."

Francisco: Well, I don't actually remember seeing the driver, but it was definitely her car.

Christina Ashcraft, a social worker who shares an office with Elena, testifies she saw her for a few minutes in the office in the early afternoon.

All the witnesses complain it is hard to remember the exact date because the events occurred so long ago.

Oscar Ramirez takes the stand. He testifies he was the one talking to Jim Martin in the morning when Washburn's car drove by. He can't recall the exact date, just that it was around March 12. However, he remembers the time being about 7:30 and not 10:00 as testified to by Martin.

Finally, O'Connor calls back Jim Martin as his last witness.

O'Connor: Mr. Martin, you recall you told this jury that you were able to remember you saw my client driving his VW toward his house on March 12 because you filed your tax return the next day, March 13?

Martin: That's right, sir.

O'Connor: Mr. Martin, I show you this document marked Exhibit 8. You recognize it?

Martin looks surprised. "Where did you get this?"

O'Connor: Please answer the question.

Martin: Wait a minute! How did you get hold of this? You have no right to this.

O'Connor: Your Honor, would you please direct the witness to answer?

Judge: You may answer, sir.

Martin: It's my tax return for last year, but how—

O'Connor: Tell the jury what date you wrote down as the filing date.

Martin: March 15.

O'Connor: Not March 13?

"No, sir." Martin looks confused. "I guess not."

The defense rests.

There are three possible verdicts in this case:

1. guilty of first-degree murder
2. guilty of second-degree murder
3. not guilty

WHAT IS YOUR VERDICT?

QUESTIONS FOR YOU TO CONSIDER

As you determine your verdict for this crime, here are some questions about the crime and the trial for you to think about.

1. What important aspect of a crime, although not a necessary element, was lacking in the prosecution's case?

2. What is the significance of finding the trash from dinner—the lamb chop bones, milk carton, and doughnut bag—next to the body?

3. What is the significance of finding all the doors and windows locked?

4. Do you think it was fair for the judge to allow the testimony of the neighbor, Jim Martin, after he had been hypnotized by the police to jog his memory?

5. Why do you think O'Connor did not put his client on the stand?

6. Why did the prosecution want to show that the necklace was the murder weapon?

7. Did the D.A. make a mistake by prosecuting solely on the theory that the victim was murdered at breakfast time?

8. An opening statement is customarily made by both attorneys at the beginning of trial. Why would O'Connor choose to waive it?

AUTHOR'S ANSWERS TO THE QUESTIONS

1. The prosecution's case lacked proof of any motive for Washburn to kill his wife. Although motive is not a required element of the crime and does not have to be shown, the defense could argue that the absence of motive was a circumstance tending to show Washburn was not guilty. He was a nonviolent, family-oriented husband and father who apparently loved Elena and their children. There was no reason shown by the prosecution why such a man would want to destroy his family.

2. The trash found near the body was important evidence because Washburn initially told the police he had fried lamb chops for dinner and soon afterward emptied the trash (including lamb chop bones, a doughnut bag, and a milk carton) into the trash can in the garage. If he did so, he certainly would have seen the body at that time, not after midnight as he told the detective. This would show he was lying as to when he found the body. The prosecutor could argue that he changed his original story about emptying the trash because he realized how damaging it was—a strong argument for conviction.

3. The significance of the locked doors and windows is that it reduces the possibility of a forced entry by a burglar or other strange intruder. It enhances the D.A.'s argument that the crime was an inside job.

4. In the past, testimony that resulted from the use of hypnosis by the police to jog the witness's memory was generally allowed. Under previously existing law, the judge's ruling to admit Jim Martin's testimony would not be considered unfair.

   Since then, however, the law has changed. Scholarly studies have led the courts to conclude that persons under hypnosis are likely to experience false memories; the subject tends to respond in the way he or she believes the hypnotist desires, and he or she is often unable to distinguish his or her true memories from pseudo memories.

5. We shall never know why O'Connor did not call Washburn to the stand to testify. That is a secret between them. However, one reason was probably that O'Connor was able to put everything before the jury that Washburn would have said, such as what he told the detective who interviewed him as well as the testimony of those who praised his character and supported his alibi. So O'Connor got what he wanted in evidence without subjecting his client to rigorous and possibly damaging cross-examination. He was also relying on the jury to follow the judge's instruction that they could not consider Washburn's failure to testify in reaching a verdict; in other words, they could not hold that against him in any way.

6. The prosecution would have liked to show that it was Elena's own necklace that was used to kill her because that too would indicate an inside job. But no murder weapon capable of strangulation was ever found. O'Connor's effective cross-examination of the investigator regarding the weakness of the necklace opened the way for him to argue that the murder weapon had to have been brought in from the outside, then removed.

7. The D.A. tried this case on the sole theory that the murder occurred in the morning while the children waited outside in the car. The coroner's opinion as to the time of death and the presence of Elena's sack lunch still in the kitchen and her car keys on the couch all supported this argument. But reliance on this theory alone turned out to be a mistake in strategy. It placed the D.A. in a weak position when defense witnesses testified they saw Elena alive that day. If the D.A. had not limited herself to this theory, she might have argued Washburn also had the chance to commit the murder when he came home at about 5:30. As it was, she was locked into her theory of the case.

8. The purpose of the opening statement is to give jurors a bird's-eye view of what the evidence will be. Sometimes a defense attorney

will defer his or her opening statement until the beginning of the defense case. In rare cases it may be waived altogether if the attorney is not sure what the evidence will show, whether certain witnesses will testify, or, if they do, what they will say. In such situations, it may be wiser not to give any opening statement at all rather than risk losing credibility with the jury because the evidence turns out to be different from what the attorney said it would be. You can be sure O'Connor knew exactly what he was doing when he waived it.

THE VERDICT

What was your verdict?

The real-life jury found the defendant not guilty.

There were simply too many unanswered questions for the jury to be convinced beyond a reasonable doubt. Why would Washburn want to kill Elena in the first place? How could the prosecution's sole theory—that the murder occurred at breakfast time—hold up when witnesses testified they saw her alive that day? Why did the police take so long to arrest him? In light of these lingering questions, the jury could not come to a decision to convict.

Did a Father Kidnap His Daughter?

STATE V. PAUL STORM AND GEORGE MCCLURE

Joan Storm, 24, is the daughter of Dr. Paul Storm, a prominent surgeon in San Diego. When her father and mother divorced, Joan lived with her mother but spent a lot of time with Dr. Storm and his new wife, often having dinner with them.

Joan became involved with a cult known as the Church of the Master, eventually joining the church but continuing to live at home. Dr. Storm objected to Joan's association with the cult and tried to persuade her, without success, that it was an evil organization. He told her he had made an investment in her life and did not want it wasted.

When Joan's interest in the cult became even stronger, Dr. Storm hired George McClure to deprogram Joan. On the pretext of taking Joan to a party, Storm and McClure took her to a private residence where they held her for over two weeks, subjecting her to videos and lectures about the danger of cults. When Joan was released on her promise to quit the church, she went to the D.A. and charged her father and McClure with kidnapping.

You wonder if you can convict a father of kidnapping his own daughter. But that is the charge, and you promised the grim-faced district attorney, John Harmon, that you would hear the evidence and be fair to the State.

Two defendants are on trial. One is Dr. Paul Storm, a prominent surgeon in your community. He is charged with kidnapping his 24-year-old daughter, Joan, in order to remove her from the Church of the Master. Dr. Storm, a distinguished, heavyset man, seems devastated by this strange situation. The codefendant is George McClure, whose name you recognize since he is known nationally for his work as a cult deprogrammer. You are still not sure what that means, but you will find out soon enough. McClure is also charged with kidnapping Joan Storm, but unlike Dr. Storm, he looks unperturbed. Squeezed between the two defendants at counsel table sits Peter Freitag, the attorney for both defendants—a smartly dressed fellow with an impeccably clipped mustache.

When Joan Storm takes the stand as the first witness for the prosecution, she does not look at her father. She turns and stares at the wall above the jury. She looks quiet and studious, and she blinks nervously.

"Why are you looking at the wall?" the D.A., Mr. Harmon, asks.

Joan Storm: Because I don't want to look at him.

Harmon: You mean your father, Dr. Storm?

Joan Storm: Yes.

Harmon: Do you love your father?

Joan Storm: I love my father.

Dr. Storm starts to get up and move toward her. "Oh, Joan," he murmurs. "Please." But his attorney restrains him.

"I love my father," Joan shouts. Already she is crying, her face bent over in her hands. "But I hate what he did to me!"

"Are you ready, Ms. Storm?" the judge asks.

She nods, sits up, and under the D.A.'s quiet direct examination, the story begins to unfold.

In 1997, at the time of this incident, Joan Storm was living with her mother, Martha Storm, and her 18-year-old brother, Jim. Her mother and father had been divorced for six years when he married his secretary, Arlene. Her father and his new wife lived in the same city. In 1995, Joan joined the Church of the Master and became a full-time student of the church, but she continued to live at home. Ever since Dr. Storm's marriage to Arlene, Joan had regularly visited her father and often had dinner with him and her stepmother. She had always been a quiet, rather withdrawn girl, dominated by her father.

Dr. Storm opposed her membership in the Church of the Master and often tried to persuade her to give it up, but she was not deterred. Nevertheless, the dinners at his home continued. The nature of their discussions changed, though. Joan began standing up to her father, would talk back to him, and would not back down as she had in the past whenever they had an argument. Her stepmother, Arlene, also tried to talk her out of being in the church.

Then one weekend when she came to Dr. Storm's house for dinner, her father and stepmother told her they were going to a surprise party for a friend of Arlene's. They all got in her father's Cadillac and drove about fifteen miles north of town, to a house she had never been to before. When they went inside, they brought her into a room where she saw two strong-looking women and George McClure, who was arranging a large TV screen for a video showing.

Harmon continues the questioning. "Did Mr. McClure say anything?"

Joan Storm: Right away he started making insults against the Church of the Master.

Harmon: What did he say?

Joan Storm: He said it was an evil cult, that I was a mindless idiot for associating with it.

Harmon: Did you respond?

Joan Storm: I was shocked.

Harmon: What did you do?

Joan Storm: I said, "I don't have to stand here and listen to this, I'm going."

Harmon: Did you try to leave?

Joan Storm: I tried to go out through the doorway, but the two women grabbed me and dragged me into the bedroom. I tried to get away. I screamed and yelled. I fought with them, but they held me down on the bed, the two of them on top of me. I was scared.

She starts to cry again. The judge hands her a box of tissues.

Harmon: Can you go on?

Joan Storm: Yes.

Harmon: What did you say to them?

Joan Storm: I said, "Why are you doing this to me?"

Harmon: Did they tell you why?

Joan Storm: They said I was a mindless robot, that George McClure was here to deprogram me.

Harmon: Had you ever heard that term *deprogram* before?

Joan Storm: I heard it once on a TV show. There was an episode about it.

Harmon: What did you understand it to mean?

Joan Storm: They were assuming I had been programmed by the church, and they were going to deprogram me.

Harmon: What happened next?

Joan Storm: One of the women, Madge, yelled in the next room, "Are you ready for her yet?" and Mr. McClure said, "Yes, bring her in."

Harmon: Did they take you into the film room?

Joan Storm: Yes, they sat me down under two big camera lights. My father was there, too. So was Arlene. George McClure sat next to me. He had a microphone in his hand.

Harmon: What did he say?

Joan Storm: He kept saying I was a mindless robot, over and over again, that I didn't know right from wrong, and that my father had hired him to stay with me until I could think straight.

Harmon: What did your father do?

Joan Storm: He was crying. I asked my father, "Why are you doing this to me?"

Harmon: What did he say?

Joan Storm: He said, "I'm protecting my investment."

Harmon: Did he say anything else?

Joan Storm: I tried to talk to him. I pleaded with him to help me, to let me go, but he just shook his head. Mr. McClure told him not to answer me, and he didn't. He just said, "I'm protecting my investment."

Harmon: How long did you remain in this room?

Joan Storm: All night until I went to bed.

Harmon: What did they do?

Joan Storm: They kept calling me names like robot; they kept saying I was a vegetable who couldn't think, that I was a zombie.

Ms. Storm tells how she was kept in the same house for several days. Sometimes McClure and the two women would lecture her; sometimes they showed her videos of other cults. The two women, Madge and Carla, guarded her all the time. When she went to the bathroom, they would go in with her. When she went to bed, one slept beside her while the other slept in front of the door, which was barricaded. She was never left alone. When Ms. Storm demonstrated no change in attitude after almost a week, McClure, Madge, and Carla seemed exasperated.

Harmon: What did Mr. McClure do?

Joan Storm: He would shake me and say, "Why are you being so difficult?"

Harmon: What else happened at these sessions?

Joan Storm: McClure and Madge and Carla and Arlene would all gather around me. They would start yelling at me and calling me these names, circling around me. Then McClure would read to me from some article criticizing the church. Then they would yell again. I was a nervous wreck.

Ms. Storm testifies that after a week of frustration, they brought in a new woman to help with the deprogramming. Her name was Anna Pettengill. She was a former member of the Church of the Master who had defected after several years and then started writing negative articles about the experience.

Harmon: What happened with Ms. Pettengill?

Joan Storm: She was supposed to be an expert on the Church of the Master and she tried to counsel me. But she didn't approve of Mr. McClure's methods of holding me prisoner, and we became friends. She said she would help me get free. She slept with me, and one night under the covers I wrote down my mother's phone number on a piece of cardboard. She whispered she'd call my mother and let her know where I was. We had to be very careful that Carla, who was sleeping by the door, wouldn't hear us.

Harmon: What happened to Ms. Pettengill?

Joan Storm: They fired her the next day because they felt she was too sympathetic, and she left.

Harmon: Did they ever suspect she was going to seek help for you?

Joan Storm: They must have suspected something because the next day they packed up and drove me to a new house several miles away. I couldn't tell where I was because they blindfolded me on the way during the drive over there.

Harmon: And did the same things happen at the new place?

Joan Storm: Yes.

Harmon: Did you see your father there?

Joan Storm: Oh, yes. He would come in from time to time to ask Mr. McClure how it was going. He still didn't talk to me because Mr. McClure asked him not to.

Harmon: Did you ever find a way to be released?

Joan Storm: I decided to fake it. I told them I was convinced that they were right. I wouldn't go back to the church if they let me go. So my father and Mr. McClure said they would let me go if I signed a general release form saying I was there of my own free will and that they hadn't done anything wrong.

Harmon: And did you sign such a statement?

Joan Storm: Yes. They drove me to the office of our family attorney, Marvin Felder.

Harmon: The statement you signed—were you truly in agreement with it?

Joan Storm: No. I just did it to get free, and that's what happened. They let me go.

Harmon: And are you still a member of the Church of the Master?

Joan Storm: Yes. A full-time student.

The D.A. turns to Defense Attorney Peter Freitag. "Your witness."

When Freitag rises to begin his cross-examination, Dr. Storm stops him and whispers something in his ear. Freitag nods reassuringly and pats the doctor on the shoulder.

Freitag: When you had dinner with your father and stepmother before this incident, did you tell them about the church?

Joan Storm: Sometimes.

Freitag: Did you ever tell them your church taught you to exteriorize yourself?

Harmon: Objection. Irrelevant.

Judge: Overruled.

Joan Storm: Yes.

Freitag: What does *exteriorize* mean?

Joan Storm: To be able to perceive yourself as a spiritual being.

Freitag: Did you tell them it meant you could get out of your own body and walk beside yourself?

Joan Storm: Not quite like that, no.

Freitag: Something like that?

Joan Storm: Well, yes.

Freitag: What else did you say?

Joan Storm: I said I was not just a body, but I had a soul, too.

Freitag: Did you tell them you could see auras of light emanating from your brother Jimmy?

Joan Storm: Yes.

Freitag: And did they seem concerned?

Joan Storm: Yes.

Freitag: They were concerned for your mental health, right?

Joan Storm: Yes, but—

Freitag: And didn't your father tell you he loved you and wanted to save you from destroying yourself?

Joan Storm: Yes. He was worried about me.

Freitag: And he tried to get you to read articles about the church, didn't he, hoping it would open your mind to the truth?

Joan Storm: Yes.

Freitag: Did you read them?

Joan Storm: No.

Freitag: Why not?

Joan Storm: Because I didn't believe them. I could see for myself what the truth was.

Freitag: Did your father tell you specifically why he didn't want you in the Church of the Master?

Harmon: Objection. Irrelevant.

Judge: Sustained.

Freitag: But Your Honor, are you denying us the right to show why Dr. Storm opposed his daughter's association with this cult?

Judge: Counsel, the benefits or detriments of that organization are not at issue. We are here to decide one thing only—whether the defendants kidnapped this woman. Nothing else.

Defense counsel asks to approach the bench, and there is a heated discussion benchside between the attorneys and the judge that you cannot hear. When they come back, Mr. Freitag looks as if he lost the argument. Finally, cross-examination resumes.

Freitag: What did your father mean when he said he was protecting his investment?

Joan Storm: He always saw everything in terms of money. I'm sure he meant he had spent a lot of money on me, and he didn't want to see it wasted.

Freitag picks up a paper from the clerk's desk and walks to the witness stand. "I show you a document marked Exhibit 5. Recognize it?"

Joan Storm: Yes.

Freitag: Is that your signature on the bottom?

Joan Storm: Yes.

Freitag: You read it carefully before you signed it?

Joan Storm: Yes.

Freitag: So you knew exactly what you were signing?

Joan Storm: Yes.

Freitag: You knew it could be used in a court of law?

Joan Storm: Well, I'm not a lawyer, but—

Freitag: In fact, you signed it under the penalty of perjury?

Joan Storm: That's what it says.

Freitag: You're not in the habit of signing false declarations, are you?

Joan Storm: No.

Freitag: This is the document you referred to in your direct examination?

Joan Storm: Yes.

Freitag: Are you telling this jury that what you said in this paper was not true?

Joan Storm: Yes.

Freitag: You lied under the penalty of perjury?

Joan Storm: Yes, but I only did it to—

Freitag: Please answer the question! Did you lie under the penalty of perjury?

Joan Storm: Yes, I had to.

Freitag: So you committed perjury?

Joan Storm: Yes.

Freitag: Your Honor, I move this document, Exhibit 5, into evidence and ask that it be reviewed by the jury at this time.

Judge: Motion granted. Exhibit 5 received in evidence. May be passed to the jury.

The paper is passed to the jury. You read it to yourself. It says:

General Release

I, Joan Storm, hereby declare that beginning September 21, 1997, my father, Paul Storm, MD, and my stepmother, Arlene Storm, together with others acting on their behalf, attempted to and did deprogram me from my beliefs in the Church of the Master. I believe their actions were justified, that I was not acting with my own free will when I was involved with the church, and now believe the church was a cult and in fact brainwashed me.

NOW THEREFORE, I hereby release all claims and causes of action, civil or criminal, I may have had against my father and all others acting on his behalf. I further acknowledge that I have not suffered any mental or physical harm by reason of this deprogramming although I first thought I might. I now realize all actions taken by my father and stepmother and George McClure were for my own good and it is now my intention to disassociate myself from the Church of the Master. I further assert my father committed no crime to my knowledge in attempting to deprogram me. I went with him of my own free will.

I declare under penalty of perjury the foregoing is true and correct.

Executed October 8, 1997

Signed, Joan Storm

When the jurors finish reading the exhibit, the defense attorney turns back to Ms. Storm.

Freitag: Isn't it true you left the house on at least two occasions the second week of your stay to go shopping?

Joan Storm: Under guard, yes.

Freitag: With Madge and Carla?

Joan Storm: Yes.

Freitag: Where did you go?

Joan Storm: Nordstrom's department store.

Freitag: Did you request to go?

Joan Storm: Yes, I needed cosmetics, underwear. Arlene brought me clothes but I needed personal things.

Freitag: And they granted your request?

Joan Storm: Under strict guard, yes.

Freitag: And you went to various counters and made purchases in the store?

Joan Storm: Yes.

Freitag: And you talked to clerks?

Joan Storm: I bought things.

Freitag: Did you ever ask them for help?

Joan Storm: No.

Freitag: Ever cry out for help? Ever say, "Help me, I'm being held prisoner." Anything like that?

Joan Storm: No, I was too frightened.

Freitag: Ever make any attempt at all to escape?

Joan Storm: No, I couldn't.

Freitag: Why not? You weren't handcuffed were you?

Joan Storm: No, but, well, I was afraid to.

Freitag: Afraid of what? You were among all those people in the store who would have helped you, isn't that true?

Joan Storm: Yes, but I was afraid no one would believe me, and if I didn't make it, Mr. McClure and his staff would do worse things to me. I'd had enough mental abuse.

Freitag: The truth is you could have run away if you wanted to, right?

Joan Storm: No. Besides, I had no money. Where would I go?

Freitag: The truth is, you really were there of your own free will, right?

Joan Storm: No, that's not the truth. I was held prisoner!

Freitag: The truth is, your mother put you up to making this charge, didn't she?

Joan Storm: Absolutely not.

Freitag: Does your mother hate your father?

Joan Storm: Yes, but what's that got to do with it?

Freitag: Didn't you talk to your mother about it after you got home?

Joan Storm: Of course.

Freitag: And didn't she encourage you to go to the D.A.?

Joan Storm: It was my idea.

Freitag: After talking to her?

Joan Storm: Well—

Freitag: Please answer my question.

Harmon: Objection, Your Honor. He's badgering the witness.

Judge: Sustained. Give the witness a chance to answer, Mr. Freitag.

Freitag: (*Speaking quietly now*) I will give you all the time you need, Ms. Storm. Please answer the question. Did you go to the D.A. after talking to your mother about it? You may answer yes or no.

Joan Storm: (*Pauses*) Yes.

Freitag: And she did suggest it, didn't she?

Joan Storm is on the verge of tears. She pauses again. "Yes."

Freitag. Thank you, no further questions.

She is crying again as she steps down. She slumps down in the back next to her mother. She is sobbing noticeably as she buries her head in her mother's shoulder.

Now Jimmy Storm, Joan's teenage brother, is called as a witness. His straight blonde hair reaches down to his shoulders. You notice his father shake his head disapprovingly as Jimmy takes the stand. He testifies that when Joan did not show up at home, he phoned their father to find out where she was. Their father replied, "I'm saving her life. She's a zombie and I'm going to have her deprogrammed."

Anna Pettengill is called to testify as to her role in the deprogramming. She corroborates Joan Storm's testimony as to what happened while she was there.

Harmon: Why did they call you?

Pettengill: They said they had a stupid girl who was acting very stubborn. They wanted me to work with her.

Harmon: Was she stupid?

Pettengill: No.

Harmon: What happened?

Pettengill: I told them right away I didn't believe in any restraints. But they held her prisoner. Mr. McClure was very forceful, and he tried to split her from her mother.

Harmon: What did he say about her mother?

Pettengill: He said her mother was evil because she allowed her to be in the church, and as long as Joan stayed in it, she was evil, too.

Ms. Pettengill testifies that after a few days, McClure asked her to leave because she was too easy on Joan. He wanted her to be more aggressive. She describes how she and Joan hid under the covers so Joan could pass her a note without the guard noticing. Since Joan did not have any paper or a pencil, she used a piece of cardboard from her pantyhose and a tube of lipstick to write her mother's phone number. As soon as Ms. Pettengill got away, she called Joan's mother to tell her where Joan was. She did not know they would move Joan the next day.

It is time to adjourn. When you go home that night, you do not turn on the news or read the local section of the paper for fear you might see something about the case.

On the second morning of the trial, the D.A. announces he has one final witness, Dr. Saul Cordero. Dr. Cordero claims he is a psychiatrist who has testified as to people's states of mind in many cases. He says he examined Joan Storm and gave her psychological testing. He has reviewed the police reports and read the transcript of Joan Storm's testimony on the stand.

Harmon: Are you familiar, Doctor, with the portion of Ms. Storm's testimony regarding her visits to the department store during her captivity?

Cordero: I have reviewed it, yes.

Harmon: I refer to those times in which it appears she had an opportunity to cry for help or even escape, but failed to do so. Remember that?

Cordero: Yes.

Harmon: Do you have an opinion, based on your training and experience, why she did not do so?

Freitag is on his feet. "Objection, Your Honor. Beyond the scope of his expertise. They tried to use this same kind of evidence in the Patty Hearst case as to why she didn't try to escape from her captors, but the judge wouldn't allow it. It's too farfetched."

Judge: Objection overruled. The doctor may respond.

Cordero: Joan Storm's behavior can be medically explained. It is perfectly understandable. She was suffering from what is popularly known as Stockholm Syndrome, a name that comes from a case in which a group of hostages in Stockholm became totally under the control of their captors to the point that they no longer wished to escape. Here Joan had been imprisoned for several weeks. They watched her every move—sleeping with her, even going to the bathroom with her. It was all a tremendous shock to her. As a result, she lost the power to make decisions. In my opinion, she lost the will and initiative to seek help, and that is why she didn't do so.

Harmon: Your witness.

Freitag wastes no time getting to the point. "You examined Joan Storm eight months after the incident, right?"

Cordero: Yes, about that.

Freitag: And you mean to tell this jury you can read her mind and tell us what she was thinking eight months before?

Cordero: I can try.

Freitag: You can try. Are you a mindreader?

Cordero: I wouldn't call it that.

Freitag: No further questions.

Dr. Cordero is excused, and the prosecution rests.

The defense begins its case by calling the lawyer Marvin Felder. He testifies he is Joan Storm's attorney, and that she came into the office with her father and stepmother one afternoon in October 1997 and asked to speak with him alone. Dr. Storm and Arlene Storm waited outside. Ms. Storm told him she had been away for several weeks with her father and others acting on his behalf in a deprogramming session, and she now wished to sign a document about her experience.

Freitag: You are aware of course of the attorney-client privilege?

Felder: I am.

Freitag: You realize of course that since you are Joan Storm's attorney, she has the right to exercise that privilege and prevent you from disclosing any part of that conversation?

Felder: I am very aware of that. Yes. And so is she.

Freitag: And has she authorized you to speak by waiving the attorney-client privilege?

Felder: She has. As to that conversation relating to the general release only. Nothing else.

Freitag shows the witness Exhibit 5, the general release. "You saw her sign this?"

Felder: I did.

Freitag: She signed it of her own free will?

Felder: She said so then.

Freitag: She knew what she was doing?

Felder: Yes.

Freitag: (*To the D.A.*) Your witness.

Harmon: Did she say anything else about this document?

Felder: Not at that time.

Harmon: At any other time?

Felder: I am not authorized to say.

Harmon: She ever tell you whether she'd been kidnapped?

Felder: I am not authorized to say.

The defense rests without calling either defendant to the stand. The D.A. goes back to talk with Joan Storm, still seated in the last row with her mother. Then the D.A. announces he has no rebuttal.

The attorneys begin their closing arguments. The D.A. cautions you not to let your sympathy for the father-daughter relationship keep you from performing your duty to follow the law.

Freitag counters by holding up the general release. He has it blown up on a screen so you can read it easily. "She swears in this document that Dr.

Storm and George McClure did nothing wrong. Under penalty of perjury. Read it for yourselves—"

Suddenly a voice from the back of the courtroom calls out: "One moment please, Your Honor." It is Joan Storm, standing up. She walks forward to D.A. Harmon and whispers in his ear.

He looks surprised. He turns to the judge. "Your Honor, a new development. Evidence has just come to my attention of which I was not previously aware."

"Objection, Your Honor," Freitag shouts. "The testimony is finished. Both sides have rested. It's too late."

A hubbub ensues between the two attorneys, and the judge calls a recess. When you return, you see Marvin Felder already seated on the stand.

Freitag: Let the record show the defense objects strenuously to this procedure. It is highly improper, unheard of—

Judge. Your objection is noted, Mr. Freitag. The district attorney may proceed.

Harmon: Mr. Felder, do you have new evidence to disclose to the jury?

Felder: I do.

Harmon: Why did you wait until now to reveal it?

Felder: Because under the attorney-client privilege with Joan Storm, I was not privileged to disclose this information until now.

He holds up a piece of paper.

Harmon: Please explain.

Felder: Ms. Storm authorized me to disclose our conversation with regard to the general release. She signed it out of sympathy for her father. She was confused as to whether she wanted him to be convicted. She told me she still loved him.

Harmon: Yes?

Felder: But she didn't authorize me to testify as to what happened two days later. Until now.

Harmon: What was that?

Felder: Two days later she returned to my office alone. She asked me to draft another document. This is it.

Harmon: Please read it to the jury.

Felder: "I, Joan Storm, hereby declare that the general release signed October 8, 1997, is void and of no consequence. It was signed under pressure and coercion. I declare under penalty of perjury this memorandum is true and correct. October 10, 1997. Signed, Joan Storm."

Harmon: (*To Freitag*) You may examine.

Freitag: What made her change her mind about waiving the privilege?

Felder: It was when she heard you making your closing argument. You were scoring points with the jury with that general release. She realized the trial would be a sham unless the truth came out.

Freitag: Anything else?

Felder: Well, yes.

Freitag: What was it?

Felder: She just learned her father cut her out of his will.

You are asked to decide whether or not Paul Storm and George McClure are guilty or not guilty of kidnapping.

WHAT IS YOUR VERDICT?

QUESTIONS FOR YOU TO CONSIDER

As you determine your verdict for this crime, here are some questions about the crime and the trial for you to think about.

1. Does a juror have the power to refuse to follow the law and vote not guilty, even if the facts support a guilty verdict?

2. What is the real reason the judge did not allow the defense to show the alleged detriments of the Church of the Master—that is, why Dr. Storm believed the church was ruining his daughter's life?

3. Should a person be allowed to commit a crime such as kidnapping when the motive is to save someone's life or well-being?

4. By signing a general release, did Joan Storm actually release her father and George McClure from all criminal liability?

5. Did the D.A. make a tactical error in prosecuting Dr. Storm and George McClure together?

AUTHOR'S ANSWERS TO THE QUESTIONS

1. The evidence against Dr. Storm and George McClure supported a guilty verdict under the law. They had no legal defense of justification or necessity. However, if a juror believes—as some jurors did in this case—that the law of kidnapping should not apply to Dr. Storm under these circumstances, or feels such sympathy for him that he or she cannot convict, then the juror has the power to vote for acquittal. This act of voting contrary to the law is called *jury nullification.*

   Jurors take an oath to follow the law. Existing law, set forth by the Supreme Court in the 1985 case of *Sparf v. United States,* says juries must follow the law as explained by the judge. But while jurors do not have the right to disregard the law, they do have the power to do so. Of course, jurors are not told of this power because courts do not wish to encourage it.

   However, there are those in the legal community, including lawyers and judges, who believe judges should inform juries of their inherent right to decide not only the facts of a case but also whether the law itself is inappropriate in this particular set of circumstances. This group is still in the minority.

   If a jury does nullify the law and votes not guilty where the facts support a guilty verdict under the law, the verdict cannot be appealed by the State no matter how strong the evidence. This is why prosecutors must take care to select jurors who will follow the law.

2. The real reason the judge did not allow defense counsel to show the alleged detriments of the Church of the Master, or all the reasons why Dr. Storm believed he had to save his daughter, is that such evidence would have turned the entire proceeding into a trial against the church. Expert witnesses then would have been called to testify on both sides as to the good or bad of the organization. The jury's attention would have been diverted from the real issue—whether

or not a kidnapping occurred. The consumption of time and the danger of confusing the jury were factors that persuaded the judge to exclude such evidence.

3. In rare cases, the court might excuse the commission of a crime such as kidnapping if it is necessary to save someone's life or prevent great bodily harm. This is called *defense of necessity*. For example, the threat of attack by other inmates on a prisoner was recognized by the California court as a possible justification for escape. However, in order for a defendant to use the defense of necessity, the physical danger must be imminent. In this case, the judge ruled that the alleged danger to Joan Storm's life was too remote to allow the defense.

4. Even if Joan Storm really intended to release her father and McClure from all criminal liability, she lacked the power to do so. The victim of a crime is not the one who decides if someone should be prosecuted. That decision lies with the D.A., who prosecutes on behalf of the people or the State. Of course, the D.A. may consider the victim's wishes, but the D.A. has the last word regardless of the victim's position.

5. See the discussion under "The Verdict."

THE VERDICT

What was your verdict?

The real-life case resulted in a hung jury as to both defendants.

By prosecuting Dr. Storm and George McClure together, the D.A. probably made a tactical error. The difficulty of persuading a jury to convict a father of kidnapping his own daughter was simply too great for the prosecution to overcome. McClure benefited from being associated in the same case. The sympathy jurors felt for Dr. Storm extended to McClure because they were tried together. Had McClure been tried separately, the State would have had a better chance of convicting him.

The case was never tried again. The D.A. had the option to go forward with a retrial, but chose not to do so.

They All Look Alike

STATE V. GARY BUCKLES

Lorraine Eberhardt, 20, a striking beauty with long blonde hair, lived with another young woman, Priscilla Mackey, on the second floor of a large apartment complex. On the night of the alleged crime, Ms. Eberhardt was awakened in the dark by a man kneeling beside her; he was wearing a white turtleneck sweater. As soon as she awoke, he pulled the sweater over his head to hide his face. Lorraine fought him as he attempted to rape her, and he eventually ran off when she screamed. When the police came, the only description Lorraine could give of her attacker was that he was a young black man wearing a white sweater.

On the witness stand, Lorraine positively identifies the defendant, Gary Buckles, a young African American male, as the one who tried to rape her. Lorraine testifies she had never seen Buckles before the attempted rape, but her roommate Priscilla tells the jury that one afternoon before the incident, she and Lorraine were walking from the swimming pool in their bathing suits when she noticed Buckles staring at Lorraine from his window. Lorraine admits that when she first talked to the police, she doubted that she could identify the attacker. When the defense attorney inquires further, Lorraine makes a reply that turns out to be the crucial evidence in the case.

This case charges Gary Buckles, a young black man, with the attempted rape of a white woman, and you have been selected as a juror after long and vigorous questioning by the defense attorney.

"Do you have any feelings about black people that would prevent you from being fair?" "Do you think blacks as a group tend to commit more crimes of violence than whites?" "Would you find this charge less offensive if the defendant were white?" "Do you have any black friends?" "What would you say if you were in a social group and someone made a racial slur against blacks?"

Finally sworn in and seated in the jury box, you look again at the defendant, Gary Buckles. He is a young African American man, slim and handsome, and well-dressed in a conservative business suit. His attorney, Marina Phelps, is also black. Judging by her appearance, she must be just out of law school, and she sits quietly, almost meekly, at her counsel table, waiting for the district attorney to call his first witness.

The burly D.A., Michael Linneman, looks very sure of himself. He has been strutting across the room like a man in charge. In a booming voice, he calls Lorraine Eberhardt to the stand.

She makes a stunning appearance in a tight-fitting dress. You watch her take her place slowly on the witness stand, like a queen. Lorraine Eberhardt. You remember the D.A. gave her name as the victim of the attempted rape. You look at her. You look at the defendant.

Ms. Eberhardt testifies she is 20 years old and lives with her roommate Priscilla Mackey in a two-bedroom apartment on the second floor of a large complex. She says she works as a restaurant hostess and that on the evening in question, she came home around midnight. Feeling tired, she went to bed at about 1:00 a.m. but was awakened an hour later by Priscilla and her boyfriend, Troy. They insisted she get up and join them for some Chinese food and beer they had just brought home. She put on her robe, went into the living room, and joined in sharing the food and beer.

Lorraine claims she went back to bed at about 4:00 a.m. Her bedroom is to one side of the living room, and Ms. Mackey's bedroom is to the other. The living room has a sliding glass door opening onto the balcony that overlooks a large patio below. Lorraine's bedroom window looks out on the balcony. Just before going to bed, she locked the window and the front door, but did not lock the sliding glass door. Since Priscilla and Troy were still up, she presumed they would take care of that.

Lorraine was wearing a T-shirt and underwear when she got in bed; she fell asleep immediately. She was awakened suddenly to find a man kneeling beside her in her bed, his face above her. He was wearing a white turtle-neck sweater, which he pulled up over his head as soon as she awoke. He had his head down, and he was grabbing at her underwear, trying to pull it off. She pushed him away, fighting him. For some reason—she does not know why—she did not scream right away. The man tried to kiss her with the sweater pulled up partly over his face. A violent struggle ensued while he kept tugging at her underwear. She was pushing him and kicking him. She kept telling him to go away. When he tried to lie on top of her, she screamed.

He ran out immediately and she could hear him climbing over the balcony. Priscilla and Troy, asleep in Priscilla's room, rushed in and learned what had happened. They ran out to the living room and noticed the sliding glass door open. They looked over the balcony but saw nothing in the dim light. Troy called the police, who arrived fifteen minutes later. The police asked Lorraine to describe her attacker, but all she could say was that he was a young black man wearing a white sweater.

Now D.A. Linneman moves to a different line of questioning.

Linneman: Had you ever seen this man before?

Eberhardt: Not to my knowledge.

Linneman: Did you authorize him to enter your apartment?

Eberhardt: Of course not.

Linneman: Did he touch any part of your body with his hands?

Eberhardt: Yes. He touched my breast, my left breast.

Linneman: Did you authorize him to touch your left breast?

Eberhardt: Absolutely not.

Linneman: Were you afraid?

Eberhardt: Yes. Of course.

Linneman: Did he ever get your underwear off?

Eberhardt: No.

Linneman: Did he ever kiss you?

Eberhardt: No.

Linneman: I want you to look around this courtroom. Do you see the man who tried to rape you?

Eberhardt: Yes. (*She points to the defendant.*) That's him.

Linneman: You're positive?

Eberhardt: Yes.

Obviously pleased with the answers, the D.A. smiles at Phelps as if to say, "See if you can get around that."

Phelps keeps her seat, checking her notes. She is a soft-spoken young woman and seems a bit intimidated by the task, but she is determined as she asks her questions. "You were very tired that morning before you went to bed?"

Eberhardt: Yes.

Phelps: How much beer did you have before you went back to bed?

Eberhardt: A couple cans.

Phelps: How many?

Eberhardt: Two or three. I didn't count.

Phelps: Could have been four?

Linneman: Objection! The witness says she doesn't know.

Judge: Sustained.

Phelps: Did you take anything else?

Eberhardt: I ate some Chinese food.

Phelps: Anything else?

Eberhardt: What do you mean?

Phelps: Did you take anything else—any other chemicals—into your system?

Eberhardt: Well, yes, we smoked.

Phelps: Smoked what?

Eberhardt: Well, yeah, we had some pot.

Phelps: Marijuana?

Eberhardt: Yes.

Phelps: Who did?

Eberhardt: Me and Troy. He gave me some.

Phelps: How did you smoke it?

Eberhardt: Through a pipe—it's called a bong.

Phelps: Tell the jury how it works.

Eberhardt: Well, it's a long vertical pipe, a water pipe. You put the marijuana in the bowl of the bong, then you light it up and inhale it.

Phelps nods as if she is very interested in how it works. "And how much did you have?"

Eberhardt: One or two hits.

Phelps: A hit? What's a hit? Tell the jury what a hit is.

Eberhardt: Each bowl is called a hit.

Phelps: And you had some hits along with the beer?

Eberhardt: Yes.

Phelps: Did you have lipstick on that night?

Eberhardt: Yes.

Phelps: Rouge?

Eberhardt: Just a little.

Phelps: Did you wash your makeup off before you went to bed?

Eberhardt: No, but it doesn't stay on that long.

Under further cross-examination, Ms. Eberhardt testifies that the bedroom was quite dark, the curtains drawn. She says that during the struggle, she may have scratched her attacker with her fingernails.

Phelps: How long was he in the room?

Eberhardt: I didn't look at my watch. It seemed like a long time. Maybe ten minutes.

Phelps: What happened for ten minutes?

Eberhardt: I was fighting him off.

Phelps: Ms. Eberhardt, isn't it true you saw him only through the opening in the sweater?

Eberhardt: No, I saw his whole face when I woke up. Then he pulled his sweater up.

Phelps walks up to the witness with a report. "I show you this police report. I ask you to read it to yourself to see if it refreshes your memory."

The witness reads it over and then says, "I've read it."

Phelps: Does it refresh your memory that you told the officer you saw the man only through the opening in the sweater?

Eberhardt: I might have said that. I was very upset. But I'm sure it's him.

Now the D.A. calls Lorraine's roommate, Priscilla Mackey. She corroborates Lorraine's account of how the two women, along with Troy, had Chinese food and beer that night. She admits that Lorraine smoked marijuana, but does not think it affected her. In Priscilla's opinion, Lorraine was not intoxicated, just tired. Priscilla says she did not smoke marijuana because she does not believe in using it. She and Troy were asleep when she heard Lorraine's screams. They rushed into Lorraine's bedroom and found her crying and hysterical. They ran to the balcony to see if they could see anyone, but the man was gone. She says she feels guilty now because she had forgotten to lock the sliding glass door.

The D.A. marches over to the defendant, stands directly behind him, and points dramatically at Buckles.

Linneman: You ever see this man before that night?

Mackey: Yes.

Linneman: Where did you see him?

Mackey: He'd just moved into our apartment complex. His apartment is just across the patio from ours, on the ground floor. Lorraine's never seen him, but I have.

Linneman: How's that?

Mackey: A few nights before this happened, Lorraine and I were walking from the pool back to our place. We were in bathing suits. I saw him standing at his window.

Linneman: What did you notice?

Mackey: Lorraine was walking ahead of me, because she was in a hurry. I noticed him looking at her. He kept watching her as she walked by. She didn't notice him, but I did.

Linneman: You are sure this is the same man you saw staring at her?

Mackey: I'm positive.

Again, the defense attorney remains seated as she conducts cross-examination. "Ms. Mackey, isn't it a fact you suspected my client was the one who tried to rape her right from the start?"

Mackey: Sure. Soon as she told me it was a black guy.

Phelps: And when the police came, you told them right away you were sure he was the one?

Mackey: Yes. He lived right there. The way he looked at her and all. He fit the description.

Phelps: The description being of a young black man?

Mackey: Yes.

Officer Joe Sampino testifies he was the first officer on the scene. He says his partner, Officer Ramon Gonzales, stayed on the ground checking out the complex for possible suspects while Sampino went upstairs to Lorraine's apartment. He took the account from her as best he could although she was still crying from fright.

He inspected the apartment for point of entry and concluded the attacker must have noticed the open sliding door, climbed up the red brick pillar to the balcony, and entered through the sliding door. He must have exited the same way. When Priscilla told him she believed it was the new neighbor across the patio, he directed Officer Gonzales over the walkie-talkie to go to the defendant's front door and ask him to come outside to a point where he and Lorraine could see him from her window. Officer Sampino explains that he wanted to see if Lorraine could make a positive identification. He and Lorraine stood at the window and watched Officer Gonzales ring the doorbell, then bang on the door, and wait for the defendant. After a long wait they saw the door open, Gonzales gesture, and the defendant, dressed in a bathrobe, step outside. As soon as he did, Lorraine gasped and said, "That's him!" Sampino immediately directed Gonzales over the radio to place the defendant under arrest.

Linneman is beaming. "Your witness, Counsel," he says to Phelps, who checks her notes carefully before she begins.

Phelps: Officer, did Ms. Eberhardt tell you that she saw the man only through the opening in the sweater?

Sampino: May I check my notes?

Phelps: Please.

Sampino: (*After checking his report*) Yes, she did.

Phelps: Did she have any doubt about her ability to identify him?

Sampino: At first she did.

Phelps: What do you mean?

Sampino: When I told her what we were going to do—that I was going to have him step outside his door to see if she could identify him—she hesitated. She said she didn't think she could. But as soon as she saw him, there was no problem.

Phelps: How far was he?

Sampino: Oh, about seventy feet.

Phelps: Was it light yet?

Sampino: It was dawn, just getting light.

Phelps: And he was standing right beside the officer in uniform?

Sampino: Yes.

Phelps pauses. She stands up for the first time and takes a deep breath. She is more aggressive now and seems more sure of herself.

Phelps: You know what a lineup is, Officer?

Sampino: Of course.

Phelps: You've conducted lineups, haven't you?

Sampino: Yes, many, many times.

Phelps: Officer Sampino, please tell the jury what a lineup is.

Linneman: Objection! Irrelevant.

Judge: Overruled. You may answer.

Sampino: A lineup is where we have the suspect stand in line with five or six others of similar appearance, and the witness is asked to look them over carefully and see if he or she can pick out the one who did it.

Phelps: And that is done to make sure you have a positive identification, right, Officer?

Sampino: Yes.

Phelps: And it's done to make sure there is no improper suggestion made by the police to the witness that might influence her?

Sampino: That's true.

Phelps: It's done in the interest of fairness, right, Officer? You wouldn't want to arrest an innocent man.

Sampino: That's right.

Phelps sits down again. There is a long pause. "This wasn't a lineup, was it, Officer?"

The officer looks at the D.A. "No," he says, "I guess not."

The last witness for the prosecution is the arresting officer, Ramon Gonzales. He testifies that after placing the defendant under arrest, he received instructions over the radio from Officer Sampino to search the defendant's apartment for a white turtleneck sweater. Gonzales says he advised Buckles of his rights, then asked him if he had a white turtleneck sweater. Buckles said he did and led the officer back to his closet, where he dug out a sweater. Gonzales immediately confiscated it for evidence. It was white and had a turtleneck. Gonzales took it outside, looking up at the window where Lorraine and Officer Sampino were still watching. He held the sweater up so they could see it, and Lorraine made a circle with her thumb and forefinger as if to say, "That's it."

The D.A. takes out a white sweater from a bag on his table, has it marked by the clerk, and shows it to Officer Gonzales. The officer identifies it as the one he took.

Later, at Sampino's request, Gonzales says he went up to the crime scene to dust for fingerprints. He found none of evidentiary value. The identifiable prints belonged to Lorraine, Priscilla, Troy, and one of Lorraine's boyfriends. The others were too smudged for identification.

Phelps now takes over. "Did you inspect the sweater?"

Gonzales: Visually, yes.

Phelps: Was it wet, as if it had just been washed?

Gonzales: No.

Phelps: See any stains on it, like lipstick or rouge?

Gonzales: I didn't see any.

Phelps: Any blonde hairs on it?

Gonzales: No.

Phelps picks up the sweater, which is still lying on the witness stand in front of the officer.

Phelps: You placed this sweater in the police evidence locker?

Gonzales: Yes.

Phelps: No one else touched it?

Gonzales: No.

Phelps: What about Mr. Buckles? See any scratches on him?

Gonzales: I didn't see any.

Phelps: Did you look him over carefully?

Gonzales: Yes.

Phelps looks satisfied.

The prosecution, having no further witnesses, rests its case.

Gary Buckles takes the stand in his defense. He answers the questions in a quiet, straightforward manner. He says he is a sophomore at State College and has a part-time job as a waiter. About two weeks before the incident, he moved into the apartment on the ground floor with another student, Max Friedrich. They each have their own bedroom. That evening, Buckles says he came home from work at about 10:00 p.m., decided to go to a late movie by himself, and went out again. He came home at about 1:00 a.m., read for a while, went to bed, and did not leave his room until he was awakened in the morning by the police banging on his door.

He acknowledges that he owns a white turtleneck sweater, which he keeps in his closet, but says he had not worn it in a while and gave it to the officer upon request. He does not know Lorraine Eberhardt but admits he saw her once when she walked by his apartment in her bathing suit, and he thought she was very attractive. He denies entering her apartment that morning and trying to rape her. He says he is willing to submit to a lie detector test.

Phelps asks him to face the jury, look the jurors in the eye, and tell them if he did it. He turns and faces you directly.

"I didn't do it," he says quietly. "I swear it. I didn't try to rape that girl. No way. You got to believe me."

The D.A. begins his cross-examination. He has a faint smirk on his face, as if he does not believe anything Buckles says.

Linneman: What went through your mind the first time you saw Lorraine Eberhardt?

Buckles: I don't understand.

Linneman: You understand all right, Mr. Buckles. A few days before this incident, you watched her walk by in her bathing suit. What were you thinking then?

Buckles: I thought she was very nice.

Linneman: She looked good to you?

Buckles: Well, yes.

Linneman: You looked at her?

Buckles: Yes. I don't deny that.

Linneman: You found her attractive?

Buckles: She's attractive, yes.

Linneman: You felt an attraction for her?

Buckles: I wouldn't say that.

Linneman: Isn't it a fact you went back inside and made a comment about her to your roommate?

Buckles: I may have.

Linneman: Didn't you make a comment to him about the size of her breasts?

Buckles: I don't remember what I said.

Linneman: Didn't you say to him, "Man, you should have seen the size of the boobs that just went by." Didn't you say that?

Buckles: I may have.

Linneman: And didn't you make a gesture with your hands describing her breasts? Didn't you do that also?

Buckles: That's possible.

Linneman: And didn't you, thereafter, form the specific intent in your mind to make sexual contact with her?

Buckles: Look, I thought she had a real nice figure. But that's it. I didn't break into her place that night, and I didn't try to rape her.

Max Friedrich, Buckles's roommate, now testifies he has been Buckles's friend for four years. They met in high school, went to the same college, then agreed to move in together in the new apartment off campus. They have separate bedrooms with one adjoining bathroom. Friedrich says he arrived home that night at about eleven o'clock, after the library closed. Buckles was not home. Friedrich went to bed and did not wake up until early the next morning, when he heard the police at the door.

He says he had seen Buckles earlier that evening, and he was not wearing his white sweater. He did not hear his roommate come in or go out. He remembers Buckles commenting to him about Lorraine Eberhardt's breast size, but they often made such comments to each other about girls who walked by in bathing suits, and he thought nothing of Buckles's remark. He is well-acquainted with Buckles's reputation for character traits of nonviolence and honesty, and he has never known Buckles to be a violent person.

Next Phelps calls Mary McElhaney, a criminologist for the police department. She states that she was trained at the University of California at Berkeley in the science of detecting various types of stains on cloth. She examined the sweater removed from the defendant's residence under a microscope and found no evidence of lipstick or rouge. She found several strands of hair on the sweater and compared them with several hairs removed from the head of Lorraine Eberhardt, but they did not match.

Phelps is poker-faced as she continues her questioning. "At my request did you also examine the red brick pillars supporting the balcony of the victim's residence?"

McElhaney: I did.

Phelps: And did you find any similar substance on the sweater?

McElhaney: I did not.

Phelps: In your opinion, would particles of the red brick pillar be likely to adhere to such a sweater worn by a person climbing up or down those pillars?

D.A.: Objection! Speculation!

Judge: Sustained. You may not answer.

As her last witness, Phelps recalls Lorraine Eberhardt, who has been sitting in the audience. The D.A. looks surprised.

Phelps: Ma'am, you remember when the officer, Officer Sampino, asked you if you thought you could identify the man who tried to rape you?

Eberhardt: Yes, we were by the window.

Phelps: Do you remember what you said?

Eberhardt: No, I don't remember what I said. I was so upset.

Phelps: I appreciate that, ma'am. But Officer Sampino has testified in this courtroom that you said you didn't think you could identify the man. Is that true?

Eberhardt: If he testified to it, I must have said it. But what's the difference? I was able to identify him when I saw him.

Phelps: Yes, I realize that, ma'am, but could you tell us why you didn't think you could identify him?

Eberhardt: Well, because—

She looks at the D.A.

Phelps: Please look at me, Ms. Eberhardt. Please tell me and tell this jury. Why didn't you think you could identify the man who attacked you?

Eberhardt: Well, because—

Phelps: Because why?

Eberhardt: Well, because—all blacks look alike to me.

Phelps stares at the witness. There is dead silence. The D.A. is grimly shaking his head.

You are asked to reach a verdict of either guilty of attempted rape or not guilty.

WHAT IS YOUR VERDICT?

QUESTIONS FOR YOU TO CONSIDER

As you determine your verdict for this crime, here are some questions about the crime and the trial for you to think about.

1. What was the single most damaging testimony to the prosecution's case?

2. Did the police use a fair identification procedure when they asked the victim to see if she could identify the suspect at a distance of seventy feet while he stood beside a uniformed police officer?

3. Why didn't the police wait to conduct a lineup at the station before they arrested the defendant?

4. What was the significance of the absence of any lipstick, rouge, hair, or particles from the red brick pillars on the sweater belonging to the defendant?

5. In the cross-examination of Lorraine Eberhardt as to her ingestion of marijuana and beer, did the defense attorney miss a good opportunity to raise a doubt as to Lorraine's identification?

6. Since the defense attorney had the criminologist available as an expert witness, should she have used the criminologist to testify as to the effect of marijuana and beer?

7. Was the intruder an experienced burglar?

AUTHOR'S ANSWERS TO THE QUESTIONS

1. The statement of six words by the victim, Lorraine Eberhardt—"All blacks look alike to me"—was the single most damaging piece of evidence to the prosecution's case. In a close case of identification, that statement was devastating to the prosecution.

2. The identification procedure was not entirely fair. Legal experts agree that showing a suspect singly beside a police officer for the victim to identify has an element of suggestiveness. Despite its potential unfairness, the courts will generally balance the interests involved, allowing the evidence of such an identification to be presented to the jury and letting the jurors decide for themselves whether it is reliable. However, if the identification is shown to be so unfair as to deprive the defendant of due process of law, the judge will suppress it altogether. To some jurors, Eberhardt's cross-racial identification of a black man under these circumstances would raise a serious question as to its reliability.

3. There is no question that a lineup at the police station, where Buckles would stand in a line of five or six men whose appearance is similar to his, would be a fairer identification procedure for him rather than the single-person showup. But generally the law does not require the police to wait for a lineup. That is because any possible unfairness is considered offset by the likelihood that a prompt identification within a short time after the crime will be more accurate than a belated identification days or weeks later. Furthermore, the police say, and the courts agree, that it is as important to free an innocent person promptly from suspicion as it is to identify a guilty person.

4. Since the victim did not wash her makeup off before going to bed, she probably still had some lipstick and blush on her face at the time of the attack. She had long, blonde hair, which might have brushed against the sweater in the struggle. The most likely point of entry and

exit was by way of the red brick pillars leading to the balcony, which the intruder would have had to rub against in climbing up and down. The lack of any such marks on the sweater was a strong point in the defense case.

5. Yes, Lorraine's admission that she smoked marijuana and drank beer just before retiring left her vulnerable to attack on cross-examination. The reason one inhales marijuana through a bong like the one she used is to obtain a stronger effect than from a marijuana cigarette. Mixing marijuana and beer together affects one's powers of observation. Phelps, lacking experience, missed an opportunity to cast doubt on Lorraine's identification when she failed to emphasize this point.

6. Yes, Phelps should have used the criminologist to testify as to scientific studies that show the effect on the mind caused by mixing marijuana and alcohol.

7. Probably not. The man who broke into the apartment and attacked Lorraine Eberhardt wore a white sweater. An experienced burglar or sophisticated criminal would probably not dress like that. Burglars tend to wear dark clothing, which aids in concealment and is less likely to pick up telltale evidence.

THE VERDICT

What was your verdict?

The real-life jury found the defendant not guilty.

The Missing Murder Victim

STATE V. MARLON BOYD

The charge is murder in the first degree. From the opening statements, you know that this case is based almost entirely on circumstantial evidence since there are no witnesses to the killing, and the body of the alleged victim has never been found.

"You will be challenged," the district attorney says. "But common sense will lead you to the only reasonable verdict—guilty of murder in the first degree." You know this D.A., Jack Drum, from the newspapers. He is a veteran of many battles in the courtroom. He has white hair, which he keeps combing back with his fingers, and thick glasses, which he is continually taking off and putting on. He is the D.A., not just a deputy. The fact that he has taken this case is an indication of its prominence.

He announces, "I call Jane Stribling as our first witness."

Jane Stribling walks gingerly into the room like a gazelle. She is an attractive young woman with long, dark blonde hair carefully styled. As she approaches the witness stand, she exudes vitality with every step. Ms. Stribling testifies that she is 21 years old and lives in the city with her parents, but previously had her own apartment. She teaches ballet at a studio and looks like a dancer. Jane Stribling is indeed a striking picture on the witness stand. But would a man kill because he could not have her?

The D.A. walks to the defense table, nods toward the defendant, Marlon Boyd, and asks, "Ms. Stribling, do you know this man?"

Stribling: I do.

Marlon Boyd sits staring at the witness. He is a tall young man in his twenties, robust, with bushy light brown hair. Adam Fields, his attorney, sits beside him. The district attorney speaks again: "Your Honor, may the record show the witness has identified the defendant?"

The judge replies, "The record may so show."

The D.A. continues to question Ms. Stribling. "How did you know him?"

Stribling: We went together once. Then he moved in with me. In my apartment.

Drum: And how did that arrangement work out?

Stribling: Well, we just didn't get along very well. Too many arguments, too many conflicts—bad feelings. It came to a point where I finally asked him to leave.

Drum: Did you tell him why?

Stribling: I told him I thought we should both start seeing other people.

Drum: And did he leave?

Stribling: Not right away. I had to get a restraining order from the court. The police came and removed him.

Drum: Was he angry?

Stribling: Very. He kept saying how much we really loved each other and I was being stupid to break up.

Drum: Did you love him?

Stribling: I thought I did at first. But that didn't last.

Drum: What was his occupation?

Stribling: Marlon was into computers. He was a computer programmer.

Drum: Did he have another job on the side?

Stribling: Oh, that. Yes. Marlon was a reserve police officer. He kept his police equipment in the apartment. Uniforms and stuff.

Drum: Guns?

Stribling: Yes, he had several guns. Two revolvers. Three rifles. But then he got dismissed—

"Objection!" The defense attorney, Adam Fields, is on his feet. "It's irrelevant!"

Judge: Sustained.

Fields: Motion to strike!

Judge: Granted.

Now the judge turns to the jury: "Ladies and gentlemen, the last statement of the witness—not the entire statement, just the last part about what happened to the defendant—that part is stricken from the record. Please strike it from your minds. Treat it as though you never heard it. You may proceed, Counsel."

The D.A. continues to question Ms. Stribling. "What happened after the defendant moved out?"

Stribling: I started going with Carl. Carl Steinmetz.

Drum: Did you hear from the defendant anymore?

Stribling: Oh yes. He kept calling me. He said he knew all about me going with Carl and he knew where Carl lived.

Drum: How long did you continue dating Carl?

Stribling: Well, that wasn't working out either, so I stopped seeing Carl.

Drum: Then what happened?

Stribling: That's when I met Max Vereno. We hit it off right away, Max and me, and we started dating. I really liked Max. Oh, God—

Tears come to Ms. Stribling's eyes. She stops speaking. The bailiff hands her a tissue and she wipes her eyes. "I'm sorry, Your Honor."

"Are you all right?" the judge asks. He is an elderly man, short and rotund with a shock of silver hair. "Can you continue?"

"Thank you. I'm all right."

D.A. Drum resumes. "Now, during the time when you were going with Max Vereno, wasn't there an incident with the defendant?

Stribling: Yes. One day Marlon came to see me at the studio. He said he wanted to get back with me.

Drum: How did you respond?

Stribling: I told him I was going with Max now. He insisted on talking to me about it. He said he would wait for me after work so we could talk. So after my last class, he was waiting for me and we went to a coffee shop nearby.

Drum: And?

Stribling: He talked a lot, went on and on. Basically said he had to get back with me. He sounded desperate—even started crying. He said he was the kind of guy who—that he couldn't accept the breakup and had to have me back in his life. He said he knew who Max was and Max was no good for me.

Drum: What did you say?

Stribling: I told him he was wrong. I said I was sorry but I was in love with someone else now. I got up to leave and then he grabbed my arm and pulled me back in the seat.

Drum: What did you do then?

Stribling: I was scared. He was so determined. I knew I had to get out of there. So I pulled away and shouted, "Let me go!" and ran out to my car. He came after me. I tried to get in my car but he was right behind me and blocked me from getting in—

Ms. Stribling is talking very fast, too fast for the court reporter. The judge has to slow her down so the reporter can take her testimony.

Drum: What did he say?

Stribling: There were tears in his eyes. He kept saying how much he loved me and needed me and he knew that I loved him. Wouldn't I give him another chance?

Drum: What was your reaction?

Stribling: I told him he had to understand. It was over between us. There was someone else. "Please let me go," I said.

Drum: Did he let you go?

Stribling: Yes. Finally. He stepped back and let me in the car. Then he said, "You'll never see me again." Then as I drove off he shouted at me.

Drum: What was it he shouted?

Stribling: He said, "You'll be sorry."

Drum: Did you ever see him again? I mean before this trial.

Stribling: Yes. Once when Max and I were driving up into my driveway. It was nighttime—morning, actually—and Marlon drove by and honked and waved at us.

Drum: He'd been following you?

Fields: Objection! Leading.

Judge: Sustained.

Drum: What time was this?

Stribling: About 2:00 a.m.

Drum: Are you sure it was Marlon Boyd who waved at you?

Stribling: Positive.

Drum: Did Max stay with you that night?

Stribling: Yes, until about 4:00 a.m. Then he had to go.

Drum: Did you make any plans before he left?

Stribling: Yes. He was going to pick me up after work the next day. We were going to drive up to Hollywood.

Drum: So what happened the next day after work?

Stribling: He never showed.

Drum: Did you hear from him?

Stribling: No. He didn't call.

Drum: Had he ever missed an appointment before?

Stribling: No, never.

Drum: Did you ever see Max Vereno again?

Stribling: No.

She is obviously near tears again.

Drum: Have you any idea what happened to him?

Stribling: I certainly do have an idea—

Fields: Objection!

Judge: Sustained!

Suddenly Ms. Stribling stands up and shouts at the defendant, "What did you do to him? Where is he? What in God's name did you do to him?"

Fields: Objection, Your Honor. The witness is out of order!

Judge: Sustained! Ms. Stribling, please contain yourself. Your conduct is entirely out of order!

Ms. Stribling sits back down, puts her head in her hands on the table, and begins to sob uncontrollably.

"We are in recess," the judge says. "Ladies and gentlemen, please remember not to discuss this incident or anything else about the case."

Fields: Move for mistrial, Your Honor.

Judge: Motion denied.

When court resumes later, Jane Stribling is back on the stand, sitting quietly, her eyes reddened. As soon as the jury is seated, she speaks. "I am sorry, Your Honor. I know I was out of order. I want to apologize to the jury for my behavior."

The judge nods. He turns to the jury. "Ladies and gentlemen of the jury, those last emotional statements by the witness to the defendant are stricken from the record. Strike them from your minds. Do not let them affect your verdict in any way. Please proceed, Counsel."

Jack Drum, the D.A., resumes. "Just a few more questions, Ms. Stribling. I know this is hard on you. What did you do when Mr. Vereno failed to appear?"

Stribling: I called his home. He was living with his mother and dad. His mother answered. She said he had not returned home. She was very worried. I called his office where he worked at the Robson plant. Nothing. Just a recorded message. So we called the police.

Drum: And?

Stribling: A police officer came over. I told him the same things I said here. And then, since I knew the route Max always took from his work to my place, I went with the officer to show him the route.

Drum: See anything?

Stribling: Yes. On Sharon Road. Parked on the side. Max's car.

Drum: What did you do when you saw that?

Stribling: We got out and went to check it out. There was nobody inside. The door was unlocked. Keys in the ignition. Other than that, nothing unusual.

Drum: No sign of any struggle, or of violence? Anything like that?

Stribling: No, nothing. We looked all around. Nothing. So that was that. The officer did some paperwork and then dropped me off at home. Starting the next day, I just kept searching by myself. All around the city. I drove around for days. Nothing.

Drum: Did there come a time when you made a phone call to Marlon Boyd?

Stribling: Yes.

Drum: Tell us about that.

Stribling: It was the police department's idea. They came to my place and recorded the conversation. They pretty much told me what to say.

The D.A. then asks permission to play the taped conversation between Ms. Stribling and the defendant. The tape is played. You hear some preliminary comments and then the following exchange:

Stribling: I've been thinking about you and wondering how you're doing. Max has deserted me. I don't see him anymore.

Boyd: Yeah, he just wanted one thing from you, and then when he got it he didn't want anything more to do with you. Why don't you give him a call?

Stribling: I'm not going to call him if he doesn't call me. I will just find someone else.

Boyd: You can always find somebody new. But call him. Go ahead. I guarantee you'll be surprised.

Stribling: What do you mean? Surprised about what?

Boyd: Go ahead. Just call him. His parents will answer and you'll be surprised.

Stribling: What, are you matchmaking for me or something? Why are you so interested in me calling him?

Boyd: You'll see. You'll be surprised and then you are really going to hate me.

Stribling: Why will I hate you? Did you do something to him?

Boyd: Call him. That's all. Just call him, baby. If you call him you're in for a big surprise. Then you are really going to get pissed off.

Stribling: I don't know what you mean.

The tape is marked for identification and admitted into evidence. The judge tells the jurors they will have the tape and the tape player in the jury room if they wish to hear it during deliberations.

The defense attorney, Adam Fields, begins cross-examination. "How long did you live with Marlon Boyd?"

Stribling: About four months.

Fields: You were in love with him, weren't you?

Stribling: I thought I was.

Fields: You told him you loved him?

Stribling: Yes.

FIELDS: Many times?

STRIBLING: Well, you know, yes.

FIELDS: You were intimate with Marlon Boyd?

STRIBLING: Uh, well—

FIELDS: You had a sexual—

DRUM: Objection!

JUDGE: Sustained!

FIELDS: Your Honor, this is a serious case. They have charged my client with first-degree murder. The jury is entitled to know every facet of this relationship.

JUDGE: Don't argue with the court, Counsel. The objection is sustained.

FIELDS: Thank you, Your Honor. Now Ms. Stribling, how did you meet Marlon Boyd?

DRUM: Objection! Irrelevant!

JUDGE: Overruled. The witness may answer.

STRIBLING: Well, he was going with one of the other dance instructors. He came to the studio one night and we got into a conversation. Then he asked me out.

FIELDS: And while you were living with him and telling him how much you loved him, you meant what you said?

STRIBLING: I thought I did.

FIELDS: You didn't lie to him about that?

Stribling: No. I didn't lie.

Fields: And when you were going with Carl Steinmetz, you told him you loved him, right?

Stribling: Well, yes, I guess I did.

Fields: And you meant what you said to Carl Steinmetz?

Stribling: At the time, yes.

Fields: As to Max Vereno, did you live with him?

Stribling: Not exactly. He didn't want that arrangement. He would stay over some nights but we didn't really live together.

Fields: And, of course, you told Max Vereno you loved him?

Stribling: Yes. I did. I really was in love with Max.

Fields: Now, you don't know, of your own knowledge, where Max Vereno is right now, do you?

Stribling: No, but—

Fields: You've answered the question, thank you. And you don't know, of your own knowledge, if Marlon Boyd ever caused Max Vereno any harm?

Stribling: It's obvious he did.

Fields: Objection, Your Honor—the witness is not responsive.

Judge: Sustained.

Fields: Motion to strike her last statement.

Judge: Motion granted. Again, ladies and gentlemen of the jury, I will direct you to disregard the witness's last statement and strike it from your minds. Ms. Stribling, please answer the question without any personal comment. Proceed, Counsel.

Fields: I will ask you again, Ms. Stribling. You may answer yes or no. Do you know of your own knowledge if Marlon Boyd ever did any harm whatsoever to Max Vereno?

Stribling: No, I don't.

Fields: You never saw Marlon Boyd strike Max Vereno, did you?

Stribling: No, I didn't.

Fields: And you never heard of anyone who said they saw Marlon Boyd kill Max Vereno, did you?

Stribling: No.

Fields: And for all you know, Max Vereno could still be alive, living in some other state or country, isn't that true?

Drum: Objection! Calls for speculation.

Judge: Sustained.

Fields: All right, I'll ask it this way. Do you know where Max Vereno is right now?

Stribling: No.

Fields: Do you know if Max Vereno is dead or alive?

Stribling: Well, I—

Fields: Please answer the question, Ms. Stribling. Do you know if Max Vereno is dead or alive? Yes or no.

The witness turns to the judge. "Do I have to answer, Your Honor?"

Judge: You do.

Stribling: Well, no. I don't know.

Fields: Thank you. No further questions.

The D.A. next calls Max Vereno Sr. to the stand. "You are the father of Max Vereno Jr.?"

Vereno Sr.: I am, yes.

Drum: Prior to his disappearance, where did your son live?

Vereno Sr.: He lived with us, my wife and me.

Drum: A few days before his disappearance, did you receive a phone call from a stranger?

Vereno Sr.: Yes. A man called. Said he knew Max from high school and wanted to talk with him.

Drum: Did he give you his name?

Vereno Sr.: He just said his name was Peter. I asked him for his phone number so Max could call him back but he said he was living in a camper and didn't have a phone.

Drum: Did he ask any questions?

Vereno Sr.: Yes, he wanted to know where Max worked, so I told him.

Drum: Any other questions?

Vereno Sr.: Yes. He did ask me one question I thought was strange.

Drum: What was that?

Vereno Sr.: Well, he wanted to know what kind of car Max drove.

Drum: Did you tell him?

Vereno Sr.: I realize now I shouldn't have. But I figured this was an old friend so I told him Max had an old BMW.

Drum: Did Max's car have any mechanical problems that might cause it to stop along the road?

Vereno Sr.: No.

Drum: Did your son have any reason whatsoever to suddenly leave the San Diego area?

Fields: Objection! Speculation.

Judge: Sustained!

Drum: All right, I'll ask it this way. As far as you know, did he have any such reason?

Vereno Sr.: No. He liked his life here. His job, his new girlfriend. He was thinking of asking Jane to marry him.

Drum: Did you and your wife initiate a search for your son?

Vereno Sr.: Yes. We did everything we could.

Drum: Ever find anything?

Vereno Sr.: Nothing. Not a clue.

Drum: Thank you. Your witness, Counsel.

Fields: Are you still searching?

Vereno Sr.: We keep trying. Any new ideas, we just keep trying.

Fields: You haven't given up hope?

Vereno Sr.: No. My wife and I, we will never lose hope. That's all we have. We can only hope he's still alive somewhere.

Fields: You believe it's possible he's still alive?

Drum: Objection, Your Honor. Anything is possible.

Judge: Sustained.

Fields: No further questions.

Eve Williston is called to the stand. Mrs. Williston is a middle-aged woman and is employed at the Robson plant.

Drum: Did you know Max Vereno?

Williston: Yes.

Drum: How did you know him?

Williston: We worked in the same office. His cubicle was next to mine.

Drum: What kind of work did you do?

Williston: We were both technical writers. The company makes airplane parts. Max and I would try to put the engineer's instructions into plain English.

Drum: How long did you know Mr. Vereno?

Williston: Oh, let's see, must have been about three years. He came after I was there for a while.

Drum: I want to ask you about the evening of August 29, 2006. Do you remember it?

Williston: I certainly do, yes.

Drum: How do you remember it?

Williston: It's the last time I saw Max.

Drum: Tell the jury the circumstances under which you saw Max Vereno that evening.

Williston: Yes. Well—(*She turns to face the jury.*) At the end of the day, we—

Drum: What time was that?

Williston: It was close to five. We always leave then. Max and I walked out to our cars in the parking lot together.

Drum: Did you see him drive off?

Williston: Yes, he left ahead of me.

Drum: Did you notice anything unusual as you were driving out of the lot?

Williston: Well, as I was driving out, I noticed a police car parked by the fence outside the lot. When Max drove out, I noticed the police car start up and appear to go in the same direction.

Drum: Could you see who was driving the police vehicle?

Williston: Just someone who looked like a police officer. That's all I can say.

Drum: Can you describe the person?

Williston: Well, um, it was a man, I can say that much, but nothing more. I only had a brief glimpse.

Drum: What happened next?

Williston: Well, I had to stop at the 7-11 to get some milk. Then as I was driving along Sharon Road, I noticed up ahead the police car on the shoulder of the road and Max's car parked in front of it.

Drum: Was it still light out?

Williston: Oh, yes. It was still sunny. I could see very clearly.

Drum: What did you see as you approached?

Williston: As I got closer, I could see the officer talking to Max next to Max's car.

Drum: Was Max outside his car?

Williston: Yes, he was standing outside and—and the officer—the officer was next to him. Oh, I'm so nervous.

Drum: Mrs. Williston, just take it easy. We just want to know the facts. Take your time and just—um, do you need a glass of water?

Williston: No, I'm fine. I'm sorry. This is such a strange experience for me.

Drum: All right, just relax. You're doing fine. Now, if you would, please tell the jury and this court what you saw.

Williston: Yes, yes, well, I slowed down and thought to myself, "Oh, poor Max, what did he do?" Max must be in some kind of trouble. Then as I got closer I saw Max walking toward the police car with the officer behind him.

Drum: Did the officer have anything in his hand?

Williston: It did look like he was holding something, yes, but I couldn't tell what it was.

Drum: What happened next?

Williston: Well, it all happened so quickly. The officer opened the door and sort of guided Max into the backseat.

Drum: What do you mean "guided"? Tell us exactly what you saw.

Williston: Well, I thought—this is what I thought—I thought the officer sort of pushed Max into the police car.

Drum: Then what happened?

Williston: I didn't know what to do. Should I stop and try to talk to the officer and ask him what was wrong? But then I thought, no, that would just embarrass Max, and so I drove on.

Drum: Did you ever see Max Vereno again?

Williston: No, bless his soul, no I didn't.

Drum: Now, Mrs. Williston, do you think you could identify the man in the police uniform you saw that night if you saw him again?

Williston: No, I can't. I wish I could, but no, the police officers at the station showed me some pictures, but I couldn't pick him out.

The D.A. turns to the judge. "Your Honor, I would like to ask the defendant to stand for the purpose of my next question."

Judge: What's the purpose?

Drum: To see if the witness can make any kind of identification from the size and build of the defendant.

Fields: Objection! She's already said she can't identify him.

Judge: Objection overruled. I will ask the defendant to stand, please.

Fields: This is highly improper, Your Honor!

Judge: The court has ruled, Counsel. The defendant will kindly stand.

You watch the defendant slowly stand and face the witness.

Drum: Now, Mrs. Williston, I ask you to look at the defendant who is now standing. I know you told us you cannot identify him as the one you saw. But can you tell us this: looking at his size and build, is it similar to the size and build of the man you saw dressed as an officer?

Williston: Similar, yes. It is similar. That's all I can say for sure.

Drum: Thank you. Your witness, Counsel.

Fields begins his cross-examination. "Mrs. Williston, I will ask you a straight question. You can answer it yes or no. Is my client the man you saw in a police uniform with Max Vereno that evening? Yes or no."

Williston: I can't say.

Fields: You say you thought the officer pushed Mr. Vereno?

Williston: Yes.

Fields: You're not sure?

Williston: Well, it looked like he kind of pushed him.

Fields: Hard? A hard push?

Williston: No, I can't say that.

Fields: You saw the officer touch him?

Williston: I thought he did. Very briefly.

Fields: You're not positive?

Williston: All I can say is what I thought.

Fields: You're not sure?

Drum: Objection! She's answered the question.

Judge: Sustained.

Fields: All right, Mrs. Williston, I know you're trying your best. It's hard to remember, isn't it?

Williston: Well, some details it's hard to be absolutely sure about.

Fields: Now, did you ever see the officer strike Mr. Vereno?

Williston: No.

Fields: Ever see the officer harm or injure Mr. Vereno in any way?

Williston: No.

Fields: See anything whatsoever of a violent nature?

Williston: No, nothing like that.

Fields: See Mr. Vereno protesting or resisting in any way?

Williston: No. No, I didn't.

Fields: For all you know, Mr. Vereno entered the police car voluntarily...

Drum: Objection! Speculation!

Judge: Sustained.

Fields: Thank you, Mrs. Williston. Nothing further, Your Honor.

The D.A. is not finished. He returns to the podium. "Mrs. Williston, you told us you saw something in the officer's hand?"

Williston: Yes, sir.

Drum: Which hand?

Williston: It was his right hand.

Drum: How was he holding it?

Williston: Oh, about waist high. In front of him.

Drum: Did he seem to be pointing it?

Williston: Mmm, can't say.

Drum: Did he seem to be pointing it like a gun?

Fields: Objection!

Judge: Sustained!

Drum: How large was this object?

Williston: All I know is he looked like he was holding something.

Drum: Was it a rifle?

Williston: Wasn't that big, no.

Drum: Thank you. You may step down.

As Mrs. Williston steps down from the witness stand, she hesitates and turns to the judge. "Your Honor, I'm sorry, but I just remembered something."

Judge: You may resume the stand.

Williston: (*Back in the witness seat*) Mr. Fields asked me if I thought Max voluntarily entered the police car.

Judge: Yes, and I sustained the objection.

Williston: Yes, but it reminded me of something I think I should mention.

Judge: Proceed.

Fields: Objection, Your Honor. The witness has been excused. No one has recalled her to the stand.

Judge: Objection overruled. We want to get at the truth here. Proceed, Mrs. Williston. You are reminded you are still under oath.

Williston: Yes, sir. Well, I remember that as the officer was walking behind Max to the police car, Max had his hands raised slightly.

Judge: Counsel may examine.

Drum: Show us, Mrs. Williston. Show us how Max had his hands raised.

Mrs. Williston stands and raises both hands at her side. "It was like this."

Drum: Your Honor, may the record show the witness has raised both hands at her side?

Fields: Only as high as her shoulders. No higher.

Judge: Yes. The record may so show.

Drum: Thank you, that's all. Your witness, Counsel.

Fields looks disturbed, then asks her, "And you just now remembered this?"

Williston: Yes, sir. I wasn't asked about it before. But when you asked if it was voluntary, well, that sort of jogged my memory.

Fields: You never told anyone about it before this moment?

Williston: No, I guess I didn't.

Fields: He didn't raise his hands above his head, did he?

Williston: No.

Fields: Just up to his shoulders?

Williston: That's right.

Fields: Could have been a little lower than his shoulders?

Williston: Could have been. I'm not sure of the height.

Fields: Did Max seem frightened?

Williston: I can't say. I couldn't tell.

Fields: Nothing further.

Drum: Our next witness will be Officer Davis.

The officer takes the stand in civilian clothes. He looks tired. He identifies himself as Wilson Davis, a police officer with twenty years of experience.

Drum: You were on duty on the night of August 29, 2006?

Davis: Yes, sir.

Drum: Describe your duties, please, on that evening.

Davis: I was one of the officers on patrol on the beat near the Robson Corporation plant. I work the shift between 15:00 hours and midnight.

Drum: In fact, you worked it last night, right?

Davis: Yes, sir.

Drum: How many officers were covering that beat on that evening?

Davis: There were six of us. We cover an assigned area.

Drum: Do you know all of them?

Davis: Yes, sir.

Drum: And on that evening around 5:00 p.m., did you notice something unusual?

Davis: Yes, sir. I was alone in my police car patrolling Sharon Road when I noticed another police car parked on the shoulder of the road ahead. As I approached, that car pulled out and drove off ahead of me. I came up on the car on the left and started to pass it to see if it was someone I knew.

Drum: Did you look at the driver?

Davis: Yes, sir.

Drum: Did you recognize him as one of the officers on your beat?

Davis: No, I didn't. I though he must be from another beat.

Drum: How far were you from the driver of that car?

Davis: We were driving parallel to each other for a few seconds until I passed him. I would say we were about twenty feet apart.

Drum: Did he look at you?

Davis: Only for an instant. Then he kept looking straight ahead. I didn't make too much of it because sometimes officers from another beat have to come into ours.

Drum: He was in uniform?

Davis: Yes, sir.

Drum: Nothing else unusual about him?

Davis: No, sir. Just that I thought I knew most of the officers and I didn't recognize him. I figured he was new on the force.

Drum: Do you think you'd recognize him if you saw him today?

Davis: Yes, sir.

Drum: I ask you to do this, Officer Davis. Would you look around this room? Take your time. Take a good look, and see if you recognize the man who was driving that police car that evening.

The witness looks about the courtroom, studying everyone. Everyone is silent.

Davis: All right.

Drum: Do you recognize the person?

Davis: Yes, sir. He is the defendant sitting right there (*pointing*).

Drum: Are you sure?

Davis: Yes, sir.

Drum: Your Honor, may the record show the witness has identified the defendant?

JUDGE: The record may so show.

DRUM: No further questions.

Fields rises for cross-examination. "As the driver of your car, you were looking at the road ahead?"

DAVIS: Yes, sir. Except when I turned to see him.

FIELDS: How long did you observe the other driver?

DAVIS: Oh, a few seconds.

FIELDS: I will ask you to do this, Officer. Will you just turn your head to the right and turn back again, just as you did that evening. In the same amount of time.

DRUM: Objection!

JUDGE: Overruled.

FIELDS: You remember looking over at the other driver, don't you?

DAVIS: Yes, sir.

FIELDS: All right, then go ahead and show us just how you did that.

He takes out a watch and looks at it.

DAVIS: Yes, sir.

He turns, looks, and turns back again.

FIELDS: That's how long you looked?

DAVIS: Yes, sir.

Fields: Your Honor, may the record show the witness's head was turned for less than a second?

Judge: About a second. All right, proceed.

Fields: What did you notice about the driver?

Davis: Looked like he had a police uniform on. He had high cheekbones, a pointed chin, dark eyes, kind of bushy hair, brownish.

You look at the defendant again. He has all those features, except his hair is close cut.

Fields: How far were you away from him?

Davis: About twenty feet.

Fields: Your window was up on the right?

Davis: Yes.

Fields: His also?

Davis: I can't be sure.

Fields: And on the basis of a one-second look, you are able to make this identification two months later?

Davis: Yes, sir. He looked at me, too. I had a full-face look.

Fields: Did he have a hat on?

Davis: A hat? Well, to be honest—

Fields: Yes, please be honest.

Davis: To be honest, I can't say for sure.

Fields: Let me ask you this, Officer. Since that evening, have you seen photographs of the defendant at the police station?

Davis: Yes, sir.

Fields: And photographs of him in the newspapers and on TV?

Davis: Yes, sir, I have.

Fields: And isn't your identification here in this courtroom based on those pictures?

Davis: No, sir.

Fields: Isn't your ID influenced and affected by the photos you saw?

Davis: No, sir.

Fields: Nothing further.

District Attorney Drum questions the witness. "Tell the jury, Officer, what your identification is based on."

Davis: On what I saw that night.

Drum: Are you positive it is this defendant you saw driving that police car?

Davis: Yes, sir, positive.

Drum: Thank you, that's all.

Officer Leah Lawton is called to the stand. The witness enters the courtroom in a police uniform. She testifies she is a fifteen-year veteran as an officer. One week after Max Vereno's disappearance, she went to the defendant's home with a search warrant, accompanied by three other officers. Marlon Boyd answered the door. The officers showed him the warrant and searched the residence. Officer Lawton found three sets of police uniforms, two revolvers of the kind issued to police, a gun belt with a revolver in the holster, a pair of handcuffs, keys to a police vehicle, and assorted police equipment. The uniforms matched the color described by the witnesses. Marlon Boyd was arrested. There was no evidence of any statement by him.

The district attorney then calls a number of police officers in quick succession. A police supervisor testifies that two weeks prior to Max Vereno's disappearance, the police department terminated Marlon Boyd as a reserve officer and ordered him to turn in his uniform and all service-related gear, which he failed to do. The witness also testifies that on the evening of Vereno's disappearance, six officers were assigned to the beat outside the Robson plant and none reported any incident of an arrest made of Max Vereno. Thereafter, the five officers who were assigned to the beat outside the Robson plant along with Officer Davis testify in succession, and none recall any arrest of Max Vereno.

The prosecution rests its case. Fields whispers to the defendant, who nods as if in agreement. Fields stands up and says, "Your Honor, in view of the People's evidence, the defense calls no further witnesses."

The judge proceeds to instruct the jury prior to argument. Adam Fields comes forward for his closing speech for the defense.

> Ladies and gentlemen, they want to convict Mr. Boyd of one of the most serious of all crimes—murder in the first degree. And yet there is not a single shred of evidence as to what happened to the alleged victim in this case. When you get back in the jury room, ask yourself these questions: Do we know beyond a reasonable doubt if Mr. Vereno is dead or alive? Is there a single witness in this case who saw Mr. Boyd strike or harm or injure Max Vereno in any way? Did a single witness claim to have seen a murder or anything close to it? Do we know beyond a reasonable doubt where Max Vereno is at this moment? If you ask yourselves those questions, you will undoubtedly answer no to every one.

Oh, yes, Mr. Boyd did something that was wrong—very wrong. We admit that. Yes, he impersonated a police officer. He could even be tried and convicted of that charge. That crime is supported by the evidence. But that is not the charge we are concerned with here today. That is not murder and certainly not murder in the first degree.

This murder charge is based on pure speculation. Where is the proof, the evidence? There has to be proof. What do we have? After evidence of the defendant placing Mr. Vereno in a police car, there is nothing. No one saw my client do anything to Max Vereno after that. Nothing but speculation. And you cannot find a man guilty of murder on mere speculation. And you know what, ladies and gentlemen...as far as we know, Max Vereno could walk right through that door (*he points to the courtroom door*) any minute.

You notice that when the defense attorney makes this statement, everyone in the courtroom turns to look at the door; that is, everyone except the defendant.

You promised during jury selection that you would follow the judge's instructions. The judge has instructed you on two vital points. First, that a finding of guilt must be based on solid proof, proof beyond any reasonable doubt, and, further, that you may not find the defendant guilty based on circumstantial evidence unless the proved circumstances not only are consistent with the theory that the defendant committed the crime, but also cannot be reconciled with any other rational conclusion. And this next part of the judge's instructions is particularly pertinent:

If the circumstantial evidence permits two reasonable interpretations, one of which points to the defendant's guilt and the other to his innocence, then you must, I repeat, you must, adopt that interpretation that points to his innocence and reject that interpretation that points to his guilt.

That is the law, ladies and gentlemen. You heard Max Vereno's father testify. He hasn't given up hope. He thinks it's reasonable to keep hoping, reasonable to believe his son is still alive—

Drum: Objection, Your Honor. Mr. Vereno didn't say that.

Judge: Ladies and gentlemen, I remind you that what counsel say in their arguments is not evidence. It is only their best memory of the evidence. It is for you, the jury, to decide what the evidence is. Proceed, Counsel.

Fields resumes:

Thank you, Your Honor. Ladies and gentlemen, you heard Max Vereno Sr. say he hasn't given up hope, that he and his wife still hope their son is alive. And I submit to you that under the circumstances of this case, it is reasonable for Mr. and Mrs. Vereno to do so.

You cannot be sure, ladies and gentlemen, and if you cannot be sure what happened to Max Vereno, then that is doubt, reasonable doubt, and your verdict must be not guilty.

Judge: You may close, Mr. Drum.

Drum gets up as if ready to explode.

What did I just hear? No shred of evidence? Defense counsel must have got this case mixed up with some other case of his. That is not the case I heard. No shred of evidence? What about the defendant stalking Jane Stribling and Max Vereno? What about the defendant masquerading as a police officer so he could stop poor Max, push him into the police car, and carry him away to God knows where? How about the defendant saying to Ms. Stribling, 'You'll hate me for what I did,' and 'You'll really be pissed off at me'? Those were his words. What was he talking about? Should we call in a rocket scientist to figure that out? You heard his voice on the tape. How he just savored what he'd done. He sounded proud of himself. No shred of evidence? What of Max's complete disappearance ever since the day he was pushed into the defendant's car? Defense counsel cries about not knowing if Max is dead or alive. Whose fault is that? Who caused that? Are you going to let the defendant benefit from putting Max's body away in a place where no one can find it? Are you going to give him credit for his clever ability to hide a dead body? Are you going to say, "Oh, that was so clever of you. We'll just have to recognize your talent by letting you off?" No shred of evidence? We know Max is dead all right. Max had no reason to leave town. He liked his life here. He wanted to marry Jane. He was close to his parents. Does it make any sense that he would suddenly decide to not call his parents?

No, he can't call his parents now. He can't call Jane now. He will never be able to do that because the poor man has been murdered. You can't bring Max back. But now you do have the opportunity to do something for Max, and for his parents, and for those who loved him. You can give them justice—some measure of retribution—by telling this man right here (*he points at Boyd*) that he is a murderer and now he must face the consequences.

Defense counsel told you of some instructions of the law on circumstantial evidence. The only trouble is he left out the important part. He didn't tell you this part, and I quote: "Both direct and circumstantial evidence are acceptable as a means of proof. Neither is entitled to any greater weight than the other." That is the law, ladies and gentlemen. So don't let the fact that the case is based partly on circumstantial evidence confuse you. It's just as good as direct evidence.

Where is Max Vereno? Only one person can tell us that.

Just use your common sense and you will do the right thing. You will come back with the only proper verdict—murder in the first degree.

The judge then gives jury instructions.

Ladies and gentlemen, a defendant in a criminal trial has a constitutional right not to be compelled to testify. You must not draw any inference from the fact that a defendant does not testify. Further, you must neither discuss this matter nor permit it to enter into your deliberations in any way. As I said, the defendant has a right not to testify and you must not hold it against him if he chooses not to testify. In deciding whether or not to testify, the defendant may choose to rely on the state of the evidence and upon the failure, if any, of the prosecution to prove beyond a reasonable doubt every element of the charge against him. The fact that the defendant does not testify will in no way make up for a failure of proof by the prosecution.

The charge is murder in the first degree. That means an unlawful killing with a specific intent to kill. There are two possible verdicts—guilty or not guilty.

WHAT IS YOUR VERDICT?

QUESTIONS FOR YOU TO CONSIDER

As you determine your verdict for this crime, here are some questions about the crime and the trial for you to think about.

1. Why didn't the district attorney argue the obvious point: if the defendant is innocent, why didn't he take the stand and tell us what he is hiding?

2. Why didn't the defense attorney call the defendant, Marlon Boyd, to the witness stand?

3. Why didn't the judge allow testimony concerning Jane Stribling's sexual relationship with Marlon Boyd?

4. Suppose the following sequence of events is true: You are the attorney for Marlon Boyd, and he told you in confidence where he hid the body of Max Vereno. Marlon Boyd is thereafter found guilty and sent to prison for life without possibility of parole. Suppose further that after Marlon Boyd is sentenced, Max Vereno's parents and Jane Stribling plead with you to tell them where the body is located so they can at least give Max Vereno a decent burial. You feel pressured by the family's wishes to obtain the body. You start to wonder if you could possibly break the attorney-client privilege on grounds that there is a moral obligation, higher than the attorney-client privilege, to reveal the secret. What would you do?

AUTHOR'S ANSWERS TO THE QUESTIONS

1. There was a time when the district attorney could have made such an argument, and usually did. However, in 1965, in *Griffin v. California,* 380 U.S. 609 (1965), the United States Supreme Court held that a defendant has a constitutional right not to testify, and that any comment on the defendant's failure to testify violates the self-incrimination clause of the Fifth Amendment. If the district attorney had made such a comment in this case, a verdict of guilty would have been set aside by the appellate court and the case would have been sent back to the trial court for a new trial. Such an argument is generally referred to as *Griffin error,* after the name of the Supreme Court case.

   The problem for the appellate courts arises when the district attorney's comment is so subtle that it becomes difficult to distinguish between proper argument and Griffin error. In this case, the comment "Where is Max Vereno? Only one person can tell us that" would probably be held to violate the rule and result in an order for a new trial. However, if the D.A. had said "Is there any evidence on the other side? None has been presented to you," the appellate court would have held the comment to be proper and a guilty verdict would be affirmed.

2. One of the toughest decisions for a defense attorney in a criminal case is whether to call his or her client as a witness. The attorney knows the jury wants to hear the defendant's story, but he or she also knows there can be great danger to his or her case in having the defendant testify. In this case the decision was not difficult. With the kind of ammunition the D.A. had, Marlon Boyd would have been destroyed on the witness stand.

3. Judges are supposed to keep out irrelevant evidence that might confuse the jury. In this case, the judge could see no connection

between Stribling's sexual activities with the defendant and the charge that he murdered Max Vereno. Another judge may have ruled otherwise, reasoning that the depth of the relationship between Stribling and Boyd was relevant to the credibility of her testimony against him.

4. The attorney-client privilege prevails, similar to the priest-penitent privilege. Whatever the client tells his or her attorney in confidence must always remain secret unless the client gives specific permission otherwise. The attorney cannot be compelled to disclose what the client revealed in confidence. However, what the attorney could do in this case is try to obtain Marlon Boyd's permission to divulge the secret. Beyond that, the location of the body cannot be revealed. The defendant retains the right to the attorney-client privilege.

THE VERDICT

What was your verdict?

In the real case, the jury found Boyd guilty of murder in the first degree, and he was sentenced to life in prison.

Although jurors were ordered not to consider the fact that Marlon Boyd did not testify, they could hardly be expected to keep Boyd's failure to explain what he did with the body out of their minds, even if they never discussed it. Boyd's biggest mistake was to allow himself to be seen with Max Vereno on a public highway.

Two Sheriffs Go Too Far

CALEB PETERS V. COUNTY OF WHEELER AND TWO DEPUTY SHERIFFS, RITA WELDON, AND GEORGE MARISAL

On a Friday evening in November 2007, two African American boys, Caleb Peters, age 13, and his brother Micah, age 12, went to a movie theater in the city. Their mother drove them to the theater and promised to pick them up before curfew at 11:00 p.m. The theater was packed with teenagers who had come to see the film *Diary of a Mad Black Woman*. When the movie ended at about 10:20 p.m., the crowd gathered outside in the street.

Caleb and Micah were conversing with four or five other African American boys when two deputy sheriffs, Rita Weldon and George Marisal, approached and asked them if they knew the curfew time. Micah replied with what the deputies considered to be a sarcastic remark. The deputies detained Micah, took him around the corner to a sheriff's storefront station, and held him there in handcuffs. They then contacted Caleb and took him to the station to phone his mother. Caleb complied peacefully. There was no evidence that Caleb had committed any crime or done anything of a suspicious nature. He told his mother what was happening and the deputies heard him say, "It's just like the last time." His mother told Caleb not to answer any questions until she got there. When Caleb hung up, the deputies demanded to know what he meant by "the last time." He refused to answer. The deputies warned him that he had to answer or he could be arrested. Caleb still refused to answer. The argument escalated to the point where the deputies placed Caleb under arrest, handcuffed him behind his back, and took him into custody.

Caleb is suing the county and the two deputy sheriffs for violation of his constitutional and civil rights. He seeks damages of $75,000.

Caleb Peters, tall for his age of 14, slender, and very dark-complected, sits at counsel's table with his mother and his attorney, John Musgrave. Seated at the defense counsel table is the attorney for the county and the two deputy sheriffs named as defendants.

The evidence begins to unfold when the plaintiff's counsel, Musgrave, calls Caleb to the stand. Caleb identifies himself and says that he lives with his mother and brother Micah, is in the eighth grade in junior high school, and is 14 now while he was 13 at the time of the incident.

Musgrave: I want to take you back to the night of November 16, 2007. You recall that evening?

Caleb Peters: I don't remember the exact date.

Defense Attorney Eric Alden: Your Honor, the defense will stipulate the incident occurred on November 16, 2007.

Judge: Thank you, Counsel. The stipulation is accepted. Proceed.

Musgrave: Did you go to a movie in town that night?

Caleb Peters: Yes, sir.

Musgrave: What was the name of the movie?

Caleb Peters: *Diary of a Mad Black Woman.*

Musgrave: Who did you go to the movie with?

Caleb Peters: My brother Micah.

Musgrave: What arrangements were made for you and Micah to get home after the movie?

Caleb Peters: My mother was to come get us. I had a cell phone to call her with.

Musgrave: What time did you get out of the movie?

Caleb Peters: I'm not sure of the exact time, but it was a little after ten o'clock.

Musgrave: What did you do when you got out of the movie?

Caleb Peters: We went across the street to get some ice cream. Then we were talking with four or five of our friends.

Musgrave: Were your friends all black—uh—African American?

Caleb Peters: Yes, sir.

Musgrave: What happened next?

Caleb Peters: Two deputy sheriffs came up to us.

Musgrave: Were there other kids in that area besides your group?

Caleb Peters: Oh, yes. There was a group of Mexican kids—Hispanic. And a group of white guys. About twenty to twenty-five kids altogether.

Musgrave: The two deputies who approached you—do you see them in the courtroom?

Caleb Peters: Yes. They are right there (*pointing*), sitting at the other table.

Musgrave: Your Honor, may the record show the witness has identified Deputy Rita Weldon and Deputy George Marisal, defendants in this case?

Judge: It may so show.

Musgrave: What did the deputies say to you?

Caleb Peters: One of them—I don't remember which one—asked if we knew the curfew time.

Musgrave: Did anyone answer?

Caleb Peters: Yes, Micah did. He said he didn't have to answer.

Musgrave: Did you know curfew was 11:00 p.m?

Caleb Peters: Yes.

Musgrave: What happened next?

Caleb Peters: The deputies took Micah off to the side. They talked to him a couple seconds. Then I saw them put handcuffs on him and lead him off.

Musgrave: Do you know why they did that?

Caleb Peters: No idea. He hadn't done anything.

Musgrave: Did you say anything when you saw them leading him off?

Caleb Peters: I sure did. I said, "Why are you taking my brother? He hasn't done anything."

Musgrave: Did they answer?

Caleb Peters: Yes, one of them said—uh—can I say the exact words?

Judge: Yes. We want the truth.

Caleb Peters: The man deputy said, "Because he's such a smart ass."

Musgrave: What did you do next?

Caleb Peters: I just kept talking with my friends.

Musgrave: Did you see the deputies again?

Caleb Peters: Yes. About five minutes later they came back without Micah. And they came up to me. They told me to come with them for questioning.

Musgrave: Did you go with them?

Caleb Peters: Yeah. We went to the sheriff's storefront office around the corner.

Musgrave: Did they tell you why they took you there?

Caleb Peters: No.

Musgrave: Had you done anything to lead them to think you were involved in any crime?

Caleb Peters: No. I was just talking to my friends.

Musgrave: Did you see Micah in the sheriff's office?

Caleb Peters: Yes. He was sitting there. He was handcuffed, hands behind his back.

Musgrave: How old was Micah?

Caleb Peters: He was 12 at the time.

Musgrave: What did the sheriffs say to you?

Caleb Peters: They told me to call my mother on my cell phone.

Musgrave: And?

Caleb Peters: So I called and told her what happened. Told her Micah was arrested. When I said that, one of the deputies said, "No, he's not arrested. He's got himself detained for being such a smart ass."

Musgrave: Did you tell your mother anything else?

Caleb Peters: I told her it was just like the last time.

Musgrave: What did you mean by that?

Caleb Peters: When I was in sixth grade, they took me out of class and took me down to the principal for questioning.

Musgrave: Had you done anything wrong?

Caleb Peters: No. Nothin'. And the principal released me right away.

Musgrave: Now, to return to the present case, what did your mother say next?

Caleb Peters: She told me not to answer any questions until she got there.

Musgrave: When you finished your phone call to your mother, did the deputies say anything?

Caleb Peters: Yes. The lady sheriff started asking me questions about what I meant when I said it was like the last time.

Musgrave: Did you answer her?

Caleb Peters: No. I told her I wasn't going to answer any questions.

Musgrave: What did she say then?

Caleb Peters: She said, "You have to answer my questions. If we tell you to answer our questions, you have to answer. You have to give us what we're asking you."

Musgrave: What did you say to that?

Caleb Peters: I just kept sayin' that I wasn't answering any questions.

Musgrave: Then what happened?

Caleb Peters: So I asked, "Can I leave? I haven't done anything." And she said "No, you can't leave." Then I said, "This got nothin' to do with me." And she told me to shut up.

Musgrave: Did you shut up?

Caleb Peters: No, uh uh. I couldn't. I kept asking if I could leave.

Musgrave: Caleb, please tell us what words you used.

Caleb Peters: Exactly? The exact words?

Musgrave: Yes. The exact words.

Caleb Peters: I told them they can't fucking arrest my brother. I said, "This is some bullshit." That's what I kept saying all the time. I said, "I can leave whenever I want to." And she said, "If you get up then we'll have to arrest you and put you in handcuffs."

Musgrave: Did you talk back to her?

Caleb Peters: Yes, I did. I told her she might as well be quiet because I'm not about to tell her anything. I was using my hands because that's the way I talk. Then she came up beside me. She was mad because I wouldn't answer. She came up to me and put a handcuff on my wrist and put it behind my back.

Musgrave: What did the other officer—the male sheriff—do?

Caleb Peters: He grabbed my other arm and they put the handcuffs on behind my back.

Musgrave: What next?

Caleb Peters: While they were putting the handcuffs on, they pushed me over the counter and I fell to the floor. I couldn't break the fall because my hands were behind me. My face got slammed onto the floor.

Musgrave: What position were you in after you fell?

Caleb Peters: I was on the floor, facedown. The lady officer had me by the ankles, holding them down. The man officer had a knee in my back. Then he fell back for some reason. He got mad, and when he got up and started to walk past me, then that's when he kicked me in the face.

Musgrave: Was it a hard kick?

Caleb Peters: Mmm, well, no, it wasn't like a football kick, but I was hit in the mouth and my lip got cut.

Musgrave: What was Micah doing all this time?

Caleb Peters: He was yelling at them to stop. He kept saying, "You all can't do him like that. He's bipolar."

Musgrave: After that, what happened?

Caleb Peters: First they tied my ankles. Then one of the sheriffs said I hadn't been searched yet. So they just went ahead and took my pants off while I was still on the floor.

Musgrave: Down to your ankles or completely off?

Caleb Peters: Completely off. They took everything out of my pants pockets. Then they used a dog leash to connect the handcuffs to the ankles.

Musgrave: They hogtied you?

Caleb Peters: Yeah, whatever it's called.

Musgrave: Did you struggle?

Caleb Peters: I guess I did.

Musgrave: So there you are. Lying facedown on the floor in your shorts. Did they pick you up finally?

Caleb Peters: Yes, sir.

Musgrave: How did they pick you up?

Caleb Peters: Like you would carry a suitcase. Two deputies grabbed the leash behind me, one on each side, picked me up, and carried me to the cop car.

Musgrave: And when the sheriff's car took off, were you still hogtied in your boxer shorts?

Caleb Peters: Yeah—yes, sir. In the backseat.

Musgrave: Where did they take you?

Caleb Peters: At first to another sheriff's station. There they untied me. Then to juvenile hall, where I was placed in custody until my hearing.

Musgrave: How long did you stay at juvenile hall before your hearing?

Caleb Peters: Twenty-six days.

Musgrave: Were you released after the hearing?

Caleb Peters: Yes, sir. The judge released me. He said—

Musgrave: Don't tell us what the judge said.

Caleb Peters: Yes, sir. My mother picked me up at juvenile hall and took me home.

Musgrave: How did this event affect you emotionally or psychologically?

Caleb Peters: Well, I had never had any contact with law enforcement officers before. I had never been questioned like that or treated like that. It made me have a different view on police or sheriff officers. Made me distrust them. I was really depressed for a long time because I couldn't be at home. I missed a lot of school. It affected me in lots of ways. People saw me getting carried outside like that—hogtied—that was embarrassing. I don't feel comfortable in public any more because I feel like I'm going to get picked out of the crowd again for no reason.

Musgrave: Did you see a psychiatrist about some of the emotional problems you sustained?

Caleb Peters: Yes I did.

Musgrave: Thank you. No further questions. Your witness, Counsel.

Eric Alden, the defense counsel, cross-examines. "Caleb, did you discuss your testimony with anyone before taking the stand today?"

Caleb Peters: Well, sure. I talked to my mom, and my attorney, and a little bit with Micah.

Alden: Did your attorney give you advice on how to answer the questions?

Musgrave: Objection! Attorney-client privilege—well, no—on second thought, I'll withdraw my objection. You may answer, Caleb.

Caleb Peters: (*Answering to his attorney*) You just said I have a good case and to just tell the truth.

Alden resumes cross-examination. "What about your mother?"

Caleb Peters: Yes, we discussed it. She said just answer the questions and don't volunteer.

Alden: Caleb, when the deputies were trying to put the handcuffs on you, you resisted, did you not?

Caleb Peters: I was yelling at them, yes. Maybe I resisted because they were arresting me when I hadn't done anything.

Alden: You were kicking and screaming, were you not?

Caleb Peters: I know I was upset. I don't recall kicking anybody. The male deputy did the kicking. Right in my face.

Alden: You wouldn't follow their orders, isn't that true?

Caleb Peters: At first I did everything they asked me to do. But they had no right to put handcuffs on me when I hadn't done anything. Yes, I resisted the handcuffs.

Alden: At one point did one of the deputies ask you for your ID?

Caleb Peters: Yes, but I didn't have it on me. I left it in my other pants.

Alden: Thank you. Nothing further.

Caleb steps down from the witness stand. Plaintiff's counsel calls one of the defendants, Deputy Rita Weldon, to the stand. She identifies herself and states she is employed as a deputy sheriff.

Musgrave: You recall the night in question?

Weldon: I do.

Musgrave: Why?

Weldon: We wanted to question him.

Musgrave: About what?

Weldon: About his brother. Also we wanted him to call his mother.

Musgrave: Did Caleb go with you to the substation?

Weldon: He did.

Musgrave: He was generally cooperative?

Weldon: At first he was, yes.

Musgrave: Was Caleb committing any crime when you saw him?

Weldon: No.

Musgrave: Curfew was 11:00 p.m., right?

Weldon: Yes.

Musgrave: Was Caleb violating curfew?

Weldon: No, but it was coming up.

Musgrave: It was 10:20, right?

Weldon: Yes.

Musgrave: Was he involved in any suspicious activity?

Weldon: No.

Musgrave: After he called his mother, did you question him?

Weldon: Yes. I heard him say to his mother that it was just like the last time. I questioned him to find out what he meant. If he had a record.

Musgrave: Did he answer you?

Weldon: No. He wouldn't answer our questions.

Musgrave: And that started an argument?

Weldon: Yes. He wouldn't cooperate.

Musgrave: So you handcuffed Caleb?

Weldon: Yes.

Musgrave: What crime did he commit?

Weldon: Well, for one thing, he didn't have ID.

Musgrave: Is that a crime?

Weldon: It's a school policy that they carry their ID.

Musgrave: Didn't that apply to school grounds?

Weldon: Well, perhaps so.

Musgrave: Was this on school grounds?

Weldon: No.

Musgrave: Is there any code, any law of any kind that says you can arrest a boy for not having his ID?

Weldon: I'm not sure.

Musgrave: Was he violating curfew?

Weldon: Not yet. But it was around 10:30 p.m. Curfew was coming up at 11:00.

Musgrave: So I'll ask you again. What crime did he commit?

Weldon: He was interfering with our duties.

Musgrave: What duties?

Weldon: Our duty to investigate.

Musgrave: Investigate what?

Weldon: What he meant when he told his mother it was like the last time. He wouldn't answer the question.

Musgrave: What else?

Weldon: He resisted arrest. He was waving his arms around when we tried to put the handcuffs on. We were afraid he would become physical. So we put him on his stomach on the counter so we could handcuff him. But he struggled with us.

Musgrave: Tell me this, Deputy Weldon, if the arrest is illegal, is it a crime to resist it?

Alden: Objection! Calls for a legal conclusion.

Musgrave: I'll withdraw the question, Your Honor. Did Caleb ever throw any punches?

Weldon: No.

Musgrave: Did he ever kick anyone?

Weldon: Not that I recall.

Musgrave: Did you help carry Caleb to the sheriff's car in a hogtied type of hold?

Weldon: It was a four-point restraint. Yes, we had to.

Musgrave: Thank you. Your witness.

Defense Counsel Alden begins his questioning. "Were you injured in the struggle with Caleb Peters?"

Musgrave: Objection! Irrelevant!

Judge: Overruled.

Weldon: Yes, I was. I sprained my left wrist.

Alden: How did that happen?

Weldon: In the struggle I fell to the ground.

Alden: Did Caleb strike you?

Weldon: No, but he was flailing his arms to keep us from putting the handcuffs on.

Alden: Did you go to the hospital with the injury?

Weldon: Yes, I did.

Alden: And what did they do at the hospital?

Musgrave: Objection, Your Honor!

Judge: Overruled.

Weldon: They X-rayed it and put it in a soft cast.

Alden: How long were you in a soft cast?

Musgrave: Your Honor, what possible relevance—

Judge: Overruled, Counsel. Proceed.

Weldon: I was on light duty for one week.

Alden: Was it necessary to place Caleb in a four-way restraint?

Weldon: Yes, sir.

Alden: Why?

Weldon: Because of the way he'd been struggling.

Alden: What was your assignment that evening?

Weldon: We were assigned to the sheriff's anti-gang violence unit.

Alden: So you were there to prevent violence?

Weldon: Yes, sir. There had been violence between gangs at that location before.

Alden: And you were there to see that it didn't happen again?

Weldon: Yes, sir. We were concerned because there was one group of African Americans, one group of Caucasians, another group of Hispanics. Like a bomb ready to go off.

Alden: And you picked Caleb out and took him to the substation to prevent any violence, right?

Weldon: Yes, sir. That was the only reason.

Alden: Thank you. Nothing further.

Musgrave: Just a few more questions if I may, Your Honor.

Judge: Proceed.

Musgrave: When you took Caleb to the storefront station, was he involved in any violence?

Weldon: No, sir.

Musgrave: Was he threatening any violence?

Weldon: No, sir.

Musgrave: Was he doing anything at all, any suspicious activity, anything to make you fear he was breaking the law or would break the law?

Weldon: No, sir.

Musgrave: He was entirely peaceful and quiet.

Weldon: At that time, yes, sir.

Musgrave: Thank you. You may step down.

Attorney Musgrave calls Caleb's mother, Edwina Peters, to the stand. She testifies she is raising the two boys by herself and has no idea where their father is. She corroborates Caleb's account of the phone call.

Musgrave: Mrs. Peters, did you notice any change in Caleb after his release from juvenile hall?

Edwina Peters: Oh, heavens, yes. Quite a bit.

Musgrave: What did you notice?

Edwina Peters: He was distraught, depressed, wouldn't go outside. Just wanted to stay home all the time. Wouldn't see his friends.

Musgrave: Did you seek treatment for Caleb?

Edwina Peters: Yes. I took him to a psychiatrist.

Musgrave: Is he better now?

Edwina Peters: Yes. But he is still afraid of being picked up for no reason.

Musgrave: Did you have a chance to observe him at juvenile hall immediately after the incident?

Edwina Peters: Yes, they let me speak to him.

Musgrave: Did you notice any injuries?

Edwina Peters: Yes, he had a swollen face on the left side. Above the left eye it was also swollen.

Musgrave: Did he ask to see a nurse?

Edwina Peters: Yes. He saw a nurse.

Musgrave: Thank you.

Defense Counsel Eric Alden now questions the mother. "Was he bleeding anywhere?"

Edwina Peters: No.

Alden: Did the nurse have to apply any bandages?

Edwina Peters: No. Like I said, his face was swollen.

Alden: If the jury grants any money damages in this case, the money would go to you, right?

Edwina Peters: I would keep it for him, yes.

Alden: Thank you, that's all.

Attorney John Musgrave calls Meyer Pearlson as a witness. Pearlson enters the courtroom in the uniform of a deputy sheriff.

Musgrave: You were present outside the movie theater on the night in question?

Pearlson: Yes. I was assigned to that site in the event of any trouble.

Musgrave: Do you know Deputy Sheriffs Rita Weldon and George Marisal?

Pearlson: I do. We're in the same anti-gang violence unit.

Musgrave: Did you observe them take Caleb Peters to the substation?

Pearlson: Yes. I was on the other side of the crowd.

Musgrave: Did you observe Caleb Peters in the crowd?

Pearlson: Oh, yes. You couldn't miss him. He's six foot two. The biggest guy on the street.

Musgrave: Before the deputies took him away, did you observe Caleb?

Pearlson: Yes.

Musgrave: Did you see him commit any crime or do anything of a suspicious nature?

Pearlson: No. I did not.

Musgrave: Do you know why they took him away?

Pearlson: No, I do not.

Musgrave: Were you then called to the substation?

Pearlson: Yes. I was immediately called in to assist in case of any trouble.

Musgrave: When you arrived at the substation, what did you see?

Pearlson: Caleb had just come in. He was still standing and they told him to sit down.

Musgrave: When he was asked to sit down, had he committed any crime?

Pearlson: No.

Musgrave: And when he called his mother, he hadn't committed any crime?

Pearlson: No.

Musgrave: Was not having his ID a violation of any law?

Pearlson: Not there, no. Only on school grounds.

Musgrave: And when the deputies questioned him about what he meant by saying to his mother, "It's just like the last time," had he committed any crime?

Pearlson: No.

Musgrave: And, when he told the deputies, "I don't have to answer your questions," was he committing any crime?

Pearlson: That's not a crime, no, sir.

Musgrave: Thank you. Nothing further.

Defense counsel cross-examines. "Did he resist when the deputies tried to put the handcuffs on him?"

Pearlson: Yes, sir.

Alden: Did the struggle become so violent that you had to assist the deputies in putting a four-point restraint on him?

Pearlson: Yes, sir.

Alden: Did you see any deputy kick him in the face?

Pearlson: No, sir.

Alden: Did you see anyone remove Caleb's pants?

Pearlson: I didn't see that.

Alden: Is resisting arrest a crime?

Pearlson: Under certain circumstances, yes, sir.

Alden: Thank you. That's all.

Musgrave: Just a moment. You said it's a crime "under certain circumstances." What circumstances would those be?

Alden: Objection, Your Honor. Calls for a legal opinion.

Musgrave: He opened it up, Your Honor. The jury is entitled to know what he meant.

Judge: Objection overruled. The witness may answer.

Pearlson: Well, it's only a crime if the arrest is legal. That's my understanding.

Musgrave: Thank you. You may step down. Your Honor, the plaintiff rests.

In the defense case, Defense Attorney Alden calls the other defendant, Deputy George Marisal, to the stand. His testimony is basically the same as that of his partner, Deputy Weldon. He never saw anyone kick Caleb and never saw anyone remove Caleb's pants. Marisal admits Caleb was put in a four-point restraint, but says it was necessary because of Caleb's resistance.

The defense rests and closing arguments begin. Eric Alden rises.

> Ladies and gentlemen, at first glance it may appear to you that the deputies acted unreasonably in this case. But I ask you to put yourselves in their place. They were out there outside the movie theater in what to them was a situation ready to explode—ready to explode with violence. Teenagers representing different ethnic groups, full of energy, and ready to fight at any moment. These deputies had been there before; they had seen violence erupting there before in exactly the same scenario. One group of African Americans, another group of Hispanics, a third group of Caucasians—all standing side-by-side. Curfew time was approaching; the deputies knew from experience what was very apt to happen. They were both assigned to the gang

suppression detail in the downtown area. They did what we have hired them to do—prevent violence, keep the peace, protect boys like Caleb and Micah from injury and getting into trouble with the law.

Was it wrong for Deputy Weldon, a half-hour before curfew, to contact the boys to make sure they had a ride home? Was it wrong for her to ask Caleb to call his mother? No. She was only trying to help them. Would you want the sheriffs to just stand aside and let the scene explode? They could have done that. But, no, they were proactive; they were doing what was reasonable under the circumstances. When Micah made a smart-aleck remark to them, it was clear that his hostile mood could get him into trouble. Caleb was bigger and taller than the other boys in his group. He would be the leader in any conflict. It was best to remove him from that situation and help him get home safely. When Caleb told his mother that it was like the "last time," the deputies felt that he had been in trouble before and that they had a duty to investigate. Caleb suffered no injury of substance. All of this was preventative action. Counsel would like to paint the deputies as monsters, but they are conscientious law enforcement officers who were only trying to protect the community. Don't punish them for trying to do what we've asked them to do. Thank you."

Caleb's attorney rises to make his closing statement.

So that's it. They were only doing what we hired them to do. They were only doing their job. That's the thrust of defense counsel's argument. I was wondering what the defense argument could possibly be in this case. Now I know. Well, ladies and gentlemen, I can assure you we never hired them to stamp on our Constitution and make a mockery of its principles. The Constitution of the United States, with its guarantees of freedom to all Americans, is the soul of this great nation. This flag hanging in our courtroom (*pointing*) is the emblem of that Constitution. Americans, men and women, have fought and died for it and they will do so again. The Bill of Rights of that Constitution says

> that every American has a right to be free from unreasonable detention and arrest—the right to be let alone.
>
> Caleb Peters had a right to be in that street, not bothering a soul, not threatening anyone, not committing violence upon anyone, not violating curfew, not doing or saying anything even remotely suspicious. He may have been only 13, and he may be of a minority race, but he had the right to be let alone as much as anyone else. When I am finished, the judge will tell you the law and you will see that the law was violated in this case by sheriffs who are supposed to uphold it. The judge will tell you in essence that the officers could not detain Caleb legally for investigation unless there was some reasonable suspicion that the boy was engaged in crime; they could not arrest Caleb unless there was—to use the legal terms—a fair probability that Caleb was involved in crime. That, ladies and gentlemen, is the law.
>
> And there is not an iota of evidence in this case, not the slightest evidence, that Caleb was doing anything criminal. All I ask you to do is follow the law. As to damages, Caleb's mother has told you how he has suffered from this experience. Who knows how much it will affect the rest of his life? We ask you to return a verdict of $75,000, but if you want 100% justice, you may decide on a greater amount. Thank you.

The judge instructs the jury on the pertinent law:

> A detention of a person by a law enforcement officer for investigation is legal only if the officer had a reasonable suspicion that the person detained was engaged in criminal activity. Otherwise the detention is illegal.
>
> An arrest of a person is legal only if the arresting officer had probable cause to believe the person committed or was committing a crime. Otherwise the arrest is illegal. Probable cause exists when

a reasonable officer concludes that there is a fair probability that the person committed or was committing a crime.

The plaintiff has the burden of proving his case by a preponderance of evidence, which means the evidence is heavier on his side than the other.

If you find for the plaintiff, then you must decide the damages to the plaintiff, Caleb Peters. Damages mean the amount of money that will fairly compensate the plaintiff for any injury caused by the defendant sheriff deputies. In assessing the amount of damages, you should consider the nature of the injuries; the loss of enjoyment of life experienced and with reasonable probability life that will be experienced in the future; and also the mental, physical, and emotional pain and suffering experienced and with reasonable probability that which will be experienced in the future.

Your verdict shall state whether you are for or against the plaintiff Caleb Peters, and if your verdict is for the plaintiff, the amount of damages.

WHAT IS YOUR VERDICT?

QUESTIONS FOR YOU TO CONSIDER

As you determine your verdict for this crime, here are some questions about the crime and the trial for you to think about.

1. In this case, the plaintiff's attorney called the defendants to the stand to testify. Why is it that in a criminal trial the prosecutor cannot call the defendant to the witness stand for cross-examination, but in a civil trial the plaintiff is generally allowed to call the defendant to the stand?

2. If you were the plaintiff's attorney in this case, what kind of person would you try to select for the jury?

3. The plaintiff's attorney asked the jury to return a verdict of $75,000 in damages or more if they found it appropriate. Suppose he asked for just $75,000 and the jury returned a verdict of $200,000. Does the jury have the power to disregard the plaintiff's request and return a much larger amount?

AUTHOR'S ANSWERS TO THE QUESTIONS

1. This being a civil case for damages, the rule in criminal trials protecting the defendant against self-incrimination does not apply. The Fifth Amendment to the United States Constitution provides that no person may be compelled in any criminal case to be a witness against him- or herself. Thus in a criminal case, the prosecutor may not call the defendant to testify. In a criminal case, the defendant always has the right to remain silent—he or she need not testify at all. This provision of the Fifth Amendment does not generally apply in civil cases, although there are exceptions. Thus in a civil case, the plaintiff may call the defendant to testify. Similarly, the defendant may call the plaintiff to the witness stand as well.

2. Parents with teenage children would be desirable for the plaintiff on the jury. Parents are likely to be outraged by the idea of their children being arrested when they had done nothing wrong.

3. The amount of damages in a civil case is a decision for the jury to make. The lawyer may request a certain amount, but what the lawyer requests is simply a suggestion. The jury has the power to decide the amount and it may be more or less than the amount suggested by either lawyer.

THE VERDICT

What was your verdict?

The real-life jury found for the plaintiff and awarded him $200,000.

A Jealous Husband Resorts to Violence

STATE V. KURT SCHAEFFER

Kurt Schaeffer and Larry Hansen were best friends and partners in a construction business. Schaeffer's wife, Vicki, worked in the office as their secretary. Hansen was not married. The Schaeffer marriage went well in the early years and produced four children. But Kurt had an addiction to gambling that worsened to the point where Vicki asked him for a divorce and he moved out. Shortly thereafter, Kurt promised Vicki he would quit gambling if she would take him back, but she said she could not because she had fallen deeply in love with Larry Hansen. Kurt became emotionally distraught over that news and at his separation from his wife and children. He also became increasingly jealous of Larry.

Kurt went back to Vicki to plead with her one more time. He told her he had to have her back, but she told him her love for Larry was too strong. Kurt testifies in tears. He says he went to the office with the intention of killing himself. When he walked in, Larry was there grinning at him. Kurt tried to shoot himself, but the gun jammed. He fired three shots at Larry, one in the arm, one in the neck, and one in the back, killing Larry instantly. But he tells the jury he cannot remember the shooting. A clinical psychologist testifies as to Kurt's state of mind, opining that Kurt was in such a heat of passion that he was incapable of exercising control, and that he could not maturely premeditate and reflect on the seriousness of his conduct.

Kurt Schaeffer was the responsible party, but for which crime—murder or manslaughter?

Samuel Ringgold introduces himself as the deputy district attorney. He looks like the chairman of the board of a major corporation and speaks slowly and deliberately. In sharp contrast is Defense Attorney Toby Cipriano, who is so light on his feet he looks as if he's constantly holding himself back, nervous and ready for the starting gun.

"There is no dispute in this case," Ringgold says in his opening statement, "that this man, Kurt Schaeffer, shot and killed Larry Hansen on the morning of June 25, 1999, in the village of Del Centro. There is also no dispute that Larry Hansen was his best friend and business partner at the time. The only reason we are here pertains to the degree of the homicide—was it murder or manslaughter? We will prove it was murder, clear and simple, caused by not one, not two, but three bullets fired into Hansen's body.

You notice Schaeffer wince as Ringgold squeezes out the words "one—two—three."

The prosecution's first witness is police officer Robert Deming. He testifies that on the morning of June 25, while on duty in his patrol car, he was told by central dispatch that a man identifying himself as Kurt Schaeffer reported he had just shot his business partner and wanted the police to come and arrest him. The officer further states that he and Detective Gordon went to the office of the S&H Construction Company and found Kurt Schaeffer waiting for them. Schaeffer indicated where his revolver was, on a shelf near the front door. The hammer of the gun was in a cocked position. Deming says Schaeffer was cooperative and full of remorse for what he had done.

Dr. Craig Fowler, the county pathologist, is the next witness. He testifies that he examined the body and found three entry bullet wounds, one in the front of the left arm, one in the side of the neck, and one in the back.

The next witness is a short man in his midsixties, Ben Simon. He is a cabinetmaker who was working in his shop next to the defendant's construction office on the morning of the shooting when he heard what sounded like firecrackers. He gives the following answers to questions by the D.A.

> **Ringgold**: How many of these firecracker sounds did you hear?

> **Simon**: Three. Bang!—Bang! Bang! Like that.

You notice a slight pause between the first and second "bangs."

> **Ringgold**: How much time went by between the three shots?

> **Simon**: I really couldn't tell you.

> **Ringgold**: Well, just in your own words, using the words "bang, bang, bang" again, tell us how you heard them with reference to the spacing between shots. Just say it to yourself, slow, like this: "bang, bang"—

Cipriano jumps to his feet. "Your Honor, counsel is coaching the witness. I'd like to remind him the witness gives evidence, not him."

The judge replies, "Let him give his testimony, he has a right to. For the record, I'll time him." Turning to the witness, he says, "Will you repeat your testimony, with particular regard to the timing of the shots, and how much time passed between shots."

> **Simon**: I said, "Bang"—I don't know, I'm confused, I don't know how fast I said it. I heard it—I don't know, I'm all mixed up.

> **Ringgold**: That's all right. For the record, I'd like the statement of the witness to be recorded as the court heard it, with a full second between the first and second—

Cipriano again jumps to his feet, furious. To the D.A., he says, "You have no right to say what the evidence is. It's for the jury to decide how much time there was between shots."

The D.A. replies, equally furious, "I was merely trying to—"

The judge pounds his gavel, and you realize that the bang-bang-bang testimony must be important. The judge states, "What the witness said has been heard by the jury, and the jury will disregard the remarks of counsel. Now we will take a ten-minute recess, during which I hope tempers will cool."

After the break, the judge returns and the trial resumes.

Ringgold: I call Mrs. Vicki Schaeffer.

She is a small, thin, sandy-haired woman, and as she sits down in the witness stand she looks daggers at her husband, the defendant.

Ringgold: You are Mrs. Kurt Schaeffer, the wife of the defendant? How long have you been married?

Vicki Schaeffer: About eleven years.

In response to various questions, she testifies she has four children with Kurt Schaeffer, all girls, the youngest now only 1 year old and the oldest 8. She says the marriage went smoothly at first. Kurt was a good father and had a good job working construction. About three years ago, he started his own construction business with Larry Hansen, his best friend. In order to save money, Vicki worked in the office as a secretary.

Ringgold: Then the three of you were often in the office together?

Vicki Schaeffer: Yes.

Ringgold: What was your relationship with Larry?

Vicki Schaeffer: At first he was just my husband's friend, but later on... (*She hesitates, searching for the right words.*) I mean—well—it became something different.

Ringgold: During this period, when Larry and your husband were running this construction company, did your married life change at all? That is, did you have any problems?

Vicki Schaeffer: Oh, you mean Kurt's gambling? That started earlier. Kurt began to gamble, heavily. Horses and the dog races. And I told him he ought to stop, so he'd stop for a few days, and then it would get worse than ever.

She becomes emotional, and she tells how Kurt bet larger and larger sums, that she tried to stop him, that they argued about it and their whole life changed. Kurt would lose his temper and yell at her. He became a different man, touchy and irritable, and although he promised to stop gambling, he never did. Finally she had to ask him for a divorce.

Ringgold: Did he agree?

Vicki Schaeffer: Not at first, but he finally gave in and moved out of the house.

Ringgold: Then what?

Vicki Schaeffer: He promised he'd join Gamblers Anonymous if I'd take him back. But I couldn't. Matters had gone too far and I—I was in love with Larry.

Ringgold: Was your husband aware of it?

Vicki Schaeffer: I don't know. I couldn't tell him. I couldn't hurt him that much.

Ringgold: Now, I'd like to go back to the night before Larry was killed. Do you recall that night?

Vicki Schaeffer: I hardly remember anything. It's all blacked out, it was such a terrible, horrible nightmare.

As she testifies, she becomes more and more upset and finally starts sobbing uncontrollably, whereupon the court orders a short recess.

After you return to the courtroom, Mrs. Schaeffer takes the stand again. She is quieter now, more in possession of herself, and the dialogue with the prosecutor continues.

Ringgold: Do you understand, Mrs. Schaeffer, that since you are legally married to Kurt Schaeffer, you do not have to testify against him if you don't want to?

Vicki Schaeffer: Yes, I understand. I want to testify.

Before the questioning of Mrs. Schaeffer can proceed, the defense attorney Cipriano rises and states, "Your Honor, I wish to advise the court that Mr. Schaeffer is aware that he has a right under the law of marital privilege to prevent his wife from testifying against him. I have discussed this right with him. Against my advice, he wishes to waive the right and allow his wife to testify. He simply wants all the truth to come out."

Judge: Thank you, Counsel. The court appreciates the defendant's wish to have the truth disclosed. The district attorney may proceed with direct examination.

Ringgold: Mrs. Schaeffer, you had a conversation with your husband in your home early on the morning of June 25, 1999. What was that about?

Vicki Schaeffer: He accused me of being out all night with Larry, and I told him it was none of his business where I was, that I had a right to do what I wanted.

Ringgold: What was the next thing you recall?

Vicki Schaeffer: He said he was going to kill me.

Ringgold: And what did you say?

Vicki Schaeffer: I don't know. It was awful, I couldn't believe it. I was hysterical, but I finally talked him out of it.

Ringgold: Then what?

Vicki Schaeffer: Then he called Larry all kinds of names and said he was going to kill him.

The prosecutor steps back and turns to Cipriano. "Your witness."

Cipriano hesitates, seems to study Mrs. Schaeffer, and then says quietly, "You hate the defendant, don't you, Mrs. Schaeffer?

She reacts with an almost hysterical outburst. "Yes, I hate him. He killed the only man I ever loved!"

The defense counsel waits for her to quiet down. "You say you lived with your husband for eleven years and bore him four children, and yet you never loved him?"

The prosecutor jumps to his feet. "Objection, Your Honor. Irrelevant!" Before the judge can rule, Cipriano says quietly, "I will withdraw the question."

Cipriano: Now, Mrs. Schaeffer, isn't it true that you told police investigators the morning after the murder that you couldn't remember anything that was said on the morning of June 25 between you and your husband?

Vicki Schaeffer: Yes, I mean, I guess so. I forgot about that at first. I was so upset over Larry's death. They tell me I tried to kill myself. That's why they put me in the hospital.

Cipriano: How long were you there, Mrs. Schaeffer?

Vicki Schaeffer: They said I tried to throw myself down the canyon.

Her mind seems to be wandering, and the question is repeated.

Cipriano: How long were you in the hospital?

Vicki Schaeffer: I think it was five weeks.

Cipriano: And how much time passed before you remembered this threat made by your husband to kill Larry?

Vicki Schaeffer: I don't know.

Cipriano: Was it after you were out of the hospital?

Vicki Schaeffer: Yes.

Cipriano: Actually, you were out of the hospital a week when you first mentioned this threat. You hadn't remembered until then, right?

Vicki Schaeffer: You know what I'm going to say. Yes, yes, yes!

Cipriano: Just one or two more questions. Did you tell your husband when he was leaving that night that Hansen was a better lover than he ever was?

Vicki Schaeffer: I don't know. I don't recall.

Cipriano: Try to recall. "Larry's a better lover than you ever were." Is it possible you said it?

Ringgold: Objection, Your Honor. Anything is possible.

Judge: Sustained.

Ringgold: All right. Is it probable you said it?

Vicki Schaeffer: I may have said it, I could have said it, I don't recall.

Cipriano stands still for a moment, letting the answer sink in. "Thank you, Mrs. Schaeffer. That is all."

The judge calls a recess for lunch.

When court resumes, the prosecution calls Mrs. Schaeffer's older sister, Adelheid Hoffman, a tall and strong-boned woman. She testifies she was babysitting Vicki's children during the evening in question and was sleeping on the couch downstairs. The children's room was upstairs, as was Vicki's. Earlier in the evening, Vicki went out to meet Larry Hansen. At about 2:00 a.m., Mrs. Hoffman woke up to find Kurt Schaeffer standing beside her. He wanted to know where Vicki was. He was upset and said he would make her feel sorry, that she had no right to do this to him.

Ringgold: They were separated at the time?

Hoffman: Yes. He had moved out.

Ringgold: Did he say how he was going to make her feel sorry?

Hoffman: He said he was going to kill her and Larry and then kill himself.

Ringgold: What did you do then?

Hoffman: I was shocked. We talked. Talked for a long time. After a while he calmed down and said he'd forget everything if only he could get her back. Then the phone rang.

Ringgold: Who was it?

Hoffman: It was Vicki, and she said she was coming home. I started to tell her that Kurt was here, but he grabbed the phone. He asked her where she was, but she hung up on him. Then without saying anything, he turned around and left the house.

Ringgold: Then what?

Hoffman: A few minutes later, Vicki came home and went upstairs to her bedroom, without even speaking to me. I lay down and tried to get some sleep, but Kurt came back. He walked right past me as if he didn't even see me and rushed upstairs, and I could hear them talking.

Ringgold: What did they say?

Hoffman: I couldn't hear their words, but they were yelling at each other, and after a while Kurt came down. He came down the stairs slowly, and Vicki came to the top of the stairs and shouted something. After he left, I heard Vicki talking to Larry on the phone and telling him that Kurt was on his way to the office.

Ringgold: Thank you, that's all.

Cipriano stands up to say he only has a few questions.

Cipriano: You and Kurt were good friends. You knew he loved Vicki very much, and you tried to bring about reconciliation. Is that right?

Hoffman: Yes.

Cipriano: You didn't like Larry?

Ringgold: Objection! Irrelevant.

Judge: Sustained!

Cipriano: You could tell Kurt was very upset that night?

Hoffman: Oh yes. Especially when he left the last time. He was shaking.

Cipriano: Out of control?

Ringgold: Objection. Calls for a conclusion.

The judge pauses. He looks undecided. Finally, he says, "Overruled. You may answer."

Hoffman: Yes. You could say that.

Cipriano: In a heat of passion?

Hoffman: Yes.

Cipriano: That's all, thank you.

Ringgold rises as if he wants to ask more questions, but then he just waves his hand and sits back. "The State rests."

Cipriano opens his case for the defense. Various witnesses, including several prominent citizens of the town of Del Centro, testify that Kurt Schaeffer had a good reputation in the community as a peaceful, law-abiding, and honest person; that he loved his wife and children very much and desperately wanted his wife back.

Now Kurt Schaeffer takes the stand amid a murmur of expectation. He is a good-looking, burly man, about 33 years old. He has a short beard and blue, glassy eyes. He tries not to look at his wife sitting in the back row.

After a few preliminary questions in which Schaeffer identifies himself and states how he and Larry Hansen started a business together and were building it up, his attorney comes to the question of the gun.

Cipriano: Did you have a permit for it?

Kurt Schaeffer: No.

Cipriano: Then you bought it illegally?

Kurt Schaeffer: No. I found it in a junk pile about two years ago. It was an old gun and I took it. It was rusty and I didn't know whether it would work, but I cleaned it and oiled it and saw that it would operate.

Cipriano: And what did you do with the gun?

Kurt Schaeffer: I kept it under my mattress, to protect my family.

Cipriano: Now, Mr. Schaeffer, I'd like to get to the day this tragedy occurred. Where were you that night?

Kurt Schaeffer: I went to a meeting of Gamblers Anonymous. I felt I was making progress, and I wanted to tell my wife, so I went to her house, only she wasn't there, but her sister Addie was, and the kids were sleeping upstairs. Addie and I talked.

Cipriano: You heard her say you talked of killing your wife and Larry, then yourself, didn't you? Is that true?

Kurt Schaeffer: If she said it, I guess it's true. I don't know—

Cipriano: But then isn't it true that you calmed down and put aside those thoughts of killing—

Ringgold jumps to his feet. "Objection, Your Honor! He is leading the witness. I have no objection to the defendant telling his story. But let it come from him, not his attorney."

Judge: Sustained. Proceed, Mr. Cipriano.

Cipriano: All right, just tell us what happened next.

Kurt Schaeffer: The phone rang. Addie answered, but I knew it was Vicki and I grabbed it. I tried to talk to her but she hung up on me. So I left.

Cipriano: Where did you go then?

Kurt Schaeffer: I figured they were at Larry's place, so I drove out that way. Then I saw our truck, the red one, coming the other way. Larry was driving. There was somebody with him. I thought it was Vicki, so I turned around and went back to the house. The truck was gone, but I knew Vicki was inside, so I went back in.

Cipriano: You talked to Vicki then?

Kurt Schaeffer: Yes. I told her I had to have her back. She said things. I don't remember. I was upset. But she—she looked at me as if she'd never seen me before. She said she was in love with Larry and wanted the divorce. I can't remember—

He stops talking. You can see the tears in his eyes. The judge waits, and Schaeffer looks up and wipes his eyes. He is staring straight ahead.

Cipriano: Can you go on?

Kurt Schaeffer: Go ahead.

Cipriano: Do you remember her saying Larry was a better lover than you?

Kurt Schaeffer: No, I mean, yes. I—she couldn't, I—

Cipriano: You don't want to remember that, do you?

Ringgold: Objection. Leading.

Judge: Sustained.

Cipriano: Did she say it?

There is a long pause.

Kurt Schaeffer: Yes. She said it.

The judge orders a recess. When the questioning resumes, Schaeffer seems like a different man. He is cold, without emotion, and he answers questions in a matter-of-fact voice.

Cipriano: What happened after you left the house?

Kurt Schaeffer: I went to the office. I was hoping Larry wouldn't be there. I just wanted to kill myself. But when I walked in and saw Larry there grinning at me and saying he wanted to talk to me, then I don't know, I shot him. I tried to shoot myself, only the gun jammed. That's all I can remember.

Cipriano turns around and speaks to the prosecutor. "You may inquire, Counselor."

On cross-examination, Schaeffer is often confused. Ringgold presses him to recall what his intentions were while he was driving around that night, while he was at the house, and after he left Vicki, but he can't remember. He can't remember at what point he got the gun. He wasn't in control of himself. He apologizes to the court for not being able to remember.

"I am sorry, sir," he says to Ringgold. "But it's all a jumble in my mind. I want to tell the truth. I—" There is a long pause. "I did it. It was wrong. I deserve to be punished."

The last witness for the defense is Dr. Basil Bernard, a clinical psychologist, who gives his opinion that Schaeffer was incapable of exercising adequate control over his responses to environmental stimuli. He testifies that tests showed Kurt's personality was noteworthy for the repeated themes of masculine inadequacy, and this feeling motivated him to keep a gun under his mattress in order to give him a sense of power. Kurt also hoped to improve his worth through gambling, but he was not successful.

The doctor then concludes his testimony by stating that Schaeffer's mental capacity was diminished at the time of the shooting to the point where he could not maturely and deliberately premeditate and reflect on the gravity of his act. He was in such a mental state—such heat of passion—that he could not really think about what he was doing or what it meant.

The cross-examination adds little, after which the defense rests.

In rebuttal, the prosecution calls a psychiatrist, Dr. Conrad Friedrich, to the stand. Unlike the younger Dr. Bernard, Dr. Friedrich is a licensed physician. He says he saw Schaeffer the day of the shooting, and he concludes that Schaeffer was legally sane at the time of the shooting in that "he could distinguish the difference between right and wrong and was aware of the nature and quality of his act." The doctor says he thought Schaeffer could meaningfully premeditate on the gravity of his act.

Cipriano starts cross-examination with a gentle voice. "Let me get this straight, Doctor. You say he could premeditate on what he was doing?"

Friedrich: He could, yes, he had the mental capacity to premeditate.

Cipriano: But you are only saying he had the ability to do so.

Friedrich: Yes.

Cipriano: You cannot say he did.

Friedrich: No. No evidence of that. I think it was an impulsive, spur-of-the-moment act.

Cipriano: In the heat of passion?

Friedrich: One might say that.

Cipriano: Thank you, Doctor.

The D.A. has further questions. "This 'heat of passion' counsel asked you about: you have no way of knowing how strong—how hot—that was, do you, Doctor?"

"Well," The doctor looks through his records. "The police gave me a letter they found in his pocket. Oh yes, here it is." Dr. Friedrich draws out a crumpled sheet of paper. "Shall I read it, Your Honor?"

Both attorneys rush to the witness stand to look at the letter in the doctor's hands. It is apparent neither has seen it before. They study it over the doctor's shoulder, then walk back to their seats.

Cipriano: No objection.

Ringgold: No objection.

The doctor reads aloud: "My heart is aching so bad since my separation from my wife and children. I cannot bear it. I keep praying night after night she will come back to me. Perhaps if my love for her was not so strong and deep I could go along. But I cannot. If I have to live apart from my family, I shall ask God, Our Father, to end my life, mercifully soon. Signed, Kurt Schaeffer."

Ringgold: The date, Doctor, of the letter?

Friedrich: June 18, 1999.

Ringgold: One week before the shooting?

Friedrich: Yes.

Ringgold: That's all.

There are four possible verdicts:

1. guilty of first-degree murder
2. guilty of second-degree murder
3. guilty of voluntary manslaughter
4. not guilty

WHAT IS YOUR VERDICT?

QUESTIONS FOR YOU TO CONSIDER

As you determine your verdict for this crime, here are some questions about the crime and the trial for you to think about.

1. What finding by the county pathologist was extremely damaging to the defense?

2. Why was the length of time between the three "bangs" so important?

3. Why did the defense attorney insist on bringing out the taunting remark by Schaeffer's wife that Hansen was a better lover?

4. How did the letter found in Schaeffer's pocket help the defense?

5. The defendant's wife, Vicki Schaeffer, took the stand as a prosecution witness against her husband. The defense attorney then told the court that, against his advice, Kurt Schaeffer would waive the marital privilege and allow Mrs. Schaeffer to testify. What is the nature of the marital privilege as it applies to this case?

AUTHOR'S ANSWERS TO THE QUESTIONS

1. The most damaging piece of evidence against the defendant was the pathologist's finding that Hansen was shot in the back. Schaeffer testified he remembered Hansen grinning at him just before the shots were fired. If so, that meant Hansen must have turned around to flee after Schaeffer opened fire and then was shot in the back, a powerful piece of circumstantial evidence tending to show a deliberate and premeditated intent to kill.

2. The length of time between the three shots was an important issue because it could show whether the defendant thought about what he was doing between each shot, or fired so rapidly he didn't have time to think. Ben Simon's testimony indicated that there was a definite pause between the first and second shots. Time to think before the fatal shot is a circumstance supporting the element of deliberation and premeditation necessary for first-degree murder.

3. The realistic goal of the defense attorney in this case was to reduce the killing from murder to manslaughter. He knew he had no chance for acquittal. In order to do this, the defense had to show that Schaeffer was provoked by some incident that would naturally arouse the heat of passion of an ordinary, reasonable man in the same circumstances. Vicki Schaeffer's remark—"Larry's a better lover than you ever were"—is arguably the kind of provocation that would make a husband act rashly in a heat of passion and thus reduce the crime to manslaughter.

4. The letter found in Schaeffer's pocket was helpful to his defense because it showed the extent of his depression over the loss of his wife. One of the laws existing at the time of this trial was that of *diminished capacity*. Under this law, jurors were told that if the defendant's mental capacity was diminished to the point where they had a reasonable doubt whether he or she could maturely and

meaningfully reflect upon the gravity of his or her act, then they could not find him or her guilty of first-degree murder. Schaeffer's suicidal depression shown by the letter might be considered some evidence of such diminished mental capacity.

5. When Mrs. Schaeffer took the stand as a prosecution witness, the situation presented the interesting legal question of when a wife can testify against her husband. The *marital privilege* protects confidential communications between husband and wife from being made public in court. Either spouse can invoke the privilege, either by refusing to testify against their spouse or by preventing their spouse from testifying against them. The privilege is based on the policy of encouraging marital harmony. Mrs. Schaeffer said she hated her husband for killing her lover and wished to testify against him, thereby waiving her privilege. The defendant still had the right to invoke his privilege and prevent her from testifying as to any private conversations between them. For some unknown reason, acting against his attorney's advice, Schaeffer waived the privilege, thereby opening the door to damaging evidence against him. He may have reasoned that her testimony would help the jury understand his conduct and thereby give him a better chance at a manslaughter verdict based on heat of passion.

THE VERDICT

What was your verdict?

The real-life jury found the defendant guilty of murder in the second degree.

There was no question in the minds of the jurors that Schaeffer intended to kill and did kill Hansen. The dispute that went on for several days in the jury room was whether the verdict should be murder in the first degree or a lesser degree of homicide, such as murder in the second degree or voluntary manslaughter.

The difference in terms of penalty can be substantial. The maximum sentence for first-degree murder in a noncapital case is generally life in prison, while the most one could get at that time for manslaughter was about ten years. The numbers vary in different states.

Certain jurors could not vote for first-degree murder because of doubts as to Schaeffer's mental state at the time of the shooting. Some could not put aside their sympathy for his position in the love triangle. As a result, the jury compromised on second-degree murder.

The argument for voluntary manslaughter based on heat of passion failed to carry the jury, because jurors felt that sufficient time elapsed between the moment Schaeffer left the house and his arrival at the crime scene for such passion to cool.

The judge sentenced the defendant to five years to life in prison.

A Prisoner's Dilemma: Escape or Die

STATE V. EDDIE CARTER

Eddie Carter, a twice-convicted felon, escaped from state prison. He had been convicted of two robberies, and at the time of his escape, he was serving out a sentence of five years for his last offense. When caught the next morning, he freely admitted to his escape and said he would do it again if similar conditions existed at the prison.

Most people would think he would have little chance of success in a jury trial charging him with the crime of escape. But Eddie Carter says he has a defense. He says he had to do it to save his life. If he had not escaped, he would be dead.

Carter has a smart woman as his attorney who believes he should be acquitted. She is determined to show you that certain conditions existed in her client's case that made it necessary for him to escape. Her theory is called the *defense of necessity*. In most criminal cases, the defendant has no burden and does not have to prove anything. But this case is different. Carter must prove his defense by a preponderance of the evidence. Eddie Carter is a man with a bad record.

In his brief opening statement, the prosecutor tells you that this is a very simple case. He only has to prove that Eddie Carter was confined in a state prison and that he left that facility without lawful authority. He calls Emery Finley as his first witness and begins direct examination. Finley testifies he is an administrative assistant at the Sundale State Prison. He states that Sundale is a minimum-security prison without the usual walls or prison bars.

D.A.: What does minimum security mean?

Finley: Prisoners are sent to Sundale who have less than a year to serve on their time. Minimum security means that prisoners live in dorms, not in cells behind bars. There is no wall or high fence around the grounds.

D.A.: So escape is not difficult?

Finley: That's true. They can walk out at their risk. But they know that if they do and get caught, they can be sent back to a real prison for many years. So they never try it.

D.A.: Except this time?

Finley: Yes. Except this time.

D.A.: Tell the jury what happened on the morning of June 2, 2007.

Finley: As was my custom every morning, I called the roll. That means that all prisoners had to come out of their rooms or wherever they were and stand in the yard in formation. I called the roll and everyone answered except Eddie Carter.

D.A.: What did you do then?

Finley: We searched his room and his locker. The locker was empty. All his belongings were gone. He was missing. No one had seen him that morning, so we immediately sent out an escape alarm to all law enforcement agencies.

D.A.: Do you see Eddie Carter in the courtroom?

Finley: I do. He is right there (*pointing*).

D.A.: Your Honor, may the record show the witness has identified the defendant?

Judge: It may.

D.A.: Did you have any inkling he would try to escape?

Finley: Oh, no. None at all.

D.A.: Was there any possible reason you knew of why he would do such a thing?

Finley: When Carter was at Marcy—that's another state prison—he complained of a death threat so we moved him to Sundale. But he seemed content at Sundale, never complained of any threats or anything like that.

D.A.: Did you ever ask him if he felt safe at Sundale?

Finley: I did. Several times. He just said everything was fine. He was looking forward to getting out soon and changing his life. He'd had enough of prisons.

D.A.: That's all I have. Thank you.

The defense attorney, Emily Conant, begins cross-examination. "Was Eddie Carter a good prisoner?"

Finley: Not only a good prisoner. He was a model prisoner. Never any trouble with him whatsoever.

Conant: You say you knew of no reason Eddie would try to escape from Sundale, is that right?

D.A.: Objection, Your Honor. I object to counsel referring to her client by his first name only.

Judge: Objection sustained. Defense counsel will kindly refrain from doing so in the future. The witness may answer the question.

Finley: That's right. I knew of no reason Carter would try to escape.

Conant: Are you familiar with an inmate at Sundale named Jeremy Brown?

Finley: Yes. Jeremy Brown was at Sundale. He's been paroled recently.

Conant: Was Jeremy Brown an inmate at Sundale at the time of Eddie Carter's escape?

Finley: Yes.

Conant: And can you tell us when Jeremy Brown became an inmate at Sundale?

Finley: One moment. I'll have to consult my files. (*He examines the file.*) Yes. Here it is. Jeremy Brown was transferred to Sundale on May 30, 2007.

Conant: Just two days before Mr. Carter left?

Finley: Yes, ma'am.

Conant: You told us in your testimony on direct examination that Carter was transferred from the Marcy Detention Center. Are you familiar with an inmate there named Darius Brown?

Finley: I don't know him. I know of him.

Conant: Were you aware that there was bad blood between Darius Brown and Eddie Carter at the Marcy prison, and that was the reason for Carter being moved to Sundale?

Finley: (*Turning to the judge*) Do I have to answer, Your Honor? The record of the incident between Darius Brown and Carter at the Marcy prison has been sealed in the prison files in the interest of security. I have been instructed not to speak of the matter in public unless Your Honor orders me to do so.

Judge: This is a criminal case. We need to hear the truth. I will have to instruct you to answer the question.

Finley: The answer is yes. There was what you call "bad blood" between them. Darius Brown made a death threat against Eddie Carter when they were both inmates at Marcy. That is why Carter had to be moved to Sundale.

Conant: Thank you. Now, when Jeremy Brown was received into custody at Sundale, were you aware that he is the brother of Darius Brown?

Finley: I was not aware of it at the time. I know it now. I will admit I should have been informed of the relationship. Somehow it slipped by us without our knowledge.

Conant: And were you aware that on the night before Eddie Carter escaped, Jeremy Brown, on behalf of his brother, sent a death threat to Eddie Carter, telling Carter he would be dead in the morning?

Finley: I was not aware of that. But that was still no reason for the escape. Eddie should have told us. If he had we would have protected him.

Conant: That's all I have. Thank you.

The next witness for the prosecution is Roberto Marquez. He testifies he is a deputy sheriff and at about 2:00 p.m. on June 3, 2007, he was alone in his vehicle patrolling the mountain area about ten miles from Sundale prison.

D.A.: Did you receive an all-points bulletin over your radio?

Marquez: Yes, sir. It said to be on the lookout for a young black man who had just escaped from Sundale, and gave a description.

D.A.: Did you see someone matching that description?

Marquez: I did. I was driving down Beaver Canyon Road when I noticed this hitchhiker walking in a direction away from the state prison.

D.A.: What did you do?

Marquez: I recognized him right away. He had his shirt off but he still had on his prison pants. As I approached, he saw me and bolted down the embankment. I exited my vehicle and yelled at him to stop or I'd have to shoot.

D.A.: Did he stop?

Marquez: Yes. He stopped right away and came back to me with his hands raised. I took him into custody.

D.A.: What did he say?

Marquez: At first he gave me some fictitious name. I said, "You're lying. I know who you are." Then he said, "All right. I'm Eddie Carter, the guy you're looking for from Sundale."

D.A.: Did he say anything else?

Marquez: He begged me not to take him back to Sundale. "For God's sake," he said. "Please. I'm begging you. A guy is going to kill me there. I would never have made it through the night. That's why I had to leave."

D.A.: When he first saw your sheriff's car, did he make any attempt at all to turn himself in?

Marquez: Oh, no. He ran off right away.

D.A.: Did he ever say anything about trying to contact the authorities to turn himself in?

Marquez: Nothing like that, no.

D.A.: Did you take him back to Sundale?

Marquez: No, I took him to the county jail.

Defense counsel proceeds to cross-examine. "Did he have any personal possessions with him other than the clothes he was wearing?"

Marquez: He didn't have a thing. No bag. Nothing.

Conant: When he came back to you with his hands up, did he cooperate with you from then on?

Marquez: Oh yes. Very much so. No trouble at all.

When the witness steps down, the prosecutor announces that he is resting his case.

The defense counsel, Conant, begins by calling Lieutenant Robert Hawkins to the stand. He lists his occupation as disciplinary hearing officer at the Marcy Detention Center, which he describes as a medium-security prison.

Conant: Sir, I want to take you back to July of 2006. Did you at that time preside over a disciplinary hearing at the Marcy prison involving an inmate by the name of Darius Brown?

Hawkins: I did.

Conant: And what was the charge against Darius Brown?

Hawkins: He was charged with assaulting several Mexican inmates during a race riot.

Conant: And during that hearing, was my client, Eddie Carter, called as a witness on behalf of the Marcy administration?

Hawkins: He was.

Conant: Please tell the jury the nature of Eddie Carter's testimony.

D.A.: Objection! This calls for hearsay.

Conant: It is not being offered for the truth of the matter being asserted, Your Honor, and therefore does not violate the hearsay rule.

Judge: Objection overruled. The witness may answer.

Hawkins: Carter testified that he saw Darius Brown lead an assault on several Mexican inmates.

Conant: Do you recall the essence of Mr. Carter's testimony?

Hawkins: Yes. Carter said he saw Darius Brown stab one of the Mexicans with a makeshift knife made from a soup spoon.

Conant: What was your decision as the hearing officer?

Hawkins: Darius Brown was determined to be the aggressor in the riot; he was docked six months of good time credit and he was placed in lockdown for six months and denied early parole.

Conant: What was the effect of that case on Eddie Carter?

Hawkins: Darius Brown had been a member of a prison gang. As a result of his testifying against Brown, Carter received several threats on his life. He had to be placed in administrative segregation for his protection and shortly thereafter was transferred from Marcy to Sundale.

Conant: Did Eddie Carter report these death threats to you?

Hawkins: He certainly did. And we reacted immediately to protect him.

Conant: Did Carter testify truthfully in your opinion?

Hawkins: Indeed he did. There was corroborative evidence. I believed him. It took courage. But in my opinion he told the truth.

Conant: Thank you, Lieutenant. The D.A. may have some questions.

D.A.: When an inmate is the target of death threats, what action does the prison staff take to protect the threatened person?

Hawkins: We take all necessary precautions to protect him.

D.A.: And if, in this case, Eddie Carter had told the prison staff at Sundale of the threat against him, would the staff have taken all necessary precautions to protect him?

Conant: Objection! He can't tell us what the staff at Sundale would do.

Judge: Sustained.

D.A.: All right, let me ask it this way. Was the staff at Sundale governed by the same policy as the staff at Marcy?

Hawkins: Absolutely. All prison staffs operate under the same rules.

D.A.: Is a prisoner ever justified in escaping?

Hawkins: Well, it would take extreme conditions but—

Conant: Objection. It's for the jury to decide if the escape was justified.

Judge: Sustained. The witness may not answer.

Finally, the witness you are waiting for, Eddie Carter, looking a bit lost and frightened, takes the stand. Under questioning from his attorney, he admits escaping from Sundale; he says he had to do it or he would be dead in the morning. He also admits having been convicted of two robberies and having served two separate stretches in state prison as punishment. He only had six months left to serve on his last offense when he ran away from Sundale.

Conant: I want to ask you about your testimony at the Marcy prison against Darius Brown. Did you do that willingly?

Carter: No, no. I was forced to do it. I wasn't so brave.

Conant: What do you mean?

Carter: They told me that if I didn't testify I would lose any reduction in my sentence and would be charged myself with the assault on the Mexicans.

Conant: Did you receive threats to your life after testifying?

Carter: Yes. They put me in protective custody and then moved me to Sundale.

Conant: Tell the jury why you escaped from the Sundale prison.

Carter: Yes, ma'am. I had no intention of escaping before that night. For God's sake, why would I escape and face four more years in the joint? I only had six months left to do on my last robbery gig. But then this guy Jeremy—Jeremy Brown—he came up to me that night.

Conant: Had you ever met him before?

Carter: No, never laid eyes on the dude before that night.

Conant: What night was that?

Carter: The night I split. He came up to me when we were waiting in line for evening chow. He asked, "Do you know who I am?" I said, "No." He said, "I'm Darius Brown's brother. I know what you did to him up at Marcy."

Conant: Then what did you say?

Carter: I said, "They forced me to do it."

Conant: Then what did he say?

Carter: He said—should I say exactly what he said?

Conant: Tell us exactly what he said.

Carter: He said, "This is payback time. You'll be a dead motherfucker by the morning."

He turns to the judge.

Carter: Excuse my language, Your Honor, but that's what he said.

Conant: Did you think he was serious?

Carter: I sure did. I could tell he meant it.

Conant: What did you do?

Carter: I was scared. I couldn't eat. I went back to my bunk. I lay back thinking about it. Hell, I didn't want to die. Then something happened that really put the cap on it.

Conant: What was that?

Carter: I went out in the hall to my locker and two guys had broken into my locker and were taking all my stuff. I mean everything. My jacket, extra underwear, toilet kit, my baseball cap, all my personal things. They were taking it away when I got there.

Conant: What did you do?

Carter: I said, "What the hell you doin'? That's my stuff!"

Conant: What did they say?

Carter: They said—I swear to God—and this is what really scared me—they said, "You won't be needing it. You'll be dead by morning." That's when I knew that Jeremy Brown had guys working with him and they meant business. That's when I decided to make a break for it.

Carter then testifies to his actions after deciding to escape—how he waited until lights out and then sneaked out of the dorm and out of the prison grounds, how he walked for miles in rural mountain country with no houses or stores around, how he was looking for a phone to call his attorney at the public defender's office to ask him what to do. He wanted to turn himself in, but was not sure how to do it. He wound up on Beaver Canyon Road trying to hitch a ride when he saw the sheriff's car approaching.

> **Conant**: What did you do when you saw the sheriff's car?

> **Carter**: I thought about giving myself up but I was afraid he would take me back to Sundale. I know it was stupid but I decided to run. One thing for sure was on my mind. I didn't want to go back to Sundale. Those guys were gonna kill me there. I wasn't sure what to do. My mind was all crazy. I guess I just panicked.

The D.A. begins cross-examination. "Why didn't you contact the staff at Sundale as soon as you received the death threat? Didn't the staff protect you at Marcy?"

> **Carter**: I didn't think I had time to tell the staff. I couldn't wait til morning. It was different at Marcy. They knew as soon as I testified that I would probably get a threat. They started to protect me right away.

> **D.A.**: You just said you intended to turn yourself in?

> **Carter**: I did. But I didn't know how to do it.

> **D.A.**: Then why did you run from the sheriff?

> **Carter**: Like I said, it was a stupid thing to do. It was just instinctive. I was so used to running from the police.

> **D.A.**: And why did you give the sheriff a false name? You lied to him. That's what you did. You lied. You want us to believe you wanted to

turn yourself in but that's not what you did when you had the chance. You lied to the sheriff and now you're lying to us. You didn't mean to turn yourself in at all.

The D.A. advances closer and closer to the witness stand.

D.A.: You just wanted to get free. Isn't that right, Mr. Carter?

Conant: Objection, Your Honor! He's badgering the witness.

Judge: Sustained. Let's keep our distance, Counsel.

D.A.: And another thing. If you wanted to turn yourself in, why did you take off your prison shirt? Wouldn't the shirt attract attention so you would be reported and be picked up? Wouldn't that be a good way to turn yourself in?

Carter: I took off the shirt because it started to get too hot, that's all.

D.A.: Too hot? Is that your answer? I'll tell you why you got rid of your prison shirt. You did that because you didn't want to be recognized as a prisoner. You wanted to escape, really escape, isn't that the real reason, Mr. Carter?

Carter: You can say what you want. I'm telling you the truth.

When the direct and cross-examination of Eddie Carter are completed, both sides rest and the judge begins his instructions of law to the jury.

Members of the jury, you have heard all the evidence and now it is my duty to instruct you on the law that applies to this case. You must accept and follow the law as I state it to you, regardless of whether you agree with the law or not. You must not be influenced by pity for the defendant or by prejudice against him.

The judge continues reading a long list of instructions, some of which apply to the case, and some of which do not. He also has the bailiff pass out the packet of instructions to each juror.

> The defendant, Eddie Carter, is charged with committing the crime of escape from prison. He claims he had to commit the crime in order to save his life and therefore he has raised the defense of necessity. I wish to define that defense to you. A prisoner is not guilty of the crime of escape if he escapes from prison because of necessity. The defendant has the burden of proving by a preponderance of the evidence all the facts necessary to establish the elements of this defense, which are as follows:
>
> 1. The prisoner was faced with a specific threat of death or great bodily harm in the immediate future.
> 2. There was no time for complaint to the authorities.
> 3. There was no time or opportunity to resort to the courts.
> 4. There was no evidence of force or violence toward prison personnel or other innocent persons in effecting the escape.
> 5. The prisoner immediately reported to authorities as soon as he attained a position of safety from immediate threat or, if apprehended before the opportunity to report arose, fully intended to report immediately to authorities after attaining a position of safety.
>
> The fact that a witness has been convicted of a felony may be considered by you only for the purpose of determining the believability of that witness. The fact of a conviction does not necessarily destroy or impair a witness's believability. It is simply one of the circumstances that you may take into consideration in weighing the testimony of that witness.

The defense counsel begins her closing argument.

> Ladies and gentlemen, let's just talk common sense. Just because you are sitting here in the formal atmosphere of the courtroom doesn't mean that you've left your common sense out in the hallway. Try to put yourself in Eddie Carter's place. There is no dispute that the threat to his life was serious. The district attorney can't dispute that fact. It was not only serious but it was imminent. It was late at night. There was no time to arrange a conference with the prison staff to get protection. He could have been killed at any moment. He had to leave to save his life. Other than that threat, Eddie had no reason to escape. With only six months to serve on a five-year sentence, that would be foolish. He had been a model prisoner. To escape would be risking another long sentence, and he was sick of prison life. He did what any reasonable person would do, what any of us would do under similar circumstances. He got out of there as soon as he could, hoping he could turn himself in and serve the rest of his time in another institution.
>
> The district attorney wants to make a big deal out of the fact that Eddie ran from the sheriff when he first saw the car. He will argue that that proves Eddie had no intention of turning himself in, that Eddie wanted to make a real escape, to be free. But Eddie has explained that. He admits it was a stupid thing to do. Eddie Carter is not an especially smart man. Never been past the eighth grade. He admits he panicked and ran. Yes it was stupid, but it was understandable. We have to try to understand Eddie's mind-set at the time. We have to try to take into account Eddie's background. He'd been running from the police most of his life. He'd spent most of his adult life in prison. Like he said, it was instinctive. You see the police, you run. Consider also what was the biggest thing on Eddie's mind. He didn't want to go back to Sundale. For a good reason. He'd just been told that he was about to die. Sundale meant death. He was afraid the sheriff would take him back to Sundale. That was a reasonable fear under those circumstances.

> The district attorney will argue that because of the incident with the sheriff, we cannot believe Eddie Carter intended to turn himself in. He wants you to believe Eddie Carter is lying to you. But consider the evidence as to Eddie's credibility. All the evidence in this case supports the fact that he is telling the truth. The hearing officer at the Marcy prison told us that Eddie was truthful; that Eddie showed courage in his testimony; and that he, Lieutenant Hawkins, the hearing officer, believed Eddie in that hearing. Consider also the incident with the locker. When Eddie didn't show up at roll call, the officer in charge, Mr. Finley, had Eddie's locker searched. It was empty. Everyone thought that Eddie had taken his things with him in his escape. But Eddie told how he saw two inmates take all his belongings and tell him he'd be dead shortly. How do we know that Eddie's account of how the locker was emptied is true? We know that because when Eddie was arrested on Beaver Canyon Road, he had nothing with him. If he had thought about really escaping, he would have planned on taking his things with him. The fact that he left the prison with just the clothes on his back supports the claim that he left in a hurry with no preplanning and also supports the inference that Eddie Carter is telling the truth.
>
> Ladies and gentlemen, when you are in the jury room deliberating the fate of Eddie Carter, put yourself in his place on the night of his escape. Then ask yourself this question: You have two choices—escape or die. Which would you choose?

The district attorney rises to being his closing argument.

> Ladies and gentlemen, let's cut right to the heart of why the defendant must be found guilty in this case. We do not dispute he received a death threat. We admit that.
>
> If that was the only fact he had to prove, then he should be acquitted. Hands down. No question. But the judge told you the law, that the defense of necessity requires five elements. They are all listed in your packet of instructions. Look them over when you are in the jury room.

The threat of death is only one of them. The judge told you that the defendant has to satisfy every one. Look at element number five. That element says that in order for the defendant to win an acquittal on the defense of necessity, he must report to authorities after his escape as soon as he has reached a position of safety, or, if arrested before he has a chance to report, must show he intended to report immediately. The defendant did neither one. What did he do when he saw the sheriff's car? Did he rush to the deputy and report to him? That is what element five requires. That is what the law requires. Oh, he rushed all right. But he rushed the other way. He took off running. Made no effort at all to report. When caught, he even gave the sheriff a phony name. Actions speak louder than words, and the defendant's actions at the time show he had no intention to turn himself in. They show he intended to escape, really escape, not just because of a death threat, but because he wanted to be free. He has failed to satisfy element number five, and therefore his defense fails and he must be found guilty.

Ladies and gentlemen, the defendant is a con artist, a twice-convicted felon trying to come up with a lame story to get away with his crime. If he had not been caught on Beaver Canyon Road, he'd be a thousand miles from here by now. Don't be fooled, ladies and gentlemen. Follow the law. The man is guilty and it is your duty to tell him so. Thank you.

WHAT IS YOUR VERDICT?

QUESTIONS FOR YOU TO CONSIDER

As you determine your verdict for this crime, here are some questions about the crime and the trial for you to think about.

1. Why did the defense attorney bring out at the beginning of the case that Eddie Carter had been convicted of two robberies, and then, when he was on the witness stand, have him admit those crimes? Wasn't that very damaging to Carter's defense?

2. What argument regarding Carter's believability as a witness could the district attorney have made but failed to make in closing argument?

AUTHOR'S ANSWERS TO THE QUESTIONS

1. Carter's felony record of two robberies was certainly damaging to the defense case. But the defense attorney knew that the only chance she had was to put him on the stand to present his defense, and she knew also that his record would come out when she did. If she didn't bring it out, the district attorney would have the right to do so. Trial attorneys generally agree that when evidence damaging to their witness is bound to come out before the jury one way or another, it is always best to bring it out first themselves to soften the blow.

2. The judge instructed the jury that they could consider Carter's two robbery convictions in judging his believability as a witness. The district attorney could have argued this point to the jury and could have reminded them that Carter's prior convictions cast a shadow over anything he said on the witness stand. For some reason, the district attorney left this point out of his closing argument.

THE VERDICT

What was your verdict?

The real-life jury found the defendant not guilty.

When jurors were interviewed after the trial, they said that it was Carter's believability on the stand that turned the tide in his favor.

A Policeman's Habit

STATE V. EDWARD MAYFIELD

On the night of December 27, 2005, Donna Nugent—a blonde, attractive woman in her early twenties—visited the apartment of her boyfriend Clay Garcia. At about 8:00 p.m., Donna phoned her mother from Clay's apartment to say she was coming home, a trip that would require her to drive about twenty miles south on the interstate highway. Donna never arrived home. Her body was found lying sixty feet below a bridge just off the highway near the Steinmetz exit ramp. She had apparently been strangled to death with a rope and thrown off the bridge.

Her light-colored Volkswagen was parked on a cul-de-sac near the bridge. A strand of hair similar to Donna's and purple fibers similar in color to Donna's slacks were found on the railing of the bridge. That evening, highway patrolman Edward Mayfield was the officer on duty in that area. A witness testifies he was driving southbound on Interstate 37 that night and saw a state police car stop a light-colored Volkswagen at the Steinmetz Road exit ramp. An attendant at a gas station a few miles from the crime scene testifies that Mayfield stopped by in his police car to buy gas that evening at about 9:30 p.m. He looked nervous, disheveled, and had scratch marks on his face. A number of female witnesses, all young and fairly attractive, testify that in the months prior to the homicide, they were stopped by Mayfield while driving alone on I-37 and directed down the same exit ramp to discuss a minor traffic violation. They say they came forward after recognizing Mayfield's picture on television. Other circumstantial evidence tends to link Mayfield to the crime, but there were no eyewitnesses. On Mayfield's behalf, several witnesses, among them high-ranking law enforcement officers, testify as to Mayfield's excellent reputation as a law-abiding citizen and public servant. Mayfield does not testify at his trial for murder in the first degree.

Deputy District Attorney Miriam Depaul rises slowly to her full height to begin her opening statement. In a strong but emotion-filled voice, she says that the defendant, state highway patrol officer Edward Mayfield, stopped young Donna Nugent on the night of December 27, 2005, as she was driving south on Interstate 37.

"Why did he stop her? We don't know. We may never know. But the evidence will show he directed her off the highway to a dark, secluded spot where he strangled her with a rope and threw her body off the bridge. When you have heard the evidence," she concludes, "I am sure you will find the defendant guilty of murder in the first degree."

You study the defendant as he listens impassively. He has the good looks of someone who could model for a clothing catalog.

"Circumstantial evidence!" the defense attorney, William Silver, a short and feisty man with a high-pitched voice, says in his opening statement. "Fibers! Bloodstains! Tire marks! Facial scratches! That's all they have. No eyewitnesses. No substantial evidence. Ladies and gentlemen of the jury"—he looks each of you in the eye—"is it enough? That's what you'll have to decide."

The first witness for the prosecution is the regional commander of the state police. He testifies that on December 27, Mayfield was working the afternoon shift on Interstate 37.

Depaul: What procedure was Officer Mayfield supposed to follow when stopping a motorist?

Police Commander: Our officers are trained to pull the motorist over to a spot that is relatively safe, to keep their conversations with the public to a minimum, and at all times to remain in view of other motorists. In other words, they're supposed to stay on the side of the highway if there is room.

Depaul: And was there enough room on Interstate 37 at the Steinmetz exit ramp?

Police Commander: Yes, ma'am. Enough to make a stop right there.

The next witness is Donna Nugent's boyfriend, Clay Garcia. He testifies that Donna was with him at his apartment on December 27. He lives about twenty miles north of where she lived with her parents. At about 8:00 p.m., she phoned her mother to let her know she was on her way home. She left in her Volkswagen wearing purple pants, a white sweatshirt, and the new white boots Clay had given her for Christmas. At about 10:30 p.m., Clay says, he received a phone call from Donna's mother, who said Donna had not returned home. He immediately set out to look for her in his car.

Donna's brother-in-law, Chris Berkley, testifies he was among those searching for Donna that night. About 2:00 a.m., he drove down the southbound exit ramp at Steinmetz Road off Interstate 37, where he found Donna's car parked in a cul-de-sac. The passenger door was locked, the keys were still in the ignition, and the driver's window was rolled down. He noticed a dirt road that ran off from one side of the cul-de-sac. He drove down the road to an old bridge but noticed nothing. There was no sign of Donna. He draws a large diagram to help those in the courtroom understand the scene. After finding Donna's car, he drove to the nearest gas station and called the police.

The first officer on the scene was Alberto Aguirre. He says he searched the area for more than an hour before he found Donna Nugent's dead body in a clump of weeds about sixty-five feet below the old bridge.

Depaul: Tell us what you observed, Officer.

Aguirre: I didn't see any blood. But there were marks—sort of like grooves, reddish marks—on her neck. Several on the left side, one on the right side.

Depaul: Did they look like rope burns?

Silver: Objection! Beyond his expertise.

Judge: Sustained.

The county pathologist, Dr. Emmet Turpin, takes the stand. He testifies that the death was caused by asphyxia due to ligature strangulation.

Depaul: What do you mean by ligature?

Turpin: I mean an object composed of various cords or strands, such as a rope, as distinguished from a wire.

The D.A. picks up a yellow rope about three feet long from the clerk's exhibit table.

Depaul: Were the marks on her neck consistent with having been caused by this rope?

Turpin: (*Examining the rope*) They were.

On cross-examination, the defense attorney, Tom Silver, shows the rope to the doctor again.

> **Silver**: Doctor, are you telling the jury that this rope caused the marks on her neck?
>
> **Turpin**: No, sir.
>
> **Silver**: You can only say it's possible—might have—is that right?
>
> **Turpin**: That's true.

As the doctor is leaving the stand, Silver stops him.

> **Silver**: By the way, Doctor, did you find any evidence of rape or any other sexual misconduct?
>
> **Turpin**: I did not, sir.

Officers Joe Petrocine and Richard Sears testify to what they found at the scene. Petrocine found a long blonde hair, similar in color to Donna's hair, on the cement railing of the bridge directly above the spot where the body was found. Sears found purple fibers on the same railing, similar in color to her purple pants.

Court adjourns for the day. The judge admonishes you not to discuss the case with anyone and not to let yourself form any opinion about it until it is finally submitted to you for deliberation.

The next morning, the first witness is Carl Waldron, who states that at some time between eight and nine o'clock on the night in question, he and his girlfriend Lynn Phillips were driving southbound on Interstate 37 when they saw a state police car stopping a light-colored Volkswagen on the Steinmetz Road exit ramp. A young woman driving alone was in the Volkswagen. He saw the emergency lights flashing on top of the police car.

"I remember," he says, "because Lynn turned to me and said, 'She's going to get busted!'"

Defense attorney Silver examines a report in his file, then says, "You were interviewed by the police on January 5?"

> **Waldron**: Yes, sir.
>
> **Silver**: And at that time you said you were not positive what night you saw a state police car stop a Volkswagen. Isn't that correct?
>
> **Waldron**: I guess so, if it's in the report.

The next witness is Charles Simpson, who says that he and his fiancée Carol Hooks left her parents' residence on the night of December 27 in a rented limousine, which suffered a mechanical breakdown on Interstate 37. The chauffeur managed to drive down the Steinmetz exit ramp, where he parked. Around 9:30 p.m., the chauffeur left to get help.

Simpson testifies that while he was waiting in the limousine, he saw a police car, traveling fast, come from under the overpass of Interstate 37 and go up the south entry ramp to the highway.

Mayfield's daily activity log for December 27 is now introduced as evidence. It shows that at 9:20 p.m., Mayfield wrote a traffic ticket to one Stephen Northcutt. A document expert testifies that the entry was originally written as 10:20 p.m. but was subsequently scratched out and touched up to read 9:20 p.m.

The log also shows that between 9:30 p.m. and 10:00 p.m., Mayfield bought gas from a Shell gas station near Marymount Boulevard and Interstate 37.

Alice Wentz takes the stand and says she works at the same Shell station. She was working there the night of December 27 when around ten o'clock a state police officer came in for gas.

Depaul: Please tell the jury what you saw when he came in.

Wentz: Well, he had some scratch marks on his face. He seemed very nervous, and he looked kind of mussed up.

Depaul: Do you see that person in the courtroom?

Wentz: I do.

She points to the defendant.

Wentz: That's him.

The next witness, Mary Knox, is also a gas station employee who was working when Mayfield drove in to get gas. She states, "While Alice was filling his tank, he was standing by the trunk of his car wiping down various objects, like he was trying to clean things."

Depaul: Just what did he do?

Knox: He wiped down something that looked like a flashlight, except I couldn't see it too clear, and then he wiped off his nightstick.

Depaul: Then what?

Knox: Well, when he went to sign his credit card receipt, he had claw marks on the side of his face, only it looked like he was trying to hide them.

Depaul: How could he hide them?

Knox: By cupping his nose with his right hand, only he had to take his hand away when he bent down to sign the receipt, so I said to him, "You must have had a bad night." He kind of looked at me like he didn't understand, and then he said, "Bad? I've had one hell of a night."

A series of state police officers then testify as to events on the night of December 27.

At about 10:25 p.m., Officer Salomino Amiel saw Mayfield in the parking lot near state police headquarters. Amiel saw three large vertical scratches on the right side of Mayfield's face.

Two other highway patrol officers came on duty at ten o'clock to work the graveyard shift. They made a preshift check of the car Mayfield had used. They said the trunk was somewhat disarrayed, the car was not in its normally clean condition, and they did not see a rope in the trunk.

At about 10:30 p.m., Sergeant Robert Mallone spoke with Mayfield. Sergeant Mallone said Mayfield had an "open, bleeding wound" on the back of his right hand, Mayfield's face was "red and puffy-looking," and there were noticeable welts.

Janet Coates, a city police officer, states she was patrolling in the vicinity of Interstate 37 on December 31, four days after the murder, when she was directed to go to the Steinmetz Road area to meet a state highway patrol officer who was detaining possible murder suspects in the Nugent case. Coates spoke there with Mayfield, who said the suspects had been riding their motorbike in the Steinmetz Road area. Mayfield said he had detained them because, "you know the crook always returns to the scene of the crime."

Officer Coates testifies that Mayfield was very curious about the Nugent murder investigation by the city police. He wanted to know "details" about it. When she explained to him what could be learned from skin samples, she noticed him cleaning his fingernails. Coates felt Mayfield was pressing her to tell him what the homicide investigators thought had "really happened down there." When she told him someone had taken Nugent to the old bridge and thrown her off the west side, Mayfield motioned to the east side of the bridge and said, "She wasn't thrown over there, she was put over here."

Mayfield asked Coates what she thought would happen to the person who committed the crime if caught. Coates said, "I hope they die a slow and painful death." Coates testifies Mayfield got angry with her, saying, "You don't know what you're talking about—it could have been something that got out of hand, it could have been something that just went too far."

The following day is devoted to expert testimony on the physical evidence.

Albert Lackner, an expert in fibers, testifies he compared a single gold thread found on Donna's sweatshirt with the threads on the shoulder patch of the defendant's uniform.

> **Depaul**: Did you form an opinion as to those threads?
>
> **Lackner**: Yes. I concluded they had the same microscopic characteristics, and therefore the fiber from the shirt could have come from the shoulder patch.
>
> **Depaul**: Did you find any distinction whatsoever between the thread on the shirt and the threads from the patch?
>
> **Lackner**: None whatsoever.

He also says that fibers found in Donna's hands were similar to fibers from the patch, and that purple fibers found on Mayfield's gun and boot could have come from Donna's purple pants.

A *serologist*, an expert in the identification of body fluids, testifies he analyzed a bloodstain found on the victim's boot and compared it to the blood of the victim and the blood of the defendant.

> **Depaul**: What blood type was found on the boot?
>
> **Serologist**: ABO Group A, Estrase D1, and PGM1.
>
> **Depaul**: And the blood type of Donna Nugent, what type was that?

Serologist: Her blood type is ABO Group O, Estrase D1, and PGM 2-1.

DePaul: What is Edward Mayfield's blood type?

Serologist: His blood type was ABO Group A, Estrase D1, and PGM1.

DePaul: And from that analysis you were able to conclude that the bloodstain found on that boot, her boot, could not have come from Ms. Nugent, but could have come from Officer Mayfield; is that right?

Serologist: That's correct.

Defense Attorney Silver looks up from a document he is studying and starts his cross-examination. "What percentage of the population has the blood type found on the boot?"

Serologist: About 18% of the general population.

Silver: Okay, so what you are saying is that about 18% of the population has that type, and that Officer Mayfield is among millions of people who have that type?

Serologist: Yes, sir.

Silver: It is not like a fingerprint, which you could say definitely came from him?

Serologist: Correct.

The witness gives similar testimony with regard to bloodstains on Donna's shirt—they could have come from the defendant; they could not have come from Donna.

An accident investigator testifies he examined fresh tire tracks on the bridge near the railing where the blonde hair and the purple fibers were found. He measured the distance between the tracks. He also measured the distance between the back tires of the Chevrolet police car Mayfield was driving that night. The distance was the same.

Upon cross-examination, Defense Attorney Silver brings out the fact that none of the expert testimony identifies Mayfield specifically.

The prosecution's final witness is a state officer who testifies that on January 6, ten days after the murder, Mayfield's patrol car was searched again. This time, a yellow rope, about three feet long—the same one counsel used in examining the pathologist—was found in the trunk.

Depaul: Is that rope standard issue equipment?

Officer: It is not, ma'am.

Silver is brief on cross-examination. "Do you know why it was not found before, when the trunk was searched?"

Officer: I don't know, sir.

The prosecution rests. D.A. Depaul offers her exhibits in evidence, and they are received without argument.

Silver opens the defense case by calling a number of character witnesses who attest to Mayfield's excellent reputation as a law-abiding citizen.

A fingerprint expert from the police department testifies none of the fingerprints found in Donna's Volkswagen belonged to Mayfield.

Mayfield's daughter, Sandra, testifies she has a purple jacket made by Mayfield's wife, who did her sewing in the living room of their home. While the sewing was going on, the purple cloth for the jacket was usually kept on the living room couch, and it was Mayfield's habit on coming home after work to put his gun and gun belt down on this same couch.

The defense calls its own expert on fibers, who testifies that the purple fibers found on the defendant's gun and boot could have come either from his daughter's purple jacket or the cloth on the couch. He also says the fibers from Mayfield's shoulder patch can be distinguished from the fibers found on Donna's shirt and hands.

Marcia Davis, a serious-looking woman wearing no makeup, takes the stand. She testifies that on the evening of December 27, she was driving her car southbound on Interstate 37 between 7:30 and 8:00 p.m. and was passing the Steinmetz Road exit.

Silver: Did anything unusual take place?

Davis: Yes. I was approaching the Steinmetz exit when I saw a man standing at the side of the highway, apparently a hitchhiker—

D.A. Depaul interrupts. "Objection, Your Honor! Irrelevant. Whether she saw a hitchhiker has absolutely nothing to do with this case."

The judge replies, "Overruled. I will hear the evidence, subject to a motion to strike." To the witness, he says, "You may proceed."

Davis: He was apparently a hitchhiker because he was waving his arms as if he wanted me to stop. Then he lunged out as if to get in my way to make me stop. I said to myself, "This guy must be crazy—"

Depaul: Objection, Your Honor. What she said to herself is irrelevant.

Judge: Sustained.

Depaul: The D.A. motions to strike, Your Honor.

Judge: Motion granted. The jury will disregard the last statement as to what the witness said to herself. Proceed.

Davis: Well, anyway, I had to swerve in order to avoid hitting him. He was waving his arms in a crazy way.

Silver: Can you describe him?

Davis: I was so upset and it happened so fast, all I remember is that he was a man.

Depaul: I move to strike the testimony, Your Honor. It's irrelevant guesswork.

Judge: Overruled. It's for the jury to decide.

Silver looks pleased with the judge's ruling. He calls three other motorists, who give similar testimony. One of the witnesses, Albert Sandoz, adds that the man was "waving money and jumping in front of cars," apparently in an effort to make them stop.

As his final witness, Silver calls one of Mayfield's fellow officers, John Bannister, who says he saw scratches on Mayfield's face the night of December 27 at about ten o'clock.

Silver: Did you ask him how he got the scratches?

Bannister: I did.

Silver: And what was his reply?

Bannister: He said he was chasing a suspect and fell against a barbed wire fence and scratched his face.

Depaul cross-examines. "Did he tell you where this happened?"

Bannister: No.

Depaul: Did he tell you if he caught the suspect?

Bannister: He said the guy got away.

The defense rests. Mayfield does not take the stand.

"Any rebuttal by the prosecution?" the judge asks.

The D.A. clears her throat. "Your Honor," she says, "I realize that it is still early on this Friday afternoon. I need the weekend to prepare my rebuttal. May we adjourn until Monday?"

On Monday morning, the D.A. begins by calling Irma Polland. She is in her early twenties, blonde, and attractive. She testifies that a month before the murder, she was stopped by Officer Mayfield while driving south along Interstate 37 at night. He directed her down the Steinmetz exit ramp and asked her to get out of her car. He told her she had been driving too slowly. After a brief conversation about her family, he let her go.

Silver jumps to his feet. "Objection, Your Honor. In the first place, it's irrelevant. Just because he stopped this lady there doesn't mean he did the same with Donna Nugent. In the second place, it's an improper rebuttal. She should have presented this evidence in her case-in-chief. The D.A.'s been lying in the weeds with this—"

"That's enough, Counsel!" the judge interrupts him. "We'll discuss it at sidebar, out of the hearing of the jury."

The attorneys go to the side of the bench, and there is a furious exchange of whispers you are not supposed to hear. You can't help but hear some of the words, however. You hear Silver say "highly inflammatory," and the judge say, "truth is what we want," but the rest is unclear. Finally the attorneys return to their places. Silver is visibly upset.

"Proceed, Counsel," the judge says. "Objection is overruled."

The witness is still on the stand. The district attorney resumes.

> **Depaul**: Ms. Polland, tell the jury how you came to be a witness in this trial.

Polland: I was watching TV last week, and I saw the news about this case. It sounded familiar, so I called your office.

Silver takes a deep breath and squares his shoulders before beginning cross-examination.

Silver: Did he tell you why he directed you off the highway?

Polland: Yes. He said it was safer. Too dangerous on the highway with all the drunk drivers these days.

Silver: Didn't touch you?

Polland: No.

Silver: Didn't do anything out of line?

Polland: No. He was very polite.

There follows a string of eighteen witnesses. Silver objects, arguing that the number of witnesses is cumulative, but the judge overrules. Most are women in their twenties who testify they were driving alone on I-37 when Mayfield stopped them and directed them down the same exit ramp for some minor violation. Nearly all say they contacted the D.A.'s office within the past few days after seeing news of the trial on television, too late to testify in the prosecution's case-in-chief. Only two were not driving alone—one had three small children asleep in the backseat, and the other was with her husband, who was slumped down in the passenger seat. Under cross-examination, all admit the defendant acted courteously at all times and never made any sexual advances.

"Let the record show my objection is a continuing one for all these witnesses," the defense attorney says.

"So noted," replies the judge.

One witness is a young man named David Bloom. He has long blonde hair, which hangs down well over his shoulders. Bloom testifies that on the night of December 2, 2005, he was driving alone on Interstate 37 when Mayfield ordered him to pull off the highway and go down the Steinmetz exit ramp.

Depaul: At the time of this stop, was your hair the same as it is now?

Bloom: A little longer.

Depaul: Was it blonde then also?

Bloom: Oh, yes.

Depaul: Was it dark at the bottom of the exit ramp?

Bloom: Real dark.

Depaul: What happened when the defendant came up to your car?

Bloom: He looked at me in surprise. He said, "Oh my goodness" when he saw me. I think he thought I was a girl—

Silver: Objection, Your Honor! What the witnesses thought is not relevant.

Judge: Sustained.

Silver: Motion to strike—

"Granted. Ladies and gentleman," the judge says to you, "the last statement of the witness as to what he thought is stricken from the record. Disregard it."

Depaul: What did he say?

Bloom: At first he seemed too confused to say anything. Then he mentioned something about my headlight. That it looked out of alignment.

Depaul: Was it?

Bloom: No. In fact, I'd just had my headlights checked a few weeks before.

Depaul: Then what?

Bloom: He let me go.

Denise Carrier, an attractive woman in her twenties, is called as the State's final witness. She testifies that on December 15, while driving south on Interstate 37, she was pulled over by a state police car. It was about 10:30 p.m. The officer told her over his loudspeaker to drive all the way down the Steinmetz exit ramp. She got out of her car and he got out of his, and they met between their two cars. It was dark and cold. He said her headlight was too low or too high—she could not remember which. He noticed she was cold, and asked her to get into his car so they could discuss it. They sat in the car for about thirty minutes talking about various things, mostly her boyfriend. Then he said he would show her the old bridge down the road.

Depaul: Did you object?

Carrier: I was too scared. I was shaking so that I could hardly talk.

The officer drove about fifty yards to the bridge, where they got out and looked down.

Depaul: Did he touch you?

Carrier: No, he was very polite.

She says the officer took her back to her car and told her she could go.

Depaul: Did he ever give you a ticket?

Carrier: No.

Depaul: What happened after you drove off?

Carrier: I was too nervous to drive. I had to pull over and stop for a while so I could calm down.

Depaul: Do you see the officer in the courtroom?

She points to the defendant. "That's him. I'll never forget him."

There are three possible verdicts in this case:

1. guilty of first-degree murder
2. guilty of second-degree murder
3. not guilty

WHAT IS YOUR VERDICT?

QUESTIONS FOR YOU TO CONSIDER

As you determine your verdict for this crime, here are some questions about the crime and the trial for you to think about.

1. Of all the circumstantial evidence presented by the prosecution, which was the most damaging to the defendant?
2. The defense attorney made a crucial decision to keep his client off the stand. Was that a mistake?
3. Does the fact that this case is based primarily on circumstantial evidence make it a bad case for the prosecution?
4. A fellow officer testified for the defense that Mayfield told him he received the scratches on his face while chasing a suspect. Shouldn't the D.A. have objected to this hearsay statement?

AUTHOR'S ANSWERS TO THE QUESTIONS

1. The defendant's strange habit of directing so many young female motorists off the highway to the same dark, secluded spot where the murder occurred was especially damaging to his case. The highly distinctive nature of this evidence pointed to Mayfield as the one who led Donna Nugent to the same place he had lured others.

2. One of the most critical decisions for any criminal defense attorney in a jury trial is whether to put his or her client on the stand. Here the jury was anxious to hear Mayfield explain why he stopped all those young women at the same place and how he got the scratches on his face. Of course, the jurors were told they could not draw any negative inference from the fact that he did not testify and they were not to permit it to enter their deliberations in any way. But could you realistically follow such an instruction? Could you keep yourself from thinking, "What's he hiding?"

   We will never know why Mayfield did not testify, or whether it was a strategic mistake not to do so. That decision remains a secret between Mayfield and his attorney. But from what we do know, it seems he would have made a poor witness. He tended to give himself away several times, when he blurted out on which side of the bridge the victim had been thrown and when he defended the killer to another officer. Moreover, the cross-examiner would have had a field day getting him to explain why he stopped so many women. Better by far to have this young, handsome officer, a family man with a clean record, sit there near his wife and children, and let the jury wonder how such a person could have done something so terrible. He may also have confessed guilt to his lawyer, making it ethically impossible for him to be called as a witness to deny guilt.

3. This case was based almost entirely on circumstantial evidence. There was no direct evidence Mayfield committed a murder: there was no

positive identification, no one saw him at the scene that night, and no confessions or admissions were recorded. However, this does not necessarily mean it was a bad case for the prosecution.

Of course, some jurors will say they can't convict on circumstantial evidence alone. Prosecutors must be wary of them in jury selection. However, most jurors like circumstantial evidence; they are challenged by it and enjoy being detectives. The judge instructs jury members that facts don't have to be proved by direct evidence; rather, both direct and circumstantial evidence are entitled to the same weight, and both are equally acceptable as a means of proof. In fact, circumstantial evidence is often the strongest. A fingerprint, for example, is really only circumstantial evidence, but it is the best proof a person was present at a certain location even if no one saw him or her. It is often better evidence than direct eyewitness identification, which could be a mistake or a lie. And when the circumstantial evidence points to only one reasonable interpretation—as it did here—jurors feel a special satisfaction in returning a guilty verdict.

4. The testimony by the officer as to what Mayfield said was definitely self-serving hearsay and should never have been admitted into evidence. But since the D.A. failed to object, the testimony came into evidence. At a second trial, the evidence was properly excluded.

THE VERDICT

What was your verdict?

The real-life jury found the defendant guilty of murder in the first degree.

Edward Mayfield was tried twice for the murder of Donna Nugent. The first trial resulted in a hung jury. In the second trial, Mayfield's hearsay statement that he received the scratches on his face while chasing a suspect and the testimony concerning the hitchhiker were both excluded. A different jury convicted Mayfield of first-degree murder. The State did not seek the death penalty, although it was within its discretion to do so.

The jury sentenced the defendant to twenty-five years to life in prison.

Who Killed Sara Parson?

STATE V. JASON TUNGSTIN

Soon after waking on the morning of March 20, 2000, the parents of 14-year-old Sara Parson were devastated to discover that Sara had been stabbed to death in her bedroom. Subsequent investigation revealed that during the previous evening, neighbors saw Jason Tungstin, a homeless transient, acting weirdly. He was roaming the neighborhood, knocking on doors, and asking for a girl named Stacy. One of the neighbors said Tungstin did not speak in a normal manner and appeared to be either drunk or on drugs. Police found Tungstin wandering the streets a few blocks from the crime scene. When questioned by police, he denied any involvement in the crime and agreed to go to the police station where he was processed for evidence. The police took hair and blood samples, fingernail scrapings, fingerprints, and footprints. They also took all of Tungstin's clothes, giving him other things to wear. After a thorough examination and questioning, detectives found nothing connecting Tungstin to the crime, and they released him.

Several days later, police detained Marcus Parson, Sara's 15-year-old brother, and Marcus's close friends, John Alter and Alan Bendix, both also 15, for questioning. After an extensive interrogation lasting many hours—which was videotaped—Marcus Parson allegedly confessed to killing Sara. John Alter allegedly admitted to police that he was the lookout and said that Marcus Parson held Sara down while Alan Bendix did the rest with a knife. Bendix denied any involvement and refused to answer any questions. The three boys were arrested and charged with murder in the first degree.

Nevertheless, detectives pursued further investigation. Criminalists conducted DNA tests of tiny blood smears discovered on the red shirt that Tungstin was wearing on the night of the crime. The tests established to a virtual certainty that Sara Parson's blood appeared on Tungstin's shirt. Marcus Parson and John Alter recanted their statements and said they had been coerced into making false confessions. The case against the three teenagers was dismissed and Tungstin was charged with the murder. At trial, an expert on police interrogation testifies that the techniques used in the interrogation of Parson and Alter were coercive and could have led to unreliable and false confessions. In the final arguments to the jury, the prosecution relies heavily on evidence of Sara's DNA found on Tungstin's shirt. The defense claims the boys were the real perpetrators and that Sara's blood was transferred to Tungstin's shirt by sloppy police work.

The courtroom is packed for this case that has rocked the community. The D.A. is a rugged-looking man who looks like he could be a linebacker.

During the opening statements, your attention is distracted by the appearance of the defendant, Jason Tungstin. He stares straight ahead and appears almost rigid, with his eyes glazed, hardly listening to the attorneys. Jason Tungstin is a young man in his twenties. His suit is too large for him and you have the feeling that he has never worn one before. His blonde hair has been trimmed but it is still unruly despite efforts to comb it back. Already you begin to wonder if he is mentally all there.

The first witness for the prosecution is Sergeant Roger Manley, who testifies that he is a firefighter and paramedic with the city fire department.

D.A.: On the morning of March 20, 2000, were you called to the Parson residence at 1620 Arcane Street in this city?

Manley: Yes. At about 6:30 a.m. that morning, my partner and I went to the residence in a medic rig.

D.A.: Who did you first see when you got there?

Manley: The girl's father, Mr. Parson, met us outside and led us in. He was very stressed out.

D.A.: Did you carry any equipment in with you?

Manley: Yes, sir. My partner Dave carried electronic equipment and an airway maintenance bag with oxygen included. I carried the EKG monitor and our first aid box.

D.A.: Tell us what you saw there.

Manley: Upon entering the girl's room, I saw Mrs. Parson kneeling over the girl's body on the floor. I asked her to move so I could look at her daughter. She moved right away. I could see a lot of blood.

D.A.: What did you do?

Manley: I placed the EKG monitor outside the room and took the paddles in with me. They were wired to the monitor.

D.A.: What did you do with those?

Manley: My purpose was to get a heart reading. I placed the paddles to where I could get skin contact. Then I held them there for five or ten seconds.

D.A.: Did she move?

Manley: Her body didn't move at all. There was no reaction.

D.A.: Meaning she was dead?

Manley: Yes, sir.

D.A.: Did you make any other assessment?

Manley: I made a carotid artery check. I placed two fingers on the left side of her neck.

D.A.: And?

Manley: I couldn't feel a pulse.

D.A.: What next?

Manley: I checked her jaw. I tried to pull down her jaw but it was stiff.

D.A.: What does that mean?

Manley: If the jaw is stiff, it means rigor mortis has set in.

D.A.: What did you do then?

Manley: Well, of course we had come out with the idea of giving medical assistance, but I told Dave that we were not going to work her as a patient. She just was not salvageable. I suspected a crime because of all the blood and the trauma that was obvious by looking at her.

D.A.: Were the police there?

Manley: No, they hadn't arrived yet.

The witness identifies photographs of the crime scene that show blood on Sara's body and on the floor.

D.A.: No further questions at this time.

The defense attorney, Anthony Carino, stands up to cross-examine the witness. He is tall and slender, with a black moustache.

Carino: Did you do anything else while waiting for the police?

Manley: Yes. I checked the window for any evidence of anyone breaking in. It was shut tight but unlocked.

Carino: See any weapon?

Manley: No.

Carino: See any evidence at all of forced entry?

Manley: No, sir.

Carino: See anything unusual in the room?

Manley: Yes, sir, I noticed two words scribbled in pencil on the windowsill.

Carino: What did they say?

Manley: They said, "Kill, kill."

Carino whispers to the D.A. and then turns to the judge.

"Your Honor, at this point the defense and the district attorney wish to enter into a stipulation as follows—the handwriting of the words "Kill, kill" found on the windowsill has been analyzed by an independent expert who also analyzed the handwriting of the defendant and found that the writing on the windowsill does not match Mr. Tungstin's handwriting."

D.A.: We so stipulate, Your Honor.

The judge turns to the jury to explain. "Ladies and gentlemen of the jury, counsel have stipulated, or agreed, to a certain fact and therefore that fact is no longer in dispute. You may accept the fact stated in the stipulation as having been conclusively proved. Proceed, Counsel."

Carino questions further on the subject of forced entry.

Carino: Did you inspect every window in the house?

Manley: We did. They were all locked except for Sara's window.

"Your Honor," Carino says to the judge, "My next question calls for hearsay but I have spoken with the district attorney and he has no objection."

Judge: Thank you. Proceed.

Carino: Sergeant, did you ask Mr. Parson about the doors?

Manley: Oh yes. He told me they all had been locked before everyone in the family retired. Except for the sliding door to the master bedroom.

Carino: Find any damage, any pry marks, anything like that?

Manley: Uh-uh, nothing.

Carino: No evidence any window had been moved?

Manley: None.

Carino: And you inspected every door?

Manley: We did.

Carino: Any indications of any attempt to break in?

Manley: No, nothing like that.

Carino: Any other possible entry or exit?

Manley: I testified to the sliding glass door in the master bedroom where Mr. and Mrs. Parson slept.

Carino: So in order to get in or out that way, any intruder would have had to pass through that bedroom?

Manley: Yes.

Carino: Did you try to move it?

Manley: We did. It made a noise, a screeching noise, when I opened it.

Carino: Loud enough to awaken Mr. and Mrs. Parson?

D.A.: Objection!

Judge: Sustained.

Carino: So what you are saying, Sergeant, is that you and your team found no evidence at all of forced entry or exit, is that correct?

Manley: That's correct.

Carino: From your interviews of the Parson family, were you able to determine who slept in the house that night?

Manley: Yes. The entire Parson family: the two parents, their son, Marcus, and the victim Sara slept there that night. Sara and Marcus each had their own room next to each other.

Carino: Thank you, that's all.

D.A.: I have one question on redirect, Your Honor. Did you find any evidence at all linking Marcus Parson or any of his friends to the crime?

Manley: No, sir. Nothing.

Carino, the defense attorney, has one last question. "Did it appear to you, Sergeant, based on your training and experience, that this crime was an inside job?"

D.A.: Objection!

Judge: Sustained.

Carino: Nothing further.

The D.A. calls Dr. Mathew Willetts to the stand. Dr. Willetts is the autopsy surgeon who examined the body of Sara Parson. After testifying to his extensive training and experience as an autopsy surgeon, Dr. Willetts says he arrived on the scene shortly after the medics and police got there. Using photographs, he points out nine stab wounds to Sara's head and chest area, front and back. He later performed an autopsy and rendered his opinion that Sara bled to death from these wounds. Dr. Willetts further states he noticed a trail of blood leading from the bed to the doorway where Sara's body was found.

D.A.: Could you tell what type of weapon was used?

Willetts: Only that it was a sharp instrument, probably a knife.

D.A.: Was there anything you observed that indicated she was killed by more than one assailant?

Willetts: There was nothing at the scene that indicated that to me, no.

D.A.: Could you determine whether she was being held down by someone while someone else stabbed her?

Willetts: No, I'm afraid I couldn't determine that.

D.A.: Isn't it true that the various wounds on Sara's body were on both her front and back?

Willetts: Yes, that's true.

D.A.: So if she was being held down, she was not being held down very effectively, was she?

Willetts: That is correct. Her body certainly moved quite a bit during the attack because different areas of the body, front and back, were struck.

D.A.: Thank you, Doctor. You have been very helpful.

Carino cross-examines. "You have testified, Doctor, that you examined the depth and width of the wounds, and that they were very different, is that correct?"

Willetts: Yes. Some were different.

Carino: So is it a possibility, Doctor, that two knives of different sizes were used?

Willetts: Yes, I suppose that's a possibility. Two different knives could have been used. I cannot rule that out.

At this point Carino goes to the clerk and whispers something to her, whereupon she unlocks her drawer and takes out a knife that she hands to him.

Carino: Your Honor, I hold in my hands a knife that has been marked Defense Exhibit A. Dr. Willetts, I hand you this knife. Have you examined it before?

Willetts: Yes. You showed it to me before the trial and I did examine it.

Carino: It appears to be a knife with a blade about six inches long, correct?

Willetts: Yes.

Carino: Is there anything unusual about that knife?

Willetts: Well, it does have two unusual incisions in the blade.

Carino: You examined the nature of the wounds carefully?

Willetts: I did.

Carino: And you examined carefully the shape of the knife with its unusual incisions?

Willetts: Uh-huh—I mean, yes.

Carino: And can you tell us, Doctor, whether it is possible that this knife caused those wounds?

D.A.: Objection! Anything is possible.

Judge: Overruled. The witness may answer.

Willetts: Possible. Yes.

Carino: Are some of the wounds consistent with having been caused by this knife?

Willetts: Consistent, yes.

Carino: Do you have an opinion, Doctor, as to whether this knife would be similar to the knife that stabbed Sara Parson?

D.A.: Objection! Beyond his expertise!

Judge: Overruled. You may answer, Doctor.

Willetts: Quite similar, yes. The knife used in the murder would have been quite similar. I cannot say anything more than that. I cannot say this was the knife used.

Carino: Thank you, Doctor. Now would you please tell this jury what a defensive wound is?

Willetts: Certainly. A defensive wound is simply a wound inflicted on someone who is trying to defend themselves. Such as grabbing the knife or bringing their hands up to cover their face.

Carino: So if a person is being held down, if their hands are being held, there would not likely be any defensive wound, is that right, Doctor?

Willetts: That is correct, assuming those circumstances.

Carino: So, just to be clear, if you have one person inflicting the stabbing and another person holding the hands down, there would be little chance of a defensive wound, correct?

Willetts: Yes. That is correct.

Carino clears his throat and pauses a moment before his next question. "Dr. Willetts, did you find any defensive wounds on the body of Sara Parson?"

Willetts: No, I did not.

Carino: So there could very well have been two people assaulting her?

D.A.: Objection! This calls for pure speculation!

Judge: Overruled.

Willetts: That is a possibility.

Carino: Thank you, Doctor. That is all.

The D.A. jumps to his feet. He is obviously upset by the cross-examination. "Dr. Willetts, can you tell this jury that this knife caused any of these wounds?"

Willetts: No, I cannot.

D.A.: Can you tell this jury that two persons assaulted Sara Parson?

Willetts: No, I cannot.

D.A.: Can you tell this jury that two knives were used in the murder?

Willetts: No, I cannot. They are only possibilities. I cannot be certain.

D.A.: Thank you, Doctor.

There follows a series of nine witnesses who live in the same neighborhood as the Parsons. Myra Brodney is called first. She states she lives at 1080 Arcane Road, in a single-family home.

D.A.: Is that just down the hill from the Parson home?

Brodney: Yes. About half a block away.

D.A.: Please try to recall the evening of March 19, 2000. Did something unusual occur at your home?

Brodney: Well, a strange-looking guy came to the door, if that's what you mean.

D.A.: Who was home at the time?

Brodney: I live with my husband and my daughter. We were all home at the time.

D.A.: How old is your daughter?

Brodney: Laura's 11.

D.A.: What were you doing when this incident happened?

Brodney: It must have been around nine o'clock. We were all watching TV when we heard a knock at the door.

D.A.: What did you do?

Brodney: I called out, "It's open, come on in."

D.A.: Why did you do that?

Brodney: We are close to our neighbors. We visit all the time. I just assumed it was one of the neighbors.

D.A.: So did the person take your invitation?

Brodney: Well, the door opened but he stayed outside. He asked if Stacy lived here.

D.A.: Did you get a good look at him?

Brodney: Oh yes. He was quite close.

D.A.: Ever see him before?

Brodney: Never.

D.A.: Describe him for us.

Brodney: Long hair. Blondish. Shoulder length. Beard and moustache. A young man. He had on a red shirt.

D.A.: What did you say when he asked for Stacy?

Brodney: I just said, "Sorry, no one here by that name."

D.A.: Did you notice anything special about him?

Brodney: Well, yes, I did think he was weird. Maybe drunk or on drugs.

D.A.: Did you see a weapon?

Brodney: Oh no, no.

D.A.: Did he leave?

Brodney: Well, he closed the door, but then—

D.A.: Yes. What happened next?

Brodney: He opened the door again. He said, "Are you sure Stacy doesn't live here?" I said, "I am sure." Then I got up. He was still standing at the door. I told him again there was no Stacy here. He continued to stand outside. I closed the door. And locked it.

D.A.: You were not used to locking your door?

Brodney: Nah, never. But I sure did this time.

D.A.: Why?

Brodney: I didn't want him bothering us again. So creepy.

D.A.: Ms. Brodney, I want you to look around this courtroom. And take your time. I want you to tell us if you see the young man who came to your door that night.

The witness nods and looks around. You know what she is going to do. You know the D.A. is doing it this way for dramatic effect. You suspect it is an act of theater coached by the D.A., but there is no reason to disbelieve the witness. She looks all around. She even looks at you. Then she stops when she turns to the defendant.

"Yes," she says, pointing at Tungstin. "That's him."

D.A.: Are you positive?

Brodney: Yes, positive. But he looks kind of different now.

D.A.: How so?

Brodney: Umm, he's been cleaned up. He's cut his hair. The beard and moustache are gone. But I know it's him.

D.A.: Your Honor, may the record show the witness has identified the defendant?

Judge: Yes. The record may so show.

D.A.: (*To the witness*) Thank you, ma'am. No further questions.

Carino has no questions. Eight other neighbors give similar accounts of how the defendant came to their homes looking for Stacy, all on the night before the murder.

Detective Tom Draper testifies for the prosecution that soon after the crime was discovered, he interviewed the neighbors who testified. Hours later, he located Tungstin wandering aimlessly in a shopping mall about a mile from the Parson residence.

D.A.: What did you say to him?

Draper: Well, I told him who I was and that I would like to talk to him about an incident that occurred earlier that day.

D.A.: How did he respond?

Draper: He just said, "Fine." He denied having anything to do with any crime. I asked his permission to take him down to the police and examine his clothing.

D.A.: You were looking for bloodstains?

Draper: Yes. And any other trace evidence. I told him he wasn't under arrest. Everything was voluntary on his part. He agreed and we took him to the station in a patrol car.

D.A.: How did he seem, I mean, his general demeanor?

Draper: Well, he seemed disoriented.

D.A.: What do you mean?

Draper: His mind—he didn't seem right to me. Ask him one question and he'd answer a question I'd asked him before. I asked him where he was born and he said, "Jason." Things like that.

D.A.: Did you get what you wanted?

Draper: Yes. He was wearing a red shirt. At the holding cell, he took off all his clothes and we put each item in a separate bag to prevent any transfer of blood or anything else. We gave him new clothes to wear. We took hair samples, body hair, fingernail clippings, fingerprints, DNA samples, photographs—things like that.

D.A.: Then what happened?

Draper: After we looked at everything, we released him. We had no cause to arrest him at that point.

D.A.: Thank you, nothing further.

Carino cross-examines. "Did you find anything connecting my client to the crime?"

Draper: No, sir.

Carino: Any knife or weapon of any kind?

Draper: No, sir.

Carino: Did you examine him for any wounds that might indicate a recent struggle?

Draper: Yes, sir.

Carino: Find any?

Draper: No, nothing like that.

Carino: Was he cooperative at all times?

Draper: Yes. Very much so.

Carino: And after you released him did he remain in town?

Draper: Yes. I saw him on the street several times later.

Carino: No attempt to run away?

Draper: No, nothing to indicate that.

Carino: Before contacting Mr. Tungstin, you were present at the crime scene, were you not?

Draper: I was.

Carino: You were in the room where Sara Parson was found on the floor?

Draper: That's right.

Carino: And you walked through that room?

Draper: Yes.

Carino: Isn't it true that some of the blood was not easily visible?

Draper: That's true.

Carino: And did you walk on the numerous bloodstains in the room?

Draper: I was being real careful not to.

Carino: That wasn't my question. I will ask it again. Did you walk on any of the bloodstains?

Draper: I suppose I may have. It's possible. But I was trying very carefully not to.

Carino: And when you went into the holding cell with Mr. Tungstin, did you walk anywhere within the holding cell?

Draper: Well, yes, I had to. I couldn't help it.

Carino: And is it possible that at that time you had blood on your boots from the crime scene?

Draper: I doubt it very much.

Carino: But it is possible?

D.A.: Objection, Your Honor. This is too much. Pure speculation!

Judge: Overruled. I will let him answer.

Draper: Well, yes, it is possible.

Carino: Thank you. And is it also possible that the blood on your shoes could have come off on the floor of the holding cell?

Draper: That too is not likely.

Carino: But possible?

Draper: Yes. Barely possible.

Carino: Was there a chair in the holding cell?

Draper: No.

Carino: So Mr. Tungstin either had to stand all the time or sit on the floor?

Draper: That's true.

Carino: Did he sit on the floor?

Draper: He may have. I do not recall.

Carino: Thank you. Nothing further.

The D.A. calls Christine Seabury. Mrs. Seabury testifies she is a forensic scientist employed by the county forensic services laboratory. She is a woman of about 60 with special expertise in the process of determining DNA information. She has impressive credentials and serves on the Board of Directors of the American Board of Criminalistics. During her career, Mrs. Seabury has qualified as an expert criminalist in about five hundred cases. She tells the jury that she examined Tungstin's red shirt for bloodstains on April 15, 2005.

D.A.: Did you examine the red shirt for DNA?

Seabury: Yes, but a lot of areas had been cut out by previous examiners and it looked like it had already been tested.

D.A.: Would you tell us what you found?

Seabury: I found bloodstains on the right front, on the right arm, and inside the right shoulder. I did that by touching the shirt with filter paper. Then, I took the filter paper off and added orthotolidine and then hydrogen peroxide.

Mrs. Seabury uses magnified photographs to illustrate the various steps she used in the examination. The process is complicated.

D.A.: Now, Mrs. Seabury, once you have done the orthotolidine test, what is the next stage in the procedure?

Seabury: The next stage is to extract the DNA. We do that by breaking open the cell wall to release the DNA to solution. That is done with an enzyme called proteinase K. We now have the DNA. The final step is to concentrate the DNA down into a small volume.

The witness speaks of using centricons and a centrifuge and putting the solution into an apparatus that spins around like a carnival ride. She describes a method called quantiblot, using a great amount of technical terms and confusing scientific jargon.

D.A.: You had samples of Sara Parson's blood and Mr. Tungstin's blood?

Seabury: Yes.

D.A.: And when you had the DNA from the red shirt, were you able to compare it to the samples?

Seabury: I compared them, yes.

D.A.: And what did you find?

Seabury: I found that the donor of the bloodstains on the red shirt was not Mr. Tungstin.

D.A.: He was excluded?

Seabury: Yes he was.

D.A.: What about Sara Parson?

Seabury: I was virtually certain she could not be excluded.

D.A.: Which means you are virtually certain she was the donor; that is, that it was her blood on the red shirt?

Carino: Objection! Leading.

Judge: Overruled. The witness may answer.

Seabury: Yes. Yes I am.

D.A.: You say you are virtually certain. Is it possible that someone else could have the same DNA as Sara Parson? That is, could it be someone else's blood on the shirt?

Seabury: I have considered that. We have calculated how rare or how common the bloodstain on the shirt was. We are talking about comparing DNA. We have calculations for three major populations: for the Caucasian population, the same DNA occurs in about one out of seven hundred billion individuals; in the African American population, it occurs in about one out of five hundred billion people; and in the Mexican American population, in about one out of five hundred billion persons.

D.A.: And that is why you are virtually certain?

Seabury: Exactly.

D.A.: Thank you.

Carino has only a few questions. "You performed these tests in 2005?"

Seabury: Yes.

Carino: Five years after the crime?

Seabury: Yes, that's right.

Carino: Do you know what testing the shirt went through during that time?

Seabury: No. Only that it had been tested before.

Carino: Do you know how many persons handled the shirt?

Seabury: No, I don't.

Carino: Thank you. That's all.

The judge turns to the D.A. "You may call your next witness."

The D.A. rises slowly and clears his throat as if to make an important pronouncement. "Your Honor, the prosecution is satisfied with the state of the evidence. The prosecution rests."

After a recess, Carino opens the case for the defense by calling Detective Brandon Webster as his first witness. Webster testifies that he has been a detective with the local police department for nineteen years, has worked in the crime lab for the last eleven years, and has had considerable training and experience in analyzing bloodstains. On the day of the murder, he and his partners thoroughly searched the crime scene for trace evidence, took many photographs (which he identifies), and used a process called fluorescein to locate bloodstains that were not visible to the naked eye. Massive amounts of evidence were taken from the house and stored in large containers.

Carino: When you took photographs in Sara's room, did you use a tripod?

Webster: Yes, sir.

Carino: And at that time, were there bloodstains on the floor?

Webster: Yes, sir.

Carino: Some visible?

Webster: Yes. And as we found out later, some not visible to the naked eye.

Carino: And did you ever place the tripod in such a way that a leg of your tripod could be in the bloodstains on the floor?

Webster: I can't say if it was on those stains or not.

Carino: How many hours did you spend searching for evidence at the house?

Webster: About eighty hours.

Carino: Did you find any footprints?

Webster: Yes, sir.

Carino: Any that belonged to Mr. Tungstin?

Webster: No, sir.

Carino: You found fingerprints? Latent prints?

Webster: Yes.

Carino: Any that belonged to Mr. Tungstin?

Webster: No, sir.

Carino: You found hair? Fibers of hair?

Webster: Yes, sir.

Carino: Any that belonged to Mr. Tungstin?

Webster: No, sir.

Carino: You found a bloody handprint on the door—Sara's bedroom door?

Webster: Yes, sir.

Carino: Did that belong to the defendant?

Webster: No, sir.

Carino: Could you match it with anyone else?

Webster: No, sir. We could not.

Carino: Detective Webster, did you find anything at all that could possibly be connected to Jason Tungstin?

Webster: No, sir.

Carino: Was Mr. Tungstin's red shirt tested for bloodstains six days after the murder?

Webster: Yes.

Carino: You used a special fluorescent process to detect latent stains?

Webster: Yes I did.

Carino: And at that time, did you find any bloodstains on the red shirt?

Webster: No, sir, we did not.

Carino: Thank you. Now with regard to the tripod in Sara's room, can you say with certainty that the leg of the tripod was not on a bloodstain?

Webster: No. I cannot.

Carino: The tripod leg could have been on a bloodstain?

D.A.: Objection! Speculation!

Judge: Overruled. The witness may answer.

Webster: It is possible.

Carino: Later on, the tripod was used to photograph Mr. Tungstin's clothing?

Webster: Yes, sir.

Carino: And can you say with certainty that while you were doing that, the tripod did not touch the red shirt?

Webster: No, sir.

Carino: Now, with regard to the clothing, you later examined Mr. Tungstin's clothing for bloodstains?

Webster: Yes, sir.

Carino: How did you do that?

Webster: We used an alternative light source and goggles. The test did not show any stains.

Carino: Did you then use another test?

Webster: Yes. We applied a process called fluorescein to detect latent or invisible stains.

Carino: Find anything?

Webster: No. We found no bloodstains.

Carino: None on the red shirt?

Webster: None. We placed the shirt in a separate bag for further testing.

Carino: Thank you. Your witness.

D.A.: Two questions regarding your examination of the shirt for bloodstains. Are you familiar with the process of DNA testing?

Webster: Of course. Although I am not an expert on that process.

D.A.: Did you test for DNA in your examination of the red shirt?

Webster: No. We didn't have the facilities for the DNA test.

D.A.: Thank you. Now, Detective Webster, about the tripod, would you please tell this jury your experience in using a tripod at crime scenes?

Webster: Used it hundreds of times.

D.A.: Sometimes where there is blood on the floor?

Webster: Yes, sir. Many times.

D.A.: And have you been trained, and have you in fact trained others, to avoid allowing any leg of the tripod to be placed on a bloodstain?

Webster: Yes, sir. We are very careful about that.

D.A.: And were you especially careful on this occasion?

Webster: I certainly was.

D.A.: And do you believe with virtual certainty that you avoided such contact in this case?

Webster: I do.

D.A.: Thank you.

Carino reacts immediately. "But it could have?"

Webster: I answered that.

Carino: It could have? In the deepest recesses of your heart, do you think it could have made such contact?

Webster: It could have, yes. That's all I can say.

Carino: Thank you.

Detective Karl Brenner is the next witness for the defense. He testifies he has investigated some forty to fifty homicide cases. Brenner testifies he went to the murder scene as the lead investigator, spoke briefly with members of the Parson family, then asked Sara's 15-year-old brother Marcus to accompany him and his partner to the juvenile center for further questioning.

Carino: Why did you do that?

Brenner: Some things he said at the house bothered me.

Carino: What things?

Brenner: He said he went to bed the night before at about 10:30 p.m. His bedroom was next to Sara's. He said he got up at about 5:00 a.m. to get some milk and then went back to bed.

Carino: Why did that bother you?

Brenner: He said he passed Sara's room and the door was closed. He didn't see Sara. That made me suspicious.

Carino: Why?

Brenner: Because we had evidence from the doctors that Sara died around midnight and she was found lying across her doorway with the door open. His story contradicted that evidence.

Carino: So what did you do?

Brenner: Since he was only 15, we asked him to come with us to the juvenile center.

Carino: And did you question him there?

Brenner: We did. For a long time.

Carino: How long?

Brenner: Six to midnight, two evenings in a row.

Carino: Did you make a videotape of that interview?

Brenner: We did.

The videotape of the entire interrogation of Marcus Parson is played for the jury. For two long days, you sit in a darkened courtroom watching the interview. The detective is friendly to Marcus, saying he just wants Marcus's help. At first Marcus denies any involvement in the crime. He says he loved his sister and would never do anything to harm her. The detective tells Marcus it would be better for Marcus if he comes clean. The detective lies to Marcus. He tells Marcus the police found Sara's fresh blood in Marcus's room, which is not true. Marcus says he respects the detective but he has no memory of doing anything to Sara. On the video, another officer takes over the interrogation. He also lies; he confirms that the police have evidence linking Marcus to the murder, such as the blood in Marcus's room. The new detective tells Marcus the police also have statements from others implicating Marcus. The detective explains to the boy that in a sense, there are two Marcuses—one that loved his sister, and one that needed to kill her.

On the second night of interrogation, Marcus begins to break down. He weakens in his denial. He says that if the police say he did it, he must have done it; if the police say Sara's blood was found in his room, it must be so; but he has no memory of being involved. Now the two detectives are talking to Marcus together. They tell him they know he did it. They tell him he will go to prison if they have to prove he did it in court, and they intimate that prison is not a good place. They tell Marcus they will see to it he will get help. Detective Brenner says that since Marcus is only 15, he would be considered a child by the judge and would not be treated like any criminal on the street. Marcus continues to weaken and changes his story. He begins to remember that when he was in seventh grade, he resented Sara's popularity, and that he once told a friend he could kill Sara. He talks oddly of reading about a Norse god named Odin who was evil and would kill anyone but was also calm and intelligent. Marcus tells the detectives he wanted to be like Odin. He reveals he had horrible nightmares the night of the murder and woke up in a rage. Possibly he killed Sara to get rid of the nightmares. Finally, Marcus appears to confess. He says on the video, "I don't remember it but I'm positive I killed her. All I know is I killed her."

When the video ends, the lights come on in the courtroom. There is a long silence. Detective Brenner is still on the witness stand. Carino resumes direct examination.

Carino: Is the video an accurate portrayal of your complete interrogation of Marcus Parson?

Brenner: It is.

Carino: Did you take Marcus into custody as a result of the interview?

Brenner: Yes.

Carino: You arrested him for murder?

Brenner: That's right. We went to the D.A. with the evidence and the murder charge was filed.

Carino: Very briefly, why did you charge him with murder?

Brenner: Because he had confessed to us.

Carino: Detective Brenner, based on your vast training and experience, and on the interview, did you believe he confessed to you voluntarily?

D.A.: Objection! That's for the jury to decide.

Judge: Sustained.

Carino: Did you force him to speak?

Brenner: No. We never forced him.

Carino: At a later time, did you and your partners interrogate one of Marcus's friends, John Alter, at his home?

Brenner: We did.

Carino: And when you entered his house, did you see an item of interest?

Brenner: Yes, I found a knife under his bed. He said it belonged to his brother but his brother told us it belonged to John.

Carino: Did you later arrest John for stealing the knife?

Brenner: Yes, because he denied it was his at first, then admitted stealing it from Alan Bendix.

Carino: Who is Alan Bendix?

Brenner: Alan Bendix was a friend of John Alter and Marcus Parson. The three boys hung out together. They were all 15 years old.

Carino: Was the knife important to you?

Brenner: Yes, because it was extremely sharp, made incisions like a scalpel.

Carino then shows the knife marked as Defense Exhibit A to the witness. "Is this the knife to which you refer?"

Brenner: That's it. From our interview of the autopsy surgeon, we realized it could have been the weapon used to kill Sara Parson.

Carino: Did you later interrogate John Alter at the juvenile center?

Brenner: Yes, and that was videotaped also. Just like we did with Marcus.

Once again, the lights in the courtroom are dimmed and for two days the jury watches the video of Detective Brenner's interrogation of John Alter. At times, another detective takes over with questioning. John at first denies any involvement in the crime, but he is more immature than Marcus, more like a child wanting to please the officers, and he succumbs readily to the officers' version of the story. Detective Brenner also lies to John Alter, telling him the police have evidence of his participation. At first, John persists in denying he did anything wrong except taking the knife from Alan Bendix.

In your notes, you record that Alter says he is Marcus's best friend. He visited the Parson home a lot, and admits to knowing the layout of the house. He says Marcus was sometimes mad at Sara and jealous of her, and once even talked of killing her, but he thought Marcus was joking. Although Alter still denies any guilt, the officers keep urging him to tell the truth. Eventually, he changes his story about the knife, saying that Alan Bendix gave it to him and told him to get rid of it because Marcus had used it to kill Sara. Alter looks tired, but the officers persist. On the second day of interrogation, he says Marcus and Alan had planned to kill Sara. The story sounds bizarre and the details keep changing, and you wonder if he is making it up. Now he seems to agree with the police, as the officers tell him it is best for him to admit to being involved in the crime. Alter says Marcus asked him to be the lookout, and on the night of the murder, he and Alan Bendix went to the Parson house around midnight. He waited in the kitchen while Marcus went into Sara's room and covered her mouth. Alan went in and stabbed her, and Alan later revealed to Alter that he and Marcus killed her.

The video finally comes to an end and the lights turn on. Again, there is a long hush in the crowd. Carino resumes examination.

Carino: Did you force him to confess?

Brenner: Not at all.

Carino: Ever threaten him or touch him?

Brenner: No. You saw the video. I never raised my voice.

Carino: Did you make any promises or use any coercion of any kind?

Brenner: No. He told us of his own free will.

D.A.: Objection!

Judge: Sustained!

D.A.: Motion to strike!

Judge: Motion granted. (*He turns slowly to the jury.*) Ladies and gentlemen, the witness's last answer is stricken and you are admonished to disregard it. Strike it from your minds.

Carino doesn't give up. "I ask you again. Please do not give us your personal opinion as to his free will. Just tell us yes or no. Did you use any methods of coercion to get him to talk against his will?"

Brenner: I did not. The tape speaks for itself.

Carino: Nothing further.

The D.A. approaches the podium to begin cross-examination. As the questioning proceeds, you recognize the unusual nature of their positions—the police detective being cross-examined by the D.A. They both represent law enforcement. Both have the prime purpose of convicting the guilty. Usually they are on the same side. But now the D.A. is trying to discredit the detective, trying to show that the detective mishandled the interrogation and coerced false confessions from the two boys. The D.A. wants you to believe Jason Tungstin committed the murder. The detective wants you to believe otherwise, that Marcus Parson and John Alter (as well as Alan Bendix) committed the crime.

The cross-examination goes on for hours. The D.A. refers to various portions of the video to show coercion and lies by Detective Brenner.

The detective admits he lied to the boys but says such tactics have been approved by the law. He says the boys' confessions came from their own mouths, not from him. "This is what they said," he explains, referring to the video. "I didn't make them say it."

The battle between the two law enforcement officers is at a stalemate. Neither scores heavily. When the examination ends, Carino announces that the defense rests. But the case is not over. The D.A. announces that he wishes to present a rebuttal.

D.A.: We call Marcus Parson to the stand.

As Marcus enters the courtroom, you hardly recognize him. Eight years have passed since the interrogation by Detective Brenner that you just witnessed on the video. He is now a grown man of 23. With his answer to the first question, you are further surprised.

"My name," he says, "is no longer Marcus Parson. My name is now Michael Carver." He explains that he changed his name to avoid the bad publicity surrounding the initial investigation, when the media branded him as the alleged confessed murderer of his sister. He states that he is now married, has a 2-year-old child, and works for a computer company. As expected, Marcus recants any admissions or confessions made in the video. He testifies that he went to bed the evening before Sara's murder at about 10:30 p.m., had a bad headache, got up at about 5:00 a.m. to get some milk, passed Sara's door but noticed nothing, and went back to bed.

At some point, he heard what sounded like a pounding on the front door, but it soon stopped and he went back to bed. At a later time, he again heard the pounding sound on the front door, but then the noise ended and he fell back asleep. The next thing that awakened him was the frantic shouts of his parents upon discovering Sara dead in her room. He denies any involvement in the homicide, insisting that he had no motive to harm his sister and that he was coerced into making false statements by a smart detective who tricked him into confessing.

D.A.: Tell the jury what possessed you to make those statements to the police.

Parson: I know it now. Not then. When they lied to me and told me they found Sara's blood in my room, I thought I must have done something that I couldn't remember.

D.A.: Did you ever actually remember committing the crime?

Parson: No. I didn't remember doing anything bad, but when they told me about the blood, I thought it must be true and I must be going crazy for not remembering.

D.A.: Was what you told the police true or false?

Parson: It was all false. I was making up stuff from what they told me.

D.A.: Did you kill Sara Parson?

Parson: No. I swear to God, I didn't do it.

Carino cross-examines Marcus. "John Alter was your good friend?"

Parson: Yes.

Carino: You often confided in him?

Parson: Yes.

Carino: And when you talked to John Alter, you weren't under pressure from the police?

Parson: No.

Carino: He didn't tell you what to say?

Parson: No.

Carino: Did you tell John Alter you wanted to kill Sara?

Parson: That was a joke.

Carino: I didn't ask you if it was a joke. Please answer the question yes or no. Did you tell John Alter you wanted to kill Sara?

Parson: I might have.

Carino: Did you say it? Yes or no?

Parson: Well, yes, but I didn't mean it.

Carino: It was just a joke?

Parson: That's right.

Carino: Did you get a good laugh out of it?

D.A.: Objection!

Judge: Sust—no. Overruled. You may answer.

Parson: No.

Carino: Does it sound like a joke now?

Parson: No, sir.

Carino: About two weeks before the murder, did John Alter call you up and ask you about that statement that you call a joke?

Parson: Yes.

Carino: Did he say to you, "Have you killed her yet?"

Parson: We were joking.

Carino: Did he ask you that? Please answer the question.

Parson: Yeah. He did ask me that. I don't know why.

Carino: Didn't you, when you were in the seventh grade with John Alter, tell him you hated your sister?

Parson: I might have.

Carino: And didn't you and John Alter often talk about killing people you didn't like?

Parson: We did that jokingly.

Carino: It was all a big joke.

Parson: Yes. I'd never harm Sara.

Carino: Nothing further.

When Marcus steps down, John Alter takes the stand. He, too, has changed in the eight years since the video—he is larger in both height and weight and has a moustache. As expected, his testimony is similar to Marcus's. He recants any confessions he made to the detectives on the video, claims he was coerced and misled by their lies, and denies any involvement in Sara's murder. He admits he took a knife from the Bendix residence but says the knife had nothing to do with Sara's death. He says that during the six-hour interrogation, the detectives denied him food when he was hungry. They told him they had evidence that Sara's blood was on the knife—which he believed because he trusted them—but he now knows that was a lie. He says that at the time of the interview, he was an innocent 15-year-old who just wanted to go home.

Carino cross-examines John Alter. "Before coming into court today, did you see the video of your interview with Detective Brenner?"

Alter: Yes.

Carino: And in the early part of that interrogation—in fact, within the first twenty minutes—did you make the following statement: "Marcus told me he hated his sister and thought of killing her"?

Alter: Yes.

Carino: The police didn't tell you to say that, did they?

Alter: No.

Carino: They didn't coerce you into saying that, did they?

Alter: No.

Carino: And that statement was true, wasn't it?

Alter: It's true that he said it, but—

Carino: Did he say, "I'm only joking," or anything like that?

Alter: No, but I know it was a joke.

Carino: And shortly afterward, about two weeks before the murder, did you call him and say, "Have you killed her yet"?

Alter: I might have. It was part of the joke.

Carino: Might have? Didn't you definitely tell Detective Brenner exactly that?

Alter: I guess I did. If it's on the video, then I said it.

Carino: Do you want to see it? I'll play it for you.

Alter: No. I believe you. I said it.

Carino: And you were not coerced into saying it, were you?

Alter: No.

Carino: You said it freely and voluntarily, right?

Alter: That's right. But I have to repeat—we were not serious.

Carino: Of course not. Thank you, that's all.

Alan Bendix is called next. Bendix is short and frail, and seems frightened by all the attention. Early in his testimony, he volunteers the information that he was never interrogated by the police because his mother told him it was better not to say anything. He testifies that he was good friends with Marcus and John Alter in junior high school and was shocked when he learned that John had implicated him in the murder as the one who did the stabbing. Alan denies any involvement whatsoever in the crime but admits that the knife marked as Defense Exhibit A was part of his collection of knives and that he did not know until after the murder that John had stolen it from his house. He further states under the D.A.'s questioning that he was often at the Parson residence with Marcus, never noticed any hostility between Marcus and Sara, and never heard Marcus say he wanted to kill or hurt Sara. Alan's situation is different from that of the other two boys because, unlike them, he never submitted to any video interrogation.

Carino begins his cross-examination, "Did you ever hear Marcus say he wanted to kill anyone?"

D.A.: Objection! Irrelevant as to anyone else.

Carino: Goes to character, Your Honor.

Judge: I'll allow it, but don't go too far with it. Witness, you may answer.

Bendix: Well, yes, he said he wanted to kill our English teacher, Ms. Miller, because she gave him a bad grade.

There is a titter in the audience.

Carino: Anyone else?

Bendix: (*Looking to the judge*) Do I have to answer, Your Honor?

Judge: Yes. I have overruled the objection.

Bendix: Well, yes, Marcus had a list. About three or four names. People he wouldn't mind killing. It was all a make-believe thing.

Carino: Who else was on it?

Bendix: I don't remember all the names, but Sara definitely was not on it. One was his former girlfriend, Becky. She'd dumped him for another guy and Marcus was mad at her. But it wasn't serious. Just a joke.

Carino: You say you had a collection of knives?

Bendix: Yes, sir. I kept a collection for a long time. Still have it. Most of them were swords but there were a couple of small knives, too, like the one John took.

Carino: What did you do with the knives?

Bendix: Oh, I liked to practice with them, different moves, attack moves, and dueling, like you see in the movies.

Carino: Ever show Marcus Parson any of those moves?

Bendix: As a matter of fact, I did a couple of times. We'd act like we were somebody in the movies.

Carino: You showed Marcus how to work with the small knife?

Bendix: We did some of that.

Carino: Showed him how to stab people with it?

Bendix: Yeah, that too.

Carino has no further questions. The D.A. announces that the jury will be glad to hear he has only one more witness.

Leo Mackey testifies as an expert on police interrogations and the use of coercive techniques by police officers. As a professor of criminology and psychology at the University of California at Berkeley, Mackey has written an authoritative book on police interrogations and has spent many hours studying the videotapes in this case. He explains that there is a difference between an interview and an interrogation. The interview applies to a witness or suspect and is not accusatorial; it allows the witness to do the talking with the purpose of obtaining as much information as possible. The interrogation, on the other hand, is founded on the presumption that the accused is guilty. Its purpose is to confirm the detective's theory that the suspect is guilty and often becomes suggestive and manipulative. The officer wants information that will lead to conviction.

D.A.: What are the techniques employed to obtain confessions?

Mackey: It often begins with accusation and reaccusation over and over. The officer is usually someone who commands respect and trust. The youthful or naïve subject tends to believe the interrogator. The officer confronts the suspect with false evidence, such as, in this case, that Sara's blood was found in Marcus's room or that her blood was found on the knife in John Alter's possession. Those statements were false.

D.A.: They were lies?

Mackey: Yes.

D.A.: Is that permissible?

Mackey: Yes. It is a popular technique in police interrogations. The courts have decided it is not unlawful. But it must not go too far. Another example is to give the subject a lie detector test and then lie to him as to the results.

D.A.: Are there other techniques?

Mackey: The longer an interrogation is, the more stress there is on the subject, and the resistance to what the officer is saying weakens. The officer's goal is to convince the subject that no one is going to believe his denials and it would be better for him to come clean.

D.A.: Are there certain tactics considered coercive that can lead to unreliable confessions?

Mackey: Yes. Such as in this case. Implying that if you don't cooperate you will go to prison and pointing out what an undesirable place prison is. That is effective with young subjects.

D.A.: Such as 15-year-old boys?

Mackey: Yes. Implying they will get leniency if they admit the officer's theory. This can be implied or expressed. The more the officer implies such promises, the more likely the subject will break down.

D.A.: What is the problem with using threats or promises?

Mackey: First of all, you can elicit an involuntary confession that way, a confession that is not of the subject's own free will. Then the courts won't allow it into evidence. Second, you can get a false confession.

D.A.: How does that happen?

Mackey: The suspect just tells the detective what the detective wants to hear. Starts making things up to please the detective. The suspect doesn't remember doing these things but says they happened because he believes the lies being told to him.

D.A.: Is there any dispute among the scientific community that false confessions occur?

Mackey: No dispute. They occur more than most people realize.

D.A.: Mr. Mackey, based on all your training and experience, do you have an opinion as to whether the confessions and admissions made by Marcus Parson and John Alter were coerced and false?

Carino: Objection! That's for the jury to decide!

Judge: Objection sustained! Do not answer.

D.A.: Your witness.

Carino: How much are you being paid for your testimony?

Mackey: Altogether, about $20,000. That includes preparation and testimony.

Carino: And of course you are being paid by the prosecution?

Mackey: Yes, but—

Carino: Thank you, you've answered the question. So, you go around the state and the country testifying as an expert on false confessions, is that right?

Mackey: Yes.

Carino: How much do you make a year doing that?

Mackey: Oh, about $75,000 a year.

Carino: Mr. Mackey, is there anything coercive in an officer saying to a subject, "The evidence shows you committed this crime"?

Mackey: No, that's not coercive.

Carino: Anything coercive in an officer saying, "We found blood in your room," whether true or not?

Mackey: No, not coercive by itself.

Carino: Why not?

Mackey: Because it is not a threat or promise. It is the use of threats or promises, especially about going to prison, that can make a statement coercive.

Carino: And nothing illegal or improper about an officer lying to the subject?

Mackey: No, not unless it involves a threat of some kind or a promise of leniency. It's perfectly legal otherwise.

Carino: You saw the two videotapes?

Mackey: Yes.

Carino: You recall that within the first thirty minutes of the Marcus tape, he said he told John Alter that he, Marcus, thought of killing his sister?

Mackey: I do. But apparently that was a joke.

Carino: So they say. But there was no coercion to get him to make that statement, was there?

Mackey: No.

Carino: Up to that time there had been no promises or threats of any kind, right?

Mackey: That's true.

Carino: And would your answers be the same as to the statements made by John Alter about hearing that statement and then calling Marcus about two weeks before the murder to ask him—and I quote his words—"Have you killed her yet?" Any coercion there?

Mackey: No. Not at that point.

Carino: And when John Alter gave the police a detailed account of how the murder went down, were any of those details suggested to him by the police?

Mackey: No.

Carino: That came from his own mouth?

Mackey: Yes.

Carino: He wasn't forced to say those things, was he?

Mackey: No.

Carino: You recall Marcus talking about being influenced by a weird god named Odin who killed people but remained calm and intelligent?

Mackey: I recall it, yes.

Carino: The detectives didn't suggest any of that, did they?

Mackey: No.

Carino: These boys, Marcus and John, they were fairly intelligent, weren't they?

Mackey: Well, average intelligence, I'd say.

Carino: Not stupid?

Mackey: Not stupid, no.

Carino: They realized the seriousness of the situation, right?

Mackey: I believe so.

Carino: Do you honestly think, Mr. Mackey, that they would confess to a murder they didn't do just so they could go home?

D.A.: Objection!

Judge: Sustained!

Carino: Thank you, nothing further.

In his closing argument, the D.A. delivers a long speech in which he meticulously reviews the testimony of each witness. He ends with these remarks:

> When I am finished, defense will have a chance to argue his case. When he has completed his argument, I shall speak to you again for the last time in rebuttal to his statement. You may think it is unfair that the prosecution gets to make two closing arguments while the defense is allowed only one. But this is the law because the prosecution has the burden of proof while the defense has no such burden. When you have heard all arguments and instructions of law, I am satisfied you will reach the only reasonable verdict—murder in the first degree.

Defense Attorney Carino rises to present his argument.

> Ladies and gentlemen of the jury, you have just seen what seemed like two trials. Who killed Sara Parson? One trial, of course, is the prosecution of Jason Tungstin. That's the one you are here to decide. The

other is the trial of three young men: Marcus Parson and John Alter and, yes, Alan Bendix. In a sense, you are here to decide that trial also. But don't be confused. There is a major difference between these two trials. In the case of Jason Tungstin, he is presumed innocent and the district attorney must prove he is guilty beyond any reasonable doubt. If you have a doubt, the slightest doubt, and it is based on reason, then you must acquit Jason Tungstin—find him not guilty. He is presumed innocent and you must hold to that presumption unless and until he is proven guilty beyond any reasonable doubt, and that has not been done in this case.

But in the case of Marcus Parson and John Alter—and Alan Bendix—the defense has no such burden. We do not have to prove anything. We do not have to prove they are guilty. We do not have to prove anyone else is guilty. You promised to follow the law, and under the law we have no burden to prove anything. That is the law, ladies and gentlemen, and I ask you to follow the law and uphold the finest and highest standards of American justice.

Please do not think you have to go into the jury room and solve this crime. No. That is not your duty. You don't have to do that. Not at all. Your only task is to determine whether my client is guilty beyond any reasonable doubt, not whether anyone else is guilty. The only reason the evidence was produced as to Marcus Parson and John Alter, and even Alan Bendix, was to raise a reasonable doubt that Jason Tungstin is guilty, and we certainly did that.

In this case, the prosecution's argument is shot full of reasonable doubt, like big holes that cannot be patched up. Reasonable doubt that has been raised, not by the defense really, but by the local police themselves, experienced police officers who represent and are supported by your community. They showed you the confessions and they showed you that they didn't force anyone or coerce anyone. Everything they did was perfectly legal. Even the prosecution's expert admitted that.

Oh, yes, the D.A. wants you to ignore those confessions, act as if they never happened. But look at them again if you want to. See for yourself that no one told the boys what to say. No one told them the details of the murder that they outlined by themselves. Yes, the boys were only 15, but they were not stupid. Does it make sense that they would confess to a murder they didn't commit just to please the officers?

You saw the detectives who interrogated the boys. They are good, honest men, experienced in their jobs, conscious of the heavy trust and responsibility we place on them. They certainly believed the boys were guilty or they would never have gone to the district attorney with murder charges. They don't charge murder on a whim or mere suspicion.

Those confessions are a big hole in the case against Jason Tungstin, but there are plenty of others. Let's name a few.

First of all, the prosecution hasn't given you a shred of evidence that Jason was ever in the Parson residence or Sara's room. The police searched the place for days and found nothing. Nothing. No fingerprints, no footprints, no hairs or fibers. Obviously there was a struggle and surely such a struggle would have left hairs or fibers from clothing. But there was absolutely nothing.

Second, the evidence leans more to an inside job than to an intruder breaking in. The front door and the laundry door were locked. An intruder would have had to come through the noisy sliding door in the parents' bedroom or through Sara's window without disturbing someone in the house. The intruder would have to have been familiar with the layout of the house, but there is no evidence Jason had ever been there.

Third, the words "Kill, kill" found scribbled on Sara's windowsill did not match Jason Tungstin's handwriting. Someone else wrote those words.

Fourth, there's the matter of the knife. John Alter hid the knife he stole from Alan Bendix but the police found it under Alter's bed. The autopsy surgeon told us that the knife had a specific size and shape, and from his examination of the stab wounds, he could say that that knife or one very similar to it was likely the one used in the murder. Coincidence?

Fifth, we don't dispute that the tiny bloodstains on the red shirt were Sara's blood; we don't dispute the testimony by the DNA expert. But the question remains as to how and when the bloodstains got there. The officers told us it was possible they could have come from the tripod leg standing in a bloodstain and later used to photograph Jason's shirt, or when Jason sat on the floor of his cell after the detective walked through the cell with bloodstains possibly on his boots.

Sixth, there is the evidence of motive. Who had the motive to kill Sara Parson? Not Jason. There is no evidence he even knew her. But Marcus Parson admitted, under no coercion whatsoever, that he thought of killing Sara. Just a joke, he says! Does that sound like a joke to you?

Finally, I come back to the confessions. When you are in the jury room, ask yourself these questions: If John Alter was innocent, how is it he could describe such details about the plan and the murder? Details about the time of the murder and entry into the home? How could he know details that were consistent with crucial aspects of the murder?

This is a circumstantial case. It's all circumstantial. No one saw Jason Tungstin do anything wrong. The judge will tell you that in a circumstantial evidence case, if there are two reasonable interpretations of the evidence, one pointing to guilt and the other pointing to innocence, then you must choose the one pointing to innocence. And that, ladies and gentlemen, is what the law requires you to do in this case.

Ladies and gentlemen of the jury, I want to thank you for your attention in this long trial. When you examine it carefully, you will see

> there is reasonable doubt splashed all over it. Please do not convict an innocent man. They have made him the scapegoat in this case. Find Jason Tungstin not guilty. Thank you.

The D.A. steps forward to make his rebuttal and final argument.

> Ladies and gentlemen, this is the last time I will have a chance to speak to you in this case. I hold in my hands all the notes I prepared for this argument. A great many of these notes go to show it was Sara's blood on the defendant's shirt. But now I can just throw these notes away. I don't need them anymore. The defense has conceded the point. They don't dispute that it was Sara's blood on his red shirt. This means you don't even have to discuss that point. It's been settled for you. Now why in the world did the defense do that? Why did they give up any fight on that point, the major point in the case? Well, it's obvious why—they had to. The DNA evidence is so strong that they would have looked ridiculous trying to dispute it. So what do they do? They take the only course left. They dream up some impossible scenario as to how the blood got there. If this case wasn't so serious, their theory would be laughable. The problem with their theory is not only that it is farfetched, but also that there is no evidence to support it. None.
>
> They want you to believe that the leg of the tripod somehow stood in Sara's blood—although there's no evidence of that—and that the blood somehow got on the tripod and then was somehow transferred to Mr. Tungstin's shirt. But there's absolutely no evidence of that. It's all fantasy. Wishful thinking. They want you to believe that the detective walked in Sara's blood at the crime scene, then walked in the defendant's cell and transferred the blood from his boots to the floor, and then that the defendant sat on that floor and in that way got the blood on his shirt. What a convoluted story! No evidence of that, either. They want you to believe that the defendant sat in the exact same spot where the blood had been transferred from the boot and thus got it on his shirt. No evidence that he ever sat down. No evidence

of any blood on the officer's boot. No evidence he ever walked in Sara's blood. You have to give them credit for trying. It's all make-believe, all fantasy. And, ladies and gentlemen, we don't let murderers off based on make-believe and fantasy.

Yes, the DNA is a big part of this trial. But there is much more to the evidence than DNA.

Just a few hours before the murder, a strange man came to the neighborhood of the Parson residence. He knocked on doors, asking for a girl named Stacy. The man was determined. He didn't stop with one or two rejections. He went from house to house. In fact, he went to at least nine homes that night. Neighbors say he looked bizarre; some say he appeared either drunk or on drugs. Several were so disturbed by his behavior that they called 911 for protection. We know who that man was. He was this man (*pointing*) sitting right here. Positively identified. This evidence places him in the vicinity of the crime scene when he had no good reason for being there.

The defense attorney told you of an instruction of law that applies to circumstantial evidence cases: if there are two reasonable interpretations of the evidence—one pointing to guilt and the other to innocence—then you must choose the one pointing to innocence. But notice one word in that instruction. *Reasonable.* Both interpretations must be reasonable. He didn't tell you of another part of that instruction, which is that if one interpretation is reasonable and the other unreasonable, then you must choose the reasonable one. And that is exactly what we have in this case. One reasonable interpretation based on scientific fact and common sense; the other based on make-believe, on guesswork.

Do your duty, ladies and gentlemen. This case has gone on long enough. Do your duty and find the defendant guilty of murder in the first degree.

You have three verdict choices in this case:

1. murder in the first degree
2. murder in the second degree
3. not guilty

WHAT IS YOUR VERDICT?

QUESTIONS FOR YOU TO CONSIDER

As you determine your verdict for this crime, here are some questions about the crime and the trial for you to think about.

1. Assume the jury's verdict was guilty. If the case had been tried thirty years earlier, would the jury's verdict have been the same?

2. Why did defense counsel give up on the question of whether it was Sara's blood on Tungstin's shirt? Wasn't that a major issue in the case?

3. The technical aspects of the procedure involved in collecting DNA evidence are difficult for the average juror to understand, but they are very important. Should such cases go to a special blue-ribbon panel or to a judge experienced in the subject rather than to the average jury, uneducated in the scientific terms of DNA?

AUTHOR'S ANSWERS TO THE QUESTIONS

1. The verdict would probably have been not guilty thirty years earlier because DNA evidence was not accepted as proof in courts of law until the mid-1980s. Without the DNA evidence in this case, the prosecution would have had an uphill battle.

   The use of DNA technology to convict criminals or eliminate innocent persons as suspects is considered to be the most significant advancement in criminal investigation since the advent of fingerprint identification. DNA analysis of blood, saliva, skin tissue, hair, and semen is now widely used by police and prosecutors as well as by defense counsel in U.S. courts.

2. Defense counsel conceded that it was Sara's blood on Tungstin's shirt because he knew he could not prevail on that point. A respected scientist had testified to the fact and the defense could offer no contrary evidence. If he tried to argue otherwise, he would appear disingenuous and would lose his credibility with the jury.

   There are, however, defense attorneys who would not have made such a concession but would instead have let the issue go to the jury, even though there was no evidence disproving that Sara's blood was on Tungstin's shirt. Their thinking would be that despite the evidence, there are still twelve individuals on the jury who have to agree and you can never tell what a jury will do. If just one of those jurors were to experience a reasonable doubt as to the guilt of the defendant, this would stand in the way of a unanimous verdict, possibly prompting the judge to declare a mistrial.

3. As new technology and science enter the courtroom more and more, such evidence becomes harder for juries to understand. The testimony, as in this case, becomes increasingly complex. This case raises a serious question as to whether juries or even many judges are the proper triers-of-fact for such subjects as DNA.

THE VERDICT

What was your verdict?

The real-life jury relied on the DNA evidence and found Jason Tungstin guilty of murder in the first degree.

Once Lovers, Now Enemies

LYNN DANIELS V. ALAN KAUFMAN, MD

Lynn Daniels, a successful businesswoman, met Dr. Alan Kaufman, a psychiatrist, as a result of an ad her mother placed in the newspaper seeking a male companion for Lynn. They fell in love and moved in together. Now Ms. Daniels is suing the doctor for the intentional infliction of emotional distress.

While still together, serious arguments arose between them after Ms. Daniels suffered two miscarriages that left her depressed. Nevertheless, they finally had a baby girl together, Chloe. When Ms. Daniels went on business trips, she would take Chloe and their Mexican governess, Filomena, with her. Upon returning from her travels, she would often accuse Kaufman of having affairs in her absence. He resented the accusations, maintaining that they were false, and decided to teach her a lesson. While she was away on one of her trips, he brought home a life-size female mannequin, and minutes before Ms. Daniels was to arrive home, he placed the doll in their bed. When he heard her drive up to the house, he got in bed beside it. Ms. Daniels walked into the bedroom, noticed the doll and Kaufman in bed together, and screamed in fright.

Although Ms. Daniels moved out immediately, the mannequin incident did not end the relationship. The couple soon resumed cohabiting but hostilities continued between them. One of their arguments arose in the car while Chloe, then 2 years old, was sitting in the back car seat. Kaufman was driving when he suddenly pulled over, boiling with rage. Ms. Daniels testifies that he tried to strangle her until she broke his hold and he calmed down. They again separated. The final straw for Ms. Daniels came when she was on an important business trip. The incident prompted her to sue Kaufman for a million dollars.

This is a civil suit brought by a woman against her former lover for the intentional infliction of emotional distress. She seeks one million dollars in damages.

As they confer with their attorneys a few feet away from you, plaintiff Lynn Daniels and defendant Alan Kaufman remind you of warriors posed for combat. They seldom look at each other, but when they do, they glare. She is an attractive woman, dressed in a tight-fitting designer suit. He is a good-looking man with horn-rimmed glasses and a receding hairline.

In this scene, she is huddling at her table with her attorney, Dan Greenberg, as the first witness is about to be called. Greenberg stands and says in a strong voice, "We call the defendant, Dr. Alan Kaufman."

The doctor looks surprised. You hear him whisper to his defense attorney, "Can they do that?" The attorney, Lee Meisner, with gray hair and a weather-beaten face, merely nods in response.

The judge notices that some of the jurors appear taken aback by the plaintiff's maneuver. "You may not be aware," the judge says to the jury, "that in a civil case, either side may call the opposing party as its witness and may cross-examine that witness. That is not true, of course, in a criminal case. There the defendant has a constitutional right to remain silent. No such right exists in a civil case except in rare circumstances. Dr. Kaufman may be sworn."

Dan Greenberg begins.

Greenberg: What is your occupation?

Kaufman: I am a licensed physician, a psychiatrist.

Greenberg: Do you have a subspecialty?

Kaufman: Yes. Sex therapy.

Greenberg: You are an expert in that field?

Kaufman: I am.

Greenberg: Where did you meet Lynn?

"Objection, Your Honor," Defense Attorney Lee Meisner says. "The use of first names is undignified."

"Sustained."

The doctor testifies he met Lynn Daniels through a personal ad. Her mother had placed it in the local newspaper ("Successful businesswoman seeks relationship with caring professional man").

Greenberg: Did you form an intimate relationship?

Kaufman: What do you mean, intimate?

Greenberg: Of a sexual nature?

Kaufman: She wanted to the first time we went out, but I—

This time it is the questioner himself, Dan Greenberg, who protests: "Objection, Your Honor! Nonresponsive."

"Sustained. Just answer the question, Doctor."

The doctor testifies that he and Lynn Daniels did indeed become sexually involved. After a few months, she moved into his six-bedroom townhouse. At his request, she agreed to pay two thousand dollars a month toward the mortgage. After two pregnancies that resulted in miscarriages, the quarreling began in earnest.

Greenberg continues the questioning. "Was she depressed over this second miscarriage?"

Kaufman: Yes.

Greenberg: Was she crying?

Kaufman: Yes. We were sitting on the bed.

Greenberg: What did she say?

Kaufman: She felt real bad. Her dreams of having a child hadn't come true.

Greenberg: What did you do?

Kaufman: I tried to console her. But then I got tired of trying to be emotionally supportive to her. It seemed like I was always doing that. I got up from the bed and walked away. I got hit in the back with the cordless phone.

Greenberg: That made you angry?

Kaufman: It sure did. I went back to her, jumped on the bed, straddled her, and held her down. I told her to stop acting like a baby. I didn't hit her.

Greenberg: Do you know why she threw the phone?

Kaufman: No.

Greenberg: No idea?

Kaufman: No.

Greenberg: Didn't you just say to her, "You killed the baby"?

Kaufman: Not in those words.

Greenberg: Words to that effect?

Kaufman: Well—

Greenberg: What words?

Kaufman: I said she'd done things to increase the possibility of miscarriage.

Greenberg: Like what?

Kaufman: She wouldn't take the thyroid medication regularly.

Greenberg: Medication that you as a doctor prescribed for her?

Kaufman: Yes.

Greenberg: Did you accuse her of doing anything else to bring on the miscarriage?

Kaufman: Yes. That she was working too hard in her business.

Greenberg: Working to pay the two thousand dollars a month you insisted she pay for the mortgage on your house?

Kaufman: We'd agreed to that.

Greenberg: This all happened the day after the second miscarriage?

Kaufman: Yes.

Greenberg: As a psychiatrist, do you think that was the proper way to react to her depression?

Kaufman: Well, I was tired of her acting like a child. She wouldn't do what she was told. I had to straighten her out.

Dr. Kaufman testifies that Ms. Daniels became pregnant a third time. This time she had the baby, a girl they named Chloe. He hired a Mexican housekeeper and governess, Filomena, to help with the baby. Ms. Daniels continued to travel in her business as a buyer and distributor of women's designer clothes. She didn't trust Dr. Kaufman with the care of Chloe, so she usually had Chloe and Filomena travel with her. There was hope that having the baby would end the hostilities, but it did not. When she returned from her business trips, she would accuse Dr. Kaufman of having affairs with other women.

Greenberg: Was it true?

Kaufman: No.

Greenberg: So did you decide to do something about her accusations?

Kaufman: Yes. I decided to teach her a lesson.

Greenberg: How did you do that?

Kaufman: Well, I'm not proud of this—

Greenberg: You mean the incident with the doll?

Kaufman: Yes.

Greenberg: You placed a life-size blow-up doll in your bed?

Kaufman: Uh, yes.

Greenberg: Describe the doll for the jury.

Kaufman: It was a sex toy. It's sold at adult stores, ostensibly for sex use.

Greenberg: Where did you get it?

Kaufman: From a patient of mine. I insisted he turn it over to me because he had become overly obsessed with it to the point where he wasn't socializing with anyone else.

Greenberg: Let me get this straight. This is a doll for performing simulated sex acts?

Kaufman: Right.

Greenberg: And while Ms. Daniels was away, you placed the doll in the bed that you and Ms. Daniels slept in?

Kaufman: Just before she got home, yes. It wasn't very attractive.

Greenberg: Oh?

Kaufman: It had yellow braids and blue eyes. It was flesh-colored.

Greenberg: So where were you immediately before Ms. Daniels came in?

Kaufman: I got in bed.

Greenberg: With the doll?

Kaufman: Yeah.

Greenberg: What time of day was this?

Kaufman: About 10 a.m.

Greenberg: Did you call out to her after you heard her enter the house to let her know you were up there?

Kaufman: I'm fairly certain I did not.

Greenberg: Did you put any clothing on it?

Kaufman: A pair of pantyhose. The legs were ugly.

Greenberg: Isn't it a fact you tied pantyhose around the doll's neck?

Kaufman: No. It didn't have a neck.

Greenberg: Didn't you do that as a threat of what could be in store for her?

Kaufman: No.

Greenberg: Had you slept with the doll while Ms. Daniels was away?

Kaufman: I don't recall if I slept with the doll or not. I think I just put it in the bed when I heard her drive up.

Greenberg: And then you got in bed with the doll?

Kaufman: Yeah. I was in bed with the doll when she came into the house, yeah.

Greenberg: Tell the jury why you did this, Dr. Kaufman.

Kaufman: I'd become frustrated with her daily allegations that I was having sexual contacts with other women, none of the allegations being true. Sure, it was probably poor judgment. I decided that since she was so certain it was happening I'd shock her a bit when she came back so she'd think she'd actually caught me at something.

Greenberg: Is this part of your sex therapy?

Meisner: Objection!

Judge: Sustained.

Greenberg: And how did she respond when she walked in?

Kaufman: She responded the way I thought she would. She screamed and yelled and didn't stop. She pulled the covers off, and acted frightened of the doll.

He testifies further that after this incident, Ms. Daniels bought her own home, moved into it, and took Chloe and Filomena with her. Soon afterward she invited Dr. Kaufman to move in with her, which he did after selling his townhouse. He admits he struck her physically once after that, but only to defend himself. He had picked her up at the airport and was driving her to his sister's house. Chloe, nearly 2 years old at the time, was in the backseat. Dr. Kaufman's father had just arrived from St. Louis and was anxiously waiting to see the baby for the first time, his only grandchild. They were all going to his sister's house for a family dinner, but Ms. Daniels did not want to go. They argued. She grabbed the steering wheel to turn it in another direction. He stopped the car on the side of the highway to avoid an accident, and she began flailing at him. He fought back to ward off her blows. Chloe was sitting up, wide-eyed, watching everything.

Greenberg: Did you grab her throat?

Kaufman: I just put my hands up to defend myself.

Greenberg: Did you see the bruises on her throat afterward?

Kaufman: I saw one or two on the side of her neck, nothing great.

This fight they had in front of Chloe and while driving on the highway made him realize they had to separate. So he moved out and bought another house. Over the years, they had bought several marriage licenses, but the licenses always expired. They had still never married. He denies he threatened to take Chloe away with him so that Lynn would never see her again. He denies he ever threatened to kill Lynn in front of Chloe.

After he moved out, the battle continued.

Greenberg: You had hired the governess Filomena?

Kaufman: Yes, on the recommendation of friends who also had Mexican servants.

Greenberg: Did you know if she was in the country legally or not?

Kaufman: Oh, I didn't know. I kind of suspected she was illegal.

Greenberg: But you went on paying her while you lived with Ms. Daniels?

Kaufman: Yes. Everyone else was doing it.

Greenberg: And shortly after you moved out, did you make a phone call to the Immigration and Naturalization Service in Miami, Florida, about Ms. Daniels and Filomena?

Kaufman: Yes.

Greenberg: You were aware of Ms. Daniels's airline schedule for her trip, so you knew when she'd be landing in Miami with Filomena and Chloe?

Kaufman: Yes.

Greenberg: What did you tell the INS?

Kaufman: I told them to watch for an illegal alien landing in Miami.

Greenberg: And you gave them Ms. Daniels's name and said she was trying to smuggle an illegal alien into the state of Florida?

Kaufman: Yes.

Greenberg: What did the INS say?

Kaufman: They thanked me for being a patriotic citizen.

Greenberg: What did you say?

Kaufman: I said, "I try to do what I can."

The doctor denies the plaintiff's complaint that he stalked or followed her or her friends. He denies ever burglarizing her home after he moved out, but admits friends offered to help him get things from her house.

Greenberg: Who were these friends?

Kaufman: Don't recall.

Greenberg: They called you on the phone.

Kaufman: Yeah. They said they would help me get my things, since there was no court restraining order on their going to the house as there was on me.

Greenberg: And did you encourage them to go into her home?

Kaufman: I just listed what the items were that were mine, and that was it.

Greenberg: And these items were later delivered to you?

Kaufman: To my house, yes.

Greenberg: And you didn't see who delivered them?

Kaufman: No.

Greenberg: Moving to another point, did you ever threaten to kill Ms. Daniels?

Kaufman: Not really, no.

Greenberg: What do you mean by, "not really"?

Kaufman: Well, she's made life miserable for me with this lawsuit—lied in court about me, won't let me see Chloe. Sure, I've told people recently that I would like to see her dead.

Greenberg: Who did you tell?

Kaufman: My attorneys—all members of my family—

Greenberg: Ever say you'd consider killing her?

Kaufman: Yes. It's something I felt. But I'm not going to act on it. Feelings and thoughts are different—different from actions.

Greenberg: So you've had homicidal thoughts about Lynn?

Kaufman: Yeah. That's a real common thing in psychiatry—homicidal ideation.

Greenberg: Must be nice to analyze your own statements and their psychological ramifications.

"Objection!" Meisner says angrily. "Counsel is making a statement. That's not a question."

Judge: Sustained. Jury will disregard counsel's last statement.

Greenberg: Thank you, Your Honor. Dr. Kaufman, did you recently say to someone in your office, "I am not going to kill myself. I might kill Lynn, but not myself"?

Kaufman: That's just what I said, yeah.

The doctor is excused and steps down from the stand. As he passes the plaintiff's table, you notice him whisper something to her under his breath, but you cannot make it out.

The next witness for the plaintiff is Anthony Pacelli of the United States Border Patrol in Miami, Florida. He testifies he received a call from a man who said he wanted to give the government a hot tip.

Greenberg: Did he give you his name.

Pacelli: No, sir. He said he wished to remain anonymous.

Greenberg: What did he say?

Pacelli: He said a female named Lynn Daniels would be arriving on an American Airlines flight—he had the number—that evening with an illegal alien she was trying to smuggle into Florida. He said there'd be a little girl with them, too.

Greenberg: What action did you take?

Pacelli: My partner and I went to the airport and spotted them when they got off the plane.

Greenberg: And did you detain them?

Pacelli: Oh, yes, sir. The lady—Ms. Daniels—was very upset. She had some meeting she was supposed to go to. But the Mexican lady didn't have papers—she was illegal all right.

Greenberg: So you held them for questioning in a detention room?

Pacelli: Yes, sir. The American lady—Ms. Daniels—broke down. She was crying uncontrollably, sobbing, very upset. She told them she thought the nanny was legal. After several hours we let Ms. Daniels go with the baby. But the nanny—we had to hold her.

Defense Attorney Meisner cross-examines.

Meisner: Officer Pacelli, you say Ms. Daniels was crying uncontrollably?

Pacelli: Yes, sir.

Meisner: She ever tell you she had acting lessons and won awards for acting?

Greenberg: Objection!

Judge: Sustained.

Now, at last, the star and catalyst of this proceeding, Lynn Daniels, is called to the witness stand. She testifies as to how she met Alan Kaufman, how her mother put the ad in the paper without her even knowing about it, how he was one of about ten men—doctors and lawyers mostly—who answered, and how she felt immediately attracted to him. He told her he owned a five-thousand-square-foot home with three acres, two cars, and a boat. She knew her mother would be extremely pleased if she were to marry a doctor. He certainly had all the things that indicated he was a successful doctor in her eyes. She was 30 years old at the time and had an income of over one hundred thousand dollars a year in her business as a buyer, but what she really wanted was a good husband and a child. The career was not important to her. When they moved in together, he demanded she pay two thousand dollars a month toward the mortgage, and she did not protest.

Near tears, she tells of the night after her second miscarriage.

Daniels: He kept telling me it was my fault for being on my feet so much. He kept yelling at me that I had killed the baby and said I never really wanted the baby.

Greenberg: Did you throw the phone at him?

Daniels: I had the phone in my hand. I'd picked it up to call my mother to ask her to come get me. I threw the phone down, he grabbed me, threw me up against the wall. I remember going down. He was on top of me, straddling me. He started to choke me—both hands. For a minute he put pressure with his hand on my neck, hard enough to leave bruises, visible bruises.

She gives a different version of the fight in the car. He picked her and Chloe up at the airport and told her he'd made plans for dinner with his father at his sister's house. He wanted to take Chloe without her.

"I said, 'I'll go too. I don't want you taking Chloe without me.'"

Greenberg: Why didn't you want him to take Chloe without you?

Daniels: Because he'd never taken care of her alone, and I wasn't sure he could.

Greenberg: What did he do?

Daniels: He pulled over and cut the engine. Chloe was sitting up in the back car seat.

Greenberg: What did he say?

Daniels: He said: "You—don't you ever tell me what I can and can't do."

Greenberg: Did he strike you then?

Daniels: He tried to strangle me. He held his hands around my throat. I started screaming for the police and he said, "You'll be dead before the police ever get here."

She points to the right side of her neck to show the jury where the bruises were.

Daniels: He had his thumbs right here, cutting off my windpipe. He held his hands like that for two minutes until I hit his arm and broke his grasp.

Greenberg: What was Chloe doing?

Daniels: She was screaming. He said, "Don't you tell me I can't take Chloe whenever I want," and he grabbed my hair and pulled my head into the gearshift. I didn't break my nose, but it was bleeding.

Greenberg: What happened after that?

Daniels: We went to dinner with his father. I cleaned up as best I could, and I don't think he noticed anything. When we were driving home after dinner, I told him to get the hell out or I was going to the police. He said if I went to the police, he would kill me.

She says the defendant testified truthfully about the doll incident except for one thing—the doll had pantyhose tied around its neck, which she understood to be a threat of what could happen to her.

For several months, she kept telling him to leave, but he wouldn't do it. "He said he would take Chloe with him and I'd never see her again. He said, "I'm not leaving until I'm good and ready, and you can't make me—and if you try anything, I'll make your life hell."

Finally, she says, she obtained a court order forcing him to leave. Then came the arrest in Miami. The Border Patrol agents told her she was being detained for smuggling an illegal alien across state lines. They took her into a little room and kept her there with Chloe and Filomena. She was not mistreated, but it was a degrading experience. After several hours, they let her go with Chloe but kept Filomena. She had to find a bail bondsman to post bail for Filomena. The agent told her she'd been set up.

Ms. Daniels calculates she lost over $60,000 in sales and commissions because of the delay. She missed several meetings and lost two major accounts at a time critical to her business. During her detention, she was unable to phone buyers to notify them.

Upon her return to San Francisco, she discovered her home had been burglarized. Liquor, toys, and gifts to Chloe were missing. The police told her that entry had been made by someone with a key, and since Dr. Kaufman was the only other person with a key, she suspected him. As a result, she had all the locks changed, installed a new security system, and even hired a guard to watch the house when she was away. The cost was $6,500.

This time she obtained a court order restraining him from coming within one hundred yards of the house, but she still saw him driving by at strange hours. She would look out the window and he would be sitting outside in his car. She called the police several times; he was gone by the time they came, but he would come back when they were gone. Sometimes when friends left her home, she would see him following them. Once she got a call from her friend Alma Dawson, who said, "Alan's following me. What should I do?"

The defense attorney, Meisner, cross-examines. "With regard to the argument in the car on the highway, you say you had bruises on your neck afterward?"

Daniels: Yes.

Meisner: You're making this up, aren't you?

Daniels: No. I am not making this up.

Meisner: Ms. Daniels, isn't it true you were bulimic at the time?

Greenberg jumps up. "Objection! Irrelevant! He's trying to embarrass the witness."

"Your Honor," Meisner says, "if the court pleases, I will show it is very relevant to her claim that my client tried to strangle her."

Judge: I will allow it subject to a motion to strike.

Daniels: Yes, I was bulimic.

Meisner: Which means you would make yourself throw up from time to time?

Daniels: Yes. It's a terrible sickness, really.

Meisner: And to do that you would stick your fingers down your throat?

Daniels: Yes.

Meisner: Show us how you would place your fingers.

Greenberg starts to object. "Your Honor—"

"Do I have to, Your Honor?" Daniels asks as she turns to the judge. "It's very—"

"All right," Meisner says, "I'll do it myself. I'll demonstrate." He stands up, places two fingers in his mouth. "Is this the way?"

Daniels: The fingers have to go in more.

Meisner: Like this?

Daniels: Farther.

Meisner: Like this?

He moves his fingers in farther.

Daniels: Farther, farther.

You can hear the sarcasm in her voice.

The judge is grinning. Meisner removes his fingers. His thumb is pressed against his throat. He has a look of triumph as he shows the jury the position of his thumb.

Meisner: And didn't you always place your thumb against your throat like this?

Daniels: No.

Meisner: And isn't this exactly how you got those bruises on your throat?

Daniels: No, Mr. Meisner, that's not how at all.

The plaintiff rests.

Meisner opens the defense case for Dr. Kaufman by calling a number of witnesses as to the doctor's character. Several members of his family testify that he has always had a reputation as a nonviolent, law-abiding citizen. His father and sister testify they were present at the dinner after the alleged strangling in the car. They sat close to Ms. Daniels and saw no bruises on her neck of any kind. She was wearing a white suit, and they did not see any blood spots on it such as might drip from a nosebleed.

The defense also calls a private investigator, Jason Holloway, who testifies he was hired by the court to supervise Dr. Kaufman's visits to see Chloe. The parties would arrive in separate cars at a prearranged spot in a parking lot. Ms. Daniels would bring Chloe. The investigator would park in the middle between them and stand by to keep the peace. He would bring Chloe to

Dr. Kaufman, where the doctor would hold her for thirty minutes, after which she would be returned to her mother and all parties would leave. Dr. Kaufman would always appear affectionate and caring during such visits.

Meisner: Did you ever hear Ms. Daniels make any threats to him at these visits?

Holloway: Yes, sir. I heard her say she'd sue him unless he promised to stay away from Chloe.

As the witness steps down, you notice Dr. Kaufman whispering to his attorney, who promptly announces he will call the doctor back to the stand.

Meisner: Dr. Kaufman, I want to ask you about these homicidal thoughts you had—

Kaufman: Yes, sir. That's all they were, just thoughts.

Meisner: You never intended to act on them?

Kaufman: Absolutely not.

Meisner: Tell me this—what's the highest level of education you've attained?

Kaufman: I've had three years of specialty residence in psychiatry following my MD degree.

Meisner: How did you do in high school?

Kaufman: I was at the top of my class.

Meisner: And how did you do in college?

Kaufman: I graduated magna cum laude with honors in two majors.

Meisner: And you've been a practicing psychiatrist now for twelve years?

Kaufman: Yes.

Meisner: And you've also been in analysis yourself?

Kaufman: Yes, sir, as part of the training.

Meisner: Now then, considering all your education and experience, do you feel you are especially aware of your thoughts, your own thought processes?

Kaufman: Oh, yes. More so than the average person. I make a strong distinction between thoughts and actions. They are two separate things.

When Dr. Kaufman leaves the stand for the last time, Meisner looks over at Daniels. He stares at her for a second, then says, "I call Lynn Daniels back for further cross-examination."

Judge: Ms. Daniels, you are reminded you are still under oath.

Daniels: Thank you, yes.

Meisner: Now tell us, what makes you think you've suffered severe emotional distress?

Daniels: I have nightmares. I'm choking in my sleep. I feel Alan's hands around my throat.

Meisner: This is still going on?

Daniels: Oh, yes. I wake up screaming and crying.

Meisner: Well, tell me this—have you ever gone to a psychiatrist for the treatment of the emotional distress that you say my client inflicted on you?

Daniels: No, sir.

Meisner: Never gone to a professional for help?

Daniels: No, sir.

Meisner: Well, if you're really suffering so much, why not?

Daniels: You really want to know?

Meisner: Yes, or is it simply that it's not been serious enough to bother?

Daniels: (*She takes a deep breath.*) You really want to know?

Meisner: Yes.

Daniels: Because Alan's a psychiatrist. And somehow I don't trust them at the moment.

Both sides rest. In closing argument, Lynn Daniels's attorney, Dan Greenberg, asks the jury for a million dollars in damages.

The judge instructs you to state your finding of liability and award of damages, if any, as to each allegation separately. You may include both compensatory damages (actual out-of-pocket losses) and punitive damages (punishment for despicable conduct). You first must determine whether or not the defendant is liable on each point. Then, if you have answered yes to any of the questions of liability, you must determine the amount of your award for each point.

The questions you must decide are:

1. Did the defendant place in the plaintiff's bed a life-size doll with a stocking tied around its neck with the intent to shock her?

2. Did the defendant try to strangle the plaintiff in front of their minor child, and did he tell the plaintiff he would kill her?

3. At another time, did the defendant tell the plaintiff he would kill her?

4. Did the defendant tell the plaintiff he would take Chloe away and that the plaintiff would never see her again?

5. Did the defendant contact the Immigration and Naturalization Service in Miami and cause the plaintiff to be detained for smuggling an illegal alien?

6. Did the plaintiff suffer a loss in her business as a result of the defendant's conduct?

7. Did the defendant burglarize or cause someone to burglarize the plaintiff's home?

8. Did the defendant so terrify the plaintiff by his burglary that she was required to install a security system?

9. Did the defendant stalk, follow, and monitor the actions of the plaintiff and her friends?

10. Did the defendant push the plaintiff's face into the gearshift of her car, causing her nose to bleed?

WHAT IS YOUR VERDICT?

QUESTIONS FOR YOU TO CONSIDER

As you determine your verdict for this crime, here are some questions about the crime and the trial for you to think about.

1. Did the fact that the defendant was a practicing psychiatrist affect the jury's decision?

AUTHOR'S ANSWERS TO THE QUESTIONS

1. It certainly did. Conversations with jurors after the trial revealed that they placed great weight on the fact that Dr. Kaufman was a psychiatrist and therefore should have known better. Although jurors were disgusted by the doctor's use of the life-size doll to frighten Ms. Daniels, they were particularly upset with the doctor's conduct in notifying INS agents in Miami of Ms. Daniels's arrival with an illegal alien, causing her to lose important business.

THE VERDICT

What was your verdict?

Here is how the real-life jury answered the questions put before them:

1. Did the defendant place in the plaintiff's bed a life-size doll with a stocking tied around its neck with the intent to shock her?

   Yes

   Award: $25,000

2. Did the defendant try to strangle the plaintiff in front of their minor child, and did he tell the plaintiff he would kill her?

   Yes

   Award: $75,000

3. At another time, did the defendant tell the plaintiff he would kill her?

   Yes

   Award: $28,000

4. Did the defendant tell the plaintiff he would take Chloe away and that the plaintiff would never see her again?

   Yes

   Award: $25,000

5. Did the defendant contact the Immigration and Naturalization Service in Miami and cause the plaintiff to be detained for smuggling an illegal alien?

   Yes

   Award: $256,250

6. Did the plaintiff suffer a loss in her business as a result of the defendant's conduct?

Yes

Award: $160,000

7. Did the defendant burglarize or cause someone to burglarize the plaintiff's home?

Yes

Award: $50,000

8. Did the defendant so terrify the plaintiff by his burglary that she was required to install a security system?

Yes

Award: $25,750

9. Did the defendant stalk, follow, and monitor the actions of the plaintiff and her friends?

Yes

Award: $25,000

10. Did the defendant push the plaintiff's face into the gearshift of her car, causing her nose to bleed?

No

Award: $0

Total Award: $670,000

A Memory Revived

STATE V. HENRY BARKER

On June 25, 1997, Edith Barker was found dead on the floor of her home, strangled with the cord of an electric iron. For years, police were unable to crack the case. Eleven years later, based on new evidence, a police detective reopened the investigation and Edith's husband, Henry Barker, with whom she had been living at the time, was charged with the murder. The alleged motive was $30,000 of insurance money on Edith's life, which was paid to Henry. The D.A. also claimed that Henry wanted to get rid of Edith so he could live with a younger woman, Sally Lester. The prosecution's evidence tended to show that Henry had hired a hit man named Leonard Keck to kill Edith.

The sticking point in the case arises with the testimony of prosecution witness Amy Gordon. Ms. Gordon testifies that she was Edith Barker's best friend; that she went to visit Edith on June 25, 1997; and, that as she got to the door, a man rushed out of the house. Upon entering, she saw Edith's dead body on the floor, blood coming from her mouth. For reasons she cannot explain, Ms. Gordon says she went home and told no one what she had seen. She further claims that, strange as it seems, she somehow forgot the incident completely. She also testifies that eleven years later, the detective jogged her memory and she remembered the event for the first time. Leonard Keck is brought into the courtroom, and in a dramatic scene, Ms. Gordon identifies him as the man she saw run out of the house the night of the murder. Henry Barker denies any involvement and denies hiring Leonard Keck to kill his wife.

Henry Barker is charged with the murder of his wife, Edith, the alleged motive being the sum of $30,000 in proceeds from a life insurance policy.

At the outset, the judge tells the jury that someone else may have been involved in the crime. "You must not give any consideration," he says, "as to why the other person or persons are not being prosecuted in this trial or whether they have been or will be prosecuted."

The D.A., Mary Walden, is noticeably pregnant. But as you will see, that does not prevent her from being a forceful prosecuting attorney. As she outlines the evidence, you think the case sounds like a piece of detective fiction. The classic elements are all here—murder for hire, a key witness with a lapsed memory, a mysterious phone call at the murder scene, and a woman suspected of being romantically involved with the defendant.

The defense attorney, Sarah Frizelle, portly and formidable-looking, rises, and in a cold, clipped voice, she derides the State's case with sarcasm.

> From the district attorney, you've all heard a lot of words, a sort of laundry list. A $5,000 payoff to a hit man? We will show such money was never paid or never even existed. Those so-called mysterious words on the phone? See for yourself if they have any meaning in this case.

At this point, she moves behind the defendant and places both hands protectively on his shoulders. He is tall, lean, and well-dressed in a gray suit. "Just remember," she says, "that this man, Henry Barker, is presumed innocent. He doesn't have to prove anything. The only burden is on the prosecution to prove him guilty beyond any reasonable doubt. That's the law. You took an oath to follow that law. I know you will do so."

District Attorney Walden calls the first witness for the prosecution. He is Milton Ordway, Henry Barker's friend and next-door neighbor. About a week before the murder, Henry came over to Ordway's house.

Walden: What did he want?

Ordway: He wanted to talk about his insurance policies. I was selling insurance then, and he wanted some advice.

Walden: Did you give him advice?

Ordway: Yes, I did. After looking over his policies, I told him he had too much life insurance on his wife and not enough on himself, since he was the breadwinner. So I advised him to reverse the amounts.

Walden: Did he agree to do that?

Ordway: Yes. I drew up an application for new policies and set up an appointment for him to take a physical. The company wouldn't approve the policy without the physical.

Walden: Did he take the physical?

Ordway: No. He missed the appointment.

Walden: So the old policies were still in effect at the time of Mrs. Barker's death?

Ordway: Yes.

Walden: For how much?

Ordway: About $30,000 on her, $10,000 on him.

Walden: And to your knowledge, was the $30,000 paid to him by the company after her death?

Ordway: Yes, it was.

Ordway testifies that on the evening of Edith Barker's death, he and his wife hosted a crystal party at their home for the purpose of selling crystalware to their friends. Henry was teaching at the Navy school that night. Edith was present at the party but seemed unusually quiet and fidgety. Ordway gave her the doctor's card to give to Henry for the physical. She fingered it nervously and looked it over, but he noticed that when she left at about nine-thirty, the card was still on the table.

Sometime after 10:30 p.m., Ordway was awakened by the ringing of the doorbell. When he answered it, Sally Lester was at the door.

Walden: Who's Sally Lester?

Ordway: She's a female boarder who rents a room at the Barkers' house. She and Henry are both in the Navy—he's an instructor, she's a student—and sometimes they ride to Navy night school together and come home together.

Walden: Ever notice any romantic involvement between them?

Ordway: Well—

Walden: Did you?

Ordway: Well, you know, the neighbors talk, but I never noticed anything.

Frizelle: Objection, Your Honor, as to what neighbors say. That's hearsay.

Judge: Sustained. The jury is admonished to disregard that part of the answer.

Walden: So, Sally Lester came to the door. What did she want?

Ordway: She said Edith was hurt, and Henry wanted me to come over right away.

Ordway says he got dressed and went next door, where Henry met him outside. They went in together and saw Edith lying on the floor. She had a cord from the iron around her neck; the iron was on the floor beside her head. She looked dead, so he did not go up to her. He asked Henry if he had called the police, and Henry said he had. Then the phone rang and Henry answered it.

Walden: Could you hear the conversation?

Ordway: It was very brief. He just said, "No, they have not got here yet and, you know, I just can't talk right now."

Walden: Do you know who he was talking to?

Ordway: No. A few seconds later, the police came and they took over.

The questioning shifts to a time several months after the murder. Ordway testifies he got out of the insurance business and organized his own company, manufacturing nameplates. Barker loaned him $15,000 to help the company get started, but the business failed and closed down within the year.

Walden: Do you know where Barker got $15,000?

Ordway: He said it came from the life insurance proceeds.

Walden: Did you ever pay him the money back?

Ordway: No, the money was gone.

Walden: Did he ever ask you for it?

Ordway: Not really. He knew we'd lost it.

Walden: So the $15,000 has still never been repaid—up to this day?

Ordway: That's right.

Defense Attorney Sarah Frizelle starts her cross-examination with a frontal attack. "Mr. Ordway, you studied first aid in the Marine Corps, didn't you?"

Ordway: Yes.

Frizelle: In fact, you taught first aid to the Marines for several years, is that true?

Ordway: Yes.

Frizelle: So you were an expert in first aid?

Ordway: You might say that.

Frizelle: When you saw Edith Barker lying on the floor, did you go over to check her?

Ordway: No.

Frizelle: Did you check to see if she was alive? Her vital signs?

Ordway: No.

Frizelle: Why didn't you do that, Mr. Ordway?

Ordway: Well, I was in shock, that's why. And besides, Henry told me she was dead.

Frizelle: Do you know if Henry checked her?

Ordway: I don't know.

Frizelle: When you saw Henry outside the house, was he upset?

Ordway: Yes, he was.

Frizelle: Was he crying?

Ordway: Yes.

Frizelle: So he was reacting as any husband would normally react upon finding his wife murdered?

Walden: Objection, Your Honor. As to how a husband normally reacts.

Judge: Overruled. You may answer.

Ordway: Yes. He was shocked.

Frizelle: What about Sally Lester?

Ordway: What about her?

Frizelle: Didn't you tell police you were surprised by her reaction?

Ordway: Yes.

Frizelle: What did you mean?

Ordway: Well, when she first came to the door, she seemed very quiet, subdued—not excited at all.

Frizelle: Did she ever ask what happened to Mrs. Barker?

Ordway: No.

Frizelle: Did she ever ask anyone to your knowledge if Edith Barker was alive or dead?

Ordway: No.

Frizelle: Did she at any time that evening express any interest in the condition of Edith Barker?

Ordway: No, that's what surprised me.

Sally Lester takes the stand for the prosecution. She is an attractive brunette in her early thirties and athletic looking. She wears a sweater and skirt. She does not look at Barker, seated at counsel's table. In fact, she keeps herself turned away from him as she speaks. Under questioning by Walden, she testifies that she met Henry Barker when they were both in the Navy thirteen years ago. She was a student at the Navy electronics school; he was an instructor. They were not in the same class, but there were several classes located close together, and during breaks students and instructors would get together in the lounge. Sally and Henry struck up a friendship. About two months before the murder, Sally asked Barker if he knew of a room she could rent. He invited her to rent the extra room in his house, so she did. Edith did not object.

Walden: Who lived in the residence when you moved in?

Lester: Henry and Edith Barker.

Walden: Were there any children?

Lester: No.

Walden: What was the house like?

Lester: Two bedrooms, one bath, living room, kitchen-dining room, garage.

Walden: You had one of the bedrooms?

Lester: Yes.

Walden: Was there ever any romantic relationship between you and Henry?

Lester: No.

Walden: You're sure?

Lester: Well, we were fond of each other. But that was it.

Several weeks before the murder, Sally says she met Leonard Keck. He was also an instructor at the Navy school, and they began having drinks together after class. Late one night, while the Barkers were asleep, she brought Keck home to her room, where he slept with her; he left before the Barkers awoke. Keck told her he was a hit man. She understood the term *hit man* to mean someone who kills people for money, but she did not take him seriously. When she told Barker what Keck said, Barker replied, "Why don't you see if he wants a job?" During one of the breaks at school, she introduced the two men to each other and observed them talking. A few days before the murder, Barker gave her a note, folded and stapled, to deliver to Keck, which she did. She had no idea what it said.

On the night of the murder, Barker and Sally arrived home from school. He opened the door with his keys. As they started inside, Barker stopped her and said, "Go get Milt and tell him to come right over." She went to get Ordway, and then stayed at his house all night while the police investigated the murder scene.

Once again Sarah Frizelle opens her cross-examination by going straight for the jugular. "You didn't like Edith, did you?"

Lester: We got along.

Frizelle: Didn't she accuse you of having an affair with Henry?

Lester: I don't remember.

Frizelle: Let me refresh your memory, Ms. Lester. Do you remember one afternoon when Edith surprised you in your room as she came in to get sheets off the bed—

Lester: What are you talking about?

Frizelle: —and you were just getting dressed and Mr. Barker was in the shower? Do you remember that?

Lester: Something like that, yes.

Frizelle: And do you remember what she said when she saw damp stains on the bottom sheet?

Lester: Yes. She made an accusation, but there was nothing to it.

Frizelle: That made you mad, didn't it?

Lester: That's true.

Frizelle: You wanted to get rid of her, didn't you?

Lester: Don't be silly.

Frizelle: You wanted to live in the house alone with Mr. Barker, didn't you?

Lester: No. That's nonsense.

Frizelle: Nonsense? Really? But isn't that just what you did? Didn't you go on living in the house with Mr. Barker after Edith's death?

Lester: Well, yes.

Frizelle: Tell the jury how long you continued to live in the house with Mr. Barker after Edith's death.

Lester: Three months.

Frizelle: Did you sleep in the master bedroom?

Walden: Objection!

Judge: Sustained!

Frizelle turns sharply to the judge. She looks upset. "But, Your Honor—" She cannot let the ruling pass. "My question goes to her motive—her motive to get Edith Barker out of the way, her motive to lie about that. If she slept with—"

"It's irrelevant," Walden shouts. "Irrelevant and ridiculous!"

The judge leans back, stroking his chin. He looks at the two attorneys, both standing, waiting anxiously.

"I'll reverse my ruling," the judge says. He leans over to Sally Lester. "You may answer the question."

"What was the question?" Lester asks. "I've forgotten the question."

"I'll gladly state it again," Frizelle replies. "Did you sleep in the master bedroom?"

Lester: No, I did not. He slept in his room. I slept in mine.

The D.A. calls Jack Wister next. He comes through the door with a swagger, shabbily dressed, unshaven, his shirt hanging partly out of his pants. He looks like a man who has had a hard night, or more likely, several hard nights. Wister testifies he used to be best friends with the Barkers. He and his wife, Jeannette, socialized with them often before Edith's death. He tells of a conversation he had with Henry Barker about a month before the murder. They'd both been drinking. Henry was upset with Edith because she had had an extramarital affair while he was on a navy cruise in the Mediterranean.

Walden: Did he ask you to kill Edith?

Wister: Not directly, but he asked if it could be done.

Walden: What did you say?

Wister: I said it was possible, but I didn't want to have anything to do with it.

Walden: Did he ask how much it would cost?

Wister: Yes, and I told him five thousand dollars.

Walden: Did he say where the money would come from?

Wister: Yes, he said it would come from the insurance.

Walden: What did he say when you said you wouldn't do it?

Wister: He said if I wouldn't do it, he'd find someone who would.

Frizelle cross-examines. "Are you still friends with Henry Barker?"

Wister: D'ya think I'd be sitting here testifying against him if I was?

Frizelle: In fact, you didn't tell this story to the police until you had a falling out with him years after the murder, isn't that right?

Wister: True.

Frizelle: Why didn't you tell police about it eleven years ago, when they first questioned you?

Wister: Because I didn't like the detective in charge.

Frizelle: Is that because he had arrested you so many times?

Wister: Yeah, he was always hassling me.

Frizelle: And some of the arrests resulted in convictions, didn't they?

Wister: Some did.

Frizelle: Such as burglary and possession of heroin?

Wister: Yeah, I guess.

Frizelle: And didn't he suspect you of being involved in this murder?

Wister: Yes.

Frizelle: In fact, he told you he had an eyewitness who saw two people running from the house at the time of the murder, and the description matched you and your wife. Isn't that right?

"Objection, Your Honor," Mary Walden says. "It's hearsay as to what the detective said."

"Your Honor," Sarah Frizelle says, "this is an exception to the hearsay rule. It goes to show why he is trying to shift the blame from himself to the defendant. It's not being offered for the truth of the matter."

Judge: For that limited purpose, I will allow it. Objection overruled. You may answer, Mr. Wister.

Wister: Yeah, that's what the detective said. But that's bull. We were both home that night.

Frizelle: You say you'd been drinking at the time Barker said this to you?

Wister: We both were.

Frizelle: Were you on drugs?

Wister: Naahh.

Frizelle: Marijuana?

Wister: Oh, yeah, I'd smoked some pot, but I don't consider that a drug.

Frizelle: And you had a few drinks before you took the stand today?

Wister: Well, yeah, a couple. I was nervous.

After Wister, several prosecution witnesses go on and off the stand quickly. The autopsy surgeon confirms Edith was strangled to death, apparently with the cord of her electric iron. The detective testifies there was no evidence of forced entry, that whoever entered apparently came through the back door with a key; the back door was ajar, with the sliding deadbolt protruding. The former wife of Leonard Keck testifies that about three months after the murder, she saw her husband open an envelope with a large amount of cash in it, but he would not tell her where it came from.

Court adjourns for the day with the announcement by D.A. Mary Walden that her first witness tomorrow will be Amy Gordon.

When the trial resumes in the morning, you notice the courtroom is filled with spectators waiting to hear Amy Gordon's testimony. A TV cameraman is in the back, and the judge asks the jurors if anyone objects to having a TV camera in the court. He promises there will be no shots of the jury. There is no response.

"I have granted the request for television coverage," the judge says, "because I believe the public has a right to know. But if it interferes with a fair trial and the dignity of this court, I will exclude it."

You wonder why this woman Amy Gordon is attracting so much media attention. Then when she enters the courtroom to take the stand, you remember having seen her picture in the newspaper recently in connection with this case.

Amy Gordon is a heavyset, timid-looking woman of about 35; she seems stagestruck by all the attention. You notice her taking a deep breath. She testifies she was best friends with Edith Barker before Edith's death. On June 25, 1997, the date Edith was killed, they went shopping together in the afternoon. Edith asked Amy to come over in the evening to keep her company while Henry was teaching. Amy says Edith was feeling depressed because she suspected Henry and Sally were having an affair. Amy promised to come, but when she got home she realized she was tired of hearing Edith's complaints about Henry and decided not to go. Later in the evening, she began to feel guilty about not keeping her promise to her best friend. She phoned Edith, but the line was busy. She called again and the line was still busy. Finally, she decided to drive over to Edith's herself, although it was past ten o'clock. She knocked at the front door but there was no answer. She heard a dull thud and ran around to the back door. The door was ajar with the sliding shaft of the deadbolt lock extended out. She called Edith's name. Still no answer.

Walden: What happened then?

Gordon: I turned around and saw a man behind me. He grabbed me around the neck, and I tried to push him off. I fell forward and hit my head. I lunged at him, but he backed away and ran off. I turned back to the door. "Edith!" I shouted. "Edith!" I remember that deadbolt sticking out of the door—something about that bolt—I looked down and saw her legs, Edith's legs. I heard a cough. I went inside. There was Edith lying on the floor. I was in a state of panic. Blood was coming out of her mouth. I couldn't tell if she was breathing or not.

Walden: What did you do?

Gordon: Nothing. I walked past her and left through the front door.

Walden: Where did you go?

There is a long pause. Gordon is shaking her head. "I went home."

Walden: Did you try to help her?

Gordon: No, I didn't. Don't ask me why. I don't know why.

Walden: Did you call the police?

Gordon: No. I went to sleep.

Walden: Did you call an ambulance?

Gordon: No.

Walden: Why not?

Gordon: I was in shock.

Walden: Did you tell your husband?

Gordon: No, no. I didn't tell anyone. Oh God.

There is a murmur through the courtroom.

Ms. Gordon states that when she awoke in the morning, she had somehow forgotten it completely. Ms. Gordon appears to be a quiet, sincere person, but you find her testimony that she forgot the incident very strange indeed. She further testifies that she heard on the radio that Edith had been murdered, and it was as if she was learning the news for the first time. She went to the police on her own that morning to tell them what Edith said, that Henry and Sally were having an affair. The police questioned her at length, but that was all she knew. She had absolutely no recollection of what happened the night before, and this lapse in memory continued for the next eleven years. During that time, no one was charged with Edith Barker's murder.

"I'm sorry," Amy Gordon says, shaking her head. "I know it must seem strange to you all."

She testifies that two months ago, Detective Dale Phillips reopened the investigation by questioning her again. He had a number of sessions with her, each lasting many hours. Then one night while he was interviewing her for the sixth or seventh time, something strange happened.

Walden: Something strange? What was that?

Gordon: He showed me a sketch of the door with the deadbolt sticking out and the feet on the floor. When I saw that deadbolt, something just broke inside me. It was like a dam bursting open. It all started to come back. The details of that night came rushing out.

Walden: And for the first time your memory of that night came back?

Gordon: Yes.

Walden: After eleven years?

Gordon: Yes.

Walden: Do you remember the man who attacked you by the back door?

Gordon: Yes. He had a scar near his eyes. He was a little taller than me.

Walden: Were you able to see his face?

Gordon: Yes, there was a yellow light from the garage.

Walden: Do you think you could recognize him if you saw him again?

Gordon: I could try.

The judge nods to the bailiff, and by a prearranged signal, the bailiff opens the back door to the courtroom. Another bailiff enters with a prisoner under guard. Amy Gordon looks at the guarded man as if in shock. "Oh my God," she shouts, "Oh my God. It looks like—oh, dear—" She twists nervously in her seat. Her face is flushed.

"You may proceed," the judge says to the D.A.

Walden: Ms. Gordon, do you see the man in the courtroom who attacked you that night?

She looks around the room. She studies the prisoner for a long time.

Gordon: Yes, he looks like him, it's coming back now, but it's been so long. He had a scar near his eyes—

She leans forward to see better.

Gordon: May I go closer?

Judge: You may.

She steps down and walks up to the prisoner. She peers closely at his face and his eyes, and she walks around him looking.

Gordon: He looks similar. He has a scar, too.

Walden: Same height?

Gordon: Yes.

Walden: Same build?

Gordon: Yes, but—

Walden: But what?

She shakes her head, returning to the stand. "It looks like him, I think it's him, but I can't be sure."

The judge nods to the guard, and he starts to remove the man.

As they reach the door, the judge stops them. "Just a minute," he says, looking at the prisoner. "Would you state your name, sir?"

"Yes, sir," the prisoner says. "My name is Leonard Keck."

"Thank you. You may go."

Amy Gordon testifies that about a month after Edith's murder, Henry contacted her to tell her she had better keep quiet "if she wanted to keep breathing." Since she had no memory then of being at the house, she understood him to be referring to what Edith had told her about Henry's affair with Sally.

She says she has never had any mental problems. Nothing like this had ever happened before. The police did not hypnotize her. She cannot explain why she did not help her friend that night or why her memory had lapsed for so long.

On cross-examination, Defense Attorney Sarah Frizelle strikes at the accuracy of Gordon's account. "You've spent many hours with the police in the past few months, right?"

Gordon: Yes.

Frizelle: They didn't believe you when you told them you weren't there, did they?

Gordon: No.

Frizelle: They kept telling you that you were at the house, that you saw something you were not telling them, right?

Gordon: Yes, they wanted the truth.

Frizelle: And these interviews went on for hours and hours, didn't they?

Gordon: Yes, a long time.

Frizelle: They kept pressing you.

Gordon: Well, yes.

Frizelle: And you were tired and exhausted?

Gordon: Yes.

Frizelle: And they kept saying you were there, that you saw something, someone?

Gordon: Yes.

Frizelle: Until you finally broke down.

Gordon: It's when I saw the deadbolt sticking out. It all just came back.

Frizelle: And what came back was what the police told you, isn't that right?

Gordon: Part of it, yes, but it was the same. I remember it now.

District Attorney Walden states she has no further witnesses and the prosecution rests.

The defense calls its first witness, William Cordrey, a neighbor of the Barkers. At about 10:15 on the night of the murder, he heard dogs barking and went out on his porch to see what was happening. He saw a large woman in Bermuda shorts running from the Barker residence. At almost the same time, he saw a man with long hair walking fast in front of the house. He is quite sure from their size and weight that neither person was Henry or Edith Barker.

Defense counsel shows him a photograph.

> **Frizelle**: I ask you to look at this picture and tell us if the man and woman shown here are the same ones you saw that night.

He studies the photograph, holds it far away, then up close.

> **Cordrey**: The guy had long hair like that, yeah. The lady was on the chubby side like this one. There's a resemblance all right. But I can't say positively. No way.

"Your Honor," defense counsel says, "the D.A. and I stipulate that this is a photograph of Jack and Jeannette Wister."

On cross-examination, the D.A. shows Cordrey a photograph of Amy Gordon as she looked eleven years ago. Cordrey says the woman in the photo also resembles the woman he saw that night in height and weight, but he cannot be sure.

Sarah Frizelle calls the defendant, Henry Barker. The tension heightens. You see him close up for the first time when he takes the stand. He makes a good appearance, but the anxiety shows in his face. He testifies he married Edith fifteen years ago in Norfolk, Virginia, when they were both in the Navy. When they moved to San Diego, she left the Navy and he reenlisted. A door-to-door salesman sold him the insurance policies, and he was not sure about the amounts until Ordway explained them. Then he wanted to change the benefits. He denies ever planning to kill Edith. He denies ever having any conversation with Jack Wister about killing Edith and says Wister has a bad reputation for honesty. He confirms Sally Lester's testimony as to the discovery of the body. He says Amy Gordon had it in for him because Edith told her he was having an affair with Sally, which was not true.

Mary Walden moves to the podium to begin her cross-examination. Her first questions focus on the life insurance policies. "You admit there was at least $30,000 insurance money on Edith's life, which you've already collected?"

Barker: Yes.

Walden: Do you remember the police asking you how much insurance there was on Edith?

Barker: I don't recall.

Walden: I'll show you this police report. See if it refreshes your memory.

She turns toward the judge.

Walden: May I approach, Your Honor?

Judge: You may.

She goes to the witness stand with a document and shows it to Barker.

Walden: Remember now?

Barker: (*Studying the paper*) I still don't remember.

Walden: Do you dispute the conversation occurred?

Barker: I guess not.

Walden: And did you tell the police, just a few days after the murder, the amount of insurance there was on Edith's life?

Barker: By looking at the report, I guess I did.

Walden: And didn't you say, "Five thousand—just enough to cover burial expenses." Didn't you say that?

Barker: According to the report, yes.

Walden: And why didn't you tell the police the truth—that it was $30,000?

Barker: Because it didn't stick in my mind.

Walden: Now, moving on, do you remember taking a Navy cruise in the summer of 1996?

Barker: I do.

Walden: And when you came back, didn't something happen that made you very angry at Edith?

Barker: Not very angry, no.

Walden: Upset?

Barker: Well, yes.

Walden: Tell the jury what it was.

Barker: Well, she'd told me she'd had an affair with somebody else while I was at sea.

Walden: And didn't that make you angry?

Barker: Well—

Walden: Betrayed?

Barker: Sort of, yes.

Walden: And didn't that make you want to get back at her, to hurt her for what she'd done to you?

Barker: No. We talked it over. We worked it out.

Walden: Now, going to the night Edith was murdered, a phone call was received at your residence. Did you ever tell the police what it was?

Barker: No.

Walden: Why not?

Barker: Because I had no recollection of it. It was a hectic time. I was very upset.

Walden: Could it have been Leonard Keck asking if the police had gotten there yet?

Barker: No, he didn't even have our phone number. We had an unlisted phone.

Walden: Nothing further.

Frizelle has a few more questions now. "Mr. Barker, at any time did you discuss with anyone a plan or intent or motive to kill Edith Barker?"

Barker: No, I've never discussed killing anybody with anyone.

Frizelle: Did you participate in any way in the murder of Edith Barker?

Barker: No, definitely not.

Barker turns and looks directly at you with his deep blue eyes.

Barker: I swear I did not!

Mary Walden stands up for one last shot. "You admit you knew Leonard Keck?"

Barker: Sure. Sally introduced us.

Walden: Did you send him a note a few weeks before the murder?

Barker: Yes.

There is a noticeable pause. You notice the other jurors leaning forward.

Walden: What did it say?

Barker: I asked him to get me some drugs. I was into drugs then.

Walden: Did you send him some money after Edith's death?

Barker: I did.

Walden: For what?

Barker: For the drugs he sent me.

Walden: That's all?

Barker: That's all.

Walden: It had nothing to do with the murder?

Barker: Nothing whatsoever.

Barker leaves the stand and both sides rest.

There are two possible verdicts you can find in this case:

1. guilty of first-degree murder
2. not guilty

WHAT IS YOUR VERDICT?

QUESTIONS FOR YOU TO CONSIDER

As you determine your verdict for this crime, here are some questions about the crime and the trial for you to think about.

1. The police detained six persons as suspects for the murder of Edith Barker. Who were they, and why were they arrested?

2. Do you find Amy Gordon's testimony that she forgot her experience at the murder scene for eleven years and then suddenly remembered it credible?

3. In the event the jury finds the defendant not guilty, would such a verdict mean the same as innocent?

AUTHOR'S ANSWERS TO THE QUESTIONS

1. The facts pointed to Henry Barker as the one who hired Leonard Keck to do the job. He had the motives: revenge for Edith's infidelity, the insurance proceeds, and possibly a desire for Sally. But it was all circumstantial evidence, and the jury was instructed that if there are two reasonable interpretations of the evidence, one pointing to guilt and one pointing to innocence, then they must choose the interpretation pointing to innocence.

   As the hit man, Leonard Keck was the primary suspect as the actual killer. Amy Gordon said he looked in every way like the man she saw, but she couldn't be positive. He was tried separately, and he never appeared as a witness in the Barker trial because he asserted his constitutional right not to testify under the Fifth Amendment.

   Sally Lester arranged the meeting between Barker and Keck, knowing Keck was a hit man. She behaved suspiciously after discovering the body and seemed uninterested in Edith's plight. She apparently had sex with Barker in her room. Was she in love with Barker? If so, she had the motive of wanting him for herself and moving into the master bedroom. In fact, she continued living in the house with Barker after the murder.

   Ordway, too, had a possible motive: he received $15,000 from Barker, which he never repaid. Was that a payoff? He also acted suspicious at the murder scene. He could not explain why he made no effort to revive Edith when he saw her unconscious, even though he was an expert in first aid.

   A man and woman observed at the scene matched the description of Jack and Jeannette Wister. Jack had a criminal record, knew several hit men, used drugs, and admitted that when Barker asked him what it would cost to have Edith killed, he told him it would be five thousand dollars.

2. Amy Gordon's loss of memory for eleven years seems bizarre, but it can be explained psychologically. Forensic experts tell us an event can be so frightening, embarrassing, or guilt-provoking that certain persons will block it out of their memory in order not to relive that terrible moment. Psychologists call this *psychogenic amnesia*, a phenomenon that is not uncommon. Suddenly a reminder may occur—in this case the sight of the deadbolt sticking out of the door—that can trigger the memory and bring it all back. The prosecution argued that this is precisely what happened to Amy Gordon. However, defense counsel had a different interpretation: the big gaps in her memory were filled in by the suggestions of others, the police in particular, and her testimony was only a rendering of what she'd been told, even though she believed it really happened—a memory implanted by suggestion.

3. See the discussion under "The Verdict."

THE VERDICT

What was your verdict?

The real-life jury found the defendant not guilty.

Henry Barker had two trials. The first resulted in a hung jury. In the second trial, the jury acquitted him and set him free. The major hurdle for the prosecution was overcoming the jury's reluctance to accept Amy Gordon's story. It could not be done. Jurors said they had a strong suspicion of Barker's guilt, but the circumstantial evidence simply did not rise to proof beyond a reasonable doubt.

The jury's verdict illustrates a common misconception by the American public. The verdict of not guilty does not mean the jury found Barker innocent. It only means he was not proven guilty beyond a reasonable doubt. *Not guilty* is not a synonym for *innocent,* and strictly speaking, there is no such verdict as *innocent* in our criminal law. However, occasionally an exception is made due to extraordinary circumstances, and a case calls out for a finding of innocent. For example, it may be shown that a defendant should never have been considered a suspect in the first place. The granting of a verdict of innocent is rare, requiring a clear showing that the defendant was not involved.

Leonard Keck likewise had two trials, with a hung jury in the first and an acquittal in the second.

Who killed Edith Barker? After eleven years of investigation and four jury trials, it is still a mystery.

Appendix: Jury Instructions

Jury instructions comprise the law of the case being tried. Most jury trials involve numerous written instructions—too numerous to include here—that are submitted by counsel, approved by the judge, read by the judge to the jury, and often submitted to the jurors for their reference while deliberating.

CRIMINAL CASES

Duties of Judge and Jury

Whether a defendant is to be found guilty or not guilty depends upon both the facts and the law.

As jurors, you have two duties to perform. One duty is to determine the facts of the case from the evidence received in this trial and not from any other source. Your other duty is to apply the rules of law that I state to you to the facts as you determine them and in this way to arrive at your verdict. It is the judge's duty to explain to you the rules of law that apply to this case. You must accept and follow the rules of law as I state them to you.

As jurors, you must not be influenced by pity for a defendant or by prejudice against him or her. You must not be biased against the defendant because he or she has been arrested for this offense, because he or she has been charged with a crime, or because he or she has been brought to trial. None of these circumstances is evidence of guilt, and you must not infer or assume from any or all of them that the defendant is more likely to be guilty than not guilty.

You must not be swayed by mere sentiment, conjecture, sympathy, passion, prejudice, public opinion, or public feeling. Both the State and the defendant have a right to expect that you will conscientiously consider and weigh the evidence and apply the law of the case, and that you will reach a just verdict regardless of what the consequences of such verdict may be.

Not All Instructions Apply

The following instructions apply to the rules of law that may be necessary for you to reach verdicts in the trials presented. Not all instructions apply to each case. Whether an instruction applies will depend on the nature of the charge and your determination of the facts.

Burden of Proof

A defendant in a criminal case is presumed to be innocent until the contrary is proved, and in case of a reasonable doubt whether his or her guilt is satisfactorily shown, he or she is entitled to a verdict of not guilty. This presumption places upon the State the burden of proving him or her guilty beyond a reasonable doubt. The defendant has no burden or proof.

Reasonable doubt is defined as follows:

> It is not a mere possible doubt, because everything relating to human affairs, and depending on moral evidence, is open to some possible or imaginary doubt. It is that state of the case that, after the entire comparison and consideration of all the evidence, leaves the minds of the jurors in that condition that they cannot say they feel an abiding conviction, to a moral certainty, of the truth of the charge.

Right to Remain Silent

It is a constitutional right of a defendant in a criminal trial that he or she may not be compelled to testify. You must not draw any inference from the fact that he or she does not testify. Further, you must neither discuss this matter nor permit it to enter your deliberations in any way.

Direct and Circumstantial Evidence

Evidence is either direct or circumstantial. *Direct evidence* is evidence that directly proves a fact without the necessity of an inference. *Circumstantial evidence* is evidence that proves a fact from which an inference of the existence of another fact may be drawn.

It is not necessary that facts be proved by direct evidence. They may be proved also by circumstantial evidence or by a combination of direct and circumstantial evidence. Both direct evidence and circumstantial evidence are acceptable as a means of proof. Neither is entitled to any greater weight than the other.

However, in any case based on circumstantial evidence, if the circumstantial evidence is susceptible of two reasonable interpretations, one of which points to the defendant's guilt and the other of which points to his or her innocence, you must adopt the interpretation that points to the defendant's innocence and reject the interpretation that points to the defendant's guilt.

If one interpretation appears reasonable and the other appears unreasonable, you must accept the reasonable interpretation and reject the unreasonable one.

Murder

Murder is the unlawful killing of a human being with malice aforethought.

Malice Aforethought

Malice means either an expressed intent to kill or an intent to commit an act dangerous to human life with knowledge of the danger to, and with conscious disregard for, human life.

Aforethought means the malice must precede the act.

First-Degree Murder

First-degree murder occurs when the killing is committed with malice aforethought and a deliberate and premeditated intent to kill.

Deliberate and Premeditated

Deliberate means determined after careful thought and weighing of the consequences. *Premeditated* means considered beforehand.

The law does not try to measure in units the length of time during which the thought must be pondered before it can ripen into an intent to kill that is truly deliberate and premeditated. The time will vary with different individuals and different circumstances.

The true test is not the duration of time but rather the extent of the reflection. A cold, calculated decision may be arrived at in a short time, but a mere unconsidered rash impulse will not amount to deliberation and premeditation, even though it includes an intent to kill.

Lesser Offenses in Homicide Cases

If you are not satisfied to a reasonable doubt that the defendant is guilty of first-degree murder, he or she may be found guilty of any lesser offense, i.e., second-degree murder, voluntary manslaughter, or involuntary manslaughter, if the evidence is sufficient to establish his or her guilt of such lesser offense beyond a reasonable doubt.

Second-Degree Murder

Second-degree murder occurs when the killing is with malice aforethought but without deliberation and premeditation.

> **Note**: There are other forms of first- and second-degree murder, but they do not apply to the cases presented.

Voluntary Manslaughter

Voluntary manslaughter is the intentional killing of a human being without malice aforethought.

An intentional killing is said to be without malice aforethought and therefore reduced to voluntary manslaughter in the following circumstances.

- Where the killing is committed during a sudden quarrel or heat of passion; where the provocation is such that it would naturally arouse such passions; and, where the killer acts under the stress of that heat of passion.

  The heat of passion that will reduce a murder to manslaughter must be such as naturally would be aroused in the mind of an ordinary reasonable person in the same circumstances.

- Where the killing is committed in the honest but unreasonable belief in the need to defend against imminent peril to life or great bodily injury.

Involuntary Manslaughter

The crime of involuntary manslaughter is the unlawful killing of a human being without the intent to kill when the fatal act involves a high risk of death or bodily harm and is done without due caution. The term *due caution* refers to a reckless act committed without proper regard for human life.

Diminished Mental Capacity

If the defendant's mental capacity was reduced by mental illness, intoxication, or any other cause, you may consider its effect on the defendant's ability to form the mental state, intent to kill, or malice aforethought.

You may not find the defendant guilty of first-degree murder if, because of his or her diminished mental capacity, you have a reasonable doubt as to whether he or she did maturely and meaningfully deliberate and premeditate upon the gravity of the act.

Further, you may not find the defendant guilty of either first- or second-degree murder if, because of a diminished mental capacity, you have a reasonable doubt that the defendant could form the mental state of malice aforethought.

Thus, a finding of diminished mental capacity can reduce a first-degree murder charge to second-degree murder, and a second-degree murder charge to voluntary manslaughter as previously outlined.

> **Note**: Among the cases in this book, the law of diminished capacity applies only to the case of *State v. Kurt Schaeffer,* since the doctrine was abolished by the state legislature after that case.

Right of Self-Defense

The killing of another person in self-defense is justifiable and therefore not unlawful when the person who does the killing honestly and reasonably believes the following.

- That there is imminent danger that the other person will kill him or her or cause him or her great bodily injury. *Imminent* means the danger must be immediate.

- That it was necessary under the circumstances to kill the other person to prevent death or great bodily injury to himself or herself.

Accident

When a person commits an act by accident under circumstances that show no criminal intent or purpose, he or she does not thereby commit a crime and must be found not guilty.

Kidnapping

Every person who unlawfully and with physical force moves any other person against his or her will and without his or her consent for a substantial distance is guilty of kidnapping.

Rape

The crime of rape is the act of sexual intercourse with a female person without her consent.

Attempted Rape

The crime of attempted rape is an attempted act of sexual intercourse with a female person without her consent.

An attempt to commit rape consists of two elements, namely, a specific intent to commit rape, and a direct but ineffectual act toward its commission.

Principals

The persons concerned in the commission of a crime who are regarded by law as principals in the crime and equally guilty thereof include:

- those who directly and actively commit the act of constituting the crime; or,

- those who aid and abet the commission of the crime.

Aiding and Abetting

A person aids and abets the commission of a crime when he or she intentionally aids, promotes, or encourages the commission of the crime with knowledge of the unlawful purpose of the perpetrator.

CIVIL CASES

Duties of Judge and Jury

It is my duty to instruct you in the law that applies to this case.

It is your duty to follow the law. As jurors, it is your duty to determine the effect and value of the evidence and to decide all questions of fact.

You must not be influenced by sympathy, prejudice, or passion.

Burden of Proof

The plaintiff has the burden of proving by a preponderance of the evidence all the facts necessary to establish the allegations in the complaint.

Preponderance of the evidence means evidence that has more convincing force than that opposed to it.

Intentional Infliction of Emotional Distress

The charge of intentional infliction of emotional distress requires proof by a preponderance of the evidence that the defendant engaged in outrageous conduct with the intent to inflict emotional distress upon the plaintiff and that the plaintiff suffered emotional distress as a result.

About the Author

The Honorable Norbert Ehrenfreund has served as a trial judge of the Superior Court in California for over thirty years. Officially retired, he continues to serve the bench on assignment.

World War II was under way when Ehrenfreund graduated from the University of Missouri's School of Journalism. He saw combat in France, Germany, and Austria as an artillery officer and was decorated with the Bronze Star for meritorious service. After the war, he worked in Europe as a reporter for the U.S. newspaper *The Stars and Stripes*. In 1952, he returned to the United States and earned a master's degree in political science at Columbia University.

His experiences in both the war and as a reporter at the Nuremberg Trials moved his life in a new direction. His view of the law evolved, and he now saw the law as mankind's most effective tool in the quest to establish universal justice and a lawful society. He earned a law degree at Stanford and began his legal career as a deputy district attorney in San Diego. Later he cofounded Defenders, Inc., a law firm committed to defending the disadvantaged, and he worked there until his appointment to the Superior Court in 1975.

While serving primarily as a criminal court judge over the years, he also brought into the family court a number of innovations that were ultimately enacted into law by the California Legislature. His contributions were recognized by the establishment of the Norby Award in his honor, awarded each year to an outstanding family law attorney. In 2001, the National Conference of State Trial Judges bestowed its Award of Judicial Excellence upon Judge Ehrenfreund at the American Bar Association's annual meeting.

Judge Ehrenfreund's interest in international law has taken him back to Europe several times, where he lectured and taught, usually under the sponsorship of the U.S. government. In addition to a previous book that he coauthored titled *You're the Jury,* he has recently published a book entitled *The Nuremberg Legacy.*

He and his wife Jill live in San Diego.